Votes from Seats

Take the number of seats in a representative assembly and the number of seats in districts through which this assembly is elected. From just these two numbers, the authors of *Votes from Seats* show that it is possible to deduce the number of parties in the assembly and in the electorate, as well as the size of the largest party. Inside parties, the vote distributions of individual candidates likewise follow predictable patterns. Four laws of party seats and votes are constructed by logic and tested, using scientific approaches rare in social sciences. Both complex and simple electoral systems are covered, and the book offers a set of "best practices" for electoral system design. The ability to predict so much from so little, and to apply to countries worldwide, is an advance in the systematic analysis of a core institutional feature found in any democracy, and points the way towards making social sciences more predictive.

Matthew S. Shugart is Professor of Political Science at the University of California, Davis, and Affiliated Professor of the University of Haifa (Israel).

Rein Taagepera is Professor Emeritus, Department of Political Science, University of California, Irvine, and Professor Emeritus, Skytte Institute, University of Tartu (Estonia).

To Huey,
with deep thanks for
all you did to make
this a better book
Matthew
Nov. 19, 2017

Votes from Seats

Logical Models of Electoral Systems

MATTHEW S. SHUGART
University of California, Davis

REIN TAAGEPERA
University of California, Irvine

CAMBRIDGE
UNIVERSITY PRESS

CAMBRIDGE
UNIVERSITY PRESS

University Printing House, Cambridge CB2 8BS, United Kingdom

One Liberty Plaza, 20th Floor, New York, NY 10006, USA

477 Williamstown Road, Port Melbourne, VIC 3207, Australia

4843/24, 2nd Floor, Ansari Road, Daryaganj, Delhi – 110002, India

79 Anson Road, #06–04/06, Singapore 079906

Cambridge University Press is part of the University of Cambridge.

It furthers the University's mission by disseminating knowledge in the pursuit of education, learning, and research at the highest international levels of excellence.

www.cambridge.org
Information on this title: www.cambridge.org/9781108417020
DOI: 10.1017/9781108261128

First published 2017

Printed in the United States of America by Sheridan Books, Inc.

A catalogue record for this publication is available from the British Library.

ISBN 978-1-108-41702-0 Hardback
ISBN 978-1-108-40426-6 Paperback

Contents

v

Tables and Figures

FIGURES

Preface and Acknowledgments

This book, *Votes from Seats*, does two things that look impossible, one in electoral studies and the other for political science more broadly.

It multiplies together the number of seats in the representative assembly (assembly size) and the number of seats in individual electoral districts (district magnitude) through which this assembly is elected. From this "seat product" it deduces the number of parties in the assembly, as well as the size of the largest, testing this logical model more fully than earlier (Taagepera 2007). Then it advances into completely novel terrain, with further logic leading to the prediction of the number of parties receiving votes once we have predicted their seats. This is why the title of the book is *Votes from Seats*. Predicting disproportionality follows.

The same fundamental logic then allows us to make some quantitative predictions for patterns where the seat product would not seem to matter at all: competition in presidential elections and inside the parties. In contrast to most prior scholarship, we find that party systems in presidential democracies are not so different from their parliamentary counterparts. At the level of an individual district, the same output indicators can be deduced from district magnitude, but surprisingly, the size of the nationwide assembly in which a district is "embedded" also matters. This finding reverses the usual way of thinking about how district and national politics connect. Rather than start at the districts and project up to the national level, we use assembly size, in conjunction with district magnitude, to predict district-level outputs.

All this vastly expands our understanding and predictive ability as compared to our earlier work on electoral, party, and presidential systems (Taagepera and Shugart 1989a and 1993; Shugart and Carey 1992; Taagepera 2007; Samuels and Shugart 2010). It takes into account the efforts of many other researchers such as Lijphart (1994); Reed (1990, 2003); Cox (1997); Clark and Golder (2006); and Hicken and Stoll (2011).

It is now possible to understand how design and reform of electoral systems will play out in practice. Actual worldwide averages fit the book's predictions remarkably well. They supply a benchmark for assessing an individual country: If a country's party constellations differ markedly from those expected on the basis of their assembly and district sizes, it would be time to look for which other country-specific political factors are at play.

This is the book's *impossible-looking* contribution to electoral studies: the ability to predict so much from so little. How is this possible? The answer leads us to the book's broader contribution to social science.

There is a huge difference between "understanding something," something "explaining" something else, having "an impact" on it, and quantitatively predicting the size of this something else. "Explaining" may mean retroactive understanding, with no hint for the future. "Having an impact" implies altering it in some direction, to an undefined extent. "Quantitatively predicting" means: "If this factor has this value, then, *ceteris paribus*, this other factor has that value," within a range of likely variation. Such prediction may come from empirical knowledge. It rises to the highest level of scientific law when it is also grounded in logic. Then it, of course, also explains.

We establish a network of "quantitatively predictive logical models." These models (Taagepera 2008) start with logical thinking about observations, rather than fitting data by regression techniques. The resulting equations connect a few variables at a time (rather than numerous input variables and "controls") and then connect these connections with each other. Having connections among connections is a hallmark of any developed science. In electricity, for instance, a network of equations connects factors such as electric charge, voltage, current intensity, resistance, force, and power. Philosophical arguments abound why this would be impossible in political science, or social sciences more generally. In *Votes from Seats* we do not argue whether it can be done; we just do it. By presenting and testing a set of interconnected quantitative connections among various factors, this book sets an example for a more *scientific* approach to society and politics. We hope this allows it to set a methodological standard for social science beyond the specific topics of electoral and party systems.

HOW THE BOOK WAS POSSIBLE

We have been working together on topics concerning electoral systems and quantitative logical modeling since Shugart was an undergraduate and then a graduate student at the University of California, Irvine, longer ago than either of us would care to remember. It thus would be an understatement to say that we both have written on electoral systems before (including Taagepera 1972, 1973, 1986, 2007; Taagepera and Shugart 1989a, 1989b, 1993; Shugart 1988,

2005a; Shugart and Carey 1992; Bergman, Shugart, and Watt 2013; Li and Shugart 2016). Yet, as the preceding overview suggests, we have extended our separate and joint work in new directions and uncovered new things along the way that find their place in this book for the first time. Moreover, we have developed findings and methods that call into question, in various ways, those of other prominent scholars in the subject area.

This book would not have been possible even a few short years ago, because the large datasets we have at our disposal simply did not exist. We owe a massive debt of gratitude to the teams of scholars who have done the work of collecting such data and providing the public good of letting other scholars use them. Following in their footsteps, we will be making public two even more expanded datasets, which we have used for the core quantitative tasks of this book.

The nationwide dataset is Li and Shugart (n.d.), "National Party Systems Dataset." This starts from Bormann and Golder (2011), "Democratic Electoral Systems Around the World, 1946-2011," and is supplemented with variables from Carey and Hix (2011), as well as several additional variables that appear in our dataset for the first time. The district level dataset is Belden and Shugart (n.d.), "District-Level Party Systems Dataset." This builds upon the Constituency Level Electoral Archive (CLEA; Kollman et al. 2016), but extends to additional countries and variables not originally in the CLEA.

Candidate-level votes for assembly elections are from Shugart's dataset, "The Intra-Party Dimension of Representation," except for data from Taiwan (generously provided by Nathan Batto) and Japan (from the "Party Personnel "dataset, collected in collaboration with Ellis Krauss and Robert Pekkanen). Shugart acknowledges two National Science Foundation grants that made his data collection possible (SES-0452573 and SES-0751662). Candidate-level data on Finland that we use in Chapters 6 and 14 were greatly improved through collaboration with Åsa von Schoultz.

Absolutely indispensable research assistance was provided by Yuhui Li (who was primarily responsible for managing the nationwide data), Nathan Rexford (who greatly enhanced our ability to analyze the intraparty data), and Cory Belden (who was the primary manager of our district-level dataset). Roi Zur provided extensive and incisive comments as well as assistance in producing the final manuscript. For support that made it possible to employ these students as researchers and data managers, Shugart acknowledges the Department of Political Science and the Dean's Office of the Division of Social Sciences at the University of California, Davis. These student researchers already have become valued colleagues and they cannot be adequately compensated either by the funding they received or by words in this preface. The book would have been impossible without them. We are deeply grateful.

We thank the anonymous reviewers for Cambridge University Press, and our acquisitions editor, Robert Dreesen for comments and encouragement, and Claire Sissen and Sri Hari Kumar Sugumaran for their expert management of the production. Scott Mainwaring helpfully provided comments on several chapters, while JD Mussel and Zirui Yang read the entire draft, helping us improve the final product. As usual, errors will remain. We trust our readers and critics will find them, and we hold no one but ourselves responsible for their having made it into print.

1

Introduction: How Electoral Systems Matter – for Politics and for the Scientific Study Thereof

Who governs? Electoral systems matter in democracies because they affect the answer to this question Robert Dahl (1961) posed in a different context. In democracies, the answer might be "those who win elections." However, it is rarely so simple. We might rephrase the question as "who wins elections?" One might immediately respond with, of course, those who win the most votes. Yet again, it is not always so straightforward. In the US presidential election of 2016, Hilary Clinton obtained over 65.8 million votes, which exceeded those of Donald Trump by almost 2.9 million (and 2.1 percentage points of the national total). Yet it was Trump, not Clinton, who became President, due to the way the electoral system takes "who got votes" and turns it into "who governs."

The US in 2016 is one recent and notable example. A reversal of which candidate won the nationwide votes and which one became president also happened in the US in 2000.[1] Yet maybe these US cases are simply aberrations. Maybe in other democracies it is always simple to say that "who governs is whoever wins the most votes." Actually it is not so simple; it is often the case that the way the electoral system works makes a difference in how the votes get turned into the important positions of power that determine who governs. A couple of other examples will demonstrate the point.

New Zealand had two consecutive elections (1978 and 1981) in which the Labour Party won the most votes nationwide, yet the rival National Party formed the government. Why? Because the Nationals won more *seats* in the national parliament. This, of course, invites the question, why did the Nationals win more seats – a majority[2], in fact – when Labour won more votes? The answer lies in the way the *electoral system* worked. There were no controversies in either of these elections over whether the outcome was correctly or "legitimately" decided. Yet these elections helped begin a process

---

[1] The significance of the US election controversy of 2000 for understanding electoral systems is discussed further in Chapter 3.

[2] We use the term, majority, strictly in the American sense as "at least one more than half." If we mean the largest share, whether or not more than half, we will say "plurality."

that, by 1996, would see the country implement a completely different electoral system.

We could also think of the case of Denmark in 2015. In this election, the Social Democrats won the most votes *and* seats. Yet when a government was formed after the election, the Social Democrats were in the opposition. The party with the second most votes and seats, the Danish People's Party, also was not in the government. Instead, the third largest party, the Venstre, provided the country's prime minister, Lars Løkke Rasmussen. His government obtained the parliamentary backing of some other parties, including the Danish People's Party, but not the Social Democrats. This example illustrates that sometimes many parties obtain representation – the three parties just mentioned combined for only slightly more than two-thirds of the votes and a similar share of seats. Six other parties obtained representation. Thus "who governs" depended on bargaining between various parties, because the electoral system made it possible for many parties to receive seats as well as votes.

Each of these examples shows that it is not enough to say there are elections. We need to know something about how votes get converted into governing power. It is the electoral system that is a key element in this conversion process. If the country has a "parliamentary" form of government, like New Zealand and Denmark, the electoral system only turns votes into seats for parties in the parliament. If one party has a majority – as in the 1978 and 1981 New Zealand examples – it forms the government (regardless of whether the party also had earned the most votes). If there is a "multiparty" system, as in the Danish example, then determining who governs involves another step – coalition bargaining. This is a step we will not consider at length in this book; many other works cover it as a topic in its own right. Instead, this book focuses on how votes become seats, and how this process varies from country to country, depending on the *electoral system*.

By electoral *system* we mean the set of rules that specify how voters can express their preferences (ballot structure) and how the votes are translated into seats. The system must specify at least the number of areas where this translation takes place (*electoral districts*), the number of seats allocated in each of these areas (*district magnitude*), and the seat allocation formula. All this will be discussed in more detail later.

This book deals only with elections that offer some choice. It bypasses fake elections where a single candidate for a given post is given total or overwhelming governmental support, while other candidates are openly blocked or covertly undermined. It also largely overlooks pathologies of electoral practices such as malapportionment and gerrymander, except for pointing out which electoral systems are more conducive to such manipulation.

The physical conditions of elections matter, such as ease of registration of voters and candidates, location and opening times of polling stations, and the timing of elections. It is presumed in this book that such conditions are satisfactory. Our only concern is to explain, in what are considered fair elections, how electoral systems affect the translation of votes into seats, how the results also affect the distribution of the votes in the next elections, and what it means for party systems. Moreover, the book largely limits itself to first or sole chambers of legislatures, although Chapters 11 and 12 will include analysis of presidential elections, and we will offer an occasional example from an elected second chamber (upper house).

This scope may look narrow, but translation of votes into seats by different electoral systems can lead to drastically different outcomes, both within a country (one election to another, or one elected body versus another) and across countries. For example, Green parties committed to more environmentally sound policies have emerged in many established democracies. The Green Party of Canada even received 6.8 percent of the votes in the national election for the House of Commons in 2008. Yet it won exactly zero seats. The Green Party of Germany in 1998 had obtained almost the same national vote share for the Bundestag, 6.7 percent, and not only won seats in parliament (forty-seven of the 669, or 7.0 percent) but also obtained seats in the cabinet including the Minister of Foreign Affairs. The difference in the outcomes, despite similar vote shares, is due to the electoral systems these countries use.

Thus, electoral systems affect party strengths in the representative assembly[3] and, if the political system is parliamentary, the resulting composition of the governing cabinet. They can encourage the rise of new parties, bringing in new blood but possibly leading to excessive fractionalization, or they can squeeze out all but two parties, bringing clarity of choice but possibly leading to eventual staleness. It is well worth discovering in quantitative detail how electoral systems and related institutions affect the translation of votes into seats. We now offer one more detailed example that introduces several themes of the book.

The Polish Election of 2015 and How the Rules Mattered

Poland has been a stable democracy since the 1989–1990 transition to democracy as the Soviet Communist bloc collapsed. Since that time and through 2015, Poland has had eight elections for Sejm and Senate, the two chambers of the national parliament, and six for its politically powerful presidency. Nonetheless, the Sejm election of 2015 stands out and led to

---

[3] Throughout this book, we will generally prefer the term, *assembly*, rather than legislature, parliament, congress, or other terms. We thus avoid any implicit commentary on the institution's precise role in a given democratic system and call attention instead to its essential feature as a plural body in which elected representatives assemble for their various tasks.

significant international concern. For the first time in the post-Communist era, a single party won a majority of seats in the Sejm, the first chamber (and the more powerful one). This party, the Law and Justice Party (known by its Polish initials, PiS), already held the presidency and thus was able to set the nation's policy agenda essentially unilaterally. This agenda was controversial, particularly a law passed near the end of 2015 that changed the procedures for the Polish Constitutional Court. This change drew an official rebuke from the European Commission as a "systemic risk to the rule of law in Poland."[4]

It is useful to situate the Polish events that troubled its neighbors into the context of political institutions, including the electoral system, which made PiS's Sejm majority possible. Poland uses one of the many examples of an electoral system that is typically called "proportional representation" (PR). Usually, under PR, no party wins a majority in the assembly, because the system is designed to make it feasible for many parties to win seats. It tends to support bargaining among parties after the election (as in the Danish case mentioned earlier). Indeed, this had been the case in Poland since the 1990s. So what changed in 2015 to allow a single-party majority?

First of all, the *timing* of the election was critical. Poland had just elected a new president in May 2015. It was a close contest. Like many countries that elect a politically powerful presidency by direct vote, Poland votes in "two rounds": in the event that no candidate has a majority in the first round, there is a runoff between the top two candidates two weeks[5] later. The winner, Andrzej Duda of PiS, won 51.6 percent to 48.5 percent, over a candidate backed by the then-governing party, Civic Platform (PO). Six months later, when the Sejm election came up, it was within the "honeymoon" of the newly elected PiS president. Presumably aided by this honeymoon period, PiS won 37.6% of the vote, which was more than Duda himself had received in the first round of his election (34.8%) and also was a 7.7 percentage-point increase in the party's vote over the previous (2011) Sejm election.

Ordinarily, the timing of assembly elections relative to presidential elections is not considered part of the "electoral system"; however, as we show in Chapter 12, such timing does indeed have systematic effects on the performance of parties. The Polish pattern in 2015, whereby the newly elected president's party enjoyed a surge in votes, is a common pattern (Shugart 1995). So, the timing of elections – an institutional feature of Polish democracy – may have helped PiS gain the most votes. How did the electoral system for Sejm turn those into a majority of seats?

---

[4] "Commission adopts Rule of Law Opinion on the situation in Poland," European Commission press release, June 1, 2016 (http://europa.eu/rapid/press-release_IP-16-2015_en.htm, accessed July 13th 2016).

[5] The time between rounds varies across countries; in Poland the rounds were May 10 and 24. We discuss some implications of two-round elections in Chapter 3.

TABLE 1.1 *Polish Sejm election result, October, 2015 (national figures)*

Party (and name or abbreviation in Polish)	Votes	Votes (%)	Seats	Seats (%)
Law and Justice (PiS)	5,711,687	37.58	235	51.09
Civic Platform (PO)	3,661,474	24.09	138	30.00
Kukiz'15 (K'15)	1,339,094	8.81	42	9.13
Modern (Nowoczesna)	1,155,370	7.6	28	6.09
United Left (ZL)	1,147,102	7.55	0	0.00
Polish People's Party (PSL)	779,875	5.13	16	3.48
KORWiN	722,999	4.76	0	0.00
Together (Razem)	550,349	3.62	0	0.00
German minority (MN)	27,530	0.18	1	0.22
others	105,191	0.69	0	0.00
Total	15,200,671		460	

The row for "others" includes no single party with more than 0.28 percent of the vote.

Table 1.1 shows the detailed results of the 2015 Sejm election. The first puzzle is the one already mentioned – the fact that the PiS won more than half the seats on only 37.6 percent of the vote. How could that be? Poland, after all, uses "proportional representation." Yet 51 percent of the seats on under 38 percent of the votes is not very "proportional." As is further shown in Table 1.1, part of the answer lies in the *thresholds*.[6] Two parties have over 3.5 percent of the votes apiece, yet no seats. This is because the electoral law required 5 percent of the nationwide votes to win seats, unless the party represents a national minority. The latter provision explains why a party for the German Minority has a seat on only 0.18 percent of the vote.[7] However, the parties called KORWiN and Together are not ethnic-minority parties. Thus the threshold excluded them from representation.

It is further visible from the table the United Left had 7.55 percent of the votes – easily clearing the 5 percent party threshold – yet no seats. How can that be? It is due to yet a further feature of Polish electoral law: if two or more parties jointly contest the election, the threshold is 8 percent, rather than 5 percent, for them. The provision is presumably intended to prevent parties from making "marriages of convenience" just to pass the threshold jointly. Yet in this case, the parties in question are a set of ideologically proximate parties that came close, but not close enough, to clearing the threshold.

---

[6] For details on Polish election laws, see Hardman (n.d.)

[7] Separate provisions for ethnic minorities will not be a theme of this book. See the excellent and detailed treatment by Lublin (2014).

We will discuss these features of the system in subsequent chapters, as we discuss electoral alliances in Chapters 6, 7, and 14 (and in passing in other chapters); we discuss thresholds in Chapter 15.

After the exclusion of parties that fell below the thresholds, PiS had around 45 percent of the total vote cast for parties that were eligible to win seats. That means its assembly majority still gives it a degree of over-representation. This is due in part to the electoral formula used – something called the D'Hondt divisor method, which will be explained in Chapter 2. A different "proportional" formula might have netted PiS less than half the seats, just as a lower threshold, or no separate threshold for alliances, might have meant more seats for smaller parties and hence fewer for PiS. An election not in the president's honeymoon, or a different outcome of the close presidential race itself, might have meant fewer votes for PiS in the first place.

While it may seem right now as if we are just making a "laundry list" of obscure provisions and Polish political idiosyncrasies, in fact, *all of these electoral rules mattered to the outcome*. With a different set of rules, then, there might not have been a PiS majority government, and the resulting international controversy that the government became embroiled in may never have occurred. In other words, electoral systems have consequences for how a country is governed, and by whom.

In Table 1.1 we saw the national outcome of Poland's 2015 Sejm election. However, Poland actually has forty-one electoral districts. With an assembly size of 460, that means each district elects *on average* just over eleven seats. As we explain further in Chapter 2, this means we can speak of Poland having an average *district magnitude* of eleven. Thus the electoral system is not really national in scope; indeed, few are. The results in Table 1.1 show the nationwide aggregation of votes and seats, but there are in fact forty-one different contests playing out, each one electing anywhere from seven to twenty members of the Sejm. Unlike many other books on electoral systems, this one will analyze not only nationwide aggregate patterns, but also district-level dynamics. In fact, Chapter 10 is devoted entirely to developing models of patterns in data disaggregated to the district level. We even go one step farther than this; in Chapters 13 and 14, we look at the *intraparty dimension* of representation, whereby individual candidates compete for votes against others of their party under certain electoral systems. Poland has one of these systems of intraparty competition, as we explain briefly here.

In **Table 1.2**, we see partial results from one of Poland's forty-one electoral districts in the 2015 election. The district is Konin, and it has a district magnitude of nine. In Poland, as in many other (but by no means all) electoral systems, the voter casts her ballot by placing a mark by the name of a single candidate. The table shows only the votes of the top fifteen candidates, including the nine winners. How is it possible that *the winners were not simply the top nine in votes*? More specifically, why

TABLE 1.2 *Votes for the leading candidates for election for members of Polish Sejm from the district of Konin, October 2015*

Number elected: 9 Candidate	Party	Votes	Votes	Elected?
Wojciech Witold Czarnecki	Law and Justice (PiS)	26399	9.52%	Yes
Zbigniew Dolata	Law and Justice (PiS)	18060	6.51%	Yes
Paul Anthony Arndt	Civic Platform (PO)	17925	6.46%	Yes
Tadeusz Tomaszewski	United Left	15350	5.53%	No
Tomasz Piotr Nowak	Civic Platform (PO)	11820	4.26%	Yes
Jan Krzysztof Ostrowski	Law and Justice (PiS)	9443	3.40%	Yes
Bartosz Jozwiak	Kukiz'15	8747	3.15%	Yes
Ryszard Bartosik	Law and Justice (PiS)	8163	2.94%	Yes
Leszek Richard Galemba	Law and Justice (PiS)	7708	2.78%	Yes
Agnieszka Mirecka-Katulska	Law and Justice (PiS)	7520	2.71%	No
Paulina Hennig-Klóska	Modern	7306	2.63%	Yes
Zofia Mariola Itman	Law and Justice (PiS)	6913	2.49%	No
Eugene Thomas Grzeszczak	Polish People's Party (PSL)	6609	2.38%	No
Kazimierz Czeslaw Broadsword	United Left	5174	1.87%	No
Maria Bychawska	Civic Platform (PO)	5053	1.82%	No

All candidates who obtained at least 5000 votes (about 1.75 percent) are shown; there were 120 additional candidates who are not shown.
Source: Authors' compilation from http://parlament2015.pkw.gov.pl/349_Wyniki_Sejm/0/0/37/3062.

did Tadeusz Tomaszewski and Agnieszka Mirecka-Katulska not win seats even when they had more votes than did other candidates who were elected?

The answer lies in an important detail that is typical of many proportional representation electoral systems, and which we explain in detail in Chapters 2, 5, and 6: the system uses "party lists." Parties, or alliances of parties, present lists of candidates. The country's system first allocates the seats to these lists.[8] Only then do the candidate votes come into play, with the top vote-earners in each list getting the seats that each list has obtained. Thus, not shown in the table, the PiS ran nine candidates, whose combined votes amounted to 37.4 percent of the district's total (quite close to the party's nationwide percentage, as Table 1.1 showed). This entitled them to five of the nine seats (55.6 percent); its winners are the five *on the PiS list* with the highest

---

[8] A vote for any candidate is also counted as a vote for the list on which the candidate is running for office.

vote totals. Similarly, the PO was collectively entitled to two seats – its top two candidates winning them – and K'15 and Modern to one each.

Tomaszewski and Mirecka-Katulska did not win a seat despite vote totals that were in the top nine because their *lists* did not have enough votes for them to win. In the case of Tomaszewski, this was due to the list of the United Left falling short of the *nationwide threshold*, as we saw in Table 1.1. Without the threshold, this list would have had sufficient votes to win a seat in the district, but in this case a rule that is applied on nationwide votes interfered. In the case of Mirecka-Katulska, she did not win even though her own votes ranked her ninth in the district overall, once Tomaszewski was excluded. Critically, however, she ranked only *sixth in her list*, which was entitled to five seats. Under a list system of proportional representation, the votes for the list of candidates are the first criterion in allocating seats. Various list systems are the most common of all electoral systems, and not just an unusual feature of Poland.[9]

Thus from Table 1.2 we see that at the district level, and even at the level of individual candidates, the electoral system affects who wins representation. This book is about all of these various ways that electoral systems matter.

How Electoral Systems Constrain and How Science Walks on Two Legs

Politics takes place in time and space – both the immutable physical space and the institutional space that politics can alter, but with much inertia. Institutions place constraints on politics. For instance, in a five-seat electoral district, at least one party and at most five parties can win seats. Within these bounds, politics is not predetermined, but the limiting frame still restricts the political game. It is rare for one party to win all seats in a five-seat district, while such an outcome is inevitable in a single-seat district. This observation may look obvious and hence pointless, but it leads to far-reaching consequences.

A key method followed in this book is the building of *logical quantitative models*. Much of contemporary social science is quantitative, in the sense of working with numbers, running and reporting statistical regressions, and so on. However, too little social science work builds its quantitative edifice on a foundation of *logic*. In this book, we will report many a regression result, but most of these are reported as tests of logical models that we derived before going to the statistical program and asking what the coefficients and standard errors (etc.) are.

In building logical models, we first ask, *what do we expect* the relationship to be between A and B? This means *thinking* about how A shapes B (and maybe vice versa). It means thinking about the shape of the relationship. Do not just

---

[9] Open lists, where candidates' votes determine the winners from the list, are less common. They are by no means rare, as we shall see in later chapters.

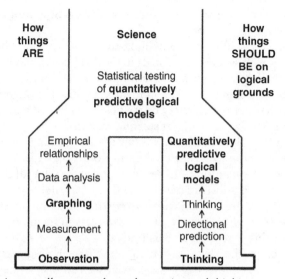

FIGURE 1.1 Science walks on two legs: observation and thinking
Source: Modified from Taagepera (2015).

run to the computer program and find out what a basic linear regression result is, because what if the relationship is not linear? We will display a lot of data graphs in the book, because it is important to see the scatterplot. This will tell us if our logic is on the right track, and whether our data need to be transformed – for instance, taking logarithms – before we enter them into regression equations.

The most important reason for thinking before you regress is that science walks on two legs, as shown schematically in **Figure 1.1**. As with any walk, the process involves *taking alternating steps on each leg*. However, the two legs of science represent different aspects of what science is. The walker can't reach the destination without using both legs. Hopping on one leg is highly inefficient!

One leg (the left in the schematic) deals with determining how things *are*. This involves careful observation, measurement, graphing of data, and statistical summaries of patterns in the data. The other leg deals with asking how things *should be*, on logical grounds? That question guides the first one. If it does not – if we jump to running statistical regressions first – we run the risk of seeing what we want to see. Or, worse, running numerous slightly different specifications of the regression equation, or different regression commands, until we see what we want to see. It is in thinking about "How things *should be*" that we come to understand *what* to look for before we use statistics. The two legs come together when expectations produced by logical modeling are tested with data, mostly using statistics. We will explain our use of statistics later, but first – because it should be first – we discuss how we start with logical model building.

Let's take the Polish district of Konin, shown previously in Table 1.2. We saw that four parties won seats in this district in the 2015 election. There were a total of nine seats available. Is four parties a lot or few? To know, we might look at other districts in Poland in 2015, and also at districts in other countries. We might see that in the UK, every district elects only one party. Again, that's obvious – there is only one seat! Yet starting with the obvious is exactly how we start to build a logical model. If there is one seat, there can be only one winning party. If there are more seats, like the nine in Konin, we expect there to be more winning parties. We can look further, perhaps at Israel and find out that ten parties won seats, in a district that has 120 seats available (see Chapter 5 for details). So, here we are dealing with *observation*: Election districts with many seats available tend to have many parties win seats in them. The second step is *thinking* about this observation. This leads to a *directional prediction*: If there are more seats in the district, the number of winning parties increases. *Measurement* of the number of seats – what we call district magnitude – and the number of parties confirms this prediction.

But a merely *directional* prediction is of limited value. Any Toscana peasant could have told Galileo in which direction things fall. They fall down! What else do you need to know? Galileo also wanted to know how fast they fall, and why. If we want to be taken seriously as scientists with results of value to offer the world of practitioners, we must ask similar questions about the number of parties, and about every other directional relationship. Yet, far too many works published in political science journals neglect to venture beyond the directional hypothesis. We should not be like the Toscana peasant who might have said, "I see which way things fall, and that is all I need to know."[10] Whenever researchers can go beyond the merely directional, they should. What is the meaning of this abstract advice? A specific example follows.

An essential step is to *graph the data*. Then really *look* at this graph and *ponder* what it wishes to tell us. In Figure 1.2, we use district-level data, from many elections around the world. We see two panels, both of which plot on the x-axis the number of seats in a district (or its magnitude, designated M) and on the y-axis the number of parties (of any size) that win in the district (designated by the strange looking label, N'_{S0}, for reasons that will become clear in later chapters). The difference in the two panels is the way the scales are drawn.

---

[10] We will accept that there are applications in which the directional hypothesis is the best a social scientist can do, and even where confirming such a hypothesis adds considerable value. However, in many applications – especially those that are the substantive topics of this book – we really must strive to be more specific in our expectations.

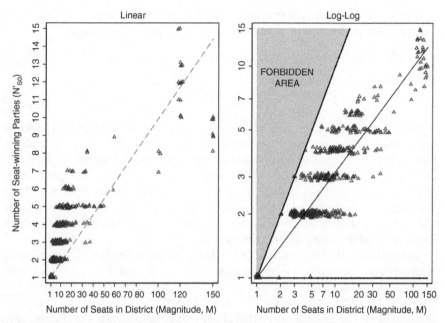

FIGURE 1.2 Two ways of visualizing the relationship between district magnitude (*M*) and the number of seat-winning parties (*N'so*)

When graphed on regular scales, as in the left panel of Figure 1.2, the pattern is not very impressive. We use elections in more than eleven thousand districts all over the world. It may not look like that many, in part because only 451 of them are districts with more than one seat. All the one-seat districts just jumble up at the lower left of the graph. (We will explain the dashed line later.) We might notice that there seems to be some curvature in the data pattern, but it is hard to tell in this format what that might be.

In the right panel of Figure 1.2, we have exactly the same data points graphed with both axes being on logarithmic scales ("log–log"). In this graph, we have added two thick dark lines to help us further our logical thinking. We should graph the data, but we should do more: *we should graph where the data cannot possibly be*. It is logically impossible for the number of winning parties to be greater than the number of seats in the district. You cannot have ten parties win in your district if there are only nine seats available, for instance. The thick diagonal line thus shows a hard constraint: $N'_{SO} \leq M$. The area above and left of this line is shaded and marked as a "forbidden area" because there simply cannot be data points here, and marking a plot area in this way can be useful for thinking through logical relationships. The thick horizontal line is the minimum: it is impossible to have fewer than one party win in the district. Perhaps that seems too obvious to say, but sometimes the obvious is the clue to a logical quantitative model of the relationship.

Further *thinking* leads to the prediction that the number of parties winning in a district should be about the square root of the district magnitude,

$$N'_{S0} = \sqrt{M},$$

which also can be written as

$$N'_{S0} = M^{0.5}. \tag{Eq.1.1}$$

We will explain the logic behind Equation 1.1 later, in Chapter 7. The short version is that this is simply the average of the maximum, $N'_{S0} = M$, and the minimum $N'_{S0} = 1$, when both variables are expressed in logarithmic format – technically known as the geometric average. Without graphing, seeing the shape of the data distribution, and thinking logically, we could not have arrived at Equation 1.1, which we first derived in one of our earlier collaborations (Taagepera and Shugart 1993). This equation is a fundamental building block for most of what comes in later chapters of this book.

Now – and only now – *statistical approaches* enter. If we ran simple linear regression on the two variables, we would get the dashed line in the left panel. It simply plots the output of a regression. Without graphing the data, we might have said our directional hypothesis is confirmed: N'_{S0} goes up as M goes up. We would be cheered that the relationship was "statistically significant" and that the R-squared measure of how well the equation fits was almost unbelievably strong for a political-science relationship, at $R^2=0.74$. How wonderful! Meanwhile, if we had not graphed it, we would not even realize that the fit is not nearly as good as the R^2 would lead us to believe. Deviation from straight line is not random but systematic: at low M almost all data points are above the line, while at high M more data points are below the line. Visibly, the straight line is not the best-fit curve, even though the statistical program suggests it is!

Instead, after having studied the graphs and done our thinking, we could run linear regression on the *logarithms* of number of parties and district magnitude – *not* on the quantities themselves. When we do that, we get Equation 1.1![11] In other words, we confirm the logical model that the number of parties winning at least one seat in a district tends to be the square root of the district magnitude. Even better, the R^2 on the log-log regression is 0.95.

The end point of the process is a *quantitatively predictive logical model*. This model is "quantitatively predictive" because it predicts not only the direction of change but also the quantity of parties, on average, at any given district magnitude. The model is "logical" in that the square-rooting of the district magnitude comes from logical considerations. Note that we took alternating steps with each of the legs on which science walks. We started with observation, the left leg of Figure 1.1, followed by directional thinking, the right leg.

---

[11] The actual coefficient is very slightly bigger than 0.5, but trivially so. The result is discussed (and the regression table displayed) in Chapter 7.

Graphing involved the observation leg. Then quantitative logical modeling took us to the thinking leg. This is the type of interaction we have in mind when saying that *whenever researchers can go beyond the merely directional, they should*. For a broader perspective on such logical approaches, see Taagepera (2008).

This section has demonstrated the interplay of logical and empirical work in finding the relationship between the number of parties and number of available seats in a district (its magnitude). It is just one example. Each of the features of how electoral institutions matter, and that we reviewed in our sketch of the Polish election result in the preceding section, can be understood through a systematic, quantitative relationship. In later chapters of this book, we develop models of, among other topics: how the relative timing of elections (such as the "honeymoon" election in Poland 2015) shapes changes in the president's party vote share; how assembly size and average district magnitude shape how many important parties there are in the assembly as a whole; how the magnitude of an individual district shapes the sizes of parties there; and how candidates' personal vote totals (i.e., what we saw in Table 1.2) are distributed in a district.

The Use of Statistics in This Book: Think Before You Regress

In the preceding subsection, we discussed the importance of undertaking graphing and logical thinking before running regressions. Ultimately, testing our quantitative logical models through statistical regression is a critical part of the enterprise of this book. However, our approach to presenting regression results is different from many standard works, as we explain here.

Statistical "analysis" is a term often used in an overly broad way. The process should be thought of as having two utterly different functions. One is statistical *description* of data: best fit to whatever is deemed a suitable mathematical format, including the values of constants in this format, measures of lack-of-scatter around this best fit (such as R^2), etc. The other is statistical *testing* of preconceived models: how well the prediction agrees with data *average*. In model testing, R^2 is far more marginal as a factor in assessing a result than it is when we do not have a logically grounded expectation before running the statistical commands. Measures of goodness of agreement with expectation, such as F-test, take precedence.

Strictly speaking, we will call it *analysis* only when we are testing a logical model, not any time we run a regression. For similar reasons, when we display results of two or more statistical tests in a table, we will use the expression, "Regression One" (etc.), rather than the common "Model One." Only when we have a prior expectation of at least some of the coefficient values will we say that we have a "model."

In addition, precisely because most of our regressions are testing a specific quantitative expectation from a logical model, we will dispense with the usual "stars" that clutter up most published regression tables. Too often most authors are interested only in whether the sign of a coefficient is "right" (i.e., the expected direction) and whether the coefficient is "significant," meaning statistically distinguishable from zero. Most regression coefficients printed in journals and books are thus "dead on arrival" (Taagepera 2008: Ch. 7). The numbers in regression tables are rarely used for any further inquiry.

By contrast, we are interested in the coefficients' values, and whether a given coefficient is distinguishable from *the value our logical model says it should be*. Thus in many of our regression tables, we will run F-tests not of whether the coefficient might actually be zero, but whether its value is the logically expected value, or is too far off to consider the model supported.[12] On the other hand, sometimes our logical model actually demands that a constant term (intercept) be zero[13]; in such cases, "statistical insignificance" is actually what we want to see! We will revert to the practice of reporting conventional tests of significance (from zero) only in cases – very rare in this book – in which we do not have a specific quantitative expectation, but only directional.

Many of our regression results are collected in chapter appendices, in order to avoid breaking of the flow of text and the all-important visual test offered by our graphs. Only some regressions most critical to demonstrating the success of our modeling will be reported in tables located within the main chapter text. Some other specific decisions we make regarding setting up regressions and transforming data beforehand are discussed in chapters (or their appendices) where the matter comes up. For a lengthier treatment of the principles, see Taagepera (2008).

What Does "Quantitative Prediction" Mean?

The term "prediction" is subject to different meanings. When we use it, it usually means "quantitative prediction": if these factors have these values, then, *ceteris paribus* (all other conditions being the same), this other factor has that value, within some range of likely variation. The following example from the realm of electricity clarifies what this means.

Ohm's law, $I=V/R$, implies that if a potential difference of $V=25$ volts is applied across a wire with known resistance $R=5$ ohms, then a current of $I=5$

---

[12] Similarly, we will report 95 percent confidence intervals on these coefficients, to enable the reader to see at a glance whether the expected value is within this interval.

[13] For example, in Equation 1.1, the regression on the logarithms of N'_{S0} and M must yield a constant of zero, in order that we get a prediction of $N'_{S0}=1$ when $M=1$. (The log of 1 is equal to 0).

amperes will flow, with a possible variation of plus or minus 1 ampere. Here a variation range of 0.7 amperes emerges already because 25 volts could mean anything between 24.5 and 25.5 volts, while 5 ohms could mean anything between 4.5 and 5.5 ohms. The *ceteris paribus* provision presumes a conducting material with no semiconductor elements mixed in, and so on. So a possible variation range of ±1 ampere could be expected, until V and R can be measured with more precision. Repeated measurements at various V and R could also establish an empirically observed range of variation.

Our Equation 1.1, $N'_{S0}=M^{0.5}$, has the same broad format $y=cx^k$, so frequent in physics. (Many more will follow in this book.) It implies that if a district has $M=25$ seats, then $N'_{S0}=5$ parties will win seats, with a likely variation range of several parties. Empirical data in Fig. 1.2 indicate that the likely range extends from three to seven parties. More generally, if one wants to be on the safe side, one might say that the number of seat-winning parties is the square root of district magnitude multiplied or divided by no more than 2. (This is equivalent to saying that $\log N'_{S0}=0.5\log M\pm0.3$.) The *ceteris paribus* provision presumes that some PR allocation rule is used. The playfield such rules allow to democratic politics does not exclude the possibility that once in a (very long) while $N'_{S0}=1$ or $N'_{S0}=25$ could materialize. It just says that $N'_{S0}=5$ is the most likely outcome for $M=5$, and that $N'_{S0}=5\pm2$ covers pretty much all the observed outcomes.

In sum, when we say "quantitatively predictive," we mean nothing more and nothing less than what physicists attribute to statements like Ohm's law: a specific value of one factor leads to a specific value of the other.

How Electoral Systems and Party Politics Are Related

In a previous subsection, we showed an exercise in how we arrived at a logical model, using the example of how the number of parties is connected logically to the district magnitude. This insight in turn allowed Taagepera (2007) to hit upon a significant breakthrough in how electoral systems and party politics are related; in this book, we take those findings several steps further.

When we are interested in party politics, we are usually interested not just in the seats, but also in the votes. Moreover, while the number of parties – of any size – turns out to be a useful building block for logical model building, it is not *intrinsically* very useful. In any real legislature or national electorate, there are bound to be some parties that are bigger than others. Do we count even the tiniest party as being just as important as the biggest? When we are looking at small districts, it may not matter. There is something intrinsically interesting about the difference between a five-seat district with four parties represented and another with just two.

When we go to the nationwide level (or a bigger district), it is not so straightforward. Take the UK parliament following the 2015 election. The biggest party had over half the seats in parliament, which is obviously consequential because this allowed it to form the governing cabinet on its own. At the same time, there were eleven other parties winning seats; six of these had just one to four seats each, in the 650-seat house. Do we really think the raw count is of interest? Well, probably not, as the relative sizes of the parties are more politically relevant than their mere number. This is where a concept called the *effective* number of parties comes in, but we will not explain what this means until Chapter 4. (Readers already versed in works on electoral and party systems will be familiar with this concept, as it has become a standard measure since its introduction by Laakso and Taagepera 1979.)

The relative sizes of parties become even more important when we turn to the votes. Take the UK 2015 election again. The largest party had about 37 percent of the votes, or more than eleven million out of over thirty million total. But how many parties won votes? It is not so easy to answer. Even if we counted only parties that ran candidates for a minimum of 5 percent of all seats – an arbitrary cutoff – we would find that this included at least one party with barely over 6,500 votes (0.02 percent). In other words, some vote-earning parties really are too small to "count." Hence the need for a measure that considers their differing sizes. Even more than for the sake of measuring, however, the greater difficulty of specifying just how many "vote-earning parties" there are becomes a fundamental insight to thinking about how electoral systems shape party politics. We go into this question in depth in Chapter 8.

Most political scientists who have attempted to connect electoral systems to the number of parties have been satisfied with directional hypotheses. Their method has been to test via statistical regression whether the ("effective") number of parties goes up, as expected, with district magnitude and other input variables posited to have either a "restrictive" or "permissive" effect on increases in the number of parties. In some influential works,[14] additional input variables that are held to explain how many parties earn votes are things like how many ethnic groups there are and how many presidential candidates ran (zero if the system is parliamentary – which is itself a problematic "measure" for reasons we explain in Chapters 7 and 12).

These standard works then take the number of vote-earning parties and enter it into a regression in which they seek to explain the number of seat-winning parties via electoral rules.[15] That is, a common scheme regarding how electoral systems and party systems are related looks something like **Figure 1.3**. The figure represents a highly stylized version of the relationship as seen by proponents of the now-standard approach: the

---

[14] For instance, Ordeshook and Shvetsova (1994), Amorim Neto and Cox (1997), Cox (1997), Hicken and Stoll (2011), and Clark and Golder (2006).

[15] In these regressions, it is again standard to use the "effective" number, not a raw count.

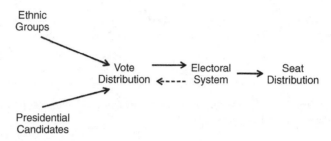

FIGURE 1.3 A common way of seeing the impact of the electoral system on votes and seats

distribution of votes is shaped by a societal feature, such as the number of ethnic groups, as well as by the number of competitors for the presidency (if there is one). The votes are also affected by the electoral system, but only indirectly, according to this standard view – hence it is depicted with a dashed line. That is, according to many authors, the electoral system effect is only fully realized in *interaction* with social factors. For instance, an electoral system favoring many parties nonetheless may result in relatively few parties unless the number of ethnic groups is large, but an electoral system that makes it hard for many parties to win may reduce the number of parties even if there are many ethnic groups. The problem with the approach depicted in Figure 1.3 is that it results in estimates that lack logical foundation, and sometimes are odd or even absurd. We discuss these problems further in Chapters 7 and 12.

The main flaw in this conventional thinking is to try to estimate the seats only after the votes have been estimated. The reason this is flawed is that votes are the *less constrained* of the two quantities. *Thus authors who do this are left with only the ability to make a directional hypothesis*: the number of vote-earning parties goes up as ethnic groups go up, if the electoral system is permissive of such increases, or similar phrasing. However, a more promising approach is to come at it from the opposite side. As we saw in the preceding section, *seats are constrained by district magnitude*. We can thus derive a logical model of the relationship (Equation 1.1). At the national level, they are further constrained by the size of the assembly, a critical consideration that we introduce in Chapter 7 (see also Taagepera 2007).

Figure 1.4 shows the opposite impacts of electoral systems and party politics on the distribution of seats and votes among parties. *Electoral systems restrict directly the way seats can be distributed.* In particular, when single-member districts are used, only one party can win a seat in the given district. *The impact on votes is more remote.* When a party fails to obtain seats in several elections, it may lose votes because voters give up on it, or it may decide not to run in the given district. The impact on party

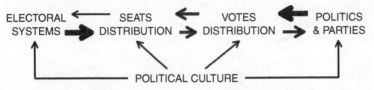

FIGURE 1.4 The opposite impacts of electoral rules and current party politics
Source: Adapted from Taagepera (2007).

systems[16] and hence on politics in general is even more remote. Still, if a party fails to win seats all across the country, over many elections, it may fold, reducing the number of parties among which the voters can choose.

The impact of the existing party system and current politics is attenuated in the reverse direction. The total number of meaningful parties may be limited by the workings of the electoral system, but current politics determines which parties obtain how many votes. The impact of current politics on the seats distribution is weaker, as the electoral system may restrict the *number* of parties that can win seats. Still, current politics determines *which* parties win seats. Finally, current politics has no impact at all on the electoral system, most of the time. Yet, infrequently, it has a major impact, when a new electoral system is worked out from scratch (for instance, in New Zealand in the 1990s – see Denmark 2001).

At all stages, political culture plays a role. The same electoral laws play out differently in different political cultures, shaping different party systems. Along with the initial party system, political culture shapes the adoption of electoral laws. If stable electoral and party systems succeed in lasting over a long time, this experience itself can alter the initial political culture – a connection not shown in Figure 1.4. This book mentions political culture rarely – we return to the issue briefly in Chapter 7. Our infrequent reference to the term is not because we underestimate it. We just do the relatively easy things first – institutions and their constraints; political culture is harder to tackle.

In the study of current politics, votes come first, and seats follow – the arrows at the top of Figure 1.4. This direction may look natural, and that is presumably why conventional approaches frame the problem this way (as in Figure 1.3). However, crucially, *the direction is reversed when we study the impact of electoral systems.* Now seats are restricted directly (as in Equation 1.1), and restrictions on votes follow in a more diffuse way – the arrows at the bottom of Figure 1.4. This is precisely why this book is entitled **Votes from Seats.** In Chapter 8, we offer a novel logical model for understanding how the votes

---

[16] In this book, when we say, "party system" it is just shorthand for how many parties there are, and their relative sizes. For a caution on the use of the word, system, see Taagepera (2007: 5–7).

follow from the seats. Recognition of such reversal of the direction of effects is essential for elucidating the impact of electoral systems.

Plan of the Book

The remainder of this book consists of five parts. In Part I, we introduce **Rules, Tools, and Context**. This section consists of five chapters. Chapter 2 introduces the main components of "simple" electoral systems, including the main rules for proportional representation. Chapter 3 delves into more complex rules, including ballots that give voters the ability to rank candidates, systems with "runoffs," and composite systems that combine two or more different components. In Chapter 4, we introduce two key measuring tools (and some others as well): the *effective number of parties* and *deviation from proportionality*. These are tools for assessing how rules work in their context. Then we have two chapters that situate rules and tools more deeply in context by exploring examples of electoral systems in countries chosen to illustrate how systems work.

The second part consists of four chapters on the **Interparty Dimension of Assembly Politics: The Seat Product Model**. When we are counting parties or measuring deviation from proportionality we are analyzing the interparty dimension, because we are concerned with how many parties there are, their relative sizes, and the relationship between their votes and seats. These concerns have been fundamental to the electoral systems literature, because they are crucial to so much of democratic politics. They get right to the question of how voters are represented and whether one party governs alone or several must cooperate.

The chapters in Part II develop the Seat Product Model, which states that the effective number of parties in the assembly has a systematic relationship to the product of a country's assembly size and mean district magnitude. This model was first proposed by Taagepera (2007), but in this book we are able to expand its scope in several ways. First, in Chapter 7, focused on nationwide assembly party systems, we test it on a large multi-country dataset of individual elections. Then in Chapter 8, we offer a novel logic that allows us to predict the effective number of vote-earning parties from the same input factors. Chapter 9 shows how the preceding chapters have allowed for the development of four *basic laws of party seats and votes*. It also offers an application of the laws to the question of how electoral systems shape one of the most important outcomes of electoral systems – their degree of proportionality – which, we find, also is affected by a country's seat product.

While Chapters 7–9 are about nationwide effects, in Chapter 10 we focus our lens on the district level. It has long been recognized that it is at the district level where the impact of rules is most felt – for exactly the reason we showed earlier in this chapter in our discussion of Equation 1.1. Of course, it is true, but we show that the reverse is true, too, and more fruitful for deriving quantitative logical predictions: *the district-level effect depends on the size of the nationwide electoral system* (i.e., the number of assembly seats) in which the district is *embedded*. The notion of embeddedness, which we extend from an earlier concept that we developed but barely were able to test at the time (Taagepera and Shugart 1993), becomes essential as a building block for several further analyses in later chapters.

The entire second part is focused principally on parliamentary systems, because those are where the number and sizes of parties directly shape government formation. However, we also are able to show that presidential systems – where there is a politically powerful executive elected separately from the assembly – are not fundamentally different from parliamentary in the way electoral systems shape assembly party systems. This is a finding at variance with the conventional literature, which claims that we must know about the number of candidates competing for the presidency (as depicted in Figure 1.3) in order to understand assembly party systems in presidential democracies.

In Part III, we explore the consequences of **Bringing the President In**. Many works on electoral systems and party systems have treated the vote for president as a factor conditioning the vote for assembly (as depicted in Figure 1.3). While such an understanding is surely correct in some sense, it is also limiting. It would be more useful if we could tie all these various party system outcomes – *including the distribution of presidential candidates' votes* – to an institutional input. In Chapter 11, we show that we can do just that. We make the shocking claim that the Seat Product Model devised for assembly party systems also can predict the effective number of presidential candidates. That is, assembly electoral systems have primacy, even in presidential systems.

A key institutional feature of presidential systems is how elections are timed relative to one another (recall our example of Poland, 2015, earlier in this chapter). Other authors have attempted to use this factor to help explain the number of parties in the assembly. Yet they have done so with only minimal theoretical logic for the notion. We show instead, in Chapter 12, that the effect of election timing is on the *votes won by the president's party*, thereby confirming an effect first shown by one us some years ago (Shugart 1995). Except when an assembly election is very late in a president's term, knowing the timing of the elections does not help us predict the number of parties in the assembly, but it critically shapes the support the president obtains in the assembly.

Part IV turns attention to the **Intraparty Dimension of Competition**. Some electoral systems pit candidates of the same party against one another, meaning there is another dimension of competition aside from that between parties – an intraparty dimension. This dimension has been less studied than the interparty. Nonetheless, we show that it, too, follows predicable patterns, and is constrained by the electoral rules. Part IV consists of two chapters. In the first of these, Chapter 13, we develop logical models of how two different types of electoral system that let voters select a candidate within a party shape the distribution of votes across multiple candidates. In Chapter 14, we look at how different rules for intraparty competition shape how parties "manage" the votes distribution across their candidates at the district level. We also address how parties divide up the nominations and the votes when forming alliances in one type of proportional representation system.

Part V is devoted to the question, **What Can We Expect From Models of Electoral Systems?** While most of the book has focused on "simple" electoral systems, many of the world's electoral systems actually are complex. So can our models help predict average outcomes in complex systems? In Chapter 15 we extend the Seat Product Model to "upper tiers."[17] This allows us to expand the range of countries to which the Seat Product Model applies, including a common class of "complex" system. We also consider ethnic diversity, which has been suggested by other works on electoral-system effects. We find that adding ethnicity does not improve much on the Seat Product predictions.

In Chapter 16, we ask whether predictions for other types of complex systems can be made using the Seat Product Model. We introduce another logical model of the impact of one common complexity – a nationwide threshold. We show that for some systems it predicts well, but most of the time our predictions from the Seat Product Model work better. The predictive power of the Seat Product Model even holds for other forms of complexity, such as ranked-choice ballots and runoffs, with some caveats. This is good news for electoral system designers, because it means that introducing some minimal complexity – sometimes desirable for specific purposes – does not mean we are flying blind in understanding the effects. We also offer some examples of overly complex systems, and the problems encountered by them.

Finally, Chapter 17 assesses what we can expect from models of votes and seats, and how they offer a baseline for evaluating country-specific deviations from model predictions. It further points out how the book's methods can contribute to advance the science of politics. We conclude with some basic recommendations for electoral-system design, drawn from our findings.

---

[17] An upper tier is a set of seats allocated based on votes accumulated across the various districts of the "basic tier."

PART I

RULES, TOOLS, AND CONTEXT

2

Components of Simple Electoral Systems

Elections determine in a democracy who the voters' representative agents will be. Before the voters can choose, however, someone has to have chosen an electoral system. This book will not focus on the reasons why a specific set of rules is found in a country. Rather, we will take them as given. Nonetheless, one of our goals with this book is to offer those who might adopt rules for elections where none exist (as in a transition from dictatorship to democracy), or reform those already in place in an established democracy, a deeper understanding of the main choices and what their consequences tend to be. In this chapter and Chapter 3, we offer a broad overview of the basic components of rules that make up the "electoral system."[1]

This chapter focuses principally on those electoral systems that can be considered "simple." We will offer a more precise definition of "simple system" (drawing on Taagepera 2007) later. The general idea is that among the many choices and components that can go into the design of an electoral system, as we review in this chapter and the next, simplicity means sticking to the basics and avoiding unusual combinations of distinct components. At times there may be valid reasons to stray from simplicity in design, but it is generally best to avoid overcomplicating an electoral system. When systems are made more complex, their effects on political parties and voters may be unpredictable.

Basic Choices

One of the biggest choices one would make in setting the rules of the electoral game is: Do we want the electoral system to enhance the seats of the largest vote-earning parties, or do we want the seat share of nearly every party to be very close to its vote share? This question lies squarely on the interparty dimension, and primarily concerns the tradeoff between "majoritarian" and

---

[1] Some portions of this chapter and Chapter 3 – particularly some of the tables – build directly off Taagepera (2007).

"proportional" systems (Lijphart 1999). Another question, which belongs mainly to the intraparty dimension, is: Do we want the primary representative agents to be parties as collective actors, or should voters be selecting candidates to represent them as individual representatives?[2]

The world of electoral systems has many ways of answering these basic questions, and the ways in which the electoral system answers them go well beyond a straightforward "this" or "that"; an almost infinite range of intermediate solutions exist. A good starting point, however, is to think of the tradeoff between plurality, also known as First-Past-The-Post (FPTP), and proportional representation (PR). If the electoral system is FPTP, only the candidate who gets the most votes in a district is chosen as a representative agent of that district. If the same party happens to have nominated the candidates who obtain these pluralities in more than half the districts, then the system is "majoritarian" in the sense of bolstering the position of a large party.

The more parties there are that run but fail to get very many district-level pluralities, the greater the tendency of the FPTP system to "manufacture" a majority, because three or more parties divide the votes, but two big ones get most of the seats. These are the dynamics that make up a tendency often known as "Duverger's law"[3]: big parties are favored in turning votes into seats under FPTP; seeing this, opponents of the leading party have an incentive to "coordinate" around one other party that can replace it.[4] Hence we might wind up with a two-party system, with not very many votes – and even fewer seats – remaining for parties other than the big two. Despite the term "law" it is not a given that such a party system will result, and in fact, several chapters of this book (especially Chapters 7–10) will cast doubt both on the empirical validity of the tendencies to which Duverger referred and on their suitability for being called "law."

On the other hand, if the system is PR, normally a party will not win a majority of seats unless it has a majority of votes. As we saw in our example of Poland, 2015, in Chapter 1, it is nonetheless possible for a party under PR to get a majority of seats despite less than half the votes. However, as reviewed there, other features aside from the PR method were involved in producing that result (notably the thresholds). Normally, PR rules reduce the chances of a majority party because even small parties can get seat shares that are quite close to their vote shares.

Additionally, the opportunity for quite small parties to win seats may encourage more of them to form, and voters will be more inclined to stick with them. Districts under PR systems need to elect more than a single legislator,

---

[2] See Carey (2009) for extensive treatment of the tradeoffs involved in collective versus individual accountability of legislators.

[3] Originally derived from the propositions laid out by Duverger (1954).

[4] For detailed analysis of electoral coordination, see Cox (1997, 1999).

in order to be able to divvy up the district's representation according to parties' vote shares. As more seats are available in a district, more opportunities exist for smaller parties to get at least one of them (as shown already in Figure 1.2 in the Introduction). Thus PR increases our odds of having a multiparty system, although the relationship is not deterministic.

On the intraparty dimension, do we prefer that voters select candidates or whole parties? In the FPTP system, every nominee of a party runs in a unique district, and hence receives votes as an individual. While parties can be cohesive and policy-focused even under FPTP, it is also very likely that the candidates and legislators elected in this way have a strong incentive to appeal to the parochial concerns of voters who reside in the district (Cain, Ferejohn, and Fiorina 1987). Thus FPTP may produce contradictory results – a majority party (interparty dimension) and local focus (intraparty). Where a given system ends up may be depend on many things other than the electoral system, such as the executive type (parliamentary or presidential), legislative rules, party rules, and so on.[5]

What about proportional systems? Here the intraparty rules make a big difference. In most PR systems, parties present *lists* of candidates. With the exception of very small parties under certain rules, parties want to nominate more than one candidate per district for the very basic reason that, by definition, PR means districts with more than one seat. A party – at least a larger one – may be able to win two or more seats in a district, but only if it nominated two or more before the election! Thus under PR rules, there is a further question that must be encountered in the design of the system: Should the voter select only a party, or should the voter be able to select one candidate (or perhaps more than one) from within a party (or sometimes from different parties)? The choice here will affect how candidates relate to voters and their party.

Rules within PR systems may allow the voter only to pick one party list, with no choice among the various candidates the party has nominated; this is called a "closed list," and is used, for example, in Israel and Portugal. The voter must take the slate as a whole, or leave it and vote for another party instead. In other systems, parties present lists, but voters may cast candidate votes, thereby having an intralist choice. Generically, these can be termed "preferential-list" systems (Shugart 2005a).

In the case of preferential-list systems, details vary in defining how the preference votes for specific candidates are counted in the process of determining winners. We explore these rules in greater detail in later chapters. One solution is the "open list," used for example in Brazil and Poland, where the identity of candidates elected from any party's list is determined entirely by the candidates' preference votes. Such rules may reduce the cohesion of the party, as candidates seek to court different groups of voters (Carey 2009). At the

---

[5] Readers wanting to explore these effects are referred to Carey (2009), Kam (2009), and Samuels and Shugart (2010).

same time it might broaden the appeal of the party by encouraging it to have candidates who can collect votes from these different groups.

Electoral systems may combine components in all sorts of ways. While this chapter is focused on "simple" systems that do not combine too many different components, it is worth noting that it is possible for a system to have all four of the basic components we just described all rolled into one. We can have a system in which some legislators are elected by FPTP yet with the overall nationwide seat allocation being proportional, thereby allowing voters to vote for both a candidate running in their local district and a party list. This complex combination typifies a type of electoral system called "mixed-member proportional," as used in Germany and, since 1996, New Zealand. These are complex systems, and are discussed in more detail in Chapter 3.

Components of Electoral Systems – Overview

Elections can apply to one position (e.g., president, governor), a few (local council) or several hundred (parliament in a large country). Voters may have to voice unqualified support for an entire party or for one or several candidates using a "categorical ballot." Alternatively, they may be able to give ranked preferences (first choice, second choice, etc.) over multiple candidates using an "ordinal ballot." There may be one or two "rounds" of voting,[6] by which voters are called back to the polls on a later date if the first round did not produce a decision, as defined by the rules.

We start by outlining the basic choices, and introducing some preliminary notation that will be needed for equations and formulas of later chapters. These basic components are: assembly size, districting arrangements, and allocation formula.

Assembly size. Some fundamental choices that pertain to elections are outside the electoral laws as such. Every democratic country needs electoral laws for the first or only chamber of its representative assembly. If a presidential regime is chosen, it also needs laws for presidential elections. If there is a two-chamber (bicameral) assembly and both chambers are elected, their electoral systems may be different in either small details or in more fundamental ways. To keep things tractable, this book focuses almost entirely on first (or sole) chambers. The book also focuses on *general elections*, rather than *primaries*, which are contests in which voters participate in the selection of candidates who will bear the party's label in the upcoming general election. Nonetheless, the basic choices of rules for general elections and first chambers also apply to primaries and second chambers.

---

[6] In principle, there could be three (or more rounds), but in contemporary elections with public participation, we do not know of cases with more than two.

The first question is: How many seats should such a representative chamber have? Given that smaller assemblies offer fewer places over which parties can compete, the choice of *assembly size* (S) is critical. For this reason, assembly size is certainly part of the electoral system, yet before Lijphart (1994) analysis of the effect of electoral systems rarely included it as a factor. Even subsequent to Lijphart, few other than Taagepera (2007) and Li and Shugart (2016) have systematically recognized the importance of assembly size to electoral system effects.[7]

Even though the assembly size is a component of the electoral system, it is probably very rare for designers of electoral systems to consider assembly size directly when deciding what provisions to incorporate. It is generally a parameter that already has been set through separate, past decisions.

Large countries are almost bound to have more seats than smaller ones. Indeed, the *cube root law* for assembly size performs well as a statement of the relationship between population and assembly size, and has a quantitative logical model to back it up (Taagepera and Shugart 1989a):

$$S = P^{1/3}. \tag{2.1}$$

In words, the assembly size, S, equals the cube root of the country's population, P. In Figure 2.1, we see a data plot of the countries whose electoral systems will be the basis of the quantitative analysis in several later chapters of this book.

The solid diagonal line in Figure 2.1 represents Equation 2.1. At a glance, the best fit slope is steeper than the law predicts. However, focus on the cases above the horizontal line at S=50. The fit is better above that line. Below the line, all cases are English-speaking Caribbean island countries.[8] We do not have a theoretical reason for why these countries have systematically "undersized" assemblies, although this fact has been noted before by Lijphart (1990), who correctly noted that their small assemblies contribute to a tendency for very large seat bonuses for the largest party.

Figure 2.1 also differentiates presidential systems (triangles) from parliamentary systems (circles). There is some tendency for presidential systems also to have smaller assemblies than the cube root of their population.[9] It is unclear why.[10] When the Caribbean countries are omitted from a regression estimation (but presidential are included), we obtain an exponent of 0.349,

[7] For the given election, assembly size is fixed in advance, although under some electoral rules it can increase slightly depending on the outcome of the election.
[8] One such country, Jamaica, is above the line, with S>60 since the 1960s.
[9] For example, the United States (see Taylor, Shugart, Grofman, and Lijphart, 2014: 209–215). The undersized nature of the US House has drawn some scholarly notice, including Frederick's (2009) study of potential consequences of the populations of individual districts.
[10] To our knowledge, the question has not been addressed in any literature on institutional design.

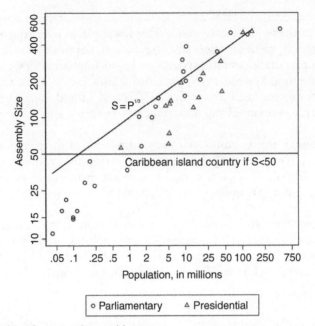

FIGURE 2.1 Population and assembly size

which is obviously a trivial difference from Equation 2.1.[11] Thus for the analysis of this book, we start off with a key parameter, assembly size, which can be thought of as, with some exceptions, exogenously set by the country's population size.

Districting arrangements. With assembly size thus essentially given, the next question is: Into how many electoral districts should the country be divided? Electoral districts mean the geographically bounded areas within which popular votes are converted into assembly seats. The number of seats allocated within a district is called *district magnitude* (M). It is arguably the single most important number for election outcomes. One can have numerous single-seat districts where $M=1$, or fewer multiseat districts where $M>1$. The limit is one nationwide district where district magnitude equals assembly size ($M=S$). All districts need not be of equal magnitude for the system to be simple; if there are overlapping districts, however, the system is complex. These matters are discussed further in Chapter 3.

---

[11] The regression has a statistically insignificant constant term of –0.189, and R^2=0.751. If the regression is run with presidential systems also dropped, the coefficient is 0.328! (And the constant becomes 0.02, also insignificant.) The insignificant constant is expected, because according to the logical-modeling techniques sketched in Chapter 1, we would be suspicious of a model with a significant constant. It would violate the obvious logical requirement that if there were only one person in a country, the assembly size would have to be $S=1$.

Many works speak of "single-member" and "multimember" districts. However, electoral rules allocate seats or memberships to candidates or parties – they do not allocate "members" as such. It is hence more logical to talk of single-seat and multiseat districts, and we shall do so throughout this book.

Allocation formula. A seat allocation formula defines the precise rules by which a party or candidate wins any one of a district's available seats, based on their votes. It is tied in with *ballot structure* and the number of *rounds* of voting, which we thus consider as subcomponents of the allocation formula.

The allocation formula stipulates how votes are to be converted into seats. At the one extreme, all seats in the district may be given to the party with the most votes (plurality rule). At the other extreme, one could use a PR formula in order to distribute the seats among multiple parties according to their votes. As we shall see, PR formula is itself a broad category including many specific variations that tend to produce more or less proportionality.

The voter may be given one or more votes. If only the first preferences are taken into account, the ballot is *categorical*. These are the simplest formulas, although more complex options exist. For instance, we already alluded to the possibility of *ordinal* (ranked) ballots. There are also electoral systems that allow voters to vote for two parties without ranking them – for instance a candidate of one party in their district and the list of another for seats allocated proportionally. We follow the suggestion of Gallagher and Mitchell (2005b, 2018) and call this a *dividual* ballot. As already noted, some allocation rules may require a second round – for instance, when no candidate obtains a majority of votes in the first round. These various features are discussed further in Chapter 3. For now, we keep the focus on simple systems.

What Makes an Electoral System Simple

Now we will begin to think about how the various components fit together, and what makes an electoral system simple or complex. Only categorical ballots and a single round of voting are simple, by our definition. The reason is that other ballot formats or multiple rounds, and the allocation rules that use them, may violate a basic criterion for simplicity of the translation of votes into seats: *the rank-size principle.* Under this principle, the relative sizes of parties in voting are reflected in the allocation of seats. That is, the first seat in a district always goes to the party with the most votes in the district. Then, if there are more seats ($M>1$), other parties that have sufficient votes may obtain seats, and they obtain them in order. That is, the next party to get a seat after the largest will be the one with the second most votes, and so on.

The rank-size principle may seem obvious. However, if an ordinal ballot is used, or there is a second round, it may be violated. For instance, under rules that use an ordinal ballot, the first seat may not go to the party that had the most first-preference votes. If there is a second round, the party that had the most votes in the first round may yet lose. There are other allocation formulas that likewise violate the rank-size principle. We discuss them in Chapter 3.

Assembly size, district magnitude, and *seat allocation formula* (plus the corresponding ballot structure) are the three indispensable features regarding which a choice cannot be avoided in designing a system to convert votes into seats. Taking the preceding factors together, a simple system is one in which:

(1) All seats are allocated in districts (as opposed to some being allocated in districts but others nationwide, for example); and
(2) The allocation rule respects the rank-size principle.[12]

Single-seat districts may look simple, but they still offer several choices for seat allocation – we will discuss some of them in Chapter 3. The simplest form of single-seat district is one in which the candidate with the most votes wins the seat – the plurality or FPTP system we mentioned earlier. This means a categorical ballot (vote for one) and a single round of voting, in which the candidate with the most votes wins the one seat. Even with these features, single-seat districts entail further complications arising from the need to delimit boundaries. We take these issues up briefly in the Chapter 3, along with other complicating factors.

In multiseat districts the options for how to elect representatives multiply; some of the options belong to the set of complex rules discussed in Chapter 3. Simple PR systems allocate seats among party lists. While it is possible to use plurality or another non-PR formula with party lists, such systems are not simple. We discuss them briefly here because they help focus our attention to the joint impact of our three essential components – assembly size (S), district magnitude (M), and allocation formula.

The plurality formula favors a large party for the very basic reason that it gives whatever number of seats are at stake in a district to the largest in that district. Usually when we think of a "plurality system" or FPTP, we mean that the country has S districts (one for every member of the assembly). The largest party in one district usually is not the largest in all districts, so two or more parties win seats in the assembly. Small parties, however, lose out unless they happen to be the largest in some districts. In Chapter 1, we gave the example from the Canadian election of 2008. In this election, under FPTP, four parties won seats in the assembly, but another party, the Green Party, won 6.8 percent of the votes nationwide, but not a plurality in any district, so no seats.

---

[12] This definition is only subtly different from that of Taagepera (2007: 19–20). The second criterion was not included in the previous definition, and Taagepera added closed lists and equal magnitude as criteria that he later relaxed.

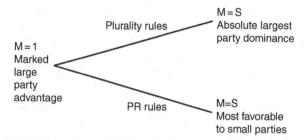

FIGURE 2.2 Contrasting effects of plurality and PR rules at the same district magnitude

Imagine instead that we had a single national district under plurality rule. Now we have *M=S* so all the seats in the assembly go to the largest party: 100 percent of seats even if there was a close race among several parties to see who would be the largest. No country uses plurality in a nationwide district. Where the multiseat plurality formula is used, it is generally in low-magnitude districts. The main exception is the US Electoral College, where plurality is used statewide with some very high magnitudes (for instance, more than 50 in California).

When a PR formula is used, the effect of magnitude is reversed. The closest we can get to pure PR (for a given *S*) is when *M=S*. This means the entire country is one district. Two such examples are Israel and the Netherlands, both of which famously have many parties. With PR, a decreasing district magnitude increases the large-party advantage and hurts the small parties. The minimum district magnitude that is possible is one; and what happens when we use PR and *M=1*? Only the largest party in the district gets a seat. Thus single-seat plurality could just as easily be called single-seat PR! This is why we prefer to designate it as First-Past-The-Post (FPTP), a relatively neutral term between plurality and PR.

Figure 2.2 shows the overall picture for party lists in single- and multiseat districts. The contrast between plurality and PR allocation rules is extreme for a nationwide single district (*M=S*). Here plurality rule would assign all *S* seats in the assembly to the winning list, while PR rules would produce highly proportional outcomes. As the electorate is divided into increasingly smaller districts (*M<S*), the contrast between the outcomes of plurality and PR rules softens, until they yield the same outcome in the case of single-seat districts (*M=1*). We do not regard multiseat plurality as a "simple" system. Simple systems thus occur along the lower branch in Figure 2.1, ranging from FPTP to nationwide PR, with a wide range of districted PR systems in between.

In simple PR systems, those that use party lists, seats are allocated among the lists of parties competing in multiseat districts. While the focus of allocation across parties is on the votes earned by the lists, the ballot may allow voters to cast votes for individual candidates. These votes may affect which candidates win from the list – that is, they affect the intraparty dimension. For instance, instead of having only the choice of party lists (*closed lists*), voters may have the option to voice preferences for one or more candidates on a list (*open lists*), or they may be even required to vote for a specific candidate (as in the Polish case discussed in Chapter 1 and in Finland, discussed in Chapter 6). The so-called *panachage* (literally, cocktail) enables voters to mix candidates from across different lists – in effect, making up their own "free" list of preferred candidates.[13] Other allocation rules for multiseat districts that do not have party lists but have only candidates votes (whether categorical, ordinal, or dividual) are discussed in Chapter 3.

In sum, choosing an electoral system involves three inevitable choices (*S*, *M*, and allocation formula) and numerous optional ones. The ways to combine and mix them are infinite in principle and extremely numerous in practice. If many different options are mixed, the system may become quite complex. In the next section, we discuss in greater detail the basic types of simple systems, FPTP and PR.

FPTP AND PR AS "SIMPLE" SYSTEMS

In the preceding section we defined an electoral system as simple when (1) all *S* seats in the assembly are allocated solely within districts, and (2) when the formula follows the relative sizes of parties in votes as it allocates seats. The basic types of systems that meet the definition of "simple" are FPTP and any "districted PR" system, the systems on the lower branch of Figure 2.2. What these have in common is *S* seats allocated in districts, the number of which can range from one to *S*. If we have one district, we have nationwide proportional representation. If we have *S* districts, we have FPTP.

When the country is divided into single-seat districts, the only system that is truly simple is plurality, or FPTP, under which the winner in each district is the candidate with the most votes. Because any given party almost without exception nominates only one candidate per district when $M=1$, a vote for a candidate is also a vote for a party. Mechanically, it makes no difference whether we call this a system with only candidate votes, or a system of party-list votes in which each "list" contains only one name. The result is the same: the party with the most votes wins the seat, and its "first-ranked" candidate takes the seat. The ballot makes the choice categoric, and because there is only one round of voting, the winner is the one with the most votes, regardless of whether its total vote is more than half, and regardless of the margin over the runner-up.

---

[13] *Panachage* is clearly a complexity, but a few such systems (Luxembourg, Switzerland, and since 2005, Honduras) remain in our subsequent analysis of "simple" systems because their complexity primarily affects the intraparty dimension rather than the allocation of seats across lists.

The FPTP system is widely used in British-heritage countries. It is often associated with a two-party system, with a "bare-majority" (Lijphart 1984, 1999) governing party and a strong opposition. However, it would be hard to speak of a "law" because there are so many exceptions. Assembly size can make a difference. Large countries with large assemblies such as the United Kingdom (S around 650) and India (S around 540) can have more than two significant parties in the assembly.[14] If a country has significant regional variation, having many districts may help region-specific parties win. In small countries like Barbados ($S=26$) one party often has about 70 percent of the seats, leaving a weak opposition (Taagepera and Ensch 2006). Examples of FPTP systems are discussed in detail in Chapter 5.

Now, we turn our attention to multiseat districts, meaning those with magnitude greater than one ($M>1$). Under proportional representation, the goal is to make the seat shares of parties reasonably proportional to their vote shares. Simple PR means that each party presents a list of candidates, typically containing at least as many candidates as there are seats allocated in the district. Thus, under any party-list system "teams" of candidates run together, and seats are allocated first among competing lists, and only then to candidates (as we showed in the Polish example in Chapter 1). When, instead of party lists, the electoral system consists of voting for individual candidates in multiseat districts, the outcome, and the voting process itself become more complex. Thus we discuss candidate-based $M>1$ systems in Chapter 3, and focus on list systems here.

Under districted (simple) PR with $M>1$, the vote for candidate and for party is one act. If the vote is a categorical one for a single party list (closed list), the vote simply endorses the full slate of candidates, with the winners being determined based on the pre-election priority ranking on the party's list. When a PR system instead gives the voter a single categorical vote for a candidate (open list), it is similarly a vote for the party as well as for that candidate;[15] either way, parties receive seats on the basis of their total votes.[16] In this way, FPTP and list PR belong to the same family, and FPTP is just one endpoint of the continuum.

We discuss the distinctions among list systems in detail, using examples, in Chapter 6. The issue of intraparty seat allocation is important, e.g., for representation of women (Matland and Taylor 1997) and local interests

---

[14] In the case of India, the number of parties is especially large. However, many parties operate under the umbrella of two or three major alliances. We discuss this phenomenon in more detail in Chapters 5 and 15.

[15] Intermediary ways to allocate seats within the party (flexible lists) are also used; see Chapter 6.

[16] As mentioned earlier, some open-list systems allow the voter to vote for more than one candidate on a list (e.g., Peru). There are also the *panachage* (free-list) systems, in which voters may vote for candidates on several lists. What unites these systems under the rubric of "list" systems is that in all of them, seats are first allocated to lists, based on their collective vote totals, before turning to the intraparty allocation.

(Crisp et al. 2004, Shugart et al. 2005); we discuss a set of questions related to these intraparty considerations in Chapters 13 and 14. Our focus here will be on different formulas used to carry out PR among party lists (rather than allocation to candidates *within* lists); there are two broad subfamilies – *quota* formulas and divisor formulas.

Proportional Representation with Quotas

How should the seats be allocated among the parties?[17] Early advocates of PR came up with various quotas that still commonly bear their names: Hare (1859) and Droop (2012 [1869]). Hare's is perhaps the simplest of all, and hence is known by the name, *Simple Quota and Largest Remainders*, as well as *Hare-LR*. Under this quota, of the M available seats, a share $100\%/M$ of the votes should entitle a party to a seat. This quota, also called exact or Hamilton quota, can be designated as q_0 for reasons of systematics that will become apparent later. Parties receive as many seats as they have full quotas of votes. These quotas are subtracted from the total vote shares, typically leaving vote remainders. Correspondingly, some seats remain unallocated; these are allocated to the parties with the largest remainders. Any party with a remainder of more than half-quota ($q_0/2$) is likely to receive such a remainder seat, but it depends on how the votes happen to be distributed among the other parties.

If we wish to have fewer remainder seats, we can reduce the quota. One might consider $100\%/(M+1)$, designated here as q_1. Now it is possible to allocate more seats by full quotas – or even all of them. But one runs just a tiny risk of allocating more seats than the district has. Suppose $M=4$, so that $q_1=20$ percent. If parties' votes happen to be exactly 60.00, 20.00, and 20.00 percent, five seats would be allocated! To guard against this admittedly unlikely outcome, the *Hagenbach-Bischoff quota* adds 1 vote to the total votes, before calculating the quota, while *Droop quota* adds 1 vote to the quota itself (NOT 1 percent of all votes!), leading to $q_{Droop}=100\%/(M+1)+1$ vote. This single vote makes overallocation of seats impossible. For practical purposes, the Droop and Hagenbach-Bischoff quotas are identical to q_1. If we are not concerned with overallocation, we can even use $q_2=100\%/(M+2)$ or $q_3=100\%/(M+3)$. Both have been referred to as *Imperiali quota* and were once used in Italy.

There also exist quotas larger than simple quota, e.g., $q_{-1}=100\%/(M-1)$, and so on, although they are not used in practice. Somewhat counterintuitively, *small quotas favor large parties*, while large quotas favor small parties. This is easiest to see when imagining extreme cases. Suppose again that $M=4$, and we decide to make use of $q_{-3}=100\%/(M-3)$ so that the quota is 100 percent. No one receives a quota seat. The four largest

---

[17] This subsection and the next draw liberally on Taagepera (2007).

parties receive one remainder seat each, even when their vote shares are as unbalanced as 60, 30, 7, 2, and 1. Of course, q_{-3} is unrealistic, but unrealistic extreme cases offer a powerful conceptual tool in disciplines such as physics (Taagepera 2008). We will use extreme examples to illustrate general patterns of interest at many points in this book.

Subtraction is the basic philosophy for all PR formulas that are based on a quota and largest remainders: each time a seat is allocated to a party, a specified amount of votes is subtracted from its total votes. Alternatively, allocation can follow a *divisor* philosophy, which brings us to the second subfamily of PR formulas.

Proportional Representation with Divisors

Under a divisor formula, each time a party is allocated a seat, the rules state that its total votes be divided by a specified amount, before the allocation of the next seat is considered. The most widely used divisors are the $D'Hondt$[18] (Jefferson) divisors, 1, 2, 3, 4 ... Table 2.1 shows how they work. Suppose $M=6$ seats are to be allocated, and the parties' percentages of the vote in the district are exactly 48, 25, 13, 9, 4, and 1. We divide all votes by the first divisor; because this is 1, it obviously does not alter the votes. Next, we allocate the first seat to the largest share, 48 percent, as indicated in Table 2.1. If this district had just one seat, we would be done! This reminds us of why FPTP is just PR (whether D'Hondt or another simple formula) in the smallest possible district. However, we have $M=6$ in our example. So now we need to divide the vote percentage of the party that won the first seat by 2. This reduces it to 24 percent for the next seat to be allocated. Now we compare this 24 percent to the other parties. The second largest party's 25 percent is larger, so it receives the second seat. Now its share is divided by 2. The next two seats go again to the largest party, with its share divided by 3 and then by 4.[19] The fifth and sixth seats go to the third and second largest parties, whose quotients (13 and 12.5, respectively) narrowly surpass the largest party's 12.

In this particular case, all major parties are overpaid: their seat shares exceed their vote shares. In general, however, D'Hondt divisors tend to favor the largest party. This advantage lessens as M increases. D'Hondt is one of the most widely used PR formulas. In addition to the Polish case discussed in Chapter 1, for example, Finland has used D'Hondt divisors for over 100 years (with mean $M=13$).

One can also use various other divisors. Faster increase in divisors reduces large party advantage. *Sainte-Laguë* (Webster) divisors (1, 3, 5, 7, ...)

---

[18] Many works, including Taagepera and Shugart (1989) and Lijphart (1994), spell the name "d'Hondt"; however, the variant we are using here has been shown to be correct. See Gallagher and Mitchell (2005a: 632).

[19] A common mistake at this point is to divide 24 by 3, instead of dividing the original 48 by 3.

TABLE 2.1 *Allocation of six seats by D'Hondt divisors (1, 2, 3, …)*

Votes,%	48 (1st seat)	25 (2nd seat)	13 (5th seat)	9	4	1
	48/2=24 (3rd seat)	25/2=12.5 (6th seat)	13/2=7.5			
	48/3=16 (4th seat)					
	48/4=12					
Seats	3	2	1	0	0	0
Seats,%	50	33	20	0	0	0

Source: First shown in Taagepera (2007).

abolish this advantage, and the so-called Danish divisors (1, 4, 7, 10, …) actually favor the smaller parties.[20] To increase their seat shares, large parties might then split their lists strategically, but doing so might risk the splits becoming permanent.

In the other direction, the divisors could be increased more slowly. This would favor heavily the largest party. *Imperiali divisors* (1, 1.5, 2, 2.5, …) have been used. (Do not confuse them with the aforementioned Imperiali quotas!) The divisor series with the slowest increase would be 1, 1, 1, 1, … where the largest party wins all the seats. Thus, surprisingly, multiseat plurality rule surfaces as the extreme member of the divisor family of the PR formulas.

It is also possible to have divisors that tend to favor middle-sized parties. The *Modified Sainte-Laguë* divisors (1.4, 3, 5, 7, …) are used in some Scandinavian countries. Here the initial divisor 1.4 (instead of 1) makes it hard for small parties to receive their first seat. The quaintest divisors ever used might be the "modified D'Hondt" divisors used in Estonia: $1^{0.9}$, $2^{0.9}$, $3^{0.9}$, $4^{0.9}$, $5^{0.9}$, … They are equivalent to 1, 1.87, 2.69, 3.48, 4.26, …

Table 2.2 illustrates the effect of the various formulas from both quota and divisor families. It shows the allocations of seats when vote shares are again exactly 48, 25, 13, 9, 4 and 1 percent, as in Table 2.1, and the district has six seats.

The perfectly proportional seat share, shown at the top of Table 2.2, is fractional and can be only approximated. Visibly, allocations 3, 2, 1, and 3, 1, 1, 1, which occur in the center of the table, come closest to proportionality.[21] These two examples, D'Hondt and Sainte-Laguë, are the only divisor rules used fairly widely. Allocation formulas at the top of the table tend to overpay the largest party and are rarely used. Those at the bottom tend to overpay the small parties and are likewise rare.

---

[20] To see why this is so, consider an extreme case: let's increase the gap between divisors and use 1, 51, 101, 151 … then all *M* largest parties may win one seat each.

[21] Operational measures for deviation from proportionality will be presented in Chapter 4.

TABLE 2.2 *Allocation of seats in a six-seat district, by various quota and divisor formulas*

Votes,%	48	25	13	9	4	1
Perfectly proportional seat share	2.88	1.50	0.78	0.54	0.24	0.06
Steady divisors (1, 1, 1, 1, …) = plurality	6	0	0	0	0	0
Imperiali divisors (1, 1.5, 2, 2.5, …)	4	2	0	0	0	0
Modified D'Hondt (1, 1.87, 2.69, 3.48, …)	4	2	0	0	0	0
Imperiali quota q_3=100%/(M+3)=11.1%	4	2	1	[overallocation!]		
Imperiali quota q_2=100%/(M+2)=12.5%	3	2	1	0	0	0
D'Hondt divisors (1, 2, 3, 4, …)	3	2	1	0	0	0
Modified Sainte-Laguë div. (1.4, 3, 5, 7, …)	3	2	1	0	0	0
Droop/Hagenbach-B. quota q_1=14.3%	3	2	1	0	0	0
Sainte-Laguë divisors (1, 3, 5, 7, …)	3	1	1	1	0	0
Hare quota q_0=100%/M=16.7%	3	1	1	1	0	0
Danish divisors (1, 4, 7, 10, …)	3	1	1	1	0	0
Quota q_{-1}=100%/(M-1)=20%	3	1	1	1	0	0
Quota q_{-2}=100%/(M-2)=25%	2	1	1	1	1	0
Quota q_{-3}=100%/(M-3)=33.3%	2	1	1	1	1	0
Divisors 1, 51, 101, 151, …	1	1	1	1	1	1
Quota q_{-4}=100%/(M-4)=50%	1	1	1	1	1	1

Source: First shown in Taagepera (2007).

Since large quotas allocate all too many seats by largest remainders, while small quotas risk overallocation of quota seats, one may look for a *sufficient quota*. Start with Droop quota and reduce the quota gradually, until all seats are allocated by quota, with no need to consider the remainders. The result may surprise: *The remainderless quota is equivalent to D'Hondt divisors.*

So the D'Hondt formula occupies a central position on the landscape of PR formulas: it is at the crossroads of quota and divisor methods. This is how Thomas Jefferson actually came to define what later came to be called D'Hondt divisors in electoral studies (Colomer 2004a: 44). But Jefferson was concerned with seat allocation to the US states according to their populations. So were Alexander Hamilton, who first defined the simple quota, and Daniel Webster, who first defined the Sainte-Laguë divisors. All these approaches were reinvented in Europe when the need arose to allocate seats to parties according to their votes.

As district magnitude increases, the choice of the particular allocation formula makes less of a difference, because all formulas in the central range of Table 2.2 tend to produce seat allocations closer to perfect PR. In principle, these formulas can be applied to any district magnitude, up to and including nationwide allocation.

Going in the opposite direction, what happens if these formulas are applied to single-seat districts? All of them allocate the only seat at stake to the party with the most votes, and hence they become equivalent to FPTP. As seen in Figure 2.2, *FPTP is a limiting case of list PR.* Sharply distinguishing between FPTP and list PR in multiseat districts is artificial.

The official descriptions of seat allocation formulas in various countries often are confusing. For instance, the D'Hondt procedure can be speeded up by first allocating seats by full Hare, Droop, or Hagenbach-Bischoff quotas and then, instead of using largest remainders, switching to D'Hondt. The outcome is the same as D'Hondt which is, as we noted above, equivalent to a remainderless quota. Variants of this combination of some standard quota first, then D'Hondt on remainders, are found in Israel (Hazan et al. 2018), the Netherlands (Jacobs 2018), and Switzerland. Such procedures invite error in classification; these should not be classified according to their initial quota, but rather by their ultimate use of D'Hondt. It is thus valuable to understand the systematics of different allocation methods, as outlined in this chapter, in order to be able to put a given example into its broader family and context.

Conclusions

The central purpose of this book is to elucidate regularities in the impact of electoral systems on party systems. To that end, we started in this chapter with the simplest electoral systems, meaning all seats allocated within districts with a formula that allocates seats among lists of candidates according to the votes cast in the district. We noted that in single-seat ($M=1$) districts, a simple system means First-Past-the-Post (FPTP), also known as plurality. As district magnitude increases beyond one ($M>1$), a simple system implies the use of one of several proportional formulas; it is also possible to use plurality with $M>1$, but doing so takes us outside the family of simple rules.

Simple systems are important for several reasons. First of all, the very features that make them simple by our definition also make them simple for voters and party officials to understand. Simplicity is itself a virtue in electoral-system design. The more complications are added, the more difficult it may be for voters and other actors to learn how to make effective use of the system to obtain desired representation. Second, simple systems are the most straightforward for developing logical predictive models, a key aim of this book. In Chapter 3, we turn our attention to more complex rules, only some of which we are able to develop logical predictions about, in subsequent chapters.

3

Components of Complex and Composite Electoral Systems

In Chapter 2, we introduced several basic features of electoral systems, with a focus on those systems that we call "simple." In this chapter, we turn our attention to several more complex rules and systems that consist of composites of different rules. Many of the world's countries have complex electoral systems, and thus it is important to work through their details. However, the complications are not only about the systems themselves. The more complex the rules are, the more we risk finding ourselves in uncharted territory. When systems are more complex, we often have fewer past cases with similar rules from which to draw empirical lessons. Further, logical predictive models might elude us or have to be made overly complex themselves.

In this book we will show that one class of "complex" systems ("two-tier PR") can be covered under a simple logical model (Chapter 15). We will have less to say about other complex systems, although in Chapter 16 we will show that some of them behave a lot like simple systems after all! The implication is that perhaps some countries or other jurisdictions using (or considering using) complex systems could get by with simpler alternatives without changing outcomes all that much.[1]

This chapter will begin by delving further into single-seat district ($M=1$) systems, discussing how they can be made more complex than plurality/FPTP by the choice of electoral formula. Then we turn to multiseat districts where the rules are candidate-based, rather than list-based. These more complicated $M=1$ and $M>1$ systems retain the feature of those discussed in Chapter 2, which is to say that all seats are allocated in a single set of districts. That is, every voter votes in just one district for any given legislative chamber. Then we turn to multitier and composite systems, a common form of complexity in which one set of district overlays another, which means that every voter actually votes in two (or more) districts for the same legislative chamber. This chapter also discusses other complications to basic rules, such as legal thresholds.

---

[1] Exceptions would be cases where complex provisions are adopted to exclude some "undesired" party or to give an unusually large boost to the leading party. These sorts of complexities can have perverse results, and we will offer some examples in Chapter 15.

TABLE 3.1 *Possible seat allocation rules in a single-seat district*

	Categorical ballot (vote for one candidate)	Ordinal ballot (rank two or more)
Plurality	First-Past-The-Post	Borda Count
Majority	Two-Round	Alternative Vote

SINGLE-TIER COMPLEX SYSTEMS

If there is a single tier of districts, any complexity comes from the formula employed. We first discuss $M=1$ systems that have complex formulas, and then turn to $M>1$, candidate-based, systems. What leaves the formulas discussed here outside of the family of simple systems is the second criterion introduced in Chapter 2. That is, as single-tier systems, they conform to the first criterion (all seats allocated solely within districts); they do not necessarily conform to the second one (following votes distributions) because they make possible one party leading in the initial vote, but a different party winning the seat.

M=1, Complex Formulas

When the country is divided into single-seat districts, there are two basic choices. The candidate with the most votes (plurality or "relative majority") in each district could be declared the winner. If this is the case, we have the simple "first-past-the-post" (FPTP) formula discussed in Chapter 2. Alternatively, an absolute majority (more than 50 percent of the votes) could be required. In either case, the voter can be asked to cast either a categorical ballot for one candidate or to rank the candidates, as shown in **Table 3.1**.

In *First-Past-The-Post* systems, the candidate with the most votes wins, but in the other examples shown in Table 3.1, the process of determining the winner is more complex. In *Two-Round* (runoff) systems, the candidate with the plurality of the vote wins only if he or she has reached a stipulated threshold of the votes. If the required threshold is not reached in the initial voting, then there is a second round of voting on a later date.[2] Participation in the second round is almost always restricted to the top two vote-earners from the first round. Often the required threshold is a majority of the vote

---

[2] Rules for many elections in the US state of California now require a second round regardless of vote shares in the first round (the so-called "primary"). Thus it is possible that a candidate could have an outright majority in the first round but still be subjected to a second round, which the initial runner-up could win (given new information or different turnout of voters in the second round). Other states likewise use two-round majority in their general elections, while also having party primaries (which are also two-round), e.g., Georgia.

(half, plus one), in which case it may be called "Majority Runoff" or "Two-Round Majority."

Other thresholds are sometimes used in two-round systems. For instance, for presidential elections in Costa Rica, if the candidate with the most votes has at least 40 percent, the election is over in one round (Lehcouq 2004). Several other variations on two-round systems for presidential elections allow a winner with less than a majority in the first round under stipulated conditions but require a second round under other situations; Colomer (2004) aptly dubs this set of rules "qualified plurality."[3]

What all two-round rules have in common is that the eventual winner may not be the candidate with the most votes in the first round. That is why it fails our definition of "simple." In a context of political fragmentation, this feature may be an advantage, by preventing an extremist candidate form winning simply by having the largest block of passionate supporters but being less preferred by a majority of voters. Few stable democracies use a two-round majority system for assembly elections, but it is fairly widespread in Africa (see tables in Reynolds, Reilly, and Ellis 2005: 30–31).[4]

While two-round systems almost always restrict a second round to the top two candidates, there can be exceptions. French rules for National Assembly elections permit multicandidate runoffs.[5] If more than two candidates remain, the candidate with only a plurality of votes in the second round may be declared the winner ("Two-Round Majority-Plurality"). In most French runoffs only two candidates compete, as parties that finish lower than second in the first round tend to drop out and endorse one of the front-runners. However, occasionally more than two candidates remain in the second round. Majority-Plurality is unusual; the only other case to have used it recently over several elections is Hungary.[6]

In the *Alternative Vote*, voters have an ordinal ballot on which they can rank the candidates. When the votes are counted, the weakest candidate is eliminated and his voters' votes are transferred according to their second preferences. The process is repeated, if necessary, possibly involving some voters' third and lower preferences (if their higher preferences have already been eliminated). Australia has used the Alternative Vote, with some variations (Farrell and McAllister, 2006; McAllister and Makkai 2018), for about a century. Australia requires

---

[3] Sometimes the criteria for first-round victory are both a vote percentage and a margin over the runner-up – for instance, 45 percent or 40 percent with a ten-point lead over the runner-up. See Shugart (2007). A proposal for a variable threshold was presented as the "double complement rule" by Shugart and Taagepera (1994). See also Jones (2018).

[4] We are not aware of thresholds lower than a majority in two-round rules for assembly elections.

[5] Under current rules, a candidate qualifies for the runoff by earning votes equivalent to at least 12.5 percent of the registered voters in the district. In French presidential elections the runoff is restricted to the top two.

[6] Where there is also a list-PR component, making it a composite system (defined later in this chapter).

TABLE 3.2 *Example of basic seat allocation options in a single-seat district*

	Left	Center-Left	Center-Right	Right	TOTAL
First or only preference	33	14	24	29	100
Second preference	14/2=7	33+24/2=45	14/2+29=36	24/2=12	100
Third preference	14/2=7	24/2+29=41	33+14/2=40	24/2=12	100
First-Past-The -Post	33 **wins**				
Two-Round, 2nd round	33+14=49	Eliminated	Eliminated	29+24=51 **wins**	
Alternative Vote, 2nd stage	33+14/2=40	Eliminated.	14/2+24=31	29	100
3rd stage	40	—	31+29=60 **wins**	Eliminated	100

Source: Modified from Taagepera (2007).

voters to rank all candidates, and thus the counting procedure ensures that one of them wins a majority; accordingly, it is called the "Majority-Preferential" system. In other jurisdictions voters have the option of ranking only as many as they wish, or are limited in how many they are allowed to rank.[7] In such cases, a majority of all votes cast may not be required to win in practice, because of voters not having ranked all candidates. As with two-round majority, sometimes the candidate who has the most first-preference votes is not the winner when later preferences of initially lower-placed candidates are transferred. Thus it is not a simple system. The Alternative Vote is used in some municipal elections in the United States, where it is often called "Instant Runoff."

In *Borda Count*, the ranked votes are weighted. When four candidates run, every 1st preference receives three points, every 2nd preference two points, and every 3rd preference one point. These weighted votes are added up, and the candidate with plurality wins. Borda Count is highly susceptible to strategic voting, and hence is a good system "only for honest men," as Jean-Charles de Borda himself put it 200 years ago (Colomer 2004: 30). Only one country country uses a variant of Borda Count for its full assembly: the small Pacific island state of Nauru (Reilly 2002). Slovenia uses Borda count for its single-seat districts that elect members of the Hungarian and Italian minorities (Lublin 2014:146). We will not discuss the Borda Count further, given its rarity.

---

[7] For instance, in Papua New Guinea, a valid vote requires ranking precisely three candidates. In municipal elections in San Francisco, California, voters may rank up to three candidates.

Table 3.2 illustrates the workings of the three most common systems for choosing a single winner. Here we compare outcomes under FPTP and more complex $M=1$ formulas for a hypothetical distribution of votes. Our scenario has one hundred voters and four candidates, assumed to line up on a simplistic left-right ideological scale. When voters are asked to rank candidates, we will assume that their second preference is the candidate closest to their first choice. In the case of equal closeness, they are assumed to split their second preferences evenly between the candidates to the left and to the right of their first preference. These assumptions are overly simplistic, but needed to make the example tractable.

Left has the most first preference votes and wins by the FPTP rule, despite only a third of the vote. By the two-round majority rule, the second round pits Left against Right, the centrist voters shift to their ideologically closest candidates, and Right wins. Finally, by the Alternative Vote rule, the process is more complex. Since no one clears fifty percent, the weakest candidate is eliminated – the Center-Left. His votes are reallocated according to the second preferences. Still, no one clears fifty percent. The weakest candidate now is Right, narrowly surpassed by Center-Right, thanks to the boost of second preferences from Center-Left. With Right eliminated, her votes are reallocated according to the second preferences, and Center-Right wins by a large margin of twenty percent.

Depending on the seat allocation formula chosen, almost any candidate could win *in this particular example*, chosen to illustrate the importance of the allocation formula. In many actual cases, however, many formulas yield the same result.

It may seem as if two-round rules permit voters to vote for their first choice in the initial round, given that they can always switch to their second-most preferred candidate of the expected runoff qualifiers. However, this can be dangerous, as voters on the French left discovered in 2002. In what would be one of the most fragmented presidential elections ever (see Chapter 11), the candidate with the most votes, Jacques Chirac (the incumbent rightist president), did not even reach 20 percent. A far-right "populist" candidate, Jean-Marie Le Pen of the National Front, came second with 16.7 percent. The main candidate of the left, then-premier Lionel Jospin, failed to crack the top two, with only 16.2 percent. Thirteen other candidates split the remaining vote. Several of these were from other left-wing parties, such as Worker's Struggle (5.7 percent), Greens (5.3 percent), and the Revolutionary Communist League (4.3 percent). It is unlikely that voters for these candidates thought they could win. It is more likely they wanted to make a statement, and that many planned to vote for Jospin in the runoff. Of course, they never got the chance. In the runoff, the combined forces of the left had little choice but to mobilize behind the right (Chirac) to stop the extreme right (Le Pen). Chirac won over 80 percent of the vote in the second round.[8] The experience shows the importance, even in two-round systems, of being aware of how split the vote may be. It does no good to plan to vote for one's second favorite if only two worse choices get top-two vote totals.[9]

Similar cases of vote-splitting can also occur in "top two" rules used in some US states. These rules stipulate that the two top in the "primary" advance to a second round. However, these candidates might be from the same party – as happened in California's US Senate contest in 2016.[10] Republicans were split among several candidates, and the November general election was a contest between two Democrats.

It is most important to realize that the casting of votes, and even the entry of specific candidates, are not rule-blind. The seat allocation formula is known ahead of time, and parties and voters will adjust. If we return to our example in Table 3.2, we see that under FPTP, Center-Right is playing a "spoiler" role, enabling Left to win. Hence, if the opinion polls offer a realistic idea of the relative strengths of the candidates, Center-Right might drop out so as not to split the votes of the wider right. If Right and Center-Right fail to coordinate in such a way in the first election, the Left victory may teach them to present a joint candidate in the next election. In turn, this could encourage Left and Center-Left to choose between presenting a joint candidate or facing sure defeat. This is how FPTP may push the party system toward two dominant parties, as claimed by the so-called Duverger's law. However, it may take time, and exceptions outnumber the cases where a balanced nationwide two-party system develops, in part because the differences among candidates and parties are rarely all about a single ideological dimension as depicted in our example. Cox (1997) discusses extensively the conditions under which such coordination can be expected to occur. In Chapter 10 we will show that even at the district level, FPTP tends to be associated systematically with more than two parties if the national assembly size is large.

Other allocation formulas from our example in Table 3.2 exert less pressure toward concentration. In two-round majority, many candidates may continue to run in the first round, with the losers hoping to bargain with their support

---

[8] Despite Chirac's sub-twenty percent showing in the first round, parties supporting him went on to win the immediately ensuing assembly election in a striking case of the "honeymoon" election pattern first mentioned in Chapter 1 and explored in detail in Chapter 12.

[9] Would Alternative Vote have prevented the French left's debacle? Perhaps. It is likely that as other left-wing candidates were eliminated, their transferred preferences would have flowed to Jospin. If so, Le Pen might have been eliminated before Jospin, despite the latter's third-place standing in initial preferences. It is impossible to say for certain that this would have been the case or, if it had been, which of the two major-party candidates would have won. However, even assuming the same distribution of first preferences, it is possible that AV could have resulted in a Jospin win (and perhaps then a Socialist win in the honeymoon assembly election).

[10] This is why the first round is not really a primary. Instead of selecting the general-election candidates of however many parties are registered to compete, it simply sends the top two, regardless of party.

prior to the second round; as cases like France in 2002 show, this can be risky. In the Alternative Vote, voters do not have to worry about playing a "spoiler" role. The voter may express support for her/his favorite, even if the latter has no chance to win, and then mark as second preference the preferred one among the top candidates.

Multi-Seat Districts with Party-Oriented Seat Allocation Formulas

In Chapter 2, we introduced the concept of *party lists*, in which parties present "teams" of candidates in a district, with $M>1$, and the allocation of seats is made first via the application of a formula to these lists. Most party-list formulas are proportional, and the broad category of list-PR makes up the most common type of electoral system worldwide.

However, there are some cases of plurality or even two-round majority list systems. In such a system, all the winners in a district come from one list. This formula is termed the *Party Block Vote* (PBV). We do not consider it a simple system, because it violates the criterion that seat allocation respects the votes of parties. By definition, PBV states that the largest list[11] gets *all* the seats, meaning that even when $M>1$, nothing matters other than which party (or alliance presenting a joint list) is the largest. Unique among electoral formulas, no second or lower-placed party can win, no matter the district magnitude or how close the parties' votes are.

Party Block Vote is used for statewide allocation in the US Electoral College.[12] In the larger states the formula greatly magnifies the advantage in electoral votes for the candidate who wins the state's voting plurality. It was this feature of the formula that was critical to the dispute over votes in the state of Florida in the US presidential election of 2000. With the electoral votes from the other forty-nine states and the District of Columbia known, Al Gore had 267 electoral votes – just three short of the number needed to win – and George W. Bush had 246. Florida's twenty-five electoral votes would go to the statewide plurality winner. When the US Supreme Court stopped a recount, Bush's declared lead in the state was 537 votes out of over 5.9 million, a margin of 0.009 percent, but sufficient to win the state's full slate of electors and clinch victory.

Stable democracies have largely abandoned this formula for electing legislative assemblies because it tends to boost the advantage of the largest party even more than FPTP, weakening the opposition to the point of making

---

[11] In the decisive round, if the rules allow for more than one. In regional and some local elections in France, the composition of lists can be changed between rounds – e.g., to include candidates from lists that did not advance to the runoff) (Hoyo 2018).

[12] Two states, Maine and Nebraska, award one elector to the plurality winner of each House district. They use party block vote for two statewide electors. Other states use statewide plurality for their full slate.

it ineffective. Such a case occurred in Mali (briefly democratic, before its breakdown in 2012); see Chapter 16.

In contrast to such a party-centered approach, one can formally ignore the existence of parties, focus on candidates, and give each voter as many votes as there are seats in the district. In such a case, we are in the realm of "nontransferable" votes, which places the system in our next category, candidate-centered formulas.

Multiseat Districts with Candidate-Based Formulas: Multiple Nontransferable Vote

There are also $M>1$ formulas that are strictly candidate-based (or *nominal*, as Shugart, 2005a, termed them). The number of votes per voter can range from one to M, or in principle higher. If the voter is permitted to vote for more than one candidate, we have a subfamily that we will call Multiple Nontransferable Vote (MNTV). These can be highly favorable to the plurality party, depending on voter behavior, with increasing odds for minority representation as the number of votes per voter is reduced, tending towards the single nontransferable vote (SNTV, discussed in the next subsection). These rules can be used with no parties at all, because votes are cast and counted solely for candidates. The rules, per se, are party blind.

If the voter may cast as many as M votes, we have the *Unlimited Vote*. This enables a voter to spread her votes among candidates without regard to the party (if any) that nominated them. However, if there is strong party loyalty, Unlimited Vote becomes akin to Party Block Vote, decimating all opposition to the dominating party.

Unlimited Vote is used in the US for some state legislatures (including New Hampshire and North Dakota) and many local jurisdictions (which are often formally nonpartisan). It was formerly used in Thailand, where it was associated with an extremely fragmented party system and weak partisan loyalties. When, on the other hand, there are parties with strong identity in the electorate, such a rule can greatly magnify the lead of the largest one. For instance, a political wing of the armed Hamas movement, running in the 2006 Palestinian election, won a large majority of seats despite a very narrow lead in votes. Hamas voters tended to vote for all or most of the Hamas candidates even though the electoral system allowed them to vote for individuals without regard to party, if they so chose; other parties' voters were less party loyal in filling out their ballots (Abdel-Ghaffar et al., n.d. 2016). The experiences in Thailand and the Palestinian Territories are discussed further in Chapter 16.[13]

---

[13] *Approval Voting* amounts to unlimited vote carried to the extreme: vote for as many candidates as you please, regardless of M, and the M candidates with the most votes win. No country has ever used approval vote, to our knowledge, though some academics have recommended it (Brams and Fishburn, 1983).

One can alleviate major party dominance by allowing *Cumulative Vote*. This formula typically gives each voter M votes, and a voter can cast more than one per candidate. As with other MNTV formulas, the winners are those with the top M vote totals. A minority in the electorate can load their votes heavily on a few candidates. The system is rare, but is found in some local elections in the US.

When the number of votes per voter is less than M, we have the Limited Vote. Under this formula, minorities may win seats even if the majority consists of voters who give all their available votes reliably in a block. The Limited Vote seems to achieve a reasonable degree of proportionality among parties when the number of votes per voter does not exceed the square root of district magnitude ($M^{0.5}$), although we are aware of no theoretical proof. Aside from some local elections, the main use of Limited Vote is in the Spanish Senate (Lijphart et al. 1986). The logically greatest limiting of the number of votes per voter is to allow just one, which brings us to SNTV.

Single-Vote Candidate-Based Systems: SNTV and STV

With the number of votes per voter limited to one, MNTV turns into the Single Nontransferable vote (SNTV), which can have effects similar to proportional representation formulas, notwithstanding that it is a purely candidate-based formula. If ranked-choice ballots are used instead of nontransferable ones, the system becomes the Single Transferable Vote (STV), which is a nonlist form of proportional representation.

SNTV may be the simplest method that could be applied in multi-seat districts. In a district with M seats, the M candidates with the most votes win. Simplicity is generally desirable, but SNTV has a unique drawback in how it affects parties. The earliest (to our knowledge) reference to this problem was that of Henry R. Droop (2012 [1869]: 3), who observed that a party,

commanding a sufficient number of voters to return several representatives, would fail to obtain as many as it was entitled to, through too many of its votes being accumulated upon its most popular candidates.

Consider a five-seat district. Suppose we have parties whose votes (in percent) are A: 45; B: 13; C: 28; D: 14. Party A's collective votes would be sufficient to win three seats.[14] Where it runs into trouble is if it has one candidate who is *too popular*. Suppose its first candidate, whom we will call $A1$, gets 23 percent of the district vote, while its other two get 11 percent each. It is now vulnerable to electing only $A1$, if four candidates from other parties each win more than 11 percent of the vote. Parties B and D can achieve this by nominating just one candidate apiece. Moreover, even Party C, with just

---

[14] For instance, it wins three under D'Hondt (see Chapter 2), because 45/3 is greater than the initial vote percentage of either B or D, and also bigger than C's votes divided by two.

28 percent of the vote, could elect two candidates if they are fairly equal in votes – say, 16 and 12 percent. Party A can elect more than one candidate only by getting some of its voters who prefer candidate $A1$ to vote for $A2$ or $A3$. It is this need of parties to coordinate their votes across candidates that prevents SNTV from being a simple system: the rule does not respect the relative sizes of parties, because parties, per se, do not matter to the allocation. A party wins seats only in accordance to how many individual candidates it has among the district's top-M vote totals. We discuss this aspect of SNTV in detail in Chapters 13 and 14;

Because of such coordination problems, SNTV is rarely applied in districts of more than three to five seats, although a system that was SNTV in its main details was used for the Colombian Senate, with $M=100$, from 1991 to 2002 (Shugart, Moreno, and Fajardo 2003). Since 2005, Afghanistan also has used SNTV, and one district has $M>30$.

Partly because of its more common use in low-magnitude districts, SNTV is often called "semiproportional." The limited proportionality, however, is not a feature of the formula itself, which actually can overrepresent small parties because all they need is to have one candidate get a top-M vote total. Especially with low M this could be a much smaller total vote share than is needed under D'Hondt or some other proportional formulas applied to party lists. For these reasons, we have referred to SNTV as a "superproportional" formula (Taagepera and Shugart, 1989a: 170n; see also Cox 1996).

Instead of having nontransferable votes, voters may be able to rank their preferences, via an ordinal ballot. In these systems a vote is "transferred" to the voter's second choice when his or her first choice is unable to be elected due to low overall support. This reduces – but does not eliminate – coordination dilemmas. Called *Single Transferable Vote* (STV), this method is the multi-seat equivalent of the aforementioned Alternative Vote. Under STV, a candidate is elected when he or she obtains a stipulated quota, which is usually the Droop quota. We identified this earlier as $q_{Droop}=100$ percent/$(M+1)+1$; while that "+1" is usually superfluous, note that it is not when $M = 1$: then the Droop quota yields exactly the definition of majority: *half the votes, plus one vote.*[15] The use of the same formula for $M>1$ is simply a generalization of the Alternative Vote (AV) procedure to $M>1$ PR. Under both AV and STV, weaker candidates are eliminated, and their voters' second preferences taken into account. Under STV, in addition, there are transfers of "surplus votes" of the successful candidates; when a candidate is over the quota, additional votes for this candidate get reallocated to voters' second

---

[15] The phrasing is worth emphasizing. Sometimes we have had students understand "half plus one" to mean 51 percent. But this would be a *super*-majority requirement. For instance, half a million is 500,000, and half plus one would be 500,001, which is only 50.0001 percent, well short of 51 percent.

choices.[16] (This latter step is unnecessary when $M=1$; no one else can use the votes after a candidate obtains the quota and is elected. Under STV, surplus votes are transferred as long as other seats remain to be filled.)

Table 3.3 follows up on the previous example of an unlucky vote constellation, where SNTV might allocate the largest party only 1 seat out of 5. How would STV allocate these seats? For sake of keeping the exposition manageable, let's assume that the second preferences go to the candidates of the same party, or to the ideologically closest party. Droop quota for $M=5$ is 100 percent/6=16.7 percent. Any candidate who reaches this quota wins a seat. Her excess votes are allocated according to her voters' second preferences. If this helps further candidates to reach a full quota, the process is repeated. If not, then the weakest candidate is eliminated, and his votes are allocated according to his voters' second preferences. In later stages, third and fourth preferences may come into play. In this particular example, the largest party wins two seats, because the transfer of ranked preferences lets it consolidate the support that was initially spread among its three candidates.

Visibly, the STV procedure is more complex than those previously described – and we have omitted some details that can make it even messier. One is the sheer number of candidates the voter may be asked to rank. There is less penalty for fielding many candidates, compared to SNTV.[17] Thus, suppose $M=5$, and six parties run. There might be an average of around four candidates per party, for a total of twenty-four. It is hard to rank that many candidates in a meaningful way.[18] Hence STV is rarely used in districts with more than five seats. This low district magnitude impedes the achievement of high proportionality.

STV offers maximal freedom of choice to the voters, reducing fear that one's vote might be wasted. For instance, if a voter's main concern is to enhance

---

[16] If the second-choice candidate already has obtained a quota, or been eliminated from the count, the vote transfers to the voter's third choice, and so on.

[17] Why would there be any penalty? After all, votes can be transferred as soon as one of the party's candidates is eliminated. One reason is that if a party has too many of its candidates eliminated in early stages of the count, it won't have them left to collect transfers later. Another reason lies in what happens if we relax the unrealistic assumption we employed in our example – that voters prefer all candidates of their first-choice candidate's party over those of other parties. In reality, voters are free to rank candidates without regard to party, so a party may not retain its votes as the count moves to further stages. Parties may guard against these risks by trying to ensure that their candidates' first-preference votes are fairly equal. See Gallagher (2005).

[18] In Ireland and some other STV jurisdictions, a ballot is valid even if a voter votes categorically for one candidate. In Australian Senate elections, voters were formerly required to rank all candidates on the ballot. Since 1983, they have been able to cast instead an "above-the-line" (or "ticket") vote for one party, which makes the system more like a closed-list system than like STV. In 2016, the rule was changed so that a ballot is valid if as few as six candidates are ranked, or a voter may rank parties above the line, rather than individual candidates. See McAllister and Makkai (2018).

TABLE 3.3 *Example of seat allocation by Single Transferable Vote (STV) in a five-seat district*

Candidates	A1	A2	A3	B	C1	C2	D
First preference votes (%)	23.0	11.0	11.0	13.0	16.0	12.0	14.0
Quota allocation	–16.7						
Remainder transfer (assumed)	6.3	–>+4.3	±2.0				
New totals		15.3		13.0			
Elimination of the weakest					±9.0<–	–12.0	–>3.0
New totals					26.0		17.0
Quota allocations					–16.7		–16.7
Remainder transfers				±8.6	<– 8.3		<–0.3
New totals				21.6			
Quota allocation				–16.7			
Remainder transfers			±4.9	<–4.9			
New totals				17.9			
Quota allocation				–16.7			
Residual remainders		15.3		1.2	[they add up to one Droop quota.]		
Seats for parties		2 seats		1 seat	1 seat		1 seat

Assume that candidates are listed in the order of placement on left-right scale
Source: First shown in Taagepera (2007).

women's representation, he could express high preference for all female candidates. Thus, STV has considerable philosophical appeal, and computer programs can handle the technical aspects easily. It remains a nonsimple system because whether parties win seats proportionate to their votes depends not on the formula, but on how voters deploy their rankings.

It bears emphasizing that each of the formulas for multiseat districts can be applied in single-seat districts, although then it normally goes by a different common name. As we noted in Chapter 2, all list-PR systems become FPTP when $M = 1$, provided that parties nominate a "list" containing just a single candidate. Open-list PR (mentioned already in Chapter 2 and considered in detail in Chapters 6, 13, and 14) with more than M candidates also can be applied with $M = 1$, but then it is not FPTP. In Uruguayan presidential elections, this was known as "Double Simultaneous Vote" in which the winner is the candidate with the most votes *within the party* that has the most votes.[19] Such rules also are used for the sole single-seat district in Finland and one in Peru.

---

[19] Uruguay later changed to two-round majority, each party settling on a single candidate via a primary.

We already noted that STV becomes the Alternative Vote. If we reduce SNTV to $M=1$ we again have FPTP.[20] In sum, the traditional distinction between single- and multiseat districts is not needed in the analysis of the impact of electoral systems on party systems. Actually, such distinction makes analysis harder. *Single-seat districts are merely the limiting cases of multiseat districts.*

BEYOND DISTRICT ALLOCATION: COMPLEX AND COMPOSITE
ELECTORAL SYSTEMS

All electoral systems previously described offer only one district magnitude and one seat allocation formula, even while this formula might be quite intricate. The possibilities for electoral design multiply when district magnitude varies from district to district; however, if all seats are allocated in districts, the system may still be "simple." Chapter 6 offers detailed examples of such systems. Here we consider features that complicate electoral systems by introducing one of two features: (1) special rules that stipulate that a party may not win seats even if applying one of the proportional formulas would have let it win in the absence of the special rule; (2) features that allow a party to win seats in the assembly even if it won none in any of the districts. The first special rule refers to thresholds of minimal votes required to win seats. The second set of features refers to two-tier or composite systems.

Legal Thresholds

While proportional representation for parties may be considered desirable in general, a profusion of tiny parties is not. Therefore, limits on minimal representation are imposed in many countries that use PR, especially those that use large-magnitude districts. Typically, parties below a given threshold of votes are not entitled to participate in seat allocation. The legal threshold used may be a low as 0.67 percent (The Netherlands, where this is the Hare quota, $1/M$, given $M=150$), but it is usually higher, for instance 5 percent (Germany). This is the sense in which legal thresholds potentially violate our second simplicity criterion: a party may have enough votes to have won a seat given the district magnitude and allocation formula, but it is denied because of the threshold. We discuss some examples from Israel in Chapter 5. Some countries apply even higher thresholds to alliance lists of several parties. For example, in Poland (as discussed in Chapter 1) a single party faces a 5 percent threshold, but an alliance list must win at least 8 percent.

---

[20] Of course, generally parties nominate only one candidate each; however, if a party had two or more candidates under $M=1$ SNTV, it is still a FPTP election but one in which the party with the most votes might fail to win the seat due to its internal split. In the Philippines it occasionally happens that a party faces a nomination battle and so declares a district a "free zone"; it then must coordinate on one of its several candidates or risk defeat (Kasuya 2009: 100–102).

It matters whether the threshold applies nationwide or in individual districts. Suppose a party has 4.9 percent of the nationwide votes. A nationwide threshold of 5 percent would bar it from obtaining seats. Something like this actually happened to two parties in the German election of 2013: there were parties with 4.76 percent and 4.70 percent of the nationwide votes,[21] but the nationwide 5 percent requirement meant no seats for either. However, the same threshold applied in individual districts almost surely would allow it to win some seats, provided districts have sufficiently high magnitude, because in some districts the party would be over 5 percent. A case in point is Spain, where there is a 3 percent threshold applied at the district level; numerous parties have won representation in Spain with less than 3 percent of the nationwide vote, because they obtain more than 3 percent in one or a few specific districts.

Rules of this sort can be highly consequential, especially if seats are allocated in districts, but the threshold is nationwide. For instance, in Turkey, district magnitude ranges from two to thirty-one (mean around 6.5), which should allow many small parties to win seats, especially given that Turkey has significant regional differences in its politics. Yet there is a threshold that must be cleared at the national level to win any seats in any district. Moreover, this threshold is the highest among arguably democratic countries, at 10 percent. Thus in several elections parties have won sizeable pluralities of the votes in some districts and yet no seats there (or anywhere). In Chapter 16 we will see that sometimes the largest party in a Turkish district has failed to win a seat, and sometimes parties present independent candidates to circumvent the threshold. When they do, they behave as though the system is SNTV, rather than list PR. The Polish system, referred to previously in this chapter as well as in Chapter 1, is another example of all seats being allocated in districts, yet thresholds based on nationwide votes. Similar rules are found also in Czechia and Peru.

District magnitude as such imposes an effective threshold. For example, when $M=5$, it is nearly impossible for a party to win a seat with less than 10 percent of the votes. For calculation of effective thresholds, see Taagepera (2007: 241–253). The key point is that a district-level legal threshold may block small parties in large districts while having no impact whatsoever in small districts. Again consider the case of Spain, with many five-seat districts but also districts for Barcelona and Madrid with $M>30$. Only the latter are affected by Spain's district-level legal threshold of 3 percent, because the effective thresholds inherent in small district magnitudes are larger than that.

A few legal thresholds contain an "or" clause. For instance, in Germany a party participates in nationwide proportional allocation if it obtains

---

[21] Respectively, the Free Democratic Party (which had been in every assembly elected since 1949) and the Alternative for Germany (a party contesting its first national election).

5 percent of the votes *or* has three of its candidates win in single-seat districts.[22] In New Zealand, a party needs 5 percent of the nationwide votes for party lists *or* just one district plurality to qualify for proportional allocation. Sweden has a provision that a party needs 4 percent of nationwide votes *or* 12 percent in any given district.[23]

Two-Tier and Composite Systems

An electoral system may consist of two (or more) components (or levels), meaning overlapping sets of districts. When these components are linked through an allocation rule that takes account of the outcome in one component when allocating seats in the other, we can speak of a two-tier or multitier system (Gallagher and Mitchell 2005b).

In such a system, there are districts as in any "simple" system but there is also another bloc of seats allocated either nationwide or in regional clusters of districts. Sets of such super-districts are commonly referred to as "upper tiers," as distinct from the "basic tier" of local districts. These systems allow parties to win seats in the assembly even if they have support that is too geographically dispersed to win in any district. In an upper tier, votes are aggregated across the districts and used for the allocation of seats in order to smooth out disproportionalities that arise from the districts. We follow the terminology of Elklit and Roberts (1996), and call these systems "two-tier compensatory."[24]

One type of two-tier compensatory system is the *mixed-member proportional* (MMP) model found in Germany and New Zealand. In these two cases, the basic tier consists of single-seat districts (using plurality) while the upper tier is nationwide[25] and uses PR rules. What makes the system "two tier" is that, on the interparty dimension where the total number of seats per party is determined, all the seats (with minor exceptions) are allocated as if it were one nationwide district. So if a party wins many single-seat districts, it will win few (or potentially no) list-PR seats, but if it wins no district seats it will still get its proportional share, all taken in the upper tier.

The way this type of system works is best illustrated with an actual example from New Zealand.[26] The MMP system was adopted in 1996, following many

---

[22] If a party wins only one or two single-seat districts, it keeps those seats. It just does not qualify for any seats from the proportional allocation if its nationwide party-list votes were under 5 percent.

[23] Unlike in New Zealand, however, qualifying for seats in one district does not also qualify the party for any national seats.

[24] A few actually have more than one layer of compensation seats, a detail we leave aside.

[25] In Germany, each state (*Land*) is its own upper-tier district, but the allocation ensures it functions as if it were one nationwide district, through a further complication that we will not elaborate on here (Zittel 2018).

[26] For more detailed treatment, see Shugart and Tan (2016) or Vowles (2018).

TABLE 3.4 *Example of an election under MMP: New Zealand, 2008*

Party	Votes (%)	Constituency seats	List seats	Total seats (%)
National Party	44.7	41	17	58 (47.5)
Labour Party	33.8	21	22	43 (35.2)
Green Party	6.7	0	9	9 (7.4)
New Zealand First Party	4.0	0	0	0
ACT New Zealand	3.6	1	4	5 (4.1)
Maori Party	2.4	5	0	5 (4.1)
Jim Anderton's Progressive	0.9	1	0	1 (0.8)
United Future New Zealand	0.9	1	0	1 (0.8)
Others	3.0	0	0	0
Total	100.0	70	52	122

decades under a FPTP system (which produced the two unusual results described at the beginning of Chapter 1). **Table 3.4** shows the 2008 election; all parties that won at least 4 percent of the vote or one seat are shown. The system consists of two tiers, one of which has seventy single-seat local constituencies. The remainder are elected from nationwide party lists. The system is a two-tier compensatory system because it is designed to ensure that the final seat allocation – taking into account both constituency and list seats – approximately matches the percentage of votes per party. It achieves this by taking the number of constituency-level plurality seats each party won and then, if necessary, allocating it further seats from the list to compensate it according to its nationwide list vote percentage.

If we take the case of National, the largest party, we see it had 44.7 percent of the votes. This entitles it to fifty-eight of the 122 seats by the application of a nationwide proportional formula (Ste.-Laguë, as defined in Chapter 2.) It won forty-one constituency seats. Thus it needs seventeen seats off its nationwide (closed) list in order to reach its proportional entitlement. Labour, which did poorly relative to its vote percentage in the constituencies (winning just twenty-one), needs twenty-two list seats to compensate it and bring it up to its proportional entitlement of forty-three out of the 122 seats.

As noted earlier, New Zealand has an "alternative" threshold – a party qualifies to participate in the allocation of compensatory list seats if it wins either 5 percent of the party-list votes or one constituency. Thus some very small parties have seats despite having less than 5 percent of the votes. Two parties (Jim Anderton's Progressive and United Future New Zealand) won one seat apiece simply because the party leader was capable of winning his own local constituency contest. ACT New Zealand likewise won in one constituency; in addition to this seat, it also has four more, because its vote share is sufficient for five seats. Had it not won the constituency seat, however, it would have had no seats, given that its list vote fell below 5 percent. This was the fate that befell the New Zealand First Party, which was actually the fourth largest party in terms of votes, but it failed to clear either alternative threshold, and hence was shut out, while parties with lower vote totals but success in at least one constituency have representation. This result demonstrates the two-tier composite nature of the system: there are two paths into parliament, a FPTP path and a list-PR path.[27]

What happens if a party wins more constituencies than its proportional share? We see this with the case of the Maori Party, which has five constituency seats despite only 2.4 percent of the party vote. This number of seats won in the FPTP tier is two more than its proportional entitlement would have been, and thus the assembly was expanded from its usual fixed 120 to 122 to accommodate what is termed an "overhang" by the Maori Party.

The set of features just described for the New Zealand system typify MMP systems, such as the one in Germany. Slightly different variations of MMP are also found for the Scottish Parliament and the Welsh Assembly (Lundberg 2018), as well as for the national assembly in Bolivia (Centellas 2015).[28]

In each of these MMP systems, the voter is given two votes, one for a candidate in their local constituency and one for a party list. Because the voter need not give both to the same party, it is an example of what Gallagher and Mitchell (2005b, 2018) call a *dividual* ballot. It is possible, however, for MMP to allow the voter only one vote, with the same vote counting for both their own constituency contest and for the party list. Germany had a one-vote MMP system in the 1949 election (Zittel 2018).

The MMP composite consists of FPTP in one tier and PR in another, with compensation to make the overall outcome close to nationwide proportional representation while retaining a local-district component. It is similarly possible for PR to be used in both tiers. For instance, in Denmark, each county serves as a multiseat district. Magnitude of these districts ranges from two to twenty, for 135 in total. There is then a forty-seat nationwide compensatory tier. Representation by party is determined as if there were one

---

[27] Because 7 percent of the votes remained unrepresented (New Zealand First and various others), all parties that received list seats were somewhat overrepresented.

[28] In Scotland and Bolivia, the key variation is that there is no nationwide compensation. Rather, compensation occurs over regional clusters of single-seat districts. Such procedure can generate substantial deviation from proportionality. However, we would still call these systems MMP because the mechanism for distributing list seats is compensatory. The factor limiting proportionality is thus the magnitude of the compensation regions, not the allocation formula. An analogy can be drawn to Spain, which all sources we know of classify as "proportional"; yet disproportionality can be relatively high in Spain, due to the use of many low-magnitude districts.

district of 175 seats (not counting an additional four from overseas territories[29]), provided that a party clears the 2 percent threshold.[30] In this way, many districts have a rather modest district magnitude, similar to some cases of districted single-tier PR, allowing for local representation. Yet parties nationally are represented in almost perfect proportion to their overall votes.

The system of South Africa likewise has a fixed compensatory tier on top of a multiseat district proportional tier (Ferree 2018). Each tier has 200 seats, with very high magnitude in most districts (averaging twenty-two, with each of the nine provinces being a district). This tier alone already would guarantee a high degree of proportionality; yet South Africa then tacks on 200 nationwide seats and allocates the entire 400-seat parliament as if it were one nationwide district. Moreover, there is no legal threshold, and thus parties with as little as 0.2 percent of the nationwide votes, and insufficient votes to win even one seat in any of the large provincial districts, have gained a seat. In all two-tier compensatory systems in which PR is used in the basic districts, the voter is allowed only one categoric vote,[31] although in principle a two-vote design could be implemented.

Another type of composite system can be thought of as part of the same "two-tier" family even though there is no set-aside block of seats for nationwide allocation. This subfamily is known as "remainder-pooling." For instance, a quota (i.e., one of those introduced in Chapter 2) is applied in districts, but the remainder seats might not be determined at the district level. Rather, the rules might say that a party wins a seat only if it gets one or more full quotas. The remainder votes and seats are then pooled at national (or regional) level, to minimize wasted votes in the districts.[32] Thus whereas some two-tier systems have a fixed number of seats in an upper tier – as with Denmark and South Africa, for example – in a remainder-pooling system it may not be possible to answer the question, "how big is the upper tier?," except to say, "as big as necessary." However, many seats are not won by quotas become upper-tier seats, and the number of seats allocated in this tier could be different from election to election (even for a constant overall assembly size).

[29] The Faeroe Islands and Greenland.

[30] There are further complex features affecting small parties' qualification for nationwide seats. See Taagepera and Shugart (1989a: 128) and Elklit (2005: 459–460).

[31] In Denmark, open lists can be used in the basic districts (Elklit 2005), whereas in South Africa the lists are closed (Ferree 2018).

[32] In the upper tier, the allocation formula may change from what it is in the districts. Some countries even have three tiers, with complex limitations. When too many seats are deemed to go to the second tier, one may alleviate the full quota rule in the districts and allocate seats by largest remainders, as long as these remainders surpass 0.9 or 0.75 of the full quota. Estonia introduced such a relaxation around 2000.

TABLE 3.5 *Example of an election under MMP: Japan, 2012*

Party	Pct. votes (party list)	Districts won	List seats	Total seats	Pct. seats
Liberal Democratic (LDP)	27.8	237	57	294	61.3
New Komeito	11.9	9	22	31	6.5
Democratic (DPJ)	15.5	27	30	57	11.9
Restoration Party	20.5	14	40	54	11.3
Your Party	8.8	4	14	18	3.8
Tomorrow Party	5.7	2	7	9	1.9
Communist	6.2	0	8	8	1.7
Social Democrat	2.4	1	1	2	0.4
People's New Party	0.12	1	0	1	0.2
Others	1.2	0	1	1	0.2
Total		300	180	480	

The LDP and Komeito contested the single-seat districts in alliance.

Composite Systems That Are Not Compensatory: Parallel Allocation and Bonus Adjustment

Instead of a compensatory composite of basic and upper tiers, it is possible to have the two components of the system operate in "parallel." If it is a *mixed-member majoritarian* (MMM) system, then seats are allocated in two independent components, one consisting of nominal (candidate-based) contests in districts[33] and the other of PR (which may be nationwide or regional). The key distinction is that the PR seats do not compensate parties in the way we saw for MMP (Table 3.4). Instead, a party's total is just the number of district seats it won, plus the number of seats it won from the PR component of the system. This combination of rules is much more favorable to large parties or those with regional concentration than is MMP. In fact, it really is more of a "softened" form of majoritarian rules, in which small nonregional parties are given a chance to win a few seats, rather than a type of PR system. Strictly speaking, the parallel components of MMM systems should not be called "tiers" because the allocation of the list seats is not linked to the outcomes in the nominal contests (see Gallagher and Mitchell 2005b).

Table 3.5 shows as an example of MMM the actual election result in Japan in 2012. We see that the largest party, the Liberal Democratic Party (LDP) won 27.8 percent of the party list votes. Despite this relatively low popularity of the party nationwide, it did exceptionally well in the single-seat districts, where it

---

[33] The districts are usually $M=1$ and the allocation rule is usually plurality. However, districts can be multiseat and can use any of the candidate-based rules discussed earlier in this chapter.

picked up 237 of the 300 seats.[34] Despite this performance making it already substantially overrepresented, it still was entitled to add a roughly proportional share of the list seats (57/180) on top of its single-seat district wins. This is a major distinction from MMP, as shown in Table 3.4, under which a party tends to have a share of the *total* assembly seats that is close to its share of list votes. By adding a party's district wins and its list wins, the MMM system preserves a substantial portion of any bonus a large party might have obtained from winning many of the single-seat districts. We see that the smaller parties were significantly underrepresented overall, because while the list tier enables them to win a block of seats, it does not compensate them in the manner of MMP.

In MMM systems, the voter may have separate votes in each component of the system, as in Japan, or just a single vote that is counted both for a candidate and the list of the party that nominated the candidate. South Korea allowed the voter only one vote from 1987 till 2004, when it was switched to two votes. When there is only one vote, it puts a voter who prefers a small party in a bind. If she votes for the small party, she is voting for a party with little chance in the single-seat district. If she votes for a large party, she is unable to boost her preferred small party's chances in the PR component.

In addition to MMP (compensatory) and MMM (parallel) systems, there are also systems that combine a component elected by plurality or majority with another using PR in ways that are "partially compensatory." Mixed-member systems with only partial compensatory rules in Hungary, Mexico, and formerly Italy (1996–2001) are often erroneously classified as MMP, but their design and outcomes substantially favor parties that win many seats in the individual districts. The details can be complex; see Shugart and Wattenberg (2001) for explanation.

A further example of a composite system that is not compensatory is *bonus-adjusted PR*. These systems typically award an initial block of seats to the party or alliance with a plurality of the vote, and then use proportional representation for the rest of the seats. For instance, a system used in Greece over several elections automatically awards fifty of the 300 parliamentary seats to the party with the most votes nationwide, and then allocates the other 250 proportionally to all parties, including the bonus recipient.[35] From 2005 through 2013, Italy's system for the Chamber of Deputies awarded a guaranteed minimum of 55 percent of seats to the alliance of parties with the most votes. It then allocated these seats proportionally among parties in the alliance, and the rest of the seats proportionally to other parties (Passarelli 2018). These systems thus

[34] Partly this was due to the New Komeito, which ran separately on the party lists, but did not compete against the LDP in districts. Rather, the two parties formed an alliance for these seats.
[35] Provided a party clears a 3 percent threshold. In addition, the proportional component of this system is itself two-tier compensatory, and most of the seats at the district level are allocated using open lists. Complexity can come in many layers!

contain a strong majoritarian element – there is a premium on being the largest political force – alongside a significant proportional one.

PATHOLOGIES OF ELECTORAL SYSTEMS

Pathologies of electoral systems are a source of increased noise. While building logical models of manageable simplicity, one has to overlook many such complications. At the same time, we must be aware of the simplifications made, so as not to mistake the models for the real world. Only then can we use these models for prediction – and know the limits on these predictions.

One common pathology is malapportionment, in which the ratio of elected representatives to voters is substantially different across districts. It may be a central design element – the US Senate has two senators per state regardless of the massive population disparity across states. The districts of single-tier PR systems typically have magnitudes that vary with population, but in some cases – such as Argentina, Brazil, and Spain– the largest population districts are significantly underrepresented (Samuels and Snyder 2001; Calvo and Murillo 2012; Hopkin 2005). [36]

Another pathology is *gerrymandering*, meaning the politically motivated drawing of district boundaries. Unlike malapportionment, gerrymandering is difficult with PR systems; it is mainly a feature of single-seat districts. With PR, the added value to a would-be boundary manipulator is small and hard to forecast accurately. When $M=1$, on the other hand, moving geographic blocks of voters from one district to another by shifting a boundary can make a difference between a safe seat for one party (or social group) and a competitive district. Most countries that use $M=1$ districts have independent actors draw boundaries and thus they do not have gerrymandering. The US, however, allows states to determine the mechanism for drawing boundaries, even for federal House elections. Many states continue to allow elected legislators to determine boundaries. In this book we leave the considerations of boundary delimitation and electoral geography to one side, not because it is unimportant, but because such topics deserve their own books (see Handley and Grofman, 2008; McGann et al. 2016).

These two pathologies should be kept conceptually distinct. Gerrymandering can exist even in the absence of malapportionment: all districts could have the same population, yet the precise location of the boundaries could be determined

---

[36] For instance, in Brazil, where the states serve as electoral districts, there are large discrepancies in population. While the districts' magnitudes cover a wide range, even the smallest states are guaranteed a minimum $M=8$. The 44 million residents of São Paulo ($M=70$) have approximately one representative for every 630,000 residents, while the 500,000 residents of Roraima ($M=8$) have approximately one representative per 60,000!

for political advantage.[37] Or, all district boundaries could be immutable, but malapportionment is entrenched through political compromise or simple inaction (failure to adjust magnitudes to keep up with population movements). The two pathologies can, of course, be combined: district boundaries could be politically manipulated (gerrymandered) to ensure unequal ratios of representatives to voters across districts (malapportionment).

CONCLUSIONS

In this chapter, we have reviewed several features of electoral rules that make them more complex than the simple types reviewed in Chapter 2. These include runoff and ordinal-ballot rules that are more complex for single-seat districts than is the plurality rule. They also include the single transferable vote (STV, which also uses an ordinal ballot), a more complex form of proportional representation than the list-PR systems discussed in Chapter 2. We further reviewed legal thresholds and two-tier or composite systems, including the mixed-member family (MMP and MMM) and bonus-adjusted PR.

Each of these more complex rules has its advantages, and some electoral systems scholars and reform advocates consider some of them, especially STV and MMP, preferable on normative grounds to simpler systems (Bowler et al. 2005). Nonetheless, these systems entail some risk if adopted in places not already accustomed to them. They may not work the same as they do in their current jurisdictions, because voters and party politicians may adapt differently. Moreover, because we have few real-world cases for many of these systems, especially those that combine several features, it is difficult for us to generalize from experience. In Chapter 15, we show that we can extend a logical model to include two-tier compensatory systems. In Chapter 16 we assess the performance of several complex systems, and note that while some of them appear to work out as if they were simple, others are so complex that they mostly exceed our modelling ability. Most of this book, however, will concern itself with simple systems, because they lend themselves to logical modelling and thus to drawing general inferences. In Chapter 4, we introduce some key tools for assessing the performance of electoral systems.

---

[37] This is basically the case in the US, within states. There is some malapportionment in the US House across states. For instance, some states with a single Representative have smaller population than the average district in the country.

4

The Number of Parties and Proportionality – Two Key Tools for Analysis

The number of parties is among the most frequent numbers in political analysis, and it is central to the study of party systems. Similarly, the "proportionality" of an electoral system is one of the most frequently discussed criteria for evaluating a system. A party system involves, of course, much more than the mere number of parties, but it is impossible to describe it without giving some idea of how many players are involved. Similarly, an electoral system can be assessed on many criteria other than proportionality. Nonetheless, these two tools for analysis – the number of parties and proportionality – are so central to the analysis of electoral systems and party systems that we devote this entire chapter to these two concepts.

THE NUMBER OF PARTIES

Characterizing the types of party systems has concerned students of party politics for a long time – see the excellent overview by Wolinetz (2006). What is a meaningful number of parties in an assembly? As we discussed already in Chapter 1, just counting parties is not always useful. Some parties are large and others small, and thus we need some way to have a count that emphasizes the number of parties that are "important" in some sense.

In this book, we will use the index known as the *effective number of parties*. This index was first proposed by Laakso and Taagepera (1979). It has become the industry standard (e.g., Lijphart 1994; Cox 1997) even as various others have been proposed and used by some scholars.[1] The effective number is a size-weighted count, devised to give more weight to the largest party and less to the smaller ones. It may be calculated on either seat shares or vote shares. The formula for calculating the effective number of seat-winning parties (which we can designate N_S) is:

---

[1] For examples, see Molinar (1991), Dunleavy and Boucek (2003), and Golosov (2009).

$N_S = 1/\sum (s_i)^2 =$ **inverse sum of squared fractional shares**.

In words, we square the seat shares for each of i parties – however many there are, starting with the largest party, s_1. Then we sum up all the squares. Once we have this sum, we take the reciprocal. In this way, the index weights each party by its size. The squaring results in a large party contributing more to the final index value than does a small one. For instance, suppose the largest party has half the seats, $s_1 = 0.5$; thus we have $0.5^2 = 0.25$. Now suppose among several remaining parties a smallest (the ith) one has only 5 percent of the seats. We take the share, 0.05, and square it, and get 0.0025. In this way, when we sum up the squared shares of all the parties, the smallest one has counted for much less than the largest. This is precisely what we want – a size-weighted count of how many parties there are. See Taagepera (2007: 47–64) for a more systematic and detailed treatment.

Alternatively, we could calculate our index on vote shares, giving us the effective number of vote-earning parties (N_V):

$$N_V = 1/\sum (v_i)^2.$$

Here v_i stands for the fractional *vote* share of the ith party. Thus for any given election result, we have two effective numbers: N_S for the seats and N_V for the votes.[2] These numbers are sometimes referred to as ENPP (Effective Number of Parliamentary Parties)[3] and ENEP (Effective Number of Electoral Parties), respectively. However, given our interest in systematically constructing logical models, we adopt the approach more typical of scientific notation: single symbols with subscripts.[4]

Table 4.1 offers a brief demonstration of how we get from vote or seat shares to the effective number of parties, using the above formula. It shows ten hypothetical examples of party systems, each consisting of two to five parties. The entries under the columns for each hypothetical parties could be either votes or seats shares. We square each share in any of these rows, sum of the squares, and then take the reciprocal of the sums. Then we have the effective number.

If we have some number of equal-sized parties, then the effective number is the same as the actual number – as it logically should be! So, in example no. 1, we have two parties, each with a share of 0.50, and we get $N=2.00$. Similarly,

---

[2] In addition, the effective number of components can be useful outside the realm of electoral and party studies, whenever well-defined components add up to a well-defined total. For instance, one can measure the effective number of polities in the world, based on their areas or populations (Taagepera 1997). One can measure the effective number of states or provinces in a federal system, and compare it to the actual number (Taylor et al. 2014). That is, the fractional shares that enter the equation for N can be shares of votes, seats, or anything else that we are interested in summarizing.

[3] Or sometimes Effective Number of Legislative Parties (ENLP).

[4] Moreover, ENP risks being mistaken for multiplication of the quantities E, N and P.

TABLE 4.1 *Examples of hypothetical party systems and resulting values for an effective number of parties*

Example	Votes (or seats) shares					Effective N
	Party 1	Party 2	Party 3	Party 4	Party 5	
1	0.50	0.50				**2.00**
2	0.667	0.333				1.80
3	0.667	0.167	0.166			2.00
4	0.50	0.25	0.25			2.67
5	**0.333**	**0.333**	**0.333**			**3.00**
6	0.50	0.33	0.17			2.58
7	0.333	0.333	0.25	0.084		3.43
8	**0.25**	**0.25**	**0.25**	**0.25**		**4.00**
9	0.25	0.25	0.25	0.13	0.12	4.57
10	**0.20**	**0.20**	**0.20**	**0.20**	**0.20**	**5.00**

with the other cases of equal sized parties in examples 5, 8, and 10, shown in bold.[5] In the second example, we still have only two parties, but one is substantially bigger than the other, yielding N=1.80. This illustrates a general pattern: if there are two unequal components, N<2. Then in example 3, the largest party stays the same size as in example 2, but there are now three parties. What should N do? It must go up! There are now three parties. However, because they are unequal, N could not be as high as the actual number. It must be in between. The formula yields N=2.00, intuitively making sense that it is between one (we have a hegemonic party) and three (we are pretty far from three equal-sized parties). In other words, N=2.00 is not always a two-party system! In most actual cases a value near 2.00 is likely to be closer to what we might mean by the vague "two-party system" than our made-up example.

The other examples in Table 4.1 illustrate the same basic points – we see N decrease when the largest party becomes larger for the same number of parties (compare example 6 to 5), but it goes up if the largest party stays the same but one of the other parties splits (compare example 7 to 5, or example 9 to both 8 and 10).[6] The effective number is never larger than the total number of parties receiving seats or votes.

---

[5] The reverse need not be the case. Thus N=2.00 might result from a balanced .50–50 (example 1), or from a very unbalanced .667–.167–.166 (example 3).

[6] At the same effective number, the parties' sizes may or may not be balanced. Compare for instance 34-33-33 and 53-15-10-10-10-2, both of which have N=3.00. Taagepera (2007: 50–53) offers a formula for an index of balance (which would result in 0.98 and 0.35, respectively, for these examples).

The formula for the effective number is "operational" in that it can be applied mechanically to any constellation of fractional shares. But the formula does not tell us which shares to use. Should the German CDU and its Bavarian "sister party" the CSU be counted as a single party or two? Either decision is justified, as the parties act as if they were one in some respects but retain their separate organizations and act independently in some other ways. The formula is not able to tell us which to do, only how to calculate once we decide whether to enter CDU and CSU shares separately or as a combined party. In the opposite direction, internal factions of a party, such as the Liberal Democratic Party in Japan, could be seen as "parties within the party" (Reed and Bolland 1999).

Lijphart (1999: 69–74) settles such dilemmas by calculating N both ways and taking the arithmetic mean. This is a reasonable solution when the two approaches are fairly close. But some cases present extra challenges. Consider the case of Chile's open-list PR system, where there are alliances, each consisting of several distinct parties. The effective number of *alliances* is close to two. However, the effective number of distinct *parties* is much higher (see our discussions of alliances in list-PR systems in Chapters 6 and 14). Both numbers make sense, in different ways, but their mean may make no sense at all. Our general practice in this book will be to count as a "party" those entities that *call themselves parties* and for which separate votes totals are reported. However, there are times when counting alliances rather than their component parties makes theoretical sense – for instance, when the alliance is essentially permanent across several elections and consistent in its membership across the country. Such is the case in Chile; India likewise has many parties that cooperate in alliances (see Chapters 5 and 15). Different researchers may make different decisions about how to count parties, alliances, and factions when calculating the effective number. The key is being consistent and transparent about what is being put into the formula.

Electoral Systems and Effective Number of Parties

It is widely understood that the electoral system somehow affects the number of parties. In particular, do multiseat PR systems produce more parties than does FPTP, in line with Duverger's (1954) propositions? It also has been claimed that presidential systems reduce the number of parties.[7] In **Table 4.2** we compare values of both N_V and N_S for FPTP and PR systems, and also for countries with parliamentary and presidential executives. We see that the ranges of N_V and N_S are definitely lower for FPTP than they are for multiseat PR. However, these are overly blunt categories, as our previous chapters already have shown. Much of the rest of the book will be about understanding more fine-grained relationships between electoral systems and party systems. As for executive types, their ranges

---

[7] Examples include Lijphart (1994), Cox (1997), Mozaffar et al. (2003) – but see Filippov et al. (1999).

TABLE 4.2 *Mean values of effective number of parties (seats and votes) by electoral system and executive binary categories*

	Parliamentary	Presidential
Effective Number of Seat-winning parties (N_S)		
FPTP mean	2.14	1.96
IQR	1.74–2.35	1.92–1.99
Number of elections	159	37
PR mean	4.23	3.60
IQR	3.22–5.04	2.27–3.90
Number of elections	261	63
Effective Number of Vote-earning parties (N_V)		
FPTP mean	2.75	2.10
IQR	2.05–3.04	2.02–2.11
Number of elections	157	37
PR mean	4.77	4.32
IQR	3.59–5.67	2.56–4.78
Number of elections	261	63

IQR = Interquartile range (the range between the 25th and 75th percentiles)

of N_V and N_S overlap heavily. While it is true in all categories (seats or votes, FPTP or PR) that the mean values are lower in presidential systems, the differences are small.[8] We will see later in the book that there is not a systematic impact of presidentialism on the (effective) number of parties in the assembly, once the electoral system variables are specified correctly.

The effective number of parties based on votes (N_V) almost always exceeds the one based on seats (N_S), as we see from the averages in Table 4.2, although exceptions occur. That the N_V is usually larger than N_S, but not by much, proves to offer an essential building block for developing a logical model of votes distribution. We develop that model in Chapter 8.

PROPORTIONALITY: BASIC INDICES

Now we turn our attention to measuring proportionality – or more precisely, *deviation* from the ideal of perfect proportionality.[9] In practice, what this

---

[8] An important caveat here is that the sample of presidential systems with FPTP is almost entirely one country, the United States. (There are two elections in Ghana and two in Sierra Leone included.)

[9] We do not mean "ideal" in a normative sense, but a scientific one. It is a standard against which to measure, regardless of one's preference over whether full proportionality is "good" or "bad" as an outcome.

means is the deviation of seat shares from vote shares of parties.[10] Two ways to measure deviation from PR have dominated. Both start with the difference between votes and seats, for each party, but they differ in how they process these differences. Loosemore and Hanby (1971) introduced into political analysis the index of deviation that we'll designate as D_1, following the systematics of Taagepera (2007: 76–79). For deviation from PR, it is

$$D_1 = 1/2 \sum |s_i - v_i|.$$

Here s_i is the i-th party's seat share, and v_i is its vote share. The index can range in principle from 0 to 1 (or 100 percent). Note that $|s_i - v_i| = |v_i - s_i|$ is never negative. D_1 dominated until Gallagher (1991) introduced what we'll designate as D_2:

$$D_2 = [1/2 \sum (s_i - v_i)^2]^{1/2}.$$

It has often been designated as the "least squares" index, but this is a misnomer. The index does involve squaring a difference but no minimization procedure so as to find some "least" squares. D_2 can range from zero to one (100 percent), but whenever more than two parties have nonzero deviations the upper limit actually remains below one – an awkward feature (Taagepera 2007: 79–82). When only two parties have nonzero deviations, the one gaining what the other is losing, then D_1 and D_2 have the same value. But when more than two parties have nonzero deviations, then D_1 is bound to be larger than D_2. In sum,

$$D_1 \geq D_2.$$

It possible, though rare, that one of these indices increases while the other decreases, from one election to the next. For further detail on various indices of deviation from proportionality, see Taagepera (2007: 65–82) and Taagepera and Grofman (2003).

Gallagher's D_2 rapidly displaced D_1 during the 1990s as the more widely used index,[11] despite grounds for doubting whether it is the best of the various measures (Taagepera and Grofman, 2003; Taagepera 2007: 76–78). In this

---

[10] We can apply the same mathematical format as deviation from PR to other features of potential interest: volatility of votes from one election to the next; the extent of ticket splitting, when voters have more than one ballot; deviations of individual district magnitudes from the system mean (see Chapter 16). All these phenomena deal with measuring *deviation from a norm* (whether it be seat shares equal to vote shares, zero ticket splitting, or equal magnitudes).

[11] It even entered popular media discourse in Canada in late 2016, when a parliamentary committee charged with considering alternative electoral systems released its report, and the Minister of Democratic Institutions mocked the formula in making her case against the committee's recommendation for greater proportionality. See "The problem with Maryam Monsef's contempt for metrics," *McCleans's*, December 3, 2016, www.macleans.ca/politics/ottawa/the-problem-with-maryam-monsefs-contempt-for-metrics/ (accessed December 15, 2016).

book's Chapter 9 we introduce a logical model that accounts for deviation from PR, defined as D_2.

Empirical Patterns of Deviation from PR

It may seem obvious that features of the electoral system would affect deviation from proportionality. After all, some electoral systems are called "proportional representation" for a reason! We can do better than just say that proportional systems have lower deviation from proportionality than majoritarian systems, such as FPTP. **Figure 4.1** shows a scatter plot of those countries from our dataset that have "simple" electoral systems. They are plotted according to their mean district magnitude on the horizontal axis and deviation from proportionality,

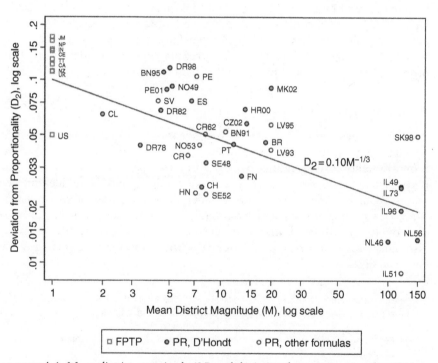

FIGURE 4.1 Mean district magnitude (M) and deviation from proportionality (D_2) Country abbreviations: BN=Benin; BR=Brazil; CA=Canada; CE=Ceylon; CH=Switzerland; CL=Chile; CR=Costa Rica; CZ=Czechia; DR=Dominican Republic; ES=Spain; FI=Finland; HN=Honduras; HR=Croatia; IL=Israel; IN=India; JM=Jamaica; LV=Latvia; MK=Macedonia; NL=Netherlands; NO=Norway; NZ=New Zealand; PE=Peru; PT=Portugal; SE=Sweden; SK=Slovakia; SV=El Salvador; TT=Trinidad and Tobago; UK=United Kingdom; US=United States. If a two-digit number follows the country abbreviation, it is to indicate the first year of a period under a different electoral system from others depicted for the same country.

D_2 (Gallagher) on the vertical axis. Both axes are on logarithmic scales. Where a country abbreviation appears with a two-digit number immediately following, it is due to some change in its electoral system.[12] Figure 4.1 differentiates systems according to allocation formula: squares for FPTP (M=1) and circles for PR (mean M>1). In addition, if the PR formula is D'Hondt, the circle is filled in, but for other formulas, it is hollow.[13]

There is clearly a strong relationship, and it can be described approximately by the solid black line, which corresponds to:

$$D_2 = 0.10M^{-1/3}.$$

The relevance of the slope, –1/3, will be explained in Chapter 9.

Figure 4.1 and its symbol patterns allow us to see that the specific formula in a PR system makes surprisingly little overall difference to the relationship between D_2 and mean M.[14] It is evident that magnitude really is the "decisive factor," as we called it in Taagepera and Shugart (1989a).[15] It is also noteworthy how low D_2 is in the United States, compared to other FPTP systems, although its use of M=1 results in higher deviation from proportionality than about half the PR systems.

CONCLUSION

Two of the most important standards conventionally used to assess electoral systems and democratic competition are the number of parties and proportionality. It is common to speak of a "two-party system" or a "multi-party system," and even casual observers of politics have some idea in their minds about how democracy differs under these categories of party system. Moreover, proportionality is such a central indicator of outcomes that an entire class of electoral system is known by the term, proportional representation, to distinguish it from other, typically quite disproportional systems such as First-Past-The-Post.

[12] We follow the definition of a new "electoral system" that Lijphart (1994) established: a change in formula or a change of at least 20 percent in mean district magnitude, assembly size, or legal threshold.

[13] Most of the non-D'Hondt PR formulas shown are either Hare quota with largest remainders or Ste.-Lague divisors.

[14] Nonetheless, see Carey (2018) for some examples of where formula has made a substantial difference in election outcomes in some newer democracies where the vote was highly fragmented after the plurality party.

[15] We see some impact of formula, independent of M: The lowest value of D_2 in Figure 4.1 is for Israel when it used Hare quota with largest remainders (1951–1969); Israel's D_2 values are strikingly higher in the periods when it has used D'Hondt. (The other separate indicators for Israel all refer to changes in legal threshold. For detail, see Chapter 5 and Hazan et al. (2018); the impact of thresholds will be discussed in Chapter 15.) In addition, the data points marked "SE48" and "SE52" show the impact of that Sweden's change from D'Hondt to Modified Ste.-Lague.

In this chapter, we took these concepts and showed how political scientists develop measures that summarize the number of parties and proportionality for any given constellation of votes and seats. The measures themselves are not new. The index for the effective number of parties, as a summary measure of the fragmentation of party support in either votes or seats, has been around since 1979. Various others had been proposed earlier, and new ones have been proposed since. All share the basic aim of indicating, with just one number, how closely a party system approximates a "two-party system" or just how "multi-party" it is. No single index ever can sum up everything we might want to know about something like a party system, where there may be many parties of wildly unequal sizes. Yet the effective number of parties has stood the test of time. More importantly, as subsequent chapters will show, it lends itself well to logical modeling that allows us to understand how institutional features of the electoral system shape party competition. Similarly, various measures of deviation from proportionality have been around for decades by now. Here, too, there is no perfect measure, but Gallagher's index has become widely used now, and we will see that it, too, has some promise for the development of logical models.

5

Examples of Electoral Systems: Nationwide PR in Israel and FPTP in Trinidad and Tobago, and India

In Chapter 4, we introduced tools for analyzing electoral system outputs – the effective number of parties and deviation from proportionality. Going back a couple of chapters further, in Chapter 2, we introduced a series of different rules that form the components of an electoral system. In this chapter and Chapter 6, we switch to a different approach. We illustrate how rules work when put together in a specific way to form an electoral system in a given political context. We use two main cases in each of these chapters, with glances at other examples where they highlight some important variation, such as the application to India, the world's largest democracy, near the end of this chapter.

In this first chapter of examples, we take the extremes in districting arrangements. The number of districts in a country may range from a minimum of one to a maximum of S, the size of the national assembly. When there is one district, it means that $M=S$, that is, the district magnitude is identical to the assembly size. At the opposite extreme, if there are S districts, then it must be the case that each of these has $M=1$, meaning a system of single-seat districts. The simplest manifestation of either of these extremes is the use of a single-round "closed list" system. As we discussed in Chapter 2, for $M=S$ this means a single nationwide district in which voters cast a single categorical ballot for one party list. Seats are then allocated proportionally among these lists – using one of the various PR formulas (see Chapter 2). Voters do not cast votes for candidates on the list that they select; rather, the candidates are selected and ranked before the election by the party.

When $M=1$, what does it mean to have a "closed list" system? It means that every party presents a list containing one candidate; this is what the FPTP system entails. Most scholars and others, when thinking of such a system, would say FPTP is a "candidate-based" system. They have a point – typically the names of the candidates are shown on the ballot, and voters may even prefer one over the other because they like the person, regardless of the party. The point we want to emphasize here, however, is that regardless of whether the voter makes her choice because she is thinking of the party or the candidate, the FPTP system is no different from closed-list PR with the district magnitude reduced to its minimum, one.[1]

Surprisingly, FPTP has one feature in common with its apparent opposite, large-magnitude closed-list PR: in either case, the voter is given a choice only among parties. Even with a single nationwide closed list, some voters may make their choice because they like the party leader, or some specific candidate on the list. Voting for the party's list because the voter likes a candidate does not change the basic constraint that FPTP and closed-list PR impose on the voter: there is no opportunity to cast a vote below the level of the party. In the case of FPTP, assuming a party nominates just one candidate (as is virtually always the case), the voter is given a choice only among parties – just as in nationwide closed-list PR.[2]

FPTP is the electoral system likely to be most familiar to readers in English-speaking countries, because it is the system used in Britain, Canada, India, and the United States, among other countries. Sometimes known as "single-member plurality," it is the system in which the country is divided into S districts, where S is the size of the national assembly (House of Commons, House of Representatives, etc.). In fact, among the major English-speaking countries, only Australia and New Zealand use systems other than this at the national level.[3] In this chapter we mainly use a lesser-known example, Trinidad and Tobago, to illustrate FPTP in context, because small country size offers several analytic advantages. We also introduce India, the world's largest FPTP system. Before turning to these examples, however, we start with the opposite example: nationwide closed-list PR.

NATIONWIDE CLOSED-LIST PR: THE CASE OF ISRAEL

We start with the Israeli case because, as we shall see, it is arguably "simpler" to elect all members in one nationwide district than it is to elect them all in their own single-seat districts. This verdict may surprise many readers, especially those accustomed to the supposed "simplicity" of elections in the UK or countries using similar electoral systems. When we turn later to the case of Trinidad and Tobago, we will see that in actual outcomes, if not in mechanics, FPTP is not so simple after all!

---

[1] If a party has a "list" of no more than M candidates, then both open and closed lists reduce to FPTP when $M=1$. In Chapter 6, we will see a case of open list where, even when $M=1$, lists may contain more than one candidate, which means it is not equivalent to FPTP.

[2] What about independent candidates? These are effectively no different from a party that happens to run only in one district.

[3] In the UK, several different electoral systems are used for other offices, such as the Scottish Parliament, Welsh Assembly, various local councils, and the European Parliament (prior to the UK's referendum calling for withdrawal from the European Union); see Lundberg (2018). In the US, some states use other systems (see Chapter 2).

Israel has a citizen population of around eight million. Israelis vote in a single nationwide district, and elect 120 Members of Knesset (MKs)–*Knesset* is simply the Hebrew word for assembly. Table 5.1 shows three recent Israeli elections, and includes all parties that win seats in at least one election, plus other parties that win over 1 percent of the vote at least once. Two things should immediately stand out, even to a reader not already familiar with electoral systems, or with Israeli politics. First, there are a lot of parties! It is noteworthy that new parties enter periodically, such as Yesh Atid in 2013 and Kulanu in 2015. The certainty of winning a share of seats commensurate to votes means that the barriers to new entrants are unusually low (Doron and Maor 1991).

Second, they all tend to have seat shares very close to their vote shares. In fact, even when they have small vote percentages, such as the 2.1 percent won by Kadima in 2013, the seat share is very similar, as long as they clear the threshold (discussed later). This is, of course, the meaning of proportional representation, and such representation can hardly be more "pure" than in a single nationwide district.

The main factor limiting proportionality is the existence of a threshold, which stipulates that a party wins no seats unless it clears the threshold percentage of votes.[4] Thresholds are common in electoral systems that have high district magnitude, as a means to put a limit on how many small parties can obtain seats. This bar was set at 2 percent in 2009 and 2013, but was increased to 3.25 percent in 2015.

Each party that clears the threshold wins seats in proportion to votes cast, after discarding votes for below-threshold parties. Deviation from proportionality tends to be low in worldwide terms. The presence of a legal threshold is the main factor in leading deviation to be higher in some elections. For instance, both the 2009 and 2013 elections were held under a 2 percent threshold. Yet deviation was considerably greater in the latter election because, as we can see in Table 5.1, there were three parties that had over 1 percent of the votes, yet less than 2 percent. By contrast, in 2009, the largest below-threshold parties had 0.8 percent and 0.4 percent of the votes. For the 2015 election, the threshold was raised to 3.25 percent; while three parties merged into one common list to clear the threshold (discussed in Chapter 6), there was also a party with 3 percent of the votes. These votes contribute to a higher deviation in 2015.

In addition to the threshold, deviation from proportionality is somewhat increased by the use of the D'Hondt method of PR (see Chapter 2). Even with such a high district magnitude, D'Hondt is somewhat advantageous to large parties. For instance, when Hare quota and largest remainders were used (with a 1 percent threshold), deviation from proportionality averaged only 0.88 percent between 1951 and 1969.

---

[4] We discussed thresholds in Chapter 3 and do so in more detail again in Chapter 16.

TABLE 5.1 *Recent elections in Israel*

Party	2009 %votes	seats	%seats	2013 %votes	seats	%seats	2015 %votes	seats	%seats
Likud	21.6	27	22.5	23.3	31	25.8	23.4	30	25.0
Yisrael Beiteinu	11.7	15	12.5				5.1	6	5.0
Labor	9.9	13	10.8	11.4	15	12.5			
Hatnuah				5.0	6	5.0			
Zionist Union							18.7	24	20.0
Joint List							10.6	13	10.8
Yesh Atid				14.3	19	15.8	8.8	11	9.2
Kulanu							7.5	10	8.3
National Union	3.3	4	3.3						
The Jewish Home	2.9	3	2.5	9.1	12	10.0	6.7	8	6.7
Shas	8.5	11	9.2	8.8	11	9.2	5.7	7	5.8
United Torah Judaism	4.4	5	4.2	5.2	7	5.8	5.0	6	5.0
Meretz	3.0	3	2.5	4.6	6	5.0	3.9	5	4.2
Yachad							3.0	0	0.0
Ale Yarok	0.4	0	0.0	1.2	0	0.0	1.1	0	0.0
United Arab List-Ta'al	3.4	4	3.3	3.7	4	3.3			
Hadash	3.3	4	3.3	3.0	4	3.3			
Balad	2.5	3	2.5	2.6	3	2.5			
Kadima	22.5	28	23.3	2.1	2	1.7			
Otzma L'Yisrael				1.8	0	0.0			
Am Shalem				1.2	0	0.0			
other	3.4	0	0.0	2.7	0	0.0	0.5	0	0.0
sum		120			120			120	
Effective N	7.37	6.77		8.68	7.28		7.71	6.94	
Deviation (D_2 %)		1.61			3.09			3.72	

Likud and Yisrael Beiteinu presented an alliance list in 2013.
Zionist Union is an alliance list of Labor and Hatnuah in 2015.
National Union joined the list of The Jewish Home in 2013.

The low entry barrier for a system of nationwide PR means new parties enter the competition frequently, and are able to win representation as long as they clear the low threshold. Several such examples of new parties are immediately noticeable in Table 5.1. In addition, the closed lists mean that parties can reserve slots on their list for prominent candidates who are known from outside politics, or for candidates who are representatives of interest groups or sectors from which the party seeks to attract votes. A party can ensure that such candidates win; yet those candidates do not have to present themselves to the voters through personal campaigns. In fact, there is little reason for candidates to campaign as individuals, given that all they can ask of the voter is to select their list rather than one of the many others running.

As for the specific MKs, these are elected solely due to their order on the list, which is determined prior to the election. For instance, when the Likud won thirty seats in 2015, it simply elected the top thirty candidates, in the order in which they were listed. Some parties determine this order via votes of their memberships (i.e., in "primaries"), whereas in other parties the leader or a small set of leaders solely determines the nominees and their list ranks (Rahat and Hazan 2001; Hazan et al. 2018). In any case, the voter is selecting only a list as presented by the party. Some voters may consider the candidates on the list (and where they are ranked) in deciding which party list to vote for, but they are unable to do anything about the order via their vote in the general election. The voter either accepts or rejects the list as offered. This is the sense in which the system is a "closed list" form of PR. It is also the sense in which it is a highly "simple" system: the voter makes one choice, and the aggregate of those choices forms the set of vote totals on which all 120 seats are determined.

The case of Yesh Atid in the 2013 election shows both the ease of entry of new parties, and the ability to construct a list of candidates who are known from nonpolitical arenas of public life. The party did not exist prior to the 2013 campaign, yet it was able to capitalize on voter sentiment for a new "centrist" alternative and win nineteen seats. Voters who wanted to vote for this new party could be sure that their votes were not mere protest votes. Due to nationwide PR, the party would win seats as long as it cleared the threshold, which it did easily.

None of the candidates on the Yesh Atid list had been members of the Knesset previously; the leader, Yair Lapid, was a former TV news anchorman. Among the candidates whom he selected to high list ranks and who were thus almost certain to gain seats unless the party totally flopped were Yaakov Perry (former head of the security service, Shin Bet) in the second rank, Ofer Shelah (a military affairs journalist), at number six,[5] and some mayors of secondary

[5] Emily L. Hauser, "Lapid's List Says It All," *The Daily Beast*, January 25, 2013 (www .thedailybeast.com/articles/2013/01/25/lapid-s-list-says-it-all.html); last accessed November 16, 2015.

cities around the country who potentially could bring their local supporters to the new party. The party's success allowed it to enter a governing coalition following the election, with Lapid as Finance Minister and four of its other winning candidates also sitting in the cabinet.

Even established parties use the strategy of setting aside list ranks for candidates with a personal reputation from outside national politics, or who represent groups the party is seeking to attract. For instance, prior to the 2015 election, the Likud Party leader and incumbent Prime Minister, Benjamin Netanyahu, "posted a request on his official Facebook page for the public to suggest candidates for the 11th and the 23rd positions" on the list.[6] These were slots that allowed Netanyahu to select candidates whose presence could help broaden the list's appeal. He chose two women who were known for their activities outside politics.[7]

Because the lists are "closed" in the sense that voters do not vote for individual candidates (see Chapter 6), parties may sometimes use a strategy of encouraging votes for the party from societal groups by placing candidates in slots where they may not win unless voters from their group turn out for the party. In 2006 Shạs, an Orthodox Jewish religious party, placed candidates from two immigrant communities "at the margins of the list" and "apparently received votes from the two communities."[8] The candidates, Rabbi Mazor Bayana from Ethiopia and Avraham Michaeli from the Republic of Georgia, were ranked 13th and 14th, respectively. The party won thirteen seats; the rankings of these candidates in marginal slots thus appeared to be a strategy to attract votes to the party from the candidates' ethnic communities.

In the ways just illustrated, parties are advertising the candidates on their list even though voters are unable to vote for candidates as individuals. Voters accept or reject the list as a whole, and the exact set of candidates who win seats is dependent on how many votes the party collectively obtains. This is a purely proportional, purely party-based, electoral system. It stands in contrast, therefore, to those systems in which every member of the assembly must win a local contest, standing as the sole candidate of the party in the district. This describes FPTP, to which we turn now.

---

[6] "Bibi Turns to Social Media to Fill Out Likud List," *JP Updates*, January 8, 2015 (http://jpupdates.com/2015/01/08/bibi-turns-social-media-fill-likud-list/); last accessed November 17, 2015.

[7] Dr. Anat Berko ("a world-renowned terrorism expert ") and Dr. Limor Samimian-Darash (a university lecturer). See Jonathan Lis, "Netanyahu Appoints Two Women to Likud Knesset Slate," *Haaretz* January 29, 2015 (www.haaretz.com/israel-news/elections/.premium-1.639625); last accessed November 17, 2015.

[8] Shahar Ilan, "Things are Different When it Comes to Shas," *Haaretz* March 3, 2006. (www.haaretz.com/print-edition/features/things-are-different-when-it-comes-to-shas-1.184162); last accessed November 17, 2015.

FPTP: THE CASE OF TRINIDAD AND TOBAGO – AND INDIA

Trinidad and Tobago is a country consisting of two main islands, which feature in the country's compound name. It is located off the coast of Venezuela in the Caribbean Sea. It is a small country, population only about 1.3 million. It is its small size that makes it an asset for illustrating its electoral system, because its small assembly size means there are not many districts to analyze if we want to see how the district level connects to the national level. In fact, making such connections is one of the core tasks of this book. Thus a small FPTP jurisdiction is ideal for illustrative purposes. The assembly size is currently forty-one. That is, we can say $S=41$, and there are forty-one electoral districts, each with a magnitude, $M=1$.

FPTP in Action in Trinidad and Tobago Elections

Trinidad and Tobago (T&T) elections since 2000 are summarized in Table 5.2. The country has been holding elections regularly since 1946, but we focus on several recent elections for sake of illustrating how FPTP works. Table 4.2 shows elections through 2010.

If one knew nothing about electoral systems, one might look at the table and be very much puzzled by some of the results. For instance, in 2001 the two leading parties wound up in an exact tie for seats despite about a three percentage-point gap between them in votes. Then in 2002, a small swing in votes between the two parties resulted in a quite large majority (over 55 percent) of seats. The 2007 election offers a very large distortion in votes and seats, with a three-fifths majority to a leading party that falls short of 46 percent of the votes, while a third party has 22.6 percent of the votes and not one seat.

What explains the rather odd outcomes seen in Table 5.2? The explanation is that *national vote totals simply do not matter for allocating seats under FPTP.* Instead, it works as if it asked each party at the end of election day: in how many individual districts did you get more votes than any other party? Consider the case of the National Alliance for Reconstruction (NAR), which won a seat in 2000 despite only 1.2 percent of the national vote, as we see in Table 5.2. How did such a small party win in a FPTP system? It had its votes highly concentrated. In fact, it ran in only two districts, both on the island of Tobago. In one of these, it had 47.2 percent of the vote, the highest among three candidates. By having a plurality – not even a majority – in one district, it obtained representation. In only a few PR systems – even those, like Israel, with a nationwide district – would a party with only 1.2 percent of the vote gain representation. It is possible under FPTP, but only if said party has strong vote concentration in one district. Even then it may need a little luck, such as a multicandidate contest allowing it to win against a divided field.

While all the elections depicted in Table 5.2, bar 2007, have an effective number of vote-earning parties (N_V) near two, the effective number by

TABLE 5.2 Election results in Trinidad and Tobago, 2000–2010

Party	2000		2001		2002		2007		2010	
	%v	seats	%v	seats	%v	seats	%v	seats	%v	seats
PNM	46.5	16 (44.4)	46.5	18 (50.0)	50.9	20 (55.6)	45.9	26 (63.4)	39.5	12 (29.3)
UNC	51.7	19 (52.8)	49.9	18 (50.0)	46.9	16 (44.4)	29.7	15 (36.6)		
COP							22.6	0		
PPC									59.8	29 (70.7)
NAR	1.2	1 (2.8)	1	0	1.1	0				
TUN			2.5	0						
CA					1	0				
Others	0.4	0	0	0	0.1	0	1.7	0	0.3	0
Ind.	0.2	0								
N_V	2.07		2.15		2.09		2.86		1.95	
N_S	2.10		2.00		1.98		1.87		1.71	
D_2 %	2.04		3.16		3.71		20.81		10.55	

seats (N_S) fluctuates over a wider range, and falls below 2.00 even when N_V goes up to 2.86. In one election, 2000, we even have $N_S > N_V$, which is an unusual occurrence globally. We also see deviation from proportionality (D_2) ranging all the way from about 2.0 percent to more than ten times as high. In each case, these are nationwide indicators, whose values and interrelationships are contingent on the way the election shakes out in each of the individual districts.

Strategic Adaptation by Parties: The Case of Trinidad and Tobago 2010

In Table 5.2, we saw that in 2007 there was a new party that won 22.6 percent of the votes. This Congress of the People (COP) was only about seven percentage points behind the United National Congress (UNC), and yet the COP won no seats while the UNC won fifteen. Meanwhile, this was an election in which the People's National Movement (PNM) won a manufactured majority: despite less than half the votes, it won well over half the seats. The combination of these outcomes in one election is not mere coincidence; the "vote-splitting" by anti-PNM voters contributed to the PNM's assembly majority.

Then in 2010, the two opposition parties, UNC and COP "coordinated" by forming an alliance called the People's Partnership Coalition (PPC). As we see in Table 5.2, the PPC won a large majority of the votes in 2010 and an even larger majority of the seats. The way the PPC operated was that the two component parties retained their distinct identities, but did not compete against one another. That is, in any given district, a candidate of one of these parties stood for the PPC and the other party in the alliance abstained from the district's contest. In this way, the parties ensured that a PNM candidate could not win through splits among its opponents, as had happened in many districts in 2007.

Table 5.3 illustrates the strategic adaptation undertaken by the UNC and COP in two districts by comparing the results of the elections in 2007 and 2010. In one of our selected examples, the district of Arima, the PNM candidate won in 2007 with a very large majority: 64.7 percent of the votes, vastly outstripping the support the party had nationally (39.5 percent, per Table 5.2). In the other example, Barataria-San Juan, the PNM candidate won with a plurality, short of half the votes. In 2010, as Table 5.3 shows, the party that came in third place in each district in 2007 did not run a candidate. Instead, it endorsed the candidate of the other party opposing the PNM. In the case of Arima, this strategy appears to have been decisive, as the COP candidate won a narrow victory over the PNM's candidate, 51.3 percent to 48.7 percent. In Barataria-San Juan, the alliance also may have been essential, as the PNM candidate's 38.3 percent of the vote (from 43.6 percent, a smaller decline than the PNM suffered nationally) potentially could have been sufficient to hold on, had the COP not abstained in favor of the UNC. In both cases, we see strategic adaptation by two parties that

TABLE 5.3 *District-level results in Trinidad and Tobago, 2007 and 2010 (selected)*

District	Party	2007 Candidate	Votes %	2010 Candidate	Votes %
Arima	PNM	**Penelope Beckles**	64.7	Laurel Lezama-Lee Sing	48.7
	UNC	Wayne Rodriguez	9.2	–	
	COP	Rodger Samuel	26.1	**Rodger Samuel**	51.3
Barataria-San Juan	PNM	**Joseph Ross**	43.6	Joseph Ross	38.3
	UNC	Nazeemool Mohammed	32.6	**Fuad Khan**	61.7
	COP	Jamal Mohammed	23.8	–	

Winner in bold.

had competed against each other in the preceding election but coordinated in an alliance in 2010. The pattern repeated itself across all districts in Trinidad and Tobago, with no district featuring both a UNC and a COP candidate in the 2010 contest. Instead, almost all districts featured a straight two-way fight between the PNM and a candidate of one of the PPC component parties.

The 2007 and 2010 elections in T&T illustrate how coordination matters, and how in a FPTP system, vote-splitting or its absence can make a difference in who wins a seat. Moreover, they demonstrate why national vote totals are not the determinant of seat winning under such an electoral system. What matters is where your votes are distributed across the territory, and how many opponents you face.

Drawing Lessons from Trinidad and Tobago for Comparative Analysis: India and Other FPTP Cases

These lessons are not unique to T&T. If they were, it would matter only to those who have a special interest in this one small country. Rather, the case offers lessons for other similar electoral systems, including in very large countries, where similar outcomes have occurred.

For instance, we saw in the T&T example that some elections result in a manufactured majority – for instance, 2007. This happens when a party wins more than half the seats despite less than half the votes. Such outcomes are the norm in many long established FPTP systems. In the UK, no party has won a majority of the national vote since 1931, and yet in all but three elections since then, one party has had a majority of seats. Consider the 1983 UK election, in which the Conservative Party, which was able to parlay 42.4 percent of the votes into a whopping 397 seats out of 650 – more than three fifths of the total. This large manufactured majority was made possible by vote-splitting of center-left parties. The Labour Party managed 209 seats on 27.6 percent of the votes, while the Alliance (of Social Democratic and Liberal parties) won only a slightly lower vote percentage, at 25.4 percent, yet only twenty-three seats.[9]

The 2010 election in Trinidad and Tobago serves as a small-scale example of what happens on a vast scale in the world's largest democracy. India uses FPTP and has a highly fragmented party system. Yet many of these parties coordinate within alliances. As we saw in Trinidad and Tobago, these alliances involve the component parties not competing against one another in any given district. Thus the large number of parties one finds in the nationwide results of recent elections in India exaggerates the fragmentation seen by the typical Indian voter, because most districts feature one candidate from each of the main national alliances.

The alliance behavior of India in a typical recent election, that of 2009, is depicted in Table 5.4. If we look only at parties' votes and seats, we see that the largest party, the Indian National Congress (INC), won only 28.6 percent of the votes, which the electoral system turned into 37.9 percent of the seats – clearly reminding us of the disproportionality of FPTP elections. The second largest party was the Bharatiya Janata Party (BJP), with only 18.8 percent of votes, and a somewhat higher percentage of seats, at 21.4 percent. The more salient feature of the election, however, is the alliances.

Several recent Indian elections have featured two big alliances that engage in what in India is often called "seat sharing," whereby parties in alliance refrain from competing against each other in any given district. It is thus exactly as we saw in T&T in 2010, only with many more parties involved across a vastly larger and more diverse country. At alliance level, the election was a contest between the United Progressive Alliance (UPA) and the National Democratic Alliance (NDA). The UPA won 48.3 percent of seats, just short of a majority, from a vote percentage of 37.2 percent for all its separate parties combined. On the other hand, the NDA won 29.3 percent of seats on 24.6 percent of the votes for its component parties. Each alliance consisted of several parties, only some of which are shown separately in the table. Each of these parties tends to run only in one or a few states; in the districts where it runs, its national partner (INC or BJP) does not put up a candidate against it. In this way, "seat-sharing" (parceling out before the election which partner will contest which districts) prevents vote-splitting (whereby parties with allied interests might lose a district to a mutual opponent if they failed to coordinate their voting bloc).

So what is the more relevant metric in India, parties or alliances? It depends. On the one hand, each party retains its separate identity and organization, and would be free to switch alliances (and such switches sometimes happen). The 2009 election featured 364 parties (not counting independent

---

[9] Seventeen of the winners were Liberals and six were Social Democrats.

TABLE 5.4 *Election results in India, 2009, by alliance and party*

Alliances	Party	Vote %	Seats won	Seat %
United Progressive Alliance				
	Indian National Congress	28.55	206	37.94
	All India Trinamool Congress	3.20	19	3.50
	Dravida Munnetra Kazhagam	1.83	18	3.31
	Nationalist Congress Party	2.04	9	1.66
	Seven other parties combined...	1.60	10	1.83
National Democratic Alliance				
	Bharatiya Janata Party	18.80	116	21.36
	Janata Dal (United)	1.52	20	3.68
	Shiv Sena	1.55	11	2.03
	Five more parties combined...	2.76	12	2.21
Third Front				
	Bahujan Samaj Party	6.17	21	3.87
	Communist Party of India (Marxist)	5.33	16	2.95
	Biju Janata Dal	1.59	14	2.58
	Eleven other parties combined...	8.06	28	5.15
Fourth Front				
	Samajwadi Party	3.42	23	4.24
	Rashtriya Janata Dal	1.27	4	0.74
	Lok Janshakti Party	0.45	0	0.00
Seven other parties combined		1.32	7	1.26
Independents		5.19	9	1.66
Total	364 Political Parties		543	

candidates), and forty-two separate parties won at least one seat. On the other hand, it is the winning alliance that forms a government if it wins the backing of a majority in parliament, and the other major alliance heads the opposition. The two biggest alliances combined for more than three-fourths of the seats. In this latter respect, the party system looks somewhat more like a "typical" FPTP system than it may seem if we count the parties separately. We take up these questions of how to count the relevant number of components – parties versus alliances – in the Indian case in more detail in Chapter 15.

While the other major FPTP countries seldom see seat-sharing alliances such as India, such strategic adaptation by parties is one way in which a multiparty system at the national level may be more streamlined for the voters, as each voter sees only the candidate of the alliance partner that contests the district, rather than all the many parties. Consider the contrast to the Israeli case: there are many parties in Israel (albeit fewer than in India), but every voter in every part of the country has the same set of choices. In India, on the other hand, alliances have limited the district-level competition, which also means that voters in different districts have a very different menu of competitors. The ability of parties to combine on alliances that differ in which party runs in given localities is a feature inherent to a system of single-seat districts, even if it is not a ubiquitous feature of such systems. In fact, as we shall see in Chapter 10, it is common under FPTP systems for the effective number of parties at district level to be higher than the expected "two-party system," due to national politics entering into district-level voting patterns.

SUMMARY: TWO "EXTREME," BUT SIMPLE SYSTEMS

In this chapter, we have seen examples of systems that are at once "simple" and "extreme." As we defined in Chapter 2, a system is simple when all seats are elected in one tier, and in one round, by party lists. As we argued earlier in this chapter, when $M=1$, as long as there is only one candidate per party (as essentially always is the case), it is equivalent to a closed list with the smallest possible number of candidates, one.

In this chapter, we looked at simple systems that sit at opposite ends of the continuum running from S districts of one seat each (FPTP, as in Trinidad and Tobago, and India) to one district with S seats (as in the nationwide PR case of Israel). Given the use of a PR formula, when the magnitude is very high, as with $M=120$ in Israel, many parties can be expected to win seats. Deviation from proportionality is low. By contrast, when magnitude is reduced all the way to one, given the single round of voting, the party whose candidate obtains a plurality of votes takes the entire representation of the district, regardless of whether this vote share was well short of a majority or even if it was just one vote ahead of the runner-up. It is this disproportional feature of FPTP that opens up the possibility of "vote-splitting" whereby two parties might share a common voter pool, but compete against one another if they both run in the same district. We saw this happen in the 2007 election in T&T. They can work around this vote-splitting by forming an alliance, under which only one of them will contest any given district, as we saw in the 2010 election, and in India.

These two systems only begin to demonstrate the diversity of electoral systems, but they define two clear pure types: an election consisting of separate contests in many districts and often producing highly disproportional results (FPTP) versus nationwide PR. In Chapter 6, we explore a common intermediate type, districted PR. We again focus the comparison on two examples, this time differing on the type of vote that voters case in those districts.

6

Examples of Electoral Systems: Districted PR and List Type in Finland, Portugal, and Elsewhere

In Chapter 5, we contrasted single-seat district FPTP against nationwide PR. We emphasized there that the key distinction between such systems is in their relationships between districts and assembly size. At one extreme, in a system of FPTP, each of S members of the assembly is elected in his or her own unique district. Each of these districts has a magnitude $M=1$. At the other extreme, there is just one district, hence $M=S$, with a simple proportional-representation (PR) formula.

In this chapter, we consider the more common intermediate case in which PR is used, and so is districting. That is, there are districts that have more than one seat, but fewer than S; it may be the case that one or a few districts have just one seat, but most have $M>1$. These are systems of districted PR. The examples that we draw on most extensively to illustrate district PR are two countries at the "corners" of Europe: in the far northeast, Finland, and in the far southwest, Portugal.

The two systems differ on another important dimension, their type of party list, with Portugal using closed lists, whereas in Finland lists are open. When a list is open, the voter has the ability to cast a vote below the level of the party, for one (or sometimes more) of the candidates included on a list and candidates are elected from a list in the order of the votes they obtain. We briefly introduced such an example from Poland in Chapter 1. The type of list may seem like a truly arcane detail of electoral systems. However, as we show, it makes a difference for who is elected within a party, and sometimes for the balance of parties themselves, in cases in which two or more parties combine in an alliance and submit a common list. Moreover, the consequences of open versus closed lists are sometimes important enough to generate mass protests, as occurred precisely over what kind of list to use in Iraq in 2009.

INTRODUCING DISTRICTED PR

Both Portugal and Finland base their electoral districts around pre-existing administrative boundaries. Because these regions differ in population, and the countries' electoral laws are designed to keep the ratio of legislators to citizens from deviating too much from region to region (minimizing malapportionment – see Chapter 3), the districts vary in their magnitude, M. In Finland, before a change in 2015, there were fifteen districts, ranging in magnitude from one to thirty-four (Raunio 2005).[1] Given an assembly size of 200, we can calculate Finland's mean district magnitude as 200/15=13.3. In Portugal, there are twenty-two districts, and they range in magnitude from two to forty-seven. Given an assembly size of 230, mean district magnitude is 230/22=10.45.

In Finland, there is a single-seat district, and it is a region that is both outlying and distinct culturally. The Åland Islands are in the Gulf of Bothnia between Sweden and mainland Finland, and have an almost entirely Swedish-speaking population. They enjoy an autonomous status, have a separate set of political parties from mainland Finland, and even issue their own postage stamps. However, the Åland Islands are part of Finland, and send a single representative to the Finnish parliament, the Eduskunta, on behalf of a voting population of just over 26,000.

The variation in district magnitude, and varying voting strength of parties across the country, results in proportionality being less "pure" than is the case under a single nationwide district, as in Israel. Table 6.1 shows examples of one recent election in Finland and one in Portugal, using nationwide statistics. We see that the party systems are very different in the two countries. While the electoral system is a crucial factor shaping party systems – as is a consistent theme of this book – they are obviously not the only factor.

In Portugal, the largest party in the 2005 election was almost exactly twice the size of the largest in Finland in 2007. Correspondingly, the effective number of parties (either votes or seats) is much higher in Finland than in Portugal. A noteworthy feature of both of these elections is that, when compared to our case of nationwide PR, Israel (shown in Table 5.1), the larger parties tend to be somewhat overrepresented, while the smaller ones tend to be somewhat underrepresented. However, the pattern is not quite as simple as that: the Swedish People's Party in Finland has about the same vote and seat percentages, while the True Finns party is considerably more underrepresented. The reason lies in the districting, and more to the point, how efficiently a party has its votes spread across different districts.

We also see that deviation from proportionality is much higher in Portugal than in Finland. In fact, the largest party in Portugal in 2005 has a manufactured majority despite the use of a "proportional" system (both countries use D'Hondt). This is due mainly to the range of district magnitudes in Portugal,

---

[1] In 2015, some smaller adjacent districts were merged to allow for higher magnitude; the mean M is now 15.4, with thirteen districts (von Schoultz 2018).

TABLE 6.1 *Examples of election results under districted PR in Finland and Portugal*

	Finland, 2007				Portugal, 2005		
Party	% votes	seats	% seats	Party	% votes	seats	% seats
Centre Party (Kesk)	23.1	51	25.5	Socialist	46.4	121	52.6
National Coalition Party (KOK)	22.3	50	25.0	Social Democrat	29.6	75	32.6
Social Democratic Party (SD)	21.4	45	22.5	Communist	7.8	14	6.1
Left Alliance (Vas)	8.8	17	8.5	People's Party	7.5	12	5.2
Green Party	8.5	15	7.5	Bloc of the Left	6.6	8	3.5
Christian Democrats	4.9	7	3.5	others	2.2	0	0.0
Swedish People's Party	4.6	9	4.5				
True Finns (PS)	4.1	5	2.5				
others	2.4	1	0.5				
total	100.1	200	100.0		100.1	230	100.0
Effective N	5.88	5.13			3.13	2.56	
Deviation (D_2 %)		3.2				5.75	

where ten of the twenty-two districts have just two to six seats apiece, whereas in Finland only one of fifteen districts has a magnitude under six.

We can consider some specific districts to get a clearer idea of how this reduced proportionality come about. Table 6.2 shows several selected districts in Portugal in 2005: Lisbon (*M*=48 at that time), Setúbal (*M*=17), Santarém (*M*=10), and Portalegre (*M*=2). Note that the same parties are running in all three districts. The Socialist Party is the largest in each of the districts shown, although the second party varies according to local preferences.

The most important thing to note about these selected districts is how the district magnitude affects the proportionality. In the very high magnitude district of Lisbon, seat percentages closely match vote percentages, despite the use of the D'Hondt formula, which somewhat favors the larger parties. We see that the Socialists won 47.9 percent of the seats on 45.6 percent of the votes – a large-party advantage, but a small one, compared to what it obtains in the smaller-*M* districts. For instance, in ten-seat Santarém it has 60 percent of seats on less than 50 percent of votes, and in two-seat Portalegre, it won both seats because it had more than twice the votes of the runner-up (see the explanation in Chapter 2 of how D'Hondt divisors work).

TABLE 6.2 *Results of selected districts in Portugal, 2005*

Party	Lisbon Votes (%)	Lisbon Seats (%)	Setúbal Votes (%)	Setúbal Seats (%)	Santarém Votes (%)	Santarém Seats (%)	Portalegre Votes (%)	Portalegre Seats (%)
Socialist	45.6	23 (47.9)	44.9	8 (47.1)	48.1	6 (60.0)	56.1	2 (100.0)
Social Dem.	24.4	12 (25.0)	16.5	3 (17.7)	27.2	3 (30.0)	20.8	0
Communist	10.1	5 (10.4)	20.5	3 (17.6)	8.9	1 (10.0)	12.4	0
Left Bloc	9.1	4 (8.3)	10.5	2 (11.8)	6.7	0	4.7	0
Peoples	8.5	4 (8.3)	5.2	1 (5.9)	7.2	0	4.3	0
Others	2.3	0	2.4	0	2.3	0	1.7	0
Effective N	3.4	3.16	3.51	3.32	3.09	2.17	2.65	1
D_2 (%)		3.25		5.34		16.0		43.9

The last line of Table 6.2 indicates the deviation from proportionality (D_2) of the seat allocation in each district. In the high-M case of Lisbon, $D_2=3.25$ percent. The values are correspondingly higher as the magnitude decreases, as is typically the case. In two-seat Portalegre, $D_2=43.9$ percent, a very high value for a "proportional representation" system. The next-to-last line indicates the effective number of parties, by both votes and seats, in each district. It is noteworthy that it is the case in each district that $N_S<N_V$, as is typical, but the $N_V–N_S$ difference is notably greater in the two districts with the lower magnitude, most strikingly in Portalegre where $N_S=1$ because only one of the parties won representation.

LIST TYPES: OPEN VERSUS CLOSED

Most proportional-representation systems entail each party (or sometimes an alliance of parties) presenting a list of candidates. The first step in determining seats in a district is to apply one of the PR formulas – D'Hondt in both Finland and Portugal, but it could be any of the formulas discussed in Chapter 2. Then the seats won by each list must be allocated to individual candidates. When lists are closed, as in the Israeli example discussed in Chapter 5, the order in which candidates are elected from the list is set by the party prior to election day. By contrast, some systems use open lists, whereby the rank order depends on votes obtained by individual candidates. There are also hybrid list types, explained later.

The choice of closed or open list may seem like a mundane matter, but evidently it is not. We take a small detour from our discussion of the Finnish and Portuguese electoral systems to look at a country where there was a significant public controversy over list type, Iraq.

Closed Versus Open Lists in Iraq

Sometimes the type of party list for a proportional-representation system becomes a matter of considerable political controversy – even internationally. When Iraq first held elections following the overthrow of the dictator Saddam Hussein by American, British, and allied military forces, it used a PR system. The first two national elections, held in January and December, 2005, used closed lists.[2] However, before the next national elections, in March 2010, the law was changed to provide for open lists. The move was marked by conflict and proved highly consequential for the balance of political and sectarian forces (Darwisha 2010).

The main political formations that emerged to contest the elections in Iraq were themselves alliances of various groups. Under the closed list, the parties and factions that came together to forge alliances, such as the United Iraqi Alliance (of mainly Shiite religious groups) and the Democratic Patriotic Alliance of Kurdistan, negotiated before the election to designate candidates from each of their component groups for specific electable ranks. In this way they could ensure an internal balance of their legislative contingents. They also used list ranking to enforce a quota of 25 percent women among the elected (Darwisha 2010).

During parliamentary debates about the electoral law in 2009 there were mass protests in several cities, organized by followers of leading Shiite cleric Grand Ayatollah Ali Husseini al-Sistani.[3] A spokesman for the Ayatollah said, "we think the open list is one of the ways to push large numbers of Iraqis to vote in the elections."[4] The leader of another major Shiite movement, the so-called Sadrist bloc, stated forthrightly, "The Sadrist bloc opposes the closed-list system in the parliamentary elections law."[5] Meanwhile, Kurdish politicians, as well as another of the Shiite factions, the Islamic Supreme Council of Iraq, "actively used the gender quota as an argument against greater openness."[6] According to the US State Department, the Iranian government preferred that Iraq continue to use a closed list, but it was outmaneuvered in domestic Iraqi politics, mainly because Sistani's very public call for open lists forced several other Shia parties to follow him.[7]

---

[2] These two elections used systems that differed in other provisions that we will leave aside here.

[3] "Iraqis Protest against Controversial Voting System," Agence France Presse, October 10, 2009.

[4] "Iraq's Top Shiite Leader May Urge Vote Boycott," Middle East Online, October 5, 2009, www .middle-east-online.com/english/?id=34719 (last accessed January 3, 2016).

[5] "Sadrists Threaten to Walk Out of Session if Vote on Closed-List System is Held," Aswat al-Iraq, October 6, 2009.

[6] Reidar Visser, "A Litmus Test for Iraq," Middle East Report Online, January 30, 2009.

[7] "Iran's Efforts in Iraqi Electoral Politics," Cable 09BAGHDAD2992, Embassy Baghdad, released by Wikileaks, November 28, 2010.

Why would these various political actors care so much about something so seemingly arcane as list type? The answer is simple: they understood the political consequences. Those that had strong mobilizational capacity would stand to benefit from open lists, because they could push many of their favored candidates into higher list positions than they could via pre-election negotiations with other factions over list ranks. Such a result was precisely confirmed by the outcome of the 2010 elections. Within the mainly Shiite Iraqi National Alliance, the Sadrist bloc won more than half the seats, substantially increasing its share over the preceding, closed-list, elections. Some other Shiite factions saw their balance within the alliance sharply reduced. Another list, known as State of Law and headed by then-Prime Minister Nuri al-Maliki, also saw a shift in its internal balance due to the open list. Reidar Visser notes:

> . . . much of the attempt by Nuri al-Maliki to build bridges to Sunnis and secularists by welding together a diverse list has been reversed by the electorate in places like Baghdad. Many Westerners hailed Maliki for bringing Sunnis and secularists . . . into his camp; however with less than a thousand votes each, [several such candidates] have all been demoted to non-winning positions on the Baghdad list for State of Law.[8]

In addition, Visser notes, the gender quota could be met only by the Electoral Commission bypassing male candidates with top preference-vote totals, because few women had been successful at obtaining sufficiently high votes.

The example of Iraq in 2005–2010 shows that even in a young democracy emerging from dictatorship and war (and still enduring internal conflict), political actors understand the consequences of electoral systems, including list type. Moreover, it shows that a list type that enhances voter choice might simultaneously undermine the representation of groups that are not among the top vote-mobilizers, such as minority factions within an alliance or women. Thus list type is an important component of proportional electoral systems. For this reason, we shall devote two chapters later in this book to matters of intraparty competition. We now return to an overview of the actual operation of closed and open lists in our two key examples of longer-term democracies using districted PR with each respective list type, Portugal and Finland.

List Types in Portugal in Finland

In Portugal, the voter casts a single categorical vote for a list, but in Finland the voter casts a single categorical vote for a candidate. Sometimes open-list systems

---

[8] Reidar Visser, "The Sadrist Watershed Confirmed," Iraq and Gulf Analysis, March 29, 2010, https://gulfanalysis.wordpress.com/2010/03/29/the-sadrist-watershed-confirmed/ (last accessed January 3, 2016).

give the voter an option of a categorical vote for a list or a candidate, while still others allow voters to vote for more than one candidate. Finland, however, offers the clearest contrast to Portugal in requiring a single candidate vote instead of a party-list vote. What makes it a case of *list* PR is that, prior to allocating any seats, the votes for all individual candidates are first summed to arrive at a list total.[9] In an open list, only after the list's seats are determined are the seats allocated according to candidates' preference votes. The procedure *within a list* then becomes akin to single nontransferable vote (SNTV), as we discuss extensively in Chapter 14.[10]

A key consequence of an open list is that it encourages "personal" campaigning. That is, the candidates seek to emphasize how they as individuals can be good representatives for some group of voters in the district. From the standpoint of the party, the "personal vote-seeking" behavior of the candidates is beneficial, because the candidates' success in attracting votes based on their personal attributes may help the party collectively win more seats than it would running on its party label and policy platform alone. Moreover, "vote splitting" is not a problem, as it is under the $M=1$ FPTP system (see Chapter 5), because all the candidates' individual votes "pool" on the list; they are summed first to determine how many seats the list wins before the individual winners are determined.

Foreign reporters covering Finnish elections have remarked on the personal nature of campaigning. For instance:

Outside [a street market] stood at least half a dozen candidates . . . *handing out their own personal campaign leaflets* and engaging, when a voter showed the slightest interest, in vigorous political discussion.[11]

In order to attract votes to their lists, parties often nominate celebrities – persons publicly known for work outside of politics (Arter 2014, von Schoultz 2018). Some examples include Juha Väätäinen, an accomplished sprinter in the late 1960s and 1970s. He ran for the True Finns Party in the Helsinki district in 2011 and finished third in preference votes on the list, enough to win a seat. Also in Helsinki in 2011, the candidate who ranked fifth in preference votes on the list of the National Coalition Party was Jaana Pelkonen, a media personality.

In contrast to Finland, in countries that have closed lists, such as Portugal, the candidates have much reduced incentive to distinguish themselves from their

---

[9] Taagepera and Shugart (1989a) referred to this as a "quasi-list" because of the absence of a provision to vote directly for the list. See also Shugart (2005a).

[10] In those open-list systems in which the voter may cast more than one preference vote, the procedure typically is akin to MNTV, although in principle the intralist allocation could follow any of the candidate-based rules outlined in Chapter 3.

[11] Jonathan Holmes, "Mature Governments are Coalitions of the Willing," *Canberra Times*, April 8, 2015 (www.canberratimes.com.au/comment/mature-governments-are-coalitions-of-the-willing-20150407-1mflw4.html); last accessed November 17, 2015. Emphasis ours.

party. The voters are unable to favor one candidate on a list over another, implying that the candidates are more likely to emphasize what their party can do for voters. There is still the possibility that parties may place "celebrity" candidates on the lists and advertise their presence as a means to attract votes. We offered some examples in Chapter 5 from the case of Israel. However, key differences from open lists are: the voters drawn by the celebrity must be willing to cast their vote for the party as a whole, because they are unable to mark a preference for any specific candidate, and, as a result, even such a candidate is presumably far likelier to emphasize his or her partisan motivations for running than to run a personal campaign.

ALLIANCES: HOW OPEN AND CLOSED LISTS DIFFER

Already in Chapter 5, we discussed how parties might choose to form pre-electoral alliances, and we saw examples from the single-seat districts in Trinidad and Tobago, and in India. Parties in proportional systems also may form alliances, in order to maximize their collective seats. Certainly they typically do not face as critical a "vote-splitting" problem as in FPTP, where each seat is decided by plurality and thus two parties splitting the vote can be especially costly – it can hand the district's only seat to a mutual opponent. Nonetheless, the problem still exists for parties under PR, especially where district magnitude is smaller. Thus parties with similar goals in national politics might band together seeking to win seats that otherwise might go to a party disliked by each. As we shall see, even in Israel and other large-M cases, some lists are presented by pre-election alliances of parties. Thus alliances are far from a feature only of FPTP cases. They are a common feature in many countries' electoral scenes.[12] Let us see how the list type alters how alliances in PR systems work.

Alliances Under Open Lists

We start with Finland, which has long experience of alliances between two or more parties. We will use as an example one of the smaller districts, partly because it makes the example easier to understand, and partly because it is the smaller districts where alliances are most relevant (von Schoultz 2018), given greater disproportionality of small M.[13]

---

[12] In our discussion of alliances we focus only on cases where two or more parties combine on a single list. Other forms of alliances are possible in some PR systems. For instance, two separate lists may be able to pool their remainders, as in Israel (Hazan, et al., 2018) and the Netherlands (Jacobs 2018). Note that these provisions may allow for more than one layer of alliance – first on a joint list, and then pooling remainders with another list.

[13] While in Israel, any alliance would be nationwide (see Chapter 5), this need not be so in a multidistrict country. Indeed, in Finland alliances typically differ from district to district.

The example shown in Table 6.3 is from the district of Southern Savo (Etelä-Savo) in 2007, which had a district magnitude of six. It shows several candidates in each of the three lists, which won two seats each. One of these lists, which we designate List One,[14] contained candidates of only one party, the Center Party of Finland. The other two lists were alliances: List Two contained candidates from the Social Democratic Party of Finland, the Green League, and the Left Alliance; List Three contained candidates from the National Coalition Party, the Christian Democrats in Finland, and the True Finns.[15]

The first point to note about open lists from this example is that the candidates who win are not necessarily those with the M highest individual vote totals, as would have been the case were the system single nontransferable vote (SNTV, as explained in Chapter 3).[16] Under SNTV instead of open-list PR, the National Coalition Party, running on List Three, would have won no seats, because its leading candidate, Nepponen, had only the eighth highest vote total in the district. So how did the National Coalition Party elect not only Nepponen but a second candidate, Toivakka, as well? Because the first criterion in determining the winners is the collective vote totals of the lists, on which a proportional formula (here D'Hondt divisors) is applied. Only then do we turn to the intralist dimension to see which candidates obtain each party's or alliance's seats. The operation of the proportional formula resulted in each of these lists' obtaining two seats, based on each list's combined votes (which are 30,759, 29,837 and 21,108, respectively). The distinction between SNTV and open lists is the central topic of Chapter 13.

When we turn to the intralist dimension, we see from Table 6.3 that List Two elected candidates of two different parties: one Social Democrat and one Green. The success of the Green Party was made possible, despite its having barely a quarter of the votes of its larger partner in the alliance, because the Green League had more than 96 percent of its own votes concentrated on one of its candidates, Järvinen. This high concentration of the Greens' votes allowed it narrowly to beat out the second Social Democrat for the second of this list's two seats.[17]

The provision for alliances, and the success of the Green League in concentrating its votes resulted in four parties winning seats in this six-seat district, on three lists. In Chapter 14 we explore in greater detail the incentives that alliance partners have to concentrate votes on a subset of their candidates, and we offer a logical model of the extent to which the provision for alliance lists tends to increase the number of parties winning seats, for a given magnitude.

---

[14] These are not the official numbers of these lists; we number them in order of their collective votes, for convenience.

[15] Four other lists contested this district in 2007, none close to winning a seat.

[16] With $M=6$, those candidates would have been, in order of their votes, Viitamies, Komi, Leppä, Järvinen, Nousiainen, and Backman – three from the Center Party (List 1) and three from List 2.

[17] A third partner, The Left Alliance, contributed some votes to the list, but was far from winning a seat.

TABLE 6.3 *The intraparty dimension in Finland: Southern Savo (Etelä-Savo), 2007.*

	List 1			List 2			List 3	
Name	Party	Votes	Name	Party	Votes	Name	Party	Votes
Komi, K.	Center	5,885	Viitamies, P.	Social Democratic	6,690	Nepponen, O.	National Coalition Party	3,728
Leppä, J.	Center	5,762	Järvinen, H.	Green League	5,525	Toivakka, L.	National Coalition Party	3,233
Nousiainen, P.	Center	5,267	Backman, J.	Social Democratic	5,259	Riikonen, T.	Christian Democrats	2,454
Korhonen, S.	Center	3,401	Seppälä, A.	Social Democratic	3,955	Linnamurto, S.	National Coalition Party	2,369
Nenonen, J.	Center	2,432	Ojala, S.	Social Democratic	1,716	Oksa, P.	National Coalition Party	2,123
Kakriainen, M.	Center	1,954	Taavitsainen, S.	Social Democratic	1,395	Pehkonen, T.	True Finns	1,865
8 others		6,058	8 others		5,297	8 others		5,336
List total		30,759	List total		29,837	List total		21,108
% of district vote		37.40			36.28			25.67
Party totals in list	Center (14)	30,759	Party totals in list	Social Democratic (10)	22,704	Party totals in list	National Coalition Party (9)	15,530
				Green League (2)	5,714		Christian Democrats (3)	2,925
				Left Alliance (2)	1,419		True Finns (2)	2,653

Numbers in parentheses indicate how many candidates each party had running on the list.
Showing only the lists that won seats, and the top six candidates in each list. Candidates who won a seat are in bold

Turning to List Three, we see that both seats were won by the leading party in the alliance, the National Coalition Party. The Christian Democrats would have remained short of winning a seat even if they had managed to pile all their votes on their top candidate, Riikonen. While neither the Christian Democrats nor the True Finns won a seat, we can determine from a close inspection of the original data that, had they run separately rather than on this alliance list, the result would have been the National Coalition Party's winning just one seat, with the Center Party's winning three.[18] Even though the two smaller partners of the National Coalition Party did not win seats on their own, presumably they preferred that an additional seat go to their big ally than to the Center Party. Thus, mission accomplished, from the standpoint of parties that are grouped into alliances, which pool their candidates' votes on Finland's open lists.

From the example in Table 6.3, we see that under the open lists used in Finland, parties that engaged in alliances with other parties win seats based on *how many candidates they have in the top ranks of the alliance's list*. This is because on each list, candidates – whether all of the same party or of different parties – win seats only according to their individual vote totals. We discuss further implications of this sort of candidate competition in Chapters 13 and 14.

Before we leave (for now) the open list system, what about the Åland Islands, which comprise a district electing just one member? Can there be an open list where only one seat is elected? Yes, under Finnish law, there can be. Each party is permitted to run up to four candidates in Åland. The winner of the district's seat is the candidate with the most votes among those in the list with the most votes. That is, it would be possible for the winner to be a candidate other than the one who had the most individual votes.[19] Why? Because, again, of the first criterion being to pool votes by list. The list with the most votes is awarded the first – here, the only – seat. Then, the rules go inside the list, seeing who has the most votes within that list. Thus we see that open-list PR is an exception to the more general rule that PR reduces to FPTP when $M=1$ (see Chapter 2); it is instead a simultaneous plurality rule within and across parties, where each party offers its voters a choice among candidates.

---

[18] One can determine this by inspecting the D'Hondt divisors. This assumes that voters' choices among parties and candidates are not affected by alliances. This is not to be taken for granted. For instance, the National Coalition alliance with the more radical True Finns may have dismayed some of their voters to the point of their shifting to a Center candidate. We assume here, for the sake of illustration, that such shifts would have been minor.

[19] This has not happened, at least recently. There is a dominant local party called, simply, the Åland List. For instance, in 2007, it won more than 85 percent of the vote. However, it had a closely fought internal contest, with its winner having 4,388 votes (45.9 percent of the list's total) against a close challenger who had 4,024 (42.1 percent).

Alliances in Closed Lists

It is also possible for parties to form alliances in closed-list systems. Because of the list type, the parties can structure the balance among themselves prior to the election, when they agree to rankings of their joint lists. As long as they do not miscalculate too badly how many seats they will win, they can ensure so many seats for party A, so many for party B, etc. We already discussed some examples of this phenomenon in Iraq earlier in this chapter, where we noted the consequences of list type for sectarian and gender balance. In the case of Portugal, a longer-term democracy, we can also see the impact of closed lists on alliance politics.

Portugal has sometimes had lists winning seats in an election that were alliances of parties. For example, prior to the 2015 assembly election, the Social Democratic Party (PSD) and the Democratic and Social Center–People's Party (CDS-PP) joined forces. The CDS-PP was itself already an existing alliance, which had won the third highest number of seats in the 2011 election. The center-right parties, PSD and CDS-PP, were attempting to ensure that they would form the largest bloc in the new assembly; as the election turned out, they did so, narrowly beating the Socialist Party for first place.[20]

An example of this alliance in action in 2015 comes from the district of Leira. The alliance won six of the ten seats, meaning that the top six candidates, as ranked on the closed list, won. Five of these were PSD, and one was CDS-PP. Of the four losers on the principal list,[21] the first two were PSD and the candidate with the list's overall ninth rank was CDS. Thus only in the extremely unlikely event that the alliance won nine of the ten seats would the CDS-PP elect two members from Leira. However, the CDS-PP was also essentially guaranteed a seat unless the alliance managed only three seats, which also presumably was unlikely. Thus, unlike in the case of open lists, the parties forming an alliance on a closed list were able to precommit to a preferred ratio of seats.[22]

As mentioned previously, even in the high-M nationwide PR case of Israel, lists are often presented by alliances. We offer two examples, to generalize the point just demonstrated in the Portuguese case of districted PR. In 2013, two center-right parties in Israel, the Likud and Yisrael Beiteinu, decided to present a joint list. In doing so they hoped to maximize their chances of being

---

[20] However, the PSD and its allies were unable to form a government, and a left-wing coalition formed after the election instead.

[21] Portuguese parties also present a "substitute" (*suplente*) list, which we do not consider here. Our information on the candidates, their ranks, and their party affiliations comes from the websites of the Portuguese National Assembly (www.parlamento.pt/deputadogp) and the Portuguese Elections Commission (www.cne.pt).

[22] In the preceding election in this district, running separately, the PSD had won six seats and the CDS-PP one.

collectively the largest bloc in the Knesset, to fend off a challenge from the new party of the center, Yesh Atid (see Chapter 5). The balance of list ranks they struck was to alternate ranks (one Likud candidate, then one Yisrael Beiteinu, etc.) through the first four slots, and then just below that following with two Likud, one Yisrael Beiteinu, etc. In this way the combined list would elect candidates in roughly the two-to-one ratio of their representation as separate parties at the preceding election.[23]

A second and politically consequential example from Israel occurred in 2015. Prior to this election, the Knesset passed a law raising the threshold to win any seats from 2.5 percent to 3.25 percent. Given that there were four parties in the Knesset elected in 2013 that had vote percentages in precisely the 2.5 to 3.25 percent range, the change was a clear threat to the representation of some existing parties. Some of these parties receive most of their votes from the Arab sector of the Israeli population, and thus in order to maximize their chances of crossing the threshold, they formed a Joint List.[24] It worked; they jointly cleared the threshold with 10.5 percent of the vote and thirteen seats, the third highest total for any list in the election. (The fourth party whose 2013 votes were below the new 2015 threshold, Kadima, went out of business.)

HYBRID LIST TYPES

This chapter thus far has considered two "pure" types of list, open and closed. There are also hybrids, usually known as "flexible" lists but sometimes as "semiopen" lists. In such lists, parties present rank-ordered lists, as in closed-list systems, but voters may give preference votes to individual candidates. (Sometimes, as in Estonia and the Netherlands, the voter must vote for a candidate.) The final ranks take into account both the pre-election rank by the party and the preference votes. Details vary with the system; there may be as many different flexible list systems as there are countries using these intermediate types.[25] For this reason, we will not attempt to generalize about them in this book. Such systems are

---

[23] For details see Matthew S. Shugart, "Likud and Yisrael Beiteinu," *Fruits and Votes* (https://fruitsandvotes.wordpress.com/2013/01/21/likud-and-yisrael-beiteinu/); last accessed November 17, 2015. The parties subsequently split and ran separately in the election of 2015.

[24] The four parties are: "Hadash, the Jewish-Arab Communist Party; Ra'am, an Islamist Group . . .; and Ta'al and Balad, Two Nationalist Groups" (http://forward.com/news/israel/215112/can-israels-new-arab-list-make-history/; last accessed November 30, 2015). Ra'am and Ta'al already had run on a combined list (the United Arab List) in several preceding elections; the other two had run separately.

[25] Typically, for a list's number of seats, s, won on the interparty dimension, the first criterion under flexible-list rules is to see if any candidates have obtained some legally stipulated quota of preference votes. Candidates with sufficient votes are elected in order of their preference votes, until s seats are filled. If seats remain unallocated, the rest go according to the order in which they were ranked on the pre-election list (skipping, obviously, any already elected on preference votes).

quite common in Europe, and therefore no treatment of electoral systems would be complete without acknowledging that "open" and "closed" lists do not exhaust the range of possibilities for list systems of PR. For details on specific provisions, the key source is Renwick and Pilet (2016). As with many features of electoral systems, there is no clear answer as to which is "best" – open, closed, or flexible – but there are different options which are conducive to achieving different goals in representation.[26]

CONCLUSIONS

This chapter has introduced systems of districted proportional representation. Focusing primarily on the cases of Finland and Portugal, we saw how variations in district magnitude affect the proportionality of the outcome in different regions of a country, given that magnitudes in these and many other districted PR systems are highly variable. Further, we introduced the distinction between closed and open lists. We saw how this distinction in list types – open, closed, and flexible – affects election of individual candidates. In the case of lists presented by alliances, the list type may alter the balance of representation of parties or factions within the alliance. These are among the issues that we will address more systematically in Chapters 13 and 14, which focus on the intraparty dimension of electoral systems.

---

[26] For empirical studies of the effects of flexible lists see André, et al., 2017; Crisp and Malecki 2013, Cahill, et al., n.d.

PART II

THE INTERPARTY DIMENSION OF ASSEMBLY POLITICS: THE SEAT PRODUCT MODEL

7

The Seat Product Model of the Effective Number of Assembly Parties

How do electoral systems shape party systems? Here we begin to address this question seriously, meaning quantitatively, walking on the two legs pictured in Figure 1.1 at the start of this book: observation and thinking. We begin with nationwide assembly parties. These are more directly affected by the institutional framework, compared to electoral parties, which will come in Chapter 8.

The tradition of such study is long in political science. Yet Clark and Golder (2006: 682) summed up the prevailing view when they concluded that "the so-called institutionalist approach does not produce clear expectations" about the number of parties, and that "everything depends on the presence or absence of social forces." Such a pessimistic claim about the "institutionalist approach" is not justified. Once the institutions themselves are more fully specified, we can have clear expectations for worldwide average patterns, which in turn can offer guidance to practitioners.[1] Demand for such guidance has been demonstrated: many political scientists have engaged in consulting missions in countries experiencing transitions from authoritarianism (Carey et al. 2013).

As a preview to what this chapter is about, we offer Figure 7.1. It deals with the effective number of seat-winning parties (N_S) in the first or sole chamber of national assemblies. This graph uses logarithmic scales and graphs N_S against a possibly surprising quantity: the product of mean district magnitude (M) and the size of the assembly (S). We can see that the relationship looks pretty tight. Our graph further shows the line that expresses the Seat Product Model for N_S:

$$N_S = (MS)^{1/6}. \tag{7.1}$$

This line visibly expresses the average trend well. We explain its derivation later in this chapter. Dashed lines indicate values that are twice, or half, the value predicted from Equation 7.1. With presidential and parliamentary

---

[1] It is not that social forces of various types such as ethnic divisions are irrelevant. Rather, their impact on the nationwide party system can be felt only within a range set by the institutional rules. Analysis of the (rather limited) impact of a common measure of ethnic diversity will be one of our themes in Chapter 15.

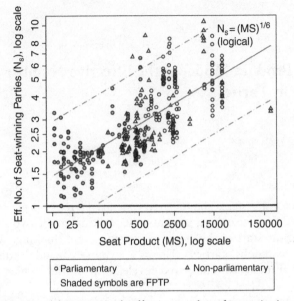

FIGURE 7.1 Relation of the nationwide effective number of seat-winning parties (N_S) to the seat product (MS)

The central line is the logical model $N_S = (MS)^{1/6}$, *not* a statistical best fit (see text). Dashed lines mark values that are double or half the logical model's predictions.

systems shown with different symbols, we can see that the scatter is greater for presidential (triangles), but the average pattern remains the same. Yet it should be apparent that, in general, presidential systems do not require a fundamentally different means of explanation – some conventional literature that we review later notwithstanding.[2]

In Figure 7.1 we also differentiate FPTP cases from PR, with the former symbols being shaded. While almost all cases of $MS < 100$ are FPTP countries, there is an intermixing of PR and FPTP when MS is greater than 100 up to 650, beyond which all systems are PR. The graphing of systems in this way allows us to see that *we do not need separate models to account for "FPTP versus PR,"* as many others might frame it. The Seat Product, MS, is more important than these two old categories. This amplifies a point from Chapter 2: *FPTP is just PR reduced to its minimum possible magnitude,* $M = 1$. If a PR system has MS around 600, perhaps due to a mean magnitude of five and $S = 120$, its impact on N_S is about the same as if it were FPTP with $S = 600$.

---

[2] Our "parliamentary" subsample in this and subsequent chapters includes Austria, Finland, Iceland, Portugal, and Switzerland, which actually have hybrid executive formats. Our results do not depend on this choice. More details on our classification of presidential systems and data results for these systems can be found in Chapter 11 and its appendix.

A crucially important point of emphasis is that the central line in Figure 7.1 is *not* a statistical best-fit line. This line represents a model (Equation 7.1) derived logically, *without using any data*. It fits remarkably well. In fact, we can summarize its average fit not only via visual inspection of Figure 7.1, but also with a series of ratios for different subsets of the data. These ratios are a given election's observed value of N_S, divided by the prediction from Equation 7.1, averaged over all elections in the given subset: r=(value observed)/(value expected). Our ideal would be r=1.00.

If we consider all parliamentary systems, the mean is r=1.07 (standard deviation, 0.34, median 0.988). For parliamentary and PR, we get r=1.125 (0.35, 1.05) and for parliamentary FPTP r=1.029 (0.33, 0.958). Turning to nonparliamentary systems, for the full subsample we get r=0.930 (0.41, 0.774). Note how these data reflect the greater scatter of presidential systems. They do not fit as well, for reasons we take up in detail in Chapter 11. On the other hand, on average, they are not wildly off the predicted values.[3]

How is Equation 7.1 obtained? This is the topic of the next section. Thereafter we test the degree of validity of this central part of the Seat Product Model, using standard statistical means. Finally, we place this model in the historical context of the "Duvergerian agenda" and comment on some other factors.[4]

THE SEAT PRODUCT MODEL FOR ASSEMBLY PARTIES: THEORY

The Seat Product Model (SPM), introduced by Taagepera (2007) and foreshadowed by Taagepera and Shugart (1993), has the important advantage of relying strictly on institutional input variables, which are in principle subject to (re-)design. It does not include rather more immutable societal variables or any variables that are themselves the product of behavior that may be shaped by the institutions, such as competition for a presidency (as in several well-known works reviewed later). The model is also unique within the broader literature of the Duvergerian agenda, to be described later on, in that it has a stable and logically supported coefficient

---

[3] We could further break the presidential cases down by electoral system, but the combination of FPTP and presidentialism is heavily dominated by one country, the US. For the several countries that combine presidentialism and PR, we find a mean r=1.025, but again evidence of greater variability from a standard deviation of 0.47 and a median value of 0.855.

[4] In Chapter 8, we develop a new logical model to explain the votes. The reason for starting with seats is that seats are most directly constrained by institutions; it is to the constraints on seats that voters and other actors adapt. Focusing first on the seats is also justified by the importance of the seats for determining who governs, if the system is parliamentary, or for who can pass legislation (in either presidential or parliamentary systems). Strictly speaking, then, seats are more important than votes to understanding a democratic polity.

for the key institutional variable. In this section, we offer a condensed overview of the logic. For the full details the reader should consult Taagepera (2007).

The Logic Underlying the Number of Seat-Winning Parties

We already introduced in Chapter 1 the fundamental building block of the relationship of the number of parties that win at least one seat in a district and the district magnitude (M). Equation 1.1 expresses this relationship:

$$N'_{S0} = M^{0.5},$$

where N'_{S0} is the actual number of parties, of any size. The apostrophe in N'_{S0} designates a district-level quantity (in contrast to nationwide); subscript S refers to seats (in contrast to votes), and 0 indicates raw count of parties (in contrast to the effective number). This is a systematic notation that we shall adopt throughout this book. In the introductory chapter, Figure 1.2 (specifically, its right panel) displayed this equation and showed it fits well. However, Equation 1.1 is something we can derive purely from logic, *without using any data!*

The model starts at the level of a single district that elects a certain number of legislators, designated as M for the district's magnitude. For any value of M seats to be allocated, the lower bound on the number of seat-winning parties is obviously one (single party wins all M seats), while the upper bound is M (each seat won by a different party). Thus the possible range of N'_{S0} is

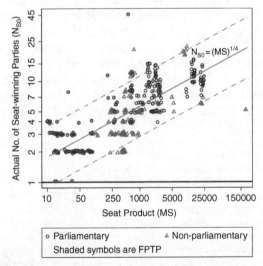

FIGURE 7.2 How the actual number of seat-winning parties (N_{S0}) relates to the seat product (MS), national level

$1 \leq N'_{S0} \leq M$. The most likely actual (not effective) number of parties to win at least one seat is the geometric mean of these boundaries (Taagepera and Shugart 1993; Taagepera 2007, 119).[5] The geometric mean of 1 and M yields what we already identified as Equation 1.1: $N'_{S0} = M^{0.5}$.

This approach does not rule out the possibility that considering other information may render a better estimate. Rather, it simply means that the geometric average of extreme values is our best estimate *in the absence of other information* – "the worst possible prediction one could make – except for all others" (Taagepera (2007: 12). We will test this district-level prediction below, but first, how do we go from the district level to the national level, thereby arriving at the Seat Product Model that yields Equation 7.1?

Suppose a country, using a nonmajoritarian formula, elects its legislators in districts of magnitude M. If it elected all its legislators in a single nationwide district, then the magnitude of this one district would be the same as the assembly size, S. By Equation 1.1, we thus would have $N'_{S0}=S^{1/2}$, when $M=S$. When $M<S$, the number of parties cannot exceed this number because that system cannot be more permissive than a national-district system. This means $S^{1/2}$ is an *upper* bound of the number of parties for any given M and S.

At the same time, the number of parties winning at least one seat *nationwide* (N_{S0}, without the apostrophe) cannot be smaller than the district-level number of parties, already estimated as $M^{1/2}$, which therefore is a theoretical *lower* bound. Thus the possible range of N_{S0} is $M^{1/2} \leq N_{S0} \leq S^{1/2}$. Then, for any given M and S, in the absence of other information we should expect the geometric mean of $M^{1/2}$ and $S^{1/2}$:

$$N_{S0} = [(M^{1/2})(S^{1/2})]^{1/2} = (MS)^{1/4}. \qquad (7.2)$$

The same logic applies for any value of M and S, provided all seats are allocated within districts and the formula is nonmajoritarian – the key features defining "simple" electoral systems (Chapter 2). Figure 7.2 shows the scatterplot of the data, with the solid line representing Equation 7.2. As in Figure 7.1, dashed lines indicate values that are twice, or half, the predicted values. The fit is visually good for worldwide average, albeit with a few cases quite scattered. Later in the chapter we offer a regression test of Equation 7.2.

---

[5] The geometric mean of two quantities is the square root of their product. But why the geometric mean rather than good old arithmetic? Ask the original question in a slightly different way: How many seats are seat-winning parties likely to win, on the average? If $M=25$, it could be from one to twenty-five, depending on the number of such parties. The geometric mean offers five parties at an average of five seats each, which multiplies to the twenty-five seats we have. In contrast, the arithmetic mean would offer thirteen parties at an average of thirteen seats each, for a total of 169 seats! Why doesn't the arithmetic mean work? See Taagepera (2007, 119, and 2008, 120–127).

Of course, most of the time we are unlikely to be interested in the raw count of parties in a legislature, which tells us nothing about their relative strengths. It was for precisely this reason that the effective number of parties was devised (Laakso and Taagepera 1979), and this has become by far the standard index of party-system fragmentation. In order to derive N_S from N_{S0}, the next step in the chain is to derive the largest party's seat share (s_1).

The Logic Underlying the Largest Seat Share

We can deduce the boundaries of this quantity's range from N_{S0}. For any given number of parties represented, the smallest possible value of s_1 is when all parties are equal-sized: $s_1 = 1/N_{S0} = N_{S0}^{-1}$. The largest is as close to 1.0 as feasible to still allow the remaining $N_{S0}-1$ parties to have one seat each.[6] Simplifying a bit, we can again try the geometric average – in this case of 1 and N_{S0}^{-1}:

$$s_1 = (1 * N_{S0}^{-1})^{1/2} = N_{S0}^{-1/2}.$$

If the largest seat share fits, then we must also have, substituting $(MS)^{1/4}$ for N_{S0} (cf. Equation 7.2),

$$s_1 = [(MS)^{1/4}]^{-1/2} = (MS)^{-1/8}. \tag{7.3}$$

Figure 7.3 shows scatterplots of the data related to both models for s_1. In the left panel, we graph s_1 against N_{S0}. We see a good fit to the expectation, $s_1 = N_{S0}^{-1/2}$, for the world average. The right panel graphs s_1 against the Seat Product, MS. Here, too, we see a good fit to our expectation, i.e., Equation 7.3. Now we are ready to turn to the final link of the chain leading us to Equation 7.1, the core expression of the Seat Product Model for the effective number of seat-winning parties.

The Logic Underlying the Effective Number of Seat-Winning Parties

The largest seat share (s_1) is the single most important component in the calculation of the effective number of parties (N_S). This is due to the way in which N_S is calculated, whereby it is a weighted index in which each party share is weighted by itself, through squaring (see Chapter 4). Because of this calculation of N_S, once we have s_1, we have tight limits on what N_S can be. The derivation of the relationship is more involved than for the previous steps – see Taagepera (2007: 160–164). Nonetheless, an expected average relationship between N_S and s_1 is quite simple:

---

[6] This additional complication is set aside, but further research on its impact might be needed. For discussion, see Taagepera and Shugart (1993) and Taagepera (2007:135).

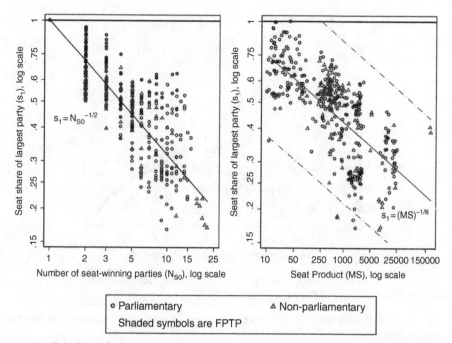

FIGURE 7.3 How the largest seat share (s_1) relates to the number of seat-winning parties (N_{S0}), left panel, and the seat product (MS), right panel

$$N_S = s_1^{-4/3}.$$

Figure 7.4 shows a strong fit of this expression; there is remarkably little scatter. Forbidden areas are marked and correspond to $N_S < 1/s_1$ (the limit when N_{S0} parties are equal sized) and $N_S > 1/s_1^2$ (a limit for the situation when all parties but the largest are infinitesimally small).[7] Now we can take the final step. Substituting $(MS)^{-1/8}$ for s_1 (cf. Equation 7.3) results in the equation we already identified as Equation 7.1:

$$N_S = [(MS)^{-1/8}]^{-4/3} = (MS)^{1/6}.$$

Conventional approaches (to be discussed at end of this chapter) are quite different. Their first step typically is to estimate the effective number of *vote-earning* parties (N_V) based on several inputs (including two that occur only in presidential systems). Then they take N_V as an input to a second equation in which the effective number of seat-winning parties (N_S) is the output variable,

---

[7] As explained by Taagepera (2007: 161–162), the actual limits for most values of s_1 are narrower still, leading to the average approximation, $N_S = s_1^{-4/3}$. Further details may be found in our online appendix. www.cambridge.org/votes_from_seats

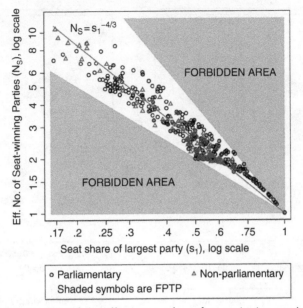

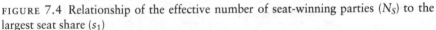

FIGURE 7.4 Relationship of the effective number of seat-winning parties (N_S) to the largest seat share (s_1)

and in which electoral-system variables are also included as further inputs shaping the votes–seats conversion.

By contrast, the SPM is based on a logic by which *votes come from seats*. The logical basis for doing so is what we demonstrated in this section – namely, that we can stipulate mandatory lower and upper bounds of seat-winning parties (ranging from 1 to M in a district and 1 to S in the assembly). From these logical starting points, we can deduce largest-party seat share (s_1) and effective number of seat-winning parties (N_S), as demonstrated here. The votes, on the other hand, are not directly constrained; that is why they do not enter into our models until Chapter 8. We now discuss one further implication of the SPM, and then devote the rest of the chapter to regression tests of the logic and comparison to the more conventional approaches.

Seat Product and the Duration of Government Cabinets

A major consequence of the effective number of assembly parties is how long government cabinets tend to last, if the executive type is parliamentary. With two major parties, single-party cabinets form and tend to last (upon re-election) around ten years. With five major parties, coalition cabinets are needed, and they tend to last less than two years.

A logical model (Taagepera 2007: 165–175) was finalized in Taagepera and Sikk (2010): $C=42$ years/N^2. It follows from $N=(MS)^{1/6}$ that $C=42$ years/$(MS)^{1/3}$. In most countries, the average cabinet duration over several decades is within a factor of two of this model (see graph in Taagepera 2007: 171).

This may be hard to believe, but the average cabinet duration is largely predetermined once a country chooses a parliamentary system with a given assembly size and district magnitude, through the intermediary of the number of parties. This is how deeply and predictably the consequences of electoral rules reach into politics. Important as this extension of the SPM is, it is outside the direct focus of the present book.

Such sets of mathematical expressions are not the typical style of the discipline, although such chains of simple bivariate expressions, one building on the other, are common in other sciences (Colomer 2007). We ask at this point that readers not object to the style, but judge it on its results. We have shown evidence in the form of graphs. Our next section carries out statistical testing of the models based on the Seat Product.

REGRESSION TESTS OF THE BASIC SPM

To test the Seat Product Model on our dataset, we first have to turn Equation 7.1 into a testable linear relationship. This is obtained by taking the decimal logarithms on both sides:

$$\log N_S = 0 + 0.167\log(MS).$$

When regressing $\log N_S$ on $\log(MS)$, we expect a simple straight line: $\log N_S = \alpha + \beta\log(MS)$. But not any such line will do; we further expect that $\alpha=0$ and $\beta=0.167$. Note that the constant of zero is equivalent to (unlogged) $N_S=1.00$, which must be the case when $MS=1$. That is, if there were only a single seat filled in a given national election, then there could be only one seat-winning party – as is the case in direct presidential elections.

Before we test the final link in the logical chain, let us see if the steps upon which the chain depends are accurate: Is it true that the physical number of parties, N'_{S0}, at the district level, nationwide N_{S0} in the assembly, and the largest party's vote share (s_1) can all be predicted from the Seat Product as claimed in Equations 7.1–7.3? Using logarithmic transformation, we turn these equations into their respective testable linear forms:

$$\log N'_{S0} = 0 + 0.5\log M \quad \text{(District level)};$$
$$\log N_{S0} = 0 + 0.25\log(MS) \quad \text{(National level)};$$
$$\log s_1 = 0 - 0.125\log(MS);$$
$$\log N_S = 0 + 0.167\log(MS).$$

To test Equation 1.1 we use the Belden and Shugart (n.d.) district-level dataset. All other models in this chapter and in Chapters 8 and 9 require nationwide data, and thus use Li and Shugart (n.d.).

The regressions in this chapter are based on parliamentary systems, because these are the systems where the connection between features of the assembly electoral system and the party system is most direct. In such systems it is the balance of parties in the assembly that determines the national executive (hence the connection to cabinet durability, mentioned in the preceding section). We already saw in Figures 7.1–7.4 that presidential systems do not stand out as requiring a different approach. We also will discuss below, in our review of prior literature, reasons why presidential-specific variables should not be included in regressions that pool the executive types. A detailed consideration of presidential systems will await Chapters 11 and 12.

Testing the District-Level Expectation

Table 7.1 reports regression results on Equation 1.1, which, to our knowledge, had never been tested prior to Li and Shugart (2016) except on a very limited set of districts by Taagepera and Shugart (1993). The unit of analysis is the district-election, and we use Ordinary Least Squares (OLS) regression,[8] with observations clustered by country.

In Regression One[9] in Table 7.1, we see a strong confirmation of the logic of the district-level foundation to the Seat Product Model (Equation 7.2). This model predicts $\log N'_{S0} = 0 + 0.5 \log M$, and Table 7.1 shows an actual result of $\log N'_{S0} = 0.00037 + 0.510 \log M$. Regression Two restricts the test to districts that elect more than one member. We run this model because a reader might be reasonably skeptical that we have "stacked the deck" by including all of those single-seat districts that appear in Regression One (note differing sample sizes).

Does the model hold within proportional systems, or is the good fit in the full sample due to artificially anchoring the intercept at the logical $N'_{S0}=1$ when $M=1$? We see from Regression Two that the constant (0.06) is only slightly greater than the expected zero, even without the single-seat districts to force the regression to yield the mandatory result of $N'_{S0}=1$ when $M=1$. The coefficient, 0.458, is a bit low, compared to the expected 0.5. However, an F test shows that we are unable to reject the null hypothesis that the

---

[8] Because the outcome variable for Equation 1.1 is a count variable, one might propose using a tool such as Poisson regression. If we do so, the results are almost identical to the models reported here, as shown in the replication materials of Li and Shugart (2016).

[9] As noted in Chapter 1, we refrain from calling a statistical test a "model," contrary to most authors. In this book, we generally perform regressions to determine whether the statistical pattern supports a *logical model*, devised prior to running the regression.

TABLE 7.1 *District magnitude and the number of seat-winning parties*

	(1) Parl.	(2) Parl. $M>1$ only
log$M$	0.510	0.458
Expected: 0.5	(0.0243)	(0.0332)
Constant	0.000373	0.0607
Expected: 0.0	(0.000304)	(0.0239)
F test that coefficient on **log$M$ = 0.5**	0.693	0.23
Observations	11,654	453
R-squared	0.955	0.738

Robust standard errors in parentheses.
Dependent variable: actual number of seat-winning parties (N'_{S0}), logged

correct value is indeed 0.5.[10] Both regressions strongly support the district-level logic that, based only on boundary conditions and taking the geometric average "in the absence of further information," the number of seat-winning parties tends to be the square root of district magnitude.

We already saw the scatterplot of N'_{S0} and M, in Figure 1.2, in which it is visible that the data points cluster mostly around that figure's gray diagonal line, which corresponds to $N'_{S0}=M^{1/2}$. Although there is scatter, the more remarkable thing is just how closely the data cloud hews to Equation 1.1. This equation, *derived without the data*, using very sparse reasoning "in the absence of other information," turns out to describe the actual relationship exceedingly well. We carry out further testing of relationships at the district level in Chapter 10. Now we turn to tests of the nationwide model.

From Districts to National Effects

At the nationwide level, first we test Equation 7.2 for the actual number of seat-winning parties, then Equation 7.3 for the size of the largest party, and finally Equation 7.1 for the main dependent variable of interest, the effective number of seat-winning parties in the national assembly. Consistent with other regression tests of party systems in the literature, but in contrast to Taagepera (2007), our unit of observation for national-level tests is the individual election. We pool the observations and use OLS, with

---

[10] The equation based on Regression Two would be $N'_{S0}=1.150M^{0.458}$, which is a very minor deviation from the logical model, $N'_{S0}=M^{1/2}$ (Equation 1.1). When we include $M=1$ districts, Regression One yields $N'_{S0}=1.0009M^{0.510}$.

TABLE 7.2 *Nationwide effects of the Seat Product, parliamentary democracies*

	1	2	3
	No. of parties (of any size) $\log(N_{S0})$	Seat share, largest party $\log(s_1)$	Effective No. of seat-winning parties $\log(N_S)$
MS, logged	0.242 (0.0210)	-0.1255 (0.0135)	0.164 (0.0163)
Expected coeff.	0.250	–0.125	0.167
F test	0.712	0.960	0.873
Constant	0.0601 (0.0614)	–0.00205 (0.0274)	0.0181 (0.0386)
Observations	265	298	298
R-squared	0.674	0.544	0.610

Robust standard errors in parentheses.

cluster-robust standard errors,[11] thereby following a methodological approach similar to that of the standard works on party-system fragmentation, including Clark and Golder (2006).

In Table 7.2 we see that all three nationwide models are supported.[12] In Regression One, we see that the coefficient on the log of the Seat Product (*MS*) is 0.242 (as compared to the expected 0.25) when the dependent variable is the log of the actual number of parties. In Regression Two, we see that the coefficient is –0.126 (as compared to the expected –0.125) for the log of the seat share of the largest party. Finally, for Regression Three we obtain a coefficient of 0.164 (as compared to the expected 0.167) in the estimated equation for the effective number of seat-winning parties (N_S).

In each case, these coefficients are almost precisely what the logical model predicts. *F* tests show that all of the reported coefficients are statistically indistinguishable from their logically expected values. Moreover, in all three regressions, the constants are indistinguishable from zero, as the logical models require. We have already seen the plots of the data for the relationship between *MS* and N_S (Figure 7.1), N_{S0} (Figure 7.2) and s_1 (Figure 7.3).

A final question concerns the electoral formula. Would considering the different PR allocation formulas (see Chapter 2), in addition to assembly size and district magnitude, affect the results? The precise answer depends on

[11] We define a cluster as a consistent set of electoral rules using the criteria of Lijphart (1994). The results are substantively the same if we simply use country as our cluster variable.

[12] These results differ trivially from those reported in Li and Shugart (2016), because we have excluded STV and SNTV elections (for reasons explained in Chapter 3), whereas Li and Shugart included them.

TABLE 7.3 *How assembly parties and seat product connect*

$N_{S0} = (MS)^{1/4}$		
$s_1 = (MS)^{-1/8}$	$s_1 = N_{S0}^{-1/2}$	
$N_S = (MS)^{1/6}$	$N_S = N_{S0}^{2/3}$	$N_S = s_1^{-4/3}$

a coding decision that is discussed in the appendix. The general answer is, effectively no. The PR formula has no systematic effect at the national level once we know the Seat Product.

Table 7.3 summarizes the relationships of N_{S0}, s_1 and N_S to MS and to each other. The one that has not previously been discussed, $N_S = N_{S0}^{2/3}$, follows from the others, through algebra.

BASELINE, NOT A THREAT

Some readers may feel threatened by the Seat Product Model. If this model worked perfectly, would it take politics out of politics? And where would that leave the political scientists? Purely statistical approaches do not pose such an apparent threat, as they only map the relationships produced *by* politics. In contrast, a logical model such as the SPM seems to impose itself *on* politics. Such fears are overblown. First, the SPM's inputs, *M* and *S*, are themselves products of past politics, and are occasionally modified by politics (although they generally remain pretty stable over time). Second, the outputs of the SPM do not freeze in the current politics but only hem them in to some degree. The values of R^2 in Table 7.2 are around 0.60. This means SPM accounts for about 60 percent of variation in the effective number of parties, leaving 40 percent to other factors, including current politics. Most important, the SPM says nothing about *which* parties will get seats. Do not worry, the SPM will not eat out politics!

Actually, the SPM puts political effects into a clearer perspective. It does so by supplying a comparison level – the effective number of parties that we would expect to materialize at a given *MS*, in the absence of any other information. The impact of politics could conceivably place all actual data points above the SPM curve – or place them all below this curve. Then we could tell that the impact of politics is the difference between the model-based expectation and the real-world effective number.

But it turns out even more interesting than that. The data points in Figure 7.1 straddle the curve. Indeed, the SPM line is close to the best statistical fit. What this intimates is that average politics produces average number of parties, given the constraints set by *M* and *S*. Now the difference between the actual and expected number of parties yields information on politics: if this difference is positive, there is something in the politics, society, current events, and history of this country that pushes the number of parties unusually high – and reverse for a negative difference. This is useful information. (During model testing, in contrast, such deviations are just an awkward nuisance.)

Of course, deviations from a statistical best-fit curve also supply a measure of where a country stands, compared to an average country. But there is a difference. Such an average depends on the sample of countries chosen, which can vary. In contrast, a baseline anchored in the seat product MS is stable. If we come across a new sample of elections in which it does not hold, the finding does not invalidate the model. Rather, it should prompt us to ask, what is it about this sample that results in deviation from the baseline?

HISTORICAL BACKGROUND: THE DUVERGERIAN AGENDA

The idea of predictable relationships between electoral systems and party-political consequences has long been around, yet has remained controversial. The study of electoral systems began with advocacy pieces for specific sets of rules, such as those written by Borda (cf. Colomer 2004: 30), Hare (1859), Mill (1861), and Droop (2012 [1869]). This tradition continued up to the mid-twentieth century. (For details, see Taagepera and Shugart 1989a: 47–50 or Colomer 2004.) A major analytical landmark was reached with Maurice Duverger's work (1951, 1954). He highlighted the possibility of predictable relationships between electoral systems and political outcomes. One broad idea underlies the line of inquiry that received a major boost from Duverger's work, although Duverger himself expressed it in a narrower form. When the electoral system is simple,

the average distribution of party sizes depends on the number of seats available.

In any given electoral district, the seats available are determined by the district's magnitude. Single-seat districts restrict the number of parties more than do multiseat districts. However, the total number of seats in the representative assembly matters, because more seats offer more room for variety. It is possible to have more than ten parties in a 500-seat assembly, but not in the ten-seat national assembly of St. Kitts and Nevis. At the same district magnitude, a larger assembly is likely to have more parties, all other factors being the same. The two size effects, district magnitude and assembly size, could in principle act separately, and one might be much stronger than the other. But it turns out, maybe surprisingly, that the logical derivation of Equation 7.2 makes them act through their product, on an equal footing.[13] This is the foundation of the Seat Product Model.

---

[13] It may seem that M and S have equal impacts on the number of parties, since they act through the product MS, but this is not so. The largest observed M (450) exceeds the smallest (one) 450-fold, while the largest observed S (around 650) exceeds the smallest (about ten) only sixty-five-fold. Thus M impacts MS more than does S.

But how did we reach this stage? This section traces the development of the Duvergerian approach since the mid-twentieth century. It highlights its achievements but also limitations.

Duverger's Propositions, Based on Mechanical and Psychological Effects

Duverger (1951, 1954) was the first to announce clearly what Riker (1982) later anointed as Duverger's "law" and "hypothesis," making a connection between electoral and party systems. Avoiding implications of unidirectional causality, they can be worded as follows:

1) Seat allocation by plurality in single-seat districts tends to go with two major parties ("law").
2) PR formulas in multiseat districts tend to go with more than two major parties ("hypothesis," because more exceptions were encountered).

Note that Duverger's propositions involve only one parameter, district magnitude.[14] They say nothing about the various complex rules that we discussed in Chapter 3 and will discuss again in Chapter 15.[15] Duverger also did not yet have the concept of *effective number of parties* (see Chapter 4), which was introduced by Laakso and Taagepera (1979).

Duverger's propositions imply a sharp break between FPTP and PR. Actually, as district magnitude increases from $M=1$ to $M=S$ (nationwide single district), the number of parties tends to increase gradually and at a decreasing rate, as first shown graphically in Taagepera and Shugart (1989a: 144). In this light, the discontinuity between the "law" and "hypothesis" should be removed, leading to a single function $N=f(M)$ for the average pattern at a given S. The question remained whether the effective number of electoral parties (N_V) or legislative parties (N_S) should be used. Taagepera and Shugart (1989a: 144, 153) presented rough empirical best-fit equations for both N_V and N_S as a "generalized Duverger's rule." However, these equations no longer should be used, because subsequent work, starting with Taagepera and Shugart (1993) and continuing with Taagepera (2007), Li and Shugart (2016), and this book, show we can do better.

What produces the outcomes noted by Duverger? Low district magnitudes – with $M=1$ being the lowest possible – arguably put a squeeze on the number of parties in two ways. In any single-seat district with plurality rule, one of the two largest parties nationwide will win, unless a third party has a local concentration of votes quite greater than its nationwide degree of support. This is what Duverger referred to as the *mechanical effect*. Hence third-party votes most often are "wasted" (for the purpose of winning seats), so that these

---

[14] Rae (1967) was the first to use the term, district "magnitude," and to carry out systematic worldwide analysis of its effects.
[15] In a retrospective essay, Duverger (1986) included mention of the "two-round majority system."

parties are underpaid, nationwide. Correspondingly, the two largest parties will be overpaid in terms of seats. This effect is observed instantaneously, for any given election, once the seat and vote shares are compared. In this sense, it is "mechanical."

In contrast, what Duverger termed the *psychological effect* may develop more slowly, over several elections. The mechanical effect means that votes for third parties are effectively wasted in most districts of low magnitude (and $M=1$ in particular). In the next election, many voters may abandon such parties – a point already noted by Droop (2012 [1869])[16] – except in the few districts where the third party won or came close. Sometimes regional or ethnic differences allow parties that are small nationwide to persist because they can win many districts in their regional strongholds. At various times, a Bloc Quebecois has been important in Canadian national politics because it could win many districts in the province of Quebec (Massicotte 2018), and the United Kingdom has its Scottish National Party and smaller regional parties in Wales and Northern Ireland (Lundberg 2018). India has a profusion of such parties, as we showed in Chapter 5 and discuss in detail in Chapter 15.

In contrast to parties that draw on regional strongholds, a nationwide third party that wins few seats may see many of its voters bleed away at the next election, causing even further voters to give up on them. Such parties may tend gradually to be reduced to insignificance or even be eliminated, according to Duverger's argument.

The psychological effect is usually presented in terms of voter strategies, but it also works on politicians and contributors. Anticipating another defeat and lacking resources, a third party may desist from running in a district even before its former voters have a chance to abandon it. Financial contributors may be hard to find, and few people may volunteer to campaign for a lost cause.

Duverger's effects apply foremost at the district level.[17] This is where the seat is lost or won and where the votes are wasted or not, regardless of nationwide results. Voters have no direct reason to abandon a third party nationwide who won in their own district – or only narrowly lost and could win in the next election. The extension of the psychological effect to the nationwide scene need

---

16 As reported by Riker (1982), Droop (2012 [1869]: 10) had called attention to these effects about eight decades before Duverger:

an election is usually reduced to a contest between the two most popular candidates or sets of candidates. Even if other candidates go to the poll, the electors usually find out that their votes will be thrown away, unless given in favour of one or other of the parties between whom the election really lies.

17 Yet, Duverger initially stipulated what came to be known as his "law" as the plurality electoral system tending to produce a two-party system *in the legislature* – see for example, the graph in Duverger (1954: 209). Other statements in his rich treatise refer to votes or to individual districts, but his preoccupation was with the nationwide assembly party system. In this chapter, so is ours.

not follow. Sometimes it does, but by no means always. Third parties have minimal presence in the United States, but such parties have survived and even made a comeback in the United Kingdom. Significant national parties other than the top two persist in Canada, and not only (as often claimed) in specific regions (see Gaines 1999).

It is thus important to emphasize that the psychological effect on nonregional third parties is only a tendency. In fact, many smaller parties persist despite winning few seats and continue to enter, and receive votes in, districts that are hopeless. Such minor-party persistence is an anomaly to those wedded to the Duvergerian tendencies, with their near-exclusive focus on district magnitude to the exclusion of assembly size.[18]

Why "Duverger's Law" Does Not Qualify as Law – but Still Is a Useful Tendency

The observation that seat allocation by plurality in single-seat districts tends to go with two major parties has passed into political science literature as "Duverger's law." Yet it does not pass the test as law in the scientific sense. It is too vague, as we will see. Maurice Duverger himself would agree. In retrospect, Duverger (1986) claimed merely a tendency, saying that it's the *American* authors, especially Riker (1982), who have called it Duverger's *law*. So, instead of "Duverger's law" we should talk of Duverger's *tendency*, until law-like firmness is demonstrated. The question is, how strong is this tendency?

This tendency would have utter firmness if two complementary conditions were satisfied. First, if FPTP always led to two-party systems; and conversely, if all two-party systems originated from FPTP rule. In contrast, suppose only one-half of all FPTP elections led to two-party systems, and only one-half of all two-party systems originated from FPTP rule. This would mean complete randomness, and Duverger's tendency would be completely rejected. Where do we actually stand, between these two extremes? The hard reality is that such a test never has been carried out.

Indeed, the very setting up of such a test runs into problems. How do we recognize a "two-party system" in operational terms? While the effective number of parties serves well in quantifying the core idea of the Duvergerian approach, it would be a poor measure of "two-partyness" for the specific

---

[18] Given that a district is "embedded" in a nationwide assembly electoral system (that may have many dozens or hundreds of other districts) the FPTP logic means our models actually predict more than two parties receiving substantial vote shares even in $M=1$ districts, if the assembly is large. This can happen because some voters may actually think nationally even when votes are turned into seats only in districts (Johnston 2017). For instance, they may want to vote for a party that they know wins seats *in other districts*, even though it has no chance in the voter's own district. This point about the national impact on the district will be the theme of Chapter 10. For now the important point is that we see no sharp break between FPTP and PR, like standard Duvergerian works do.

purpose of testing the validity of "Duverger's law." This is so because $N=2.00$ can originate not only from 50-50-0, which expresses pure two-partyness, but also from constellations such as 70-(five parties at), 4-(five at) 2, which is pure one-party hegemony. Such $N=2.00$ could also come from 66.6–16.7–16.7, which combines features of one-party hegemony and a three-party constellation that do not meaningfully "average out" to two parties. Gaines and Taagepera (2013) offer better ways to distinguish two-party constellations from one-party and multiparty combinations, but problems remain.

By the way, are we talking about votes or seats? Is it *votes* parties receive in electoral districts, or *seats* they win in the national assembly? Duverger implied both, at different points in his original treatise. First, in each electoral district only two parties emerge to compete for votes. Then, by some quite fuzzy process (what Cox, 1997, termed "linkage"), these parties supposedly turn out to be the *same* two parties in each district, so that assembly seats go only to these two parties. OK, such a connection may exist. But we would have to test the presumed tendency at both levels – district votes and assembly seats.

As one surveys the literature on FPTP systems, several desirable outcomes are claimed for what would be an ideal Duvergerian two-party system. They go beyond just having two major parties. *First*, such an ideal system leads to a comfortable single-party majority, so that the government can act decisively. *Second*, it leads to a single vigorous opposition party that keeps the government on its toes and can take over after new elections. *Third*, FPTP rule favors regular alternation in power, so that neither major party becomes stale. *Fourth*, it even offers proportional representation of sorts in the long run, as the two major parties tend to win an equal number of elections. A test along these lines (Taagepera, 2015) brings mixed results. Indeed, the Australian Alternative Vote would seem more Duvergerian than FPTP (see Chapter 16).

In sum, we are left with a tendency that falls short of qualifying as law. *The SPM is a major step beyond the so-called Duverger's law*, because the latter offers no equation between operationally measurable quantities and hence can offer no quantitative predictions. The SPM does. But this in no ways reduces Duverger's enormous contribution to the field. He was the first one to announce clearly some basic tendencies that have guided much of the work in electoral systems ever since. This is the basis for the Duvergerian agenda, to which we come next.[19]

The Duvergerian Agenda

The "Duvergerian Agenda" (as termed by Shugart 2005a) refers to the scholarly work that builds on Duverger's tendencies regarding institutional effects on

---

[19] Remarkably, we could develop the Seat Product Model without explicit reference to Duvergerian tendencies and effects. However, they are implicit there. The SPM is very much a product of the Duvergerian agenda.

party system fragmentation. This agenda has evolved into a "mature" and active subfield for an ever-growing set of scholars despite having been considered "underdeveloped" just over three decades ago (Lijphart 1985).

The Duvergerian agenda consists of explaining and predicting the results and causes of Duverger's effects. It includes "micro" and "macro" dimensions. Micro considerations underlie the psychological effect and related strategic considerations and "coordination" (see Cox 1997). Our focus is principally on the macro perspective – the systemic relationship between institutional rules and party-system outcomes.[20] This macroscopic approach tries to make use of the restrictions imposed by electoral rules (low district magnitude and small assembly size, in particular) to explain and predict the number and relative sizes of parties, as well as the degree of disproportionality of seats to votes. In many works, some measure of social diversity or "issue dimensions" is taken into account (Taagepera and Grofman 1985, Ordeshook and Shvetsova 1994, Amorim Neto and Cox 1997, Cox 1997, Clark and Golder 2006, van de Wardt 2017, Moser, et al., 2018). The macro dimension of the Duvergerian agenda has been called the "core of the core" of electoral studies (Shugart 2005a).

For many decades, the understanding of the macro level of electoral-system effects was dominated by the idea that *seats come from votes*. This view, which has retained substantial currency, primarily sees the electoral system as a black box in between the votes and seats (cf. Taagepera and Shugart 1989a: 64 and 202). In one of our earlier collaborations (Taagepera and Shugart 1993), we observed instead that votes and the electoral system *both* affect seats, from opposite directions.

Due to the actual impact on seats from these two directions, the concept of the electoral system as an "intervening control box" between votes and seats is *wrong*! Progress in furthering the Duvergerian agenda required specifying how the number of available seats constrains electoral outcomes, including the votes. **Votes come from seats**, although that is not to say that they come *only* from seats. Current politics and deeper cultural and historical factors of the country are important, too, but these are country-specific rather than systematic cross-national factors like institutional variation.

More recent works, starting with Amorim Neto and Cox (1997) and Cox (1997) have explicitly recognized that the electoral system shapes the votes. However, their dominant theoretical approach remains one that sees the distribution of seats entirely as an output of the electoral system, *after* the votes are fed in (recall our depiction of this approach in Figure 1.3).

---

[20] We will not get into a philosophical debate on whether the macro level can be understood at all without solving the micro level. Let the results speak for themselves. Note that in physics thermodynamics was developed (and continues to serve) much before statistical physics explained its micro level underpinnings.

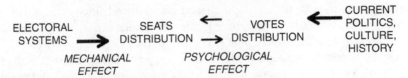

FIGURE 7.5 The opposite impacts of current politics and electoral systems
Source: Adapted from Taagepera (2007).

The more theoretically fruitful approach is the one that sees the seats distribution as affected by both the votes and the electoral system. We already depicted this in Figure 1.4, but we amplify it in Figure 7.5 with the addition of Duverger's notions of mechanical and psychological effects.[21]

For individual elections, votes come first, based on current politics and, more remotely, on the country's historical peculiarities. They will determine the seats, in conjunction with the mechanical effect of the electoral system. But for the average of many elections, and for the purpose of elaborating systematic cross-national models, we need to recognize that the causal arrow reverses direction. Through the mechanical effect, the electoral system pressures the distribution of seats to conform to what best fits in with the total number of seats available. Through the psychological effect, the electoral system eventually also impacts the distribution of votes. In the process, it might even counteract culture and history to some degree by rendering some parties nonviable.

The Duvergerian agenda continues to be salient because of the impact of party fragmentation on the wider pattern of governance, such as the balance between accountable governments and broadly representative political inclusion (Cheibub et al. 1996; Carey and Hix 2011; Lijphart 1999), and because political scientists continue to be commissioned for their advice on electoral-system design (Carey et al. 2013). Although there are still disagreements over how much fragmentation is optimal for a party system, no one will deny that we can hardly make any normative judgment on an electoral system without knowing its impact on the distribution of seats among parties.

SOME OTHER FACTORS OF PARTY-SYSTEM FRAGMENTATION

The Seat Product Model accounts for about 60 percent of the variation in the effective number of assembly parties (cf. Table 7.2). This leaves 40 percent to other causes and randomness. It would be welcome, if further factors could be located. Socioethnic diversity could be one, acting by itself or in conjunction with seat product, as could be presidential factors in the case of such regimes.

---

[21] For simplicity, it omits political culture. In Chapter 8, we will discuss how it can be brought back in.

Unfortunately, we will see here and in Chapters 11, 12, and 15 that such factors add little explanation and prediction ability, once the seat product has been accounted for.

Socioethnic Diversity

It is reasonable to suspect that the tendency of PR systems to be associated with multipartism is conditional on social cleavages – a point made by Ordeshook and Shvetsova (1994) and extended by Amorim Neto and Cox (1997). Several scholars, including Clark (2006), Clark and Golder (2006), and Hicken and Stoll (2012), have estimated models of these effects. While each study differs in important respects, a key conclusion of all of them is summarized by the statement in Clark and Golder (2006: 682) that "absent any knowledge concerning the social pressure for the multiplication of parties, it is not possible to predict whether multiple parties will actually form in permissive electoral systems."

In other words, they see no direct relationship between permissive (i.e., substantively proportional) electoral systems and fragmented party systems, and only when high social heterogeneity and permissive rules interact do they claim we will find fragmentation. In contrast to the Seat Product Model, these approaches did not include assembly size, using only district magnitude (mean or median) and the size of upper tiers (if any) of seat-allocation as measures of system permissiveness. The question of the impact of ethnic diversity is one that we turn to in Chapter 15. We will spoil the suspense a bit here, however, by noting that the reason we come back to it so late in the book is that ethnic diversity has only very limited impact on the predictions we derive from the Seat Product Model, which uses only institutional inputs.

Previous regression-based works on electoral systems and party systems broke important ground in furthering knowledge about statistical patterns via broad cross-national datasets. Unfortunately, they come up short in offering guides to real-world institutional design. For instance, Table 2 in Clark and Golder (2006: 698) shows that their most preferred regression model has highly unstable coefficients on key independent variables depending on the sample to which it is applied. This may not be a problem if all we are curious about is *which* factors matter. But if we were tasked with offering advice on the likely impact of a proposed electoral system on party-system fragmentation, our most honest answer, based on the existing statistical methods, would be "we can't say." One can only imagine how frustrating it would be if Newton's Laws of Motion showed only *what* can change an object's speed, but without giving a stable formula: most industrial products in our time would not have been possible.

Presidential Impact on Assembly Parties

When it comes to the effective number of assembly parties in presidential democracies, some works include as an input variable the effective number of presidential candidates as well as the temporal "proximity" of legislative and presidential elections (see our depiction in Figure 1.3).[22] On the one hand, this would imply that presidential systems are fundamentally different from parliamentary. On the other hand, it has forced some regression analyses to treat parliamentary systems essentially as if they were *special cases of presidential systems*, with the effective number of presidential candidates being zero.[23] The approach requires us to know the votes distribution in the presidential election in order to understand the number of parties in the assembly or the votes distribution for assembly elections. Yet, Figures 7.1 and 7.2 suggest that assembly party systems in presidential democracies can be explained by the same fundamental institutional input as those in parliamentary – the Seat Product.

The inclusion of variables specific to presidential systems in regressions that pool all democracies has already been called into question. Elgie et al. (2014) show that the conclusions of such models do not hold for presidential systems when the parliamentary systems are removed from the sample. Then, Li and Shugart (2016) showed that the widely accepted interactive effect of social and institutional factors also does not hold for parliamentary systems, when they attempted to replicate Clark and Golder's (2006) regressions.[24] If the conclusions about either executive type hold only when the other is included, along with variables specific only to presidential systems, then the overall conclusions themselves might be due for a serious rethink. Fortunately, once we conceptualize the electoral system via the Seat Product, we do not need to separate the samples by executive format, or incorporate presidential-specific variables, in order to make sense of the statistical patterns.

CONCLUSION

In this chapter, we show the value of the Seat Product Model for predicting the effective number of seat-winning parties in the national assembly (N_S). For simple systems, N_S tends to be around the sixth root of the product of mean district magnitude and assembly size. This formula was introduced by Taagepera (2007). Here we extended its applicability by testing it on a much wider set of cases; in Chapter 15 we will extend it farther to include complex two-tier systems and the role of ethnic diversity (see also Li and Shugart, 2016).

[22] These works include the following: Amorin, Neto, and Cox 1997, Cox 1997, Clark and Golder 2006, Hicken and Stoll 2012. We return to them (and others) again in Chapter 12.

[23] Even though an "effective" number, by definition, cannot be less than one.

[24] More specifically, the finding of Clark and Golder (and others using similar approaches) is not robust to the exclusion of India, by far the case with the highest ethnic diversity. We discuss the Indian case further in Chapter 15. By contrast, the SPM is statistically robust to whether we include or exclude India. See Li and Shugart (2016).

A key message we can deliver at the conclusion of this chapter is that institutional theories should no longer be considered just a thought game played in the academic community that have failed to produce robust expectations. Rather, the Seat Product Model can have genuine real-world impact when applied to the institutional-design process in newer democracies. This is a valuable contribution, because political scientists are often called to advise on electoral system design in emerging democracies (Carey et al. 2013).

Of course, just predicting party fragmentation in the legislature cannot satisfy us; we want to know if the Seat Product can lead us to a prediction of electoral fragmentation. This is the task of Chapter 8. There we offer a completely novel theory of how the SPM applies to nationwide elective party systems.

Appendix to Chapter 7

THE IMPACT OF ALLOCATION FORMULA

Does the precise allocation formula of a PR electoral system (see Chapter 2) affect the relationship of the seat product, MS, to the output quantities of interest in this chapter? We can test this by calculating ratios of the actual output to the value expected under a simple system, as follows:

$$N_{S0}/(MS)^{1/4};$$
$$s_1/(MS)^{-1/8};$$
$$N_S/(MS)^{1/6}.$$

We then perform difference-of-means tests on these ratios for PR systems, depending on whether they use D'Hondt or another PR formula. In all cases but two, the allocation formula, if not D'Hondt, is either Hare quota with largest remainders, or Modified Ste.-Laguë. The exceptions are Brazil and Finland, which require further explanation.

As we demonstrated in Chapter 6, many lists in Brazil and Finland contain candidates of more than one party in alliance. Under the rules used in these countries the parties *within the list* win their seats as if the formula were SNTV. That is, each list wins some number of seats, which we can designate s, via the application of D'Hondt, then the top s candidates on the list are elected, without regard to the party affiliations of the candidates on the list.

Depending on how many different parties have candidates in a given list's top s vote totals, the number of parties winning may be two or more per list. Thus the provision for alliances in these countries potentially inflates the number of parties. We go into the impact of these provisions in more detail in Chapter 14, which focuses on intralist allocations at the district level.

TABLE 7.A1 *Impact of formula on ratios of actual values to Seat Product predictions*

Ratio	If Brazil and Finland are considered to be D'Hondt		If Brazil and Finland are not considered to be D'Hondt	
	D'Hondt	Other PR formula	D'Hondt	Other PR formula
$N_{S0}/(MS)^{1/4}$	**1.156**	*1.014*	**1.119**	1.109
$s_1/(MS)^{-1/8}$	0.984	1.086	*1.036*	*0.978*
$N_S/(MS)^{1/6}$	*1.096*	1.072	*1.022*	*1.190*

Statistically significant differences (at $p<0.05$) are in bold. Those in the expected direction are in italics.

In the sense that they effectively use D'Hondt for lists and then switch to SNTV within lists, Brazil and Finland do not actually have a "pure" D'Hondt system. The way we code these cases affects our answer to our question of whether the PR allocation formula matters.

Table 7.A1 summarizes the results, which contain some surprises. We expect D'Hondt to lead to lower $N_{S0}/(MS)^{1/4}$ and $N_S/(MS)^{1/6}$ but higher $s_1/(MS)^{-1/8}$. Regardless of our coding of Brazil and Finland, the effect on the nationwide number of parties winning at least one seat, N_{S0}, is opposite of expectation. There is no reason why, in any given district, D'Hondt (without alliances) would permit more parties to win seats than other PR formulas. The result must be due to quirks of cross-district politics.[25]

If, however, we recode the "impure" D'Hondt formulas in Brazil and Finland, we see that the effects on the nationwide effective number of parties, N_S, or on the seat share of the largest party, s_1, are as expected. The difference for N_S is also statistically significant (so is the difference for s_1 if we adopt a $p<0.065$ standard). That is, D'Hondt, without alliances, has a significantly lower N_S and higher s_1 than other PR formulas.

Because it depends on how we treat these two unusual cases, we do not consider the findings on the impact of formula to be robust. We are on safer grounds estimating these quantities from the Seat Product, and considering deviations from expectation as matters of individual country or election politics. One of those country-level (or even election-specific) variations is whether alliances are allowed, and how many lists elect candidates of more than one party. We return to this question in more detail in Chapter 14.

---

[25] When Brazil and Finland are not considered D'Hondt, the difference between D'Hondt and other PR formulas is insignificant if Spain is excluded. Indeed, Spain's districted PR system features a plethora of regional parties, each of which wins seats in one or a few districts only (as detailed in Hopkin 2005).

8

Winners Plus One: How We Get Votes from Seats

Now we literally deduce votes from seats, in line with the book's title. We take a completely novel step and extend the Seat Product Model to votes distribution. This transition was hard to come by. For instance, the chapter on "The institutional impact on votes" in Taagepera (2007) is in retrospect a total flop, and the approach to estimating votes fragmentation taken by Li and Shugart (2016) lacked a theoretical foundation. Yet the additional assumption needed will be seen to be of utmost simplicity.

When a given number of parties wins seats in a representative assembly, how many more are likely to try their luck? How are these two numbers connected logically? If a logical model can be proposed, does it agree with the empirical average pattern? We can expect, of course, that the actual worldwide data will show variation over a wide range. In fact, we can expect any data on vote-earning parties to show more variation than comparable data on seat-winners, for the same reason that we argue for starting the analysis with the seats and only then extending votes: the seats are ultimately constrained by the institutions, whereas the votes actually are not. Whatever total number of seats comprise the assembly, we can be certain that there are no more parties than this number that gain representation. But how many others may run, and earn votes? The only constraint is that obviously there could not be more parties earning votes than there are voters, but that observation is hardly helpful. The extent to which the number of parties earning votes is greater than that winning seats is softly constrained, and only by the willingness of voters to tolerate "wasted votes" and the elites who form parties to keep running and losing.

Despite the expectation of wide variation in the number of electoral parties, the average value for a given country or a given institutional setup can offer a useful benchmark. When establishing a logically expected number of parties competing, we implicitly also ask: *Given the number of parties that won seats, was the number of parties competing for seats in a particular country unusually high or low, or as expected?* If there is marked deviation from expectation, then one may wish to look for the reason. In the absence of such a benchmark, anything goes and nothing gets explained.

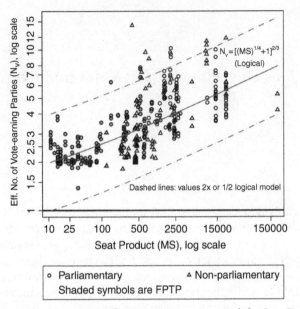

FIGURE 8.1 The effective number of vote-earning parties and the Seat Product

As a preview to what this chapter is about, we offer Figure 8.1. This graph shows how Seat Product, *MS*, affects the effective number of *vote-earning* parties (N_V). The data points represent 285 individual elections in thirty-two countries. The solid curve shows the logically based model we are going to develop:

$$N_V = [(MS)^{1/4} + 1]^{2/3}. \tag{8.1}$$

This equation is a good deal more complex than the one for seats, $N_S=(MS)^{1/6}$. This is the nature of cumulative science: we start with simple building blocks like $N'_{S0}=M^{1/2}$ (Equation 1.1, tested in Chapter 7) and build up complex structures. The solid curve in Figure 8.1 that follows Equation 8.1 is visibly a good fit, even though it is not a regression estimate.

The dashed curves represent observed values of N_V twice or one-half the prediction of Equation 8.1. Most cases are well within the range delimited by the dashed curves, but there are a few elections that are outside the range, on the high side. Several of these are presidential systems (depicted with triangles). We will discuss the reasons for why presidential systems are sometimes more fragmented than parliamentary systems in Chapter 11.

Votes are only indirectly and incompletely constrained by a purely institutional input like the Seat Product (*MS*). Therefore, we would expect more scatter for vote-based N_V than for seat-based N_S in Figure 7.1. Surprisingly, scatter is only slightly heavier here.

The amount of scatter should not detract from the bigger picture, which is that the overall fit is good. The degree of fit in Figure 8.1 shows that we can make progress in predicting average outcomes from institutional inputs. We discuss in the next section how we build the model just previewed; a later section of this chapter subjects it to a regression test on simple systems. Complex systems will be discussed in passing in this chapter, but not systematically analyzed till Chapter 15.

"PLUS ONE," BUT NOT $M+1$

The now fairly well-established idea of an "$M+1$ rule" for the number of "serious" or "viable" *candidates* offers a useful starting point. This rule was elaborated by Reed (1990, 2003) and Cox (1997). A recent review summarizes it as follows: "The $M+1$ rule, whereby the number of parties or candidates in a district is capped by the district magnitude (M) plus one" (Ferree, et al., 2013: 812). This "parties *or* candidates" becomes problematic when M is large and the number of parties is thus sure to be smaller than M.

The original notion behind the $M+1$ rule was that it generalized the so-called Duverger's law. When $M=1$, it hardly matters whether we think of the competing agents as parties or candidates – each party generally presents just one candidate, so the concepts merge. "Duverger's law" predicts two parties (two candidates) when $M=1$. Reed's contribution was to say that under single nontransferable vote (SNTV) rules (see Chapter 3) formerly used in Japan, the number of "serious" candidates also was near $M+1$. Reed operationalized "serious" via the effective number, and he explicitly meant candidates, not parties. Under SNTV, larger parties typically nominate more than one candidate per district (but fewer than M – see Chapter 13). Because there are M winners, and they are those with the highest individual vote totals regardless of party, there are $M+1$ viable candidates,[1] according to Reed's argument. In other words, the district has M winners, and one close loser. The rest tend to fall farther behind, at least under certain conditions specified by Reed and extended by Cox.

Cox himself recognizes the limits of applicability of the $M+1$ rule to larger magnitudes and to the (effective) number of parties, saying it specifies an "upper bound" rather than a prediction. It is obvious that it would be a poor prediction of the number of parties. For instance, in the single nationwide district of $M=150$ seats in The Netherlands, 151 parties is an overkill.[2] Above some moderate level of M – Cox (1997: 100) suggests "about five" seats – the $M+1$

---

[1] Cox (1997: 99) defines viable as "proof against strategic voting."

[2] By the same token, 151 viable candidates presumably would be too low, as many a party that wins seats also likely has one or more viable losing candidates. (The Netherlands uses a "flexible" list – see Chapter 6 for definition – and thus individual candidates can enhance their own viability if they successfully campaign for preference votes.)

rule is not the principal factor limiting proliferation of parties (Cox 1997: 122). Further, Cox (1997: 102n) states that the application of the $M+1$ rule to lists in PR systems is "substantially less compelling." Thus, he concludes, "something else" other than the strategic voting that leads to $M+1$ viable candidates under FPTP and SNTV must be at work when we are concerned with the number of vote-earning parties in PR systems (Cox 1997: 110).[3]

For making sense of the number of viable vote-earning parties, we agree that the "plus one" is an important logical building block. However, we suggest the "plus one" should be added to the *number of seat-winning parties*, not the total number of seats in a district. The objective of this chapter is to understand how electoral systems shape the effective number of vote-earning parties for elections to national assemblies. The Reed and Cox notion of viability being conditioned by competition for seats is logically correct. We take this key insight a step further. As already sketched in Figures 1.4 and 7.5 the total numbers of seats available in a district and nationwide impose physical constraints on the number of winning parties. No district can have more than M winning parties (or fewer than one), nor can the assembly have more than S winners (or fewer than one). This was the logic behind the Seat Product, MS, explained and successfully tested in Chapter 7.

Unlike seat-winning parties, however, the number of vote-earners is not strictly constrained. It is challenging to specify *ex ante* how tolerant of "wasted votes" the country's politicians, election financiers, and voters will be. While we know the actual upper bound on the number of seat-winning parties (M in any district, S nationwide), the upper bound on parties that might be viable vote-earners is not knowable. However, it is surely constrained by the number of parties with seats. The number of vote-earning parties clearly is not lower than the number with seats. It likely tends not to be greatly higher, as most voters and other actors will not long tolerate voting for a hopeless party.

With this logical foundation, we can specify a new concept that will be crucial to this chapter and again in Chapter 10 (which deals with district-level effects): *the number of pertinent vote-earning parties*. We will use the term, "pertinent," rather than "viable," in order to differentiate our concept from those of preceding authors. We mean something subtly, but importantly, different. We are not asking whether some number of parties, beyond the winners, is perceived as sufficiently viable so as not to suffer from strategic defection. We are asking how many are sufficiently important to contribute to our prediction of the effective number of vote-earning parties (N_V). They are "pertinent" if counting them helps us estimate N_V. Thus our logical basis for model building is:

The number of pertinent vote-earning parties (N_{V0}) is the number of seat-winning parties (N_{S0}), plus one. More briefly: strivers are winners plus one.

---

[3] Cox goes on to suggest the answer is "economies of scale" that lead actors to "coordinate" around a smaller number of *party lists*.

The statement defines N_{V0} as deriving from a quantity that we already know can be logically predicted: N_{S0} (as we saw in Chapter 7). The rest of the logical model building, leading to Equation 8.1, then follows, as we shall see in the next sections of this chapter. While the $M+1$ rule is restricted to a single electoral district, this "winners plus one" model can also apply to electoral parties nationwide. In this chapter we will test the plausibility of this notion at the national level; we extend it to the district level in Chapter 10.

We will test "winners plus one" using the known number of assembly parties (of any size), which we have already shown in Chapter 7 to be a quantity about which we can build systematic models. Perhaps surprisingly, given how blunt the notion of winning parties, plus one, might appear, it works well. Given that it does, we can also connect the concept later in this chapter to the purely institutional input, the Seat Product, MS, thereby providing the logical basis behind Equation 8.1.

Connecting Vote-Based and Seat-Based Effective Numbers

We show the hypothesis "successful parties plus one" in bold, because this is a major advance first published in this book. Several later chapters hinge on this simple relationship. It applies to N_0, the *actual* number of parties:

$$N_{V0}=N_{S0}+1. \tag{8.2}$$

It does *not* apply to the *effective* numbers. What we add is one real party that barely fails to win a seat, not an abstract "effective" quantity. This equation is the crucial link where the average patterns for **votes** are deduced **from** the average patterns for **seats**, and hence from the purely institutional Seat Product MS.

The reasoning that took us in Chapter 7 from the actual number of seat-winning parties to the largest seat share and then on to the effective number of assembly seats remains valid when we substitute votes for seats. So, in parallel with $s_1 = N_{S0}^{-1/2}$ and $N_S = s_1^{-4/3}$ (Table 7.3), we get

$$v_1 = N_{V0}^{-1/2} \quad \text{and} \quad N_V = v_1^{-4/3}$$

for the largest vote share, and the effective number of vote-earning parties.

Figure 8.2 compares the fit of $N_S = s_1^{-4/3}$ for seats in the left panel (as reproduced from Figure 7.4) to the fit of $N_V = v_1^{-4/3}$ for votes in the right panel. Forbidden areas are shown in both panels, corresponding to those depicted in Figure 7.4. Votes show slightly more scatter, but the agreement with the logical model is still very good.

From $v_1 = N_{V0}^{-1/2}$ and $N_{V0}=N_{S0}+1$ it follows that

$$v_1 = (N_{S0} + 1)^{-1/2}.$$

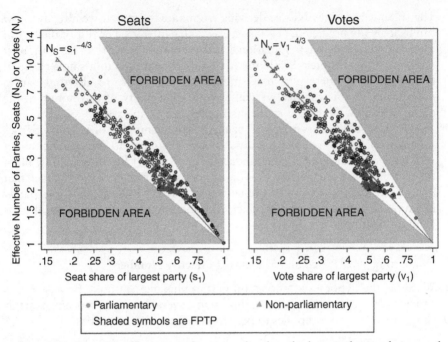

FIGURE 8.2 How the effective numbers are related to the largest shares of seats and votes

Figure 8.3 compares the impact of the number of seat-winning parties (N_{S0}) on the largest seat and vote shares, respectively. The left panel reproduces the left panel of Figure 7.3 for the largest seat share. The right panel shows the impact of N_{S0} on the largest vote share. Due to the "+1" the relationship is curved. The degree of fit is comparable for seats and votes, confirming that the model $v_1=(N_{S0}+1)^{-1/2}$ fits the data.

This is an important connection, as we are unable to measure "actual vote-earning parties" directly in a meaningful way. We surely do not mean any party that earns even a single vote the same way that for "actual seat-winning parties" we do indeed mean to include even a party that wins only one seat. Thus we need a "phantom" quantity for how to measure how many parties are serious – or, as we call them, *pertinent*. This is what Equation 8.2 represents – the number of pertinent vote-earning parties, represented by the number of winners with at least one seat (N_{S0}) plus one serious striver that came up just short.

If the logic is on the right track, it means we can also connect the effective numbers for votes and seats, using basic algebra. Inserting $v_1=(N_{S0}+1)^{-1/2}$ into $N_V=v_1^{-4/3}$, we get $N_V=(N_{S0}+1)^{2/3}$. Reversing $N_S=N_{S0}^{2/3}$ (Table 7.3) leads to $N_{S0}=N_S^{3/2}$. Inserting this into

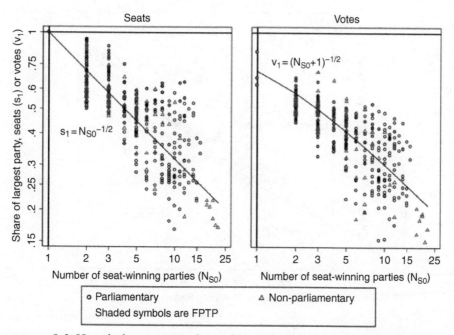

FIGURE 8.3 How the largest seat and vote shares relate to the number of seat-winning parties

$$N_V = (N_{S0} + 1)^{2/3}$$

yields

$$N_V = [N_S^{3/2} + 1]^{2/3} \tag{8.3}$$

Equation 8.3 offers a powerful test of the underlying logic of how we get votes from seats, bypassing the major uncertainties surrounding the "real" value of N_{V0} in Equation 8.1. The effective numbers, N_V and N_S, can be measured unambiguously – at least in principle.

In Figure 8.4 we plot the data for a visual test of Equation 8.3. We plot several institutional variations with different symbols, in order to see if the relationship between N_V and N_S is somehow fundamentally different when the rules are different. The symbols differentiate FPTP ($M=1$), nationwide PR ($M=S$), two-tier PR systems, as well as presidential democracies.[4]

The graph has the effective number of seat-winning parties (N_S) on the x-axis and the effective number of vote-earning parties (N_V) on the y-axis, both on logarithmic scales. The light gray line represents $N_V = N_S$. Visibly, very few data points fall below this equality line, although many come close when the number of parties is large.

---

[4] We do not further differentiate the presidential cases by electoral system.

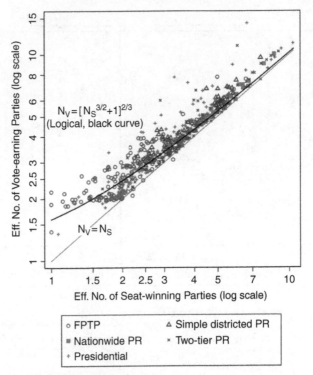

FIGURE 8.4 The effective numbers of parties, votes versus seats

The curve plotted in black corresponds to the logical model, $N_V = [N_S^{3/2} + 1]^{2/3}$. We see that the fit is strong. In fact, it is so strong that few cases, *regardless of electoral system or executive type*, are outside of a narrow band that follows the logical model. The logical model, Equation 8.3, clearly fits the pattern well, thereby offering support for our theory of "strivers are winners, plus one."

Among the relatively few cases that are outside the main data cloud, it is noteworthy that many are presidential systems and a few have two-tier rules. (We will discuss the additional considerations that affect presidential democracies in Chapters 11 and 12.) Moreover, there is some tendency for N_V to be higher than expected in those $M=1$ systems in which N_S is less than about 1.5. More noteworthy, however, is that $M=1$, districted PR, two-tier, and $M=S$ (nationwide PR) systems are intermixed. It may seem surprising that less proportional electoral systems do not have a tendency to have N_V substantially greater than their typically low N_S, but in fact, Equation 8.3 accurately assesses the relationship of votes to seats independent of electoral system. (We show regression results later.) Thus the regression and graph both support our logical model – "strivers are winners plus one."

So far we have considered the fit of Equation 8.3, which has the effective number of seat-winning parties on the right hand side: $N_V = [N_S^{3/2} + 1]^{2/3}$. However, what we really should ask is, can we connect N_V to the Seat Product, MS? Of course, we have already spoiled the suspense! We showed in Figure 8.1 at the beginning of this chapter that such a connection works. In the following section we discuss this finding in more detail.

Predicting the Effective Number of Vote-Earning Parties: Are Institutions Sufficient?

If we are able to connect N_V to the Seat Product (MS), as we previewed as a promising task at the start of this chapter, it would permit an estimation of the fragmentation of the vote in a country based solely on its institutions. This is advantageous because such a prediction would be based on inputs that are, in principle, subject to design and reform: the average district magnitude and the assembly size. Given that we have previously established $N_V = [N_S^{3/2} + 1]^{2/3}$ and, even earlier (Chapter 7), $N_S = (MS)^{1/6}$, we expect Equation 8.1 to result for simple systems[5]:

$$N_V = [(MS)^{1/4} + 1]^{2/3}.$$

This was the curve plotted in Figure 8.1. Similarly, it follows from $v_1 = (N_{S0}+1)^{-1/2}$ that the largest vote share can be estimated from the Seat Product:

$$v_1 = [(MS)^{1/4} + 1]^{-1/2}.$$

However, data plot in Figure 8.1 showed some nontrivial scatter. In particular, there were several countries with a tendency to have elections with $N_V >> [(MS)^{1/4} + 1]^{2/3}$. Such cases raise the question of whether we should consider inclusion of the factor of ethnic diversity. After all, it is generally agreed by other authors (reviewed in Chapter 7), that countries with greater social diversity have a systematically higher effective number of parties, at least if they combine such diversity with "permissive" electoral institutions (i.e., high MS). We will present tests that include ethnic diversity in Chapter 15; we find that the impact of this additional factor is less than commonly believed, but it does help understand some countries' party systems. For now, we stick to the institutional variables, to uncover the generalizable patterns that form a baseline against which country-level deviation can be compared.

---

[5] Extension to two-tier systems will be done in Chapter 15.

Statistical Testing of the Connection Between the Effective Numbers of Parties for Votes and Seats

In this section, we begin undertaking empirical testing of the model that ultimately leads to Equation 8.1, introduced at the beginning of this chapter. In the preceding subsection, we proposed Equation 8.3, $N_V = [N_S^{3/2} + 1]^{2/3}$. We can test it by running the following OLS regression:

$$LogN_V = \alpha + \beta log(N_S^{3/2} + 1).$$

We should obtain a coefficient of $\beta=2/3$, and a constant, $\alpha=0$. What we actually find is remarkably close. First, if we run it on just the parliamentary systems with the simple electoral systems – the set to which the model is designed to apply – we obtain:

$$LogN_V = 0.00093 + 0.687 \; log(N_S^{3/2} + 1) \quad [R^2 = 0.920, \; 288 \text{ obs.}].$$

This is a remarkably good fit, confirming the logic behind Equation 8.3. We can then double the number of observations by including presidential democracies and two-tier proportional electoral systems (as defined in Chapter 3). The result is:

$$LogN_V = -0.0322 + 0.722 \; log(N_S^{3/2} + 1) \quad [R^2 = 0.904, \; 598 \text{ obs.}].$$

Now we have added a large number of observations where we could expect the distribution of votes to parties to be less adjusted to the seats – either because the assembly election is not also the source of executive authority (due to direct presidential election) or because nationwide compensation from a second tier may make voters less aware of institutional constraints. Yet the inclusion of these cases only slightly alters the fit of the empirical regression to our logical model.[6]

Statistical Testing of the Connection Between the Effective Numbers of Vote-Earning Parties and the Seat Product

Following our usual procedure, we can test Equation 8.1 as follows:

$$logN_V = \alpha + \beta log[(MS)^{1/4} + 1].$$

We should find $\alpha=0$ and $\beta=2/3$. The right-hand side of this equation is our proxy for the *number of pertinent vote-earning parties* (N_{V0}), logged. As explained earlier in the chapter, N_{V0} cannot be measured directly, hence we estimate it from the Seat Product.

---

[6] If we include the two-tier systems, but discard the presidential systems, the coefficient is 0.689. Thus the complexity of two-tier allocation does not affect the accuracy of the result, even though some are visible outliers in Figure 8.4. Rather, it is presidential systems that perturb it somewhat – as we would already expect from these systems' greater visible scatter in Figure 8.1, at the start of this chapter.

TABLE 8.1 *Regression for the effective number of vote-earning parties* (N_V)

	(1) Institutions only parl., simple	(2) Institutions only all execs., simple
log[(MS)¼ +1] **Expected: 0.667**	0.679*** (0.0722) [0.533–0.825]	0.706*** (0.0747) [0.557–0.855]
Constant **Expected: 0.000**	0.0148 (0.0481) [–0.0826–0.112]	–0.0275 (0.0550) [–0.137–0.0823]
Observations	285	389
R-squared	0.618	0.486
rmse	0.108	0.132

Robust standard errors in parentheses.
95 percent confidence intervals in brackets.

In Table 8.1 we see output of two regression tests of Equation 8.1. In Regression One, the sample consists of parliamentary democracies with simple electoral systems. This is the subset for which we have the strongest expectations, because we derived the Seat Product Model, including the extension to nationwide electoral party systems in this chapter, with simple parliamentary systems in mind. The result confirms Equation 8.1, as 0.679 is hardly different from the expected 0.667 and constant of 0.0148 is not statistically distinguishable from zero.

Regression Two adds in the presidential systems. The result does not change greatly; the expected coefficient of 2/3 remains within the 95 percent confidence interval of the regression's coefficient, even though the latter increases to 0.706. The constant remains effectively zero. The somewhat reduced fit reminds us again that presidential systems are more variable than parliamentary. We will discuss this matter in some detail in Chapter 11. Nonetheless, both regressions show that for simple electoral systems, if we know average district magnitude (M) and assembly size (S), we can estimate its effective number of vote-earning parties (N_V). The degree of accuracy of the fit to worldwide averages of many systems is remarkable.

So far then, we have achieved much, as existing approaches to explaining the effective number of vote-earning parties in national elections offer only quite vague answers to the question of how high we should expect N_V to be. Moreover, they typically include some index of social heterogeneity in their models, which has various problems for generalizability of results: it is difficult to measure accurately, is only a proxy for the various social factors that might lead to demand for additional parties, and is not always available for all countries. If we can have success predicting electoral party systems from just a country's assembly size and its mean district magnitude, we should regard that as a significant advance. In Chapter 15, we will offer extended tests that include two-tier systems as well as ethnic diversity.

HOW ELECTORAL SYSTEM IS CONGRUENT WITH CURRENT POLITICS

In Chapter 7, we showed a schematic, Figure 7.1, which suggested that the electoral system has a direct impact on seats and only an indirect impact on votes. The latter effect is indirect because votes are more directly affected by current politics and culture. Why then does the purely institutional model $N_V=[(MS)^{1/4}+1]^{2/3}$ (Equation 8.1) almost agree with the statistical best-fit (as reported in Table 8.1)? Does the psychological effect of the electoral system reach even beyond votes, into current politics and culture? Partly this is so indeed: politicians, voters, and commentators are very much aware of the limitations imposed by electoral rules. But there is also another reason.

Rather than put history into the same box with current politics, maybe we should place a separate box, "Original political culture," underneath the scheme in Figure 7.1, as we do now in Figure 8.5. This means political culture at the time the values of S and M were chosen, which includes many factors that are difficult to measure. We will attempt one such measure in Chapter 15, through the inclusion of the effective number of ethnic groups in our regression tests. While assembly size is rather tightly constrained by size of population (Taagepera and Shugart, 1989a: 173–183; see also Figure 2.1 of this book), original political culture very much determined the choice of district magnitude. Here we mean more than a country's ethnic diversity, which is the noninstitutional factor most often included in cross-national regressions by other authors. We mean something more difficult to theorize about systematically, such as prior political legacies of the country or enduring attitudes about how politics should work.

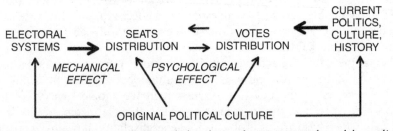

FIGURE 8.5 How current politics and the electoral system are shaped by political culture

For example, countries that were once colonies of the UK tend to retain a majoritarian culture and opt for $M=1$, FPTP. Notably, this is so whether ethnic diversity is unusually low (as in Jamaica) or the highest of any long-term democracy (India). One key exception is New Zealand, which changed to a proportional system in the 1990s; there are various indications that the country's norms about how politics should work were shifting in a more consensual direction around the time that the process of electoral reform was underway (Blais and Shugart, 2008; Vowles, 2008).

On the other hand, countries with a deeper tradition of political and social accommodation typically opted for large-M or two-tier systems, often early in their process of democratization. The precise reasons for why some countries adopted proportional representation remain controversial, and are not of direct concern to us (see Boix 2003, Colomer 2005, Ahmed 2013). The political culture that stands behind the adoption of majoritarian or proportional rules becomes the basis of the current culture as well. Thus, the point that is of more immediate concern for us is that part of the success of the Seat Product Model, for both seats and votes, is due to this congruence between M and present culture.

CONCLUSIONS

We have seen that the rule, "strivers are winners plus one," a modified form of Reed's and Cox's well-known $M+1$ rule, provides a reasonable starting point for estimating the effective number of vote-earning parties at the national level (N_V). The model that we derive from this starting point leads to a new concept that we will use again in future chapters: *the number of pertinent vote-earning parties* (N_{V0}). We showed that a model proxies this "phantom" quantity by the actual number of seat-winning parties (N_{S0}), plus one. When we replaced N_{S0} with $(MS)^{1/4}$, which we already had confirmed in Chapter 7, we were able to derive an institutions-only logical model for predicting N_V. Thus we are able to predict worldwide average N_V quite accurately from solely the assembly size and the mean district magnitude. It may seem that it could not be that straightforward – after all, many factors might motivate the formation of political parties and voter response to them. Yet, as shown in this chapter and the preceding one, the seat-winning parties are conditioned by the electoral institutions, and the vote-earning parties tend to follow from the seat-winners in a predictable fashion. Some individual countries deviate from the model appreciably. In these cases the model supplies a benchmark and flags the need to look for factors that cause the deviation.

So far we have modeled the number of parties at the nationwide level, primarily focused on parliamentary democracies with simple electoral systems. Presidential systems will be treated systematically in Chapters 11 and 12, while extension to two-tier systems and consideration of the impact of ethnic diversity is the topic of Chapter 15. Chapter 9 ties the nationwide effects all together into a series of four "basic laws" and extends the logic to another key output variable: deviation from PR.

9

Basic Laws of Party Seats and Votes – and Application to Deviation from Proportionality

What we have reached at this point in the book is a set of *basic laws of party seats and votes*. Each of these laws has been derived in preceding chapters. In this chapter we summarize them and explain how they qualify as laws in the strongest scientific sense of the term. Then we explore how they can be applied to a further quantity of interest, deviation from proportionality. We do not (yet) have a law of how electoral systems connect to deviation, but we have a mathematical expression that draws on the basic laws.

BASIC LAWS OF PARTY SEATS AND VOTES

1 Law of Largest Party Seats

The most likely seat share of the largest party in an elected assembly is $s_1=(MS)^{-1/8}$, where S is the number of seats in the assembly and M is the number of seats in the average district.

2 Law of Number of Assembly Parties

The most likely effective number of parties in an elected assembly is $N_S=(MS)^{1/6}$, where S is the number of seats in the assembly and M is the number of seats in the average district.[1]

In social sciences, the term "law" has been at times conferred rather loosely to empirical quantitative regularities the cause of which remains unknown and even to directional tendencies lacking any quantitative content. The laws above are stronger than that. *First*, they have a logical underpinning. Indeed, they can be derived from probabilistic considerations without any data input. *Second*,

---

[1] What about the number of seat-winning parties, $N_{S0}=(MS)^{1/4}$? While the largest seat share and the effective number of parties can be determined fairly unambiguously, the operational determination of the number of parties winning at least one seat is at the mercy of local parties and independent candidates. Thus we would not claim $N_{S0}=(MS)^{1/4}$ as a law, even while it is an indispensable link in deriving the two laws.

they are confirmed empirically, as being as close to the world median outcomes as one could hope.

These laws are deterministic regarding the average outcome: if you carry out sufficiently many measurements on reasonably fair elections worldwide, the averages will approach $s_1=(MS)^{-1/8}$ and $N_S=(MS)^{1/6}$, respectively. These laws are probabilistic for individual cases, with about one half of outcomes falling short of the average expectation values and about one half exceeding them; however, outcomes far from expectation values are rarer than those close to them.

So far we have applied these laws only to a select group of countries using "simple" electoral rules. There is nothing inherently problematic with that: after all, the law of ideal gases, so basic to physics and chemistry, applies only to a nonexisting ideal entity! In Chapters 15 and 16 we will probe their applicability to other systems that are more complex, but in this chapter the focus remains on simple systems.

These laws enable us to calculate the most likely outcome in a country, *in the absence of any further information* beyond M and S. If we do have further information, we may make further inferences on the direction in which this country would tend to deviate from worldwide expectations.[2]

With more caution, we also put forward two further potential laws.

3 Law of Largest Party Votes

The most likely vote share of the largest party in assembly elections is $v_1=[(MS)^{1/4}+1]^{-1/2}$, where S is the number of seats in the assembly and M is the number of seats in the average district.

4 Law of Number of Electoral Parties

The most likely effective number of parties in assembly elections is $N_V=[(MS)^{1/4}+1]^{2/3}$, where S is the number of seats in the assembly and M is the number of seats in the average district.[3]

The reasons for caution are wider scatter in data and less thorough testing, especially trying to extend these laws to complex systems. Note, however, that this testing has already been more stringent than is the case for many a tendency

---

[2] How do these laws relate to the so-called Duverger's law? Suppose we have $S=256$ and $M=1$. We would expect a largest seat share of 50.0 percent and an effective number of seat-winning parties 2.52. Is the largest party sufficiently large and the number of parties sufficiently low to confirm Duvergerian expectation? This would be a matter of taste, given that the so-called Duverger's law lacks quantitative specificity. Note that an expectation of $s_1=0.50$, as an average, would imply, if the executive were parliamentary, about one half of the time there would be either a minority or coalition government.

[3] Here we have even more reason not to propose $N_{V0}=(MS)^{1/4}+1$ as a law, given the phantom nature of the "pertinent" number of electoral parties, even while $N_{V0}=(MS)^{1/4}+1$ is an indispensable link in deriving the two laws.

loosely called law in social sciences. We prefer to be more demanding in what we call a law, starting with the requirement that it be based on logical deduction and estimation of a specific quantitative relationship, before determining whether it also might be an empirical regularity.

Now, having summarized these basic laws, let us see if we can extend in further directions. The first extension is to another nationwide outcome, deviation from proportionality. Then there will be several further extensions in subsequent chapters.

ELECTORAL RULES AND DEVIATION FROM PROPORTIONALITY

A central concept in the analysis or design of electoral systems is proportionality. In this chapter, we turn our attention to how nationwide electoral system characteristics affect this important outcome of elections. *Deviation from proportionality* means a summary index of the differences between the seat shares and vote shares of parties. Recall from Chapter 4 that the two most widely used measures are:

Loosemore and Hanby's $(1971) D_1 = 0.5\sum|s_i - v_i|$, and

Gallagher's $(1991) D_2 = [0.5\sum(s_i - v_i)^2]^{1/2}$.

Deviation, by either measure, tends to be largest in elections using one-seat districts, especially when assemblies are small, so that Seat Product MS is less than 100. Deviation tends to be smallest for nationwide seat allocation, where S is more than 100 and MS thus more than 10,000. Table 9.1 shows a clear impact of the Seat Product.

Developing a model of just what that effect looks like, however, turns out to be somewhat challenging. In this chapter, we show an approximation that does reasonably well, even though it is not as complete a logical prediction as we have been aiming for with other quantities.

How might we make the relationship between Deviation from PR and MS more specific and quantitative? In Chapter 4, we showed a graph (Figure 4.1) of D_2 against a country's mean district magnitude, M. We suggested that the best fit was approximately

$$D_2 = 0.10M^{-1/3}.$$

TABLE 9.1 *Deviation from PR tends to decrease with increasing Seat Product* MS

MS	Less than 100	100 to 10,000	Over 10,000
Average D_2	0.153	0.069	0.0157
No. of elections	102	155	35

This expression, of course, leaves out the assembly size, S. Moreover, it is purely empirical. Logically a connection to MS should exist, but what would it be? At this stage, we are stretching the limits of our basic approach. We are now several logical steps removed from where we began, going from the number of seat-winning parties to the vote share of the largest. Each step piles up more random scatter. On top of that, taking differences of almost equal values such as s_1 and v_1 makes relative error explode.[4] Such scatter could blur out any impact of Seat Product MS. For successive individual elections, deviation from PR is notoriously fickle, even while the effective number of parties remains practically the same.

Toward Logical Model of Deviation from Proportionality

So far, we are unable to provide a precise logical model for either measure of deviation from proportionality. However, we can approximate one for Gallagher's D_2, as explained in this section.[5] We base it on (s_1-v_1), the difference between the seat and vote shares of the largest party nationwide. The largest party typically has the biggest impact of all parties on D_2. When only one party has a greater share of seats than of votes and only one other party has a lesser share of seats than of votes, then $D_2=[0.5\Sigma(s_i-v_i)^2]^{1/2}$ boils down to this difference, $|s_1-v_1|$. Most often the party with the most votes gets a bonus in seats, making the difference a positive value. Then $D_2=s_1-v_1$. This is our base line.[6] If several other parties have losses ($s_i<v_i$), then D_2 is less than s_1-v_1. But it also may happen that several large parties have bonuses ($s_i>v_i$,) at the expense of a single major loser; then D_2 is more than s_1-v_1. So we settle on

---

[4] Assume $M=10$ and $S=100$, so that $MS=1000$. The expected largest seat share is $s_1=0.42$, and the largest vote share is $v_1=0.39$, so that $s_1-v_1=0.03$. Assume a relative error of just ±2 percent on s_1 and v_1: they can range from 0.412 to 0.429, and from 0.382 to 0.398, respectively. Then s_1-v_1 could range from as little as 0.014 to as much as 0.047. Indeed, an error range of ±4 percent on s_1 and v_1 could turn s_1-v_1 negative.

[5] While we consider Loosemore-Hanby's index to be at least as good a measure as D_2, we have found no way to start a logical model for D_1. Empirically, Taagepera (2007: 79) observes that $D_1 \approx D_2^{.863}$, on the average, but we have no logical model to account for such relationship. Taagepera and Shugart (1989a: 270–273) show a good fit between D_1 and the ratio $r=(N_V-N_S)/N_V$; namely $r=(D_1-.02)^{0.7}$. We still do not know the logical reason behind it.

[6] Lijphart (1994: 160–162) listed stable period averages in various countries for D_2 and also for an even simpler measure of deviation from PR: the largest single gap, $D_\infty=\max|s_i-v_i|$. Taagepera (2007: 67) observed that the values of D_2 and D_∞ are fairly close. Most often D_2 falls slightly short of D_∞, but sometimes even exceeds it. So we take a leap of faith and assume that $D_2 \approx D_\infty$. Often the largest party supplies this maximum gap: $D_\infty=s_1-v_1$. Yet it also happens that the losses of a third party exceed the gains of the largest party. It can even happen that s_1-v_1 is negative in an individual election. As we strive for general average relationships, we'll ignore these very rare cases.

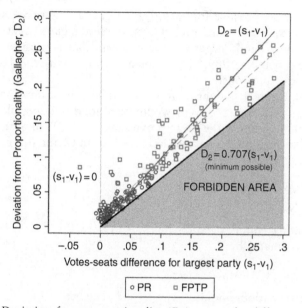

FIGURE 9.1 Deviation from proportionality (D_2) versus the difference between the largest party's seat and vote shares (s_1-v_1)

$$D_2 \approx s_1 - v_1,$$

even though this assumption is quite questionable.[7]

Despite being questionable, $D_2 \approx s_1-v_1$ is clearly close to being accurate, as seen in Figure 9.1. This figure also shows the minimum possible D_2, for given s_1-v_1, as the thick black line. This line represents the equation,

$$D_2 = 0.707(s_1 - v_1).$$

No election result could be below this line.[8] The statistical best fit, $D_2=0.0138 + 0.845(s_1-v_1)$ [$R^2=0.913$]. This best fit is depicted in Figure 9.1 as the dashed line. It deviates from $D_2=s_1-v_1$ in an expected way. Indeed, when (s_1-v_1) happens to be a perfect 0, it makes sense for D_2 to be slightly positive (hence intercept 0.0138), because s_i-v_i is still likely to be off perfect 0 for other parties. On the other hand, a very large s_1-v_1 materializes most easily when a large party faces split opposition. Evenly split opposition would lead to $D_2=0.867(s_1-v_1)$; the observed slope, 0.845, is close.

---

[7] When relationships cannot be firmly modeled, one has the choice: give up or do one's best. Giving up leaves us with nothing. Trying may lead to partial advance, because the disparities between the tentative model and the actual average pattern may offer hints of how to improve the model.

[8] Mathematically, this lower limit is approached when the large party faces a profusion of tiny parties that win no seats, so that $(s_i-v_i)^2$ approaches 0 for each of them. Then $D_2=[0.5(s_1-v_1)^2]^{1/2}=0.707(s_1-v_1)$.

It is, of course, possible for s_1-v_1 to be negative. Figure 9.1 shows a light vertical line at $s_1-v_1=0$ in order to allow us to see at a glance that most cases of $s_1-v_1<0$ are only barely negative. The one case that is most visibly into the negative range is India 1989.[9] The graph also shows, with the dashed line, the best fit, reported previously.

In general, Figure 9.1 confirms, it is not as ridiculous as it might have seemed initially to suggest that $D_2 \approx s_1-v_1$ would be a good building block. Thus we might be able to connect the average expectation for D_2 to Seat Product MS. This should be possible because we have seen (from Chapters 7 and 8) that, on the average,

$$s_1 = (MS)^{-1/8} \text{ and}$$
$$v_1 = (N_{S0} + 1)^{-1/2} = [(MS)^{1/4} + 1]^{-1/2}.$$

The resulting complex expression $s_1 - v_1 = (MS)^{-1/8} - [(MS)^{1/4} + 1]^{-1/2}$ can be approximated by

$$s_1 - v_1 = (1/3)(MS)^{-1/3}. \tag{9.1}$$

This approximation holds within ±6 percent of the value of $(MS)^{-1/8} - [(MS)^{1/4} + 1]^{-1/2}$, throughout the observed range of MS. The coefficient and exponent (which just happen to have the same numerical value) are not empirical (data based) but result from a purely mathematical transformation.[10] To the extent $D_2=s_1-v_1$ holds, we would then also expect

$$D_2 = (1/3)(MS)^{-1/3}. \tag{9.2}$$

We can graph both the MS-derived expectation for largest party seat–vote difference (s_1-v_1) and the complete value of deviation from proportionality (D_2) against the Seat Product, MS. Figure 9.2 shows the direct graphing of s_1-v_1 against MS. The actual values of s_1-v_1 tend to exceed slightly the logical expectation at low MS and to fall slightly below it at very high MS.[11]

Figure 9.2 also differentiates by electoral formula. The FPTP systems are shown with squares. PR systems are with circles; the circles are filled in if the formula is D'Hondt, but open otherwise.[12] The impact of PR formula is not

---

[9] In this election, the Indian National Congress party won only 36.15 percent of the seats despite 39.5 percent of the votes. The other cases, all with $-0.004<(s_1-v_1)<0$, are Finland, 1951, and the Swiss elections of 1959 and 1963.

[10] A slightly better fit to $(MS)^{-1/8}-[(MS)^{1/4}+1]^{-1/2}$ is possible, but keeping to simple values of coefficients has its advantages.

[11] It is worth calling attention to the significant outlier at $MS=36$, $s_1-v_1=0.001$, as this is Trinidad and Tobago, 2001, one of the elections discussed in Chapter 5.

[12] The non-D'Hondt PR formulas are all either Hare quota with largest remainders or Modified Ste.-Laguë, with the exception of Brazil and Finland, which use hybrid D'Hondt/SNTV as explained in the appendix to Chapter 7.

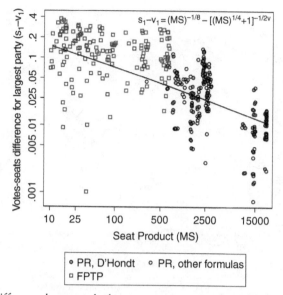

FIGURE 9.2 Difference between the largest party's seat and vote shares (s_1-v_1) and the seat product (MS)

obvious, although there is some tendency of non-D'Hondt cases to be lower, for a given MS, than are the D'Hondt elections.

In Figure 9.3, we graph D_2 against MS. Equation 9.2, plotted as the dashed line, is visibly too low. However, the important thing is that the slope, $-1/3$, that we showed in Figure 9.2 still clearly works. What we find is that the fit is better fit with approximately $D_2=1.5(s_1-v_1)$, hence

$$D_2 = 0.50(MS)^{-1/3}, \qquad\qquad (9.3)$$

shown as the solid line in Figure 9.3. (See regression in the chapter appendix.)

Figure 9.3 again differentiates FPTP (squares) from PR (circles), and uses filled-in circles for D'Hondt.[13] It is again apparent that PR formula is less important than the Seat Product. Nonetheless, note that the data points for Israel (labeled in the graph), which is among the few countries to have used D'Hondt and Hare quota and largest remainders in different times periods with the same Seat Product (Hazan et al., 2018), shows a clear differentiation by formula, with the D'Hondt elections exhibiting higher D_2.

It is from the connection to MS in Equation 9.3 that we derived the expression, $D_2=0.10\ M^{-1/3}$, reported way back in Chapter 4, before we had

---

[13] Only parliamentary systems are shown; a regression in the appendix includes presidential systems and provides support for Equation 9.3.

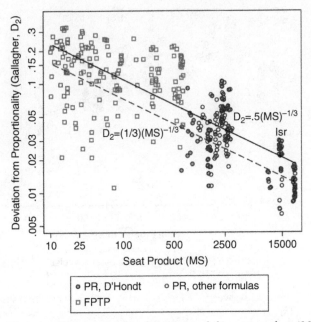

FIGURE 9.3 Deviation from proportionality (D_2) and the seat product (MS)

introduced the concept of the Seat Product. Thus the same slope works to connect D_2 to a country's mean magnitude or to its Seat Product.[14] The slope itself is, within the range of actual assembly sizes, an almost precise match to a logically derived difference of seats and votes for the largest party – that is, derived from MS, the Seat Product (Equation 9.2).

In both Figures 9.2 and 9.3 we see one noteworthy cluster of data points under FPTP that are especially far off the graph's solid line. The set of points with $MS>450$ and both s_1-v_1 and D_2 greater than 0.125 consists entirely of elections from India and the UK. These are the FPTP parliamentary systems with the largest assemblies, although other elections in these countries are not so far off the line. Among the PR systems, a few elections in Spain have unusually high s_1-v_1 and D_2. In Spain, as in India and the UK, low magnitude and a large number of districts both tend allow individual district-level deviations to accumulate if the leading party performs unusually well at converting votes into seats.

Recall that $N_S=(MS)^{1/6}$, as our best average estimate (Chapter 7). It then would follow from $D_2=0.50(MS)^{-1/3}$ that

$$D_2 = 0.50/N_S^2 \tag{9.4}$$

---

[14] More specifically, for this sample, mean S is around 200. Applying Equation 10.3 with this value yields $D_2 =0.09M^{-1/3}$; we round the constant to 0.10 for purposes of the discussion in Chapter 4.

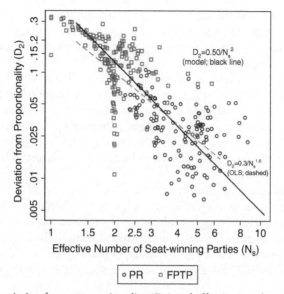

FIGURE 9.4 Deviation from proportionality (D_2) and effective number of seat-winning parties (N_S)

The causal linkage between D_2 and N_S is as indirect as it could be. Indeed, the closest common "ancestor" that enters their derivation from MS is N_{S0} (and partly, s_1). Therefore, one might expect enormous scatter when graphing D_2 against N_S. However, the fit is quite good, even if a best fit from an OLS regression (the output of which is in the chapter appendix) diverges somewhat from Equation 9.4, as we see in Figure 9.4. The solid line in the figure is Equation 9.4.

Thus we have a systematic relationship between D_2 and N_S, although we hesitate to call it a law, because the relationship of D_2 to MS is itself somewhat short of a law (as shown earlier in this chapter). In retrospect, some inverse relationship between D_2 and N_S makes sense. A very low number of assembly parties – which is most likely to result from FPTP (see square symbols in Figure 9.4) – is likely to result from heavy disproportionality, while a very high number of parties can make it into the assembly only when disproportionality is low.[15]

CONCLUSION: CONNECTIONS AMONG CONNECTIONS

Starting with the institutional Seat Product, we have been able to identify four basic laws of party votes and seats. These have been derived and tested on

---

[15] Previous graphing of disproportionality against the number of parties (e.g., Taagepera and Shugart 1989a:107 and Taagepera 2007: 68) missed this relationship because they graphed against the number of electoral parties, N_V, rather than N_S.

nationwide party systems in the preceding two chapters, and were summarized at the beginning of the present chapter. Then, in this chapter, we apply them to an index that indicates a core question for assessing electoral-system performance: proportionality.

When we apply the laws to the index of Deviation from PR (D_2, introduced by Gallagher, 1991), we step on shakier ground. Seat structure follows directly from the Seat Product (Chapter 7). Vote structure follows from seat structure and from the bold and risky "plus one" hypothesis (Chapter 8). Whatever discrepancies occur at the seats level will be transmitted to the votes level, possibly magnified. When we reach deviation from PR, the subtraction of vote shares from seat shares can have two effects.

First, it can cause random error to explode. We find that scatter increases indeed, but remains manageable. Second, tiny but systematic deviations from the "plus one" hypothesis regarding votes can systematically shift even the average of the pattern for deviation from PR, especially in conjunction with deviations from the assumption that D_2 equals $s_1 - v_1$. We do observe such a shift: in Figure 9.3, D_2 tends to be systematically larger than expected, by a factor of 1.5.

Further fine-tuning of the model for D_2 would be potentially useful.[16] Yet this should not obscure the fact that the broad dependence of deviation from PR on the number of seats that are available in the assembly and districts has become predictable. If a country with given M and S considers altering either of them, we can estimate the extent to which it would change the deviation from PR. Note that much of the scatter in Figure 9.3 is due to country-specific factors that would remain the same for the given country. When its MS is altered, its D_2 can be expected to move on a curve parallel to the worldwide average curve.

We thus stand at a point at which a panoply of nationwide party system effects can be linked together, all back to the most basic of institutional inputs, assembly size (S) and mean district magnitude (M) – at least for simple systems. In Chapter 15 we will offer an extension with one more parameter, which allows us to estimate values in two-tier compensatory PR systems. In Chapter 16 we consider other complex types of electoral systems, and find that at least some of them show patterns that are predictable as if they were simple after all.

In Figure 9.5, we offer a schematic of how the various quantities derive ultimately from the Seat Product, MS. Table 9.2 summarizes the key equations linking the quantities together. Table 9.3 gives examples of what the equations would produce as expected outputs for given values of MS. We already have seen that these generally conform to real-world averages (in previous chapters, except for D_2, which was shown in this chapter).

---

[16] Plus we lack a model to predict Loosemore-Hanby's D_1. This is not too severe a deficiency, given that D_2 has become the more prevalent measure.

TABLE 9.2 *Nationwide equations for the Seat Product Model*

Nationwide seats

$N_{S0} = (MS)^{1/4}$

$s_1 = (MS)^{-1/8}$ BASIC LAW 1 $\qquad\qquad s_1 = N_{S0}^{-1/2}$

$N_S = (MS)^{1/6}$ BASIC LAW 2 $\qquad\qquad N_S = N_{S0}^{2/3} \qquad\qquad N_S = s_1^{-4/3}$

Nationwide vote-seat interaction

$N_{V0} = N_{S0} + 1$

$v_1 = (N_{S0}+1)^{-1/2} \qquad\qquad\qquad v_1 = (s_1^{-2} + 1)^{-1/2}$

$N_V = (N_{S0}+1)^{2/3} \qquad\qquad\qquad N_V = (s_1^{-2} + 1)^{2/3} \qquad N_V = [N_S^{3/2}+1]^{2/3}$

Nationwide votes

$N_{V0} = (MS)^{1/4} + 1$

$v_1 = [(MS)^{1/4}+1]^{-1/2}$ BASIC LAW 3 $\qquad v_1 = N_{V0}^{-1/2}$

$N_V = [(MS)^{1/4}+1]^{2/3}$ BASIC LAW 4 $\qquad N_V = N_{V0}^{2/3} \qquad\qquad N_V = v_1^{-4/3}$

Nationwide deviation from proportional representation

$s_1 - v_1 = (1/3)(MS)^{-1/3}$ [theoretical]

$D_2 = 0.50(MS)^{-1/3}$ [empirically adjusted coefficient]

The four basic laws and their antecedents are shown in bold; the rest follows from algebra.

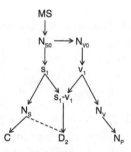

FIGURE 9.5 Schematic of quantities deriving from the Seat Product

The basic sequence shown on the left side of Figure 9.5, $MS \rightarrow N_{S0} \rightarrow s_1 \rightarrow N_S$, was tested in Chapter 7 (see also Taagepera 2007). Once "winners plus one" is introduced (Chapter 8), we repeat the basic sequence $N_{S0} \rightarrow s_1 \rightarrow N_S$ on the right side of the schematic, for measures based on votes: $N_{V0} \rightarrow v_1 \rightarrow N_V$. Finally, $s_1 - v_1$ joins the two strands, and D_2 needs further and fuzzier juggling. The pattern is symmetrical, apart from MS directly impacting seats, not votes.

Each step involves noise (data scatter). We are estimating predictions from predictions. Thus, as one graphs and regresses against each other factors several steps away, one might expect increasing scatter, as the number of

TABLE 9.3 *Average expectations at various levels of* **MS**

MS	1	10	100	1000	10,000	100,000
$s_1 = (MS)^{-1/8}$	1	0.750	0.562	0.422	0.316	0.237
$v_1 = [(MS)^{1/4}+1]^{-1/2}$	0.707	0.600	0.490	0.389	0.302	0.231
$N_S=(MS)^{1/6}$	1	1.468	2.154	3.162	4.642	6.813
$N_V=[(MS)^{1/4}+1]^{2/3}$	1.587	1.976	2.588	3.527	4.946	7.066
$D_2=0.5(MS)^{-1/3}$	0.5	0.232	0.108	0.050	0.023	0.011

steps increases. But this is not quite so. Since N_S and N_V are five steps removed, huge scatter might be expected on this account. Yet it stands to reason that they cannot diverge widely and just randomly. The same applies to s_1 and v_1, three steps removed. The parallel nature of $N_{S0} \rightarrow s_1 \rightarrow N_S$ and $N_{V0} \rightarrow v_1 \rightarrow N_V$ may keep their fluctuations in line, even though this is hard to demonstrate.

In contrast, $s_1 - v_1$, so close to both s_1 and v_1, would offer much more scatter, when graphed against either s_1 or v_1, compared to s_1 graphed against v_1. This is the effect of subtracting rather similar quantities. Indeed, the closer the systematic parts of s_1 and v_1 are, the more random their relative difference becomes.

The eagle-eyed reader might notice an entirely new quantity connected to N_V out on the right of Figure 9.5: "N_P." This refers to the effective number of presidential candidates. We have noted in both Chapters 7 and 8 that quantities such as N_S and N_V in presidential systems are somewhat more scattered than is the case for parliamentary systems. Nonetheless, we have stressed, there is no need for a systematically different approach to presidential systems. The existence of a politically significant, elected office of the presidency has consequences for the party system, but they are less distinct in their patterns than may be expected. In fact, in Chapter 11 we are able to support the very bold claim that the Seat Product can predict the values of N_P, too. This is remarkable, given that the Seat Product is a feature of the assembly, not of the presidency. Yet what we will show in Chapter 11 is that for presidential democracies the Seat Product actually predicts trends in N_P better than it predicts assembly party-system quantities such as N_S and N_V! The two core institutional parameters, M and S, really are fundamental.

The last feature on the lower left in Figure 9.5 is cabinet duration (C), derived from the effective number of assembly parties, as indicated in Chapter 7. While it is outside the direct focus of the present book, cabinet duration extends the predictive power of the Seat Product from electoral to governmental realm, if the executive type is parliamentary. Note also the dashed line joining

N_S to D_2: while there is no direct causal link between the two, the previous logical relationships imply a simple equation joining the two (as in Figure 9.4).

We have now completed our set of chapters on the basic models for nationwide party systems, although we will come back to them in Part III (on presidential systems) and Part V (where we analyze complex systems). While understanding the nationwide level is critical, it is nonetheless the case that most electoral systems consist of numerous districts, in each one of which a contest among several parties takes place. To account for the district level, Chapter 10 shows how to model the impact of these nationwide factors on those multiple districts that comprise what we think of as "the electoral system".

What we will demonstrate in Chapter 10 is that same schematic depicted for the nationwide party system in Figure 9.5 also recurs at the district level. It is perhaps obvious that one of the core institutional parameters, M, would be critical at the district level. What is less obvious is that S – a nationwide feature by definition – also would be. Yet we will see that the impact of M depends on how much of a share of the country's total S any given district represents.

Appendix to Chapter 9

In this chapter we observe that

$$s_1 - v_1 = (MS)^{-1/8} - [(MS)^{1/4} + 1]^{-1/2} \approx (1/3)(MS)^{-1/3} \qquad (9.1)$$

as a close approximation.[17] We further suggest

$$D_2 = (1/3)(MS)^{-1/3} \qquad (9.2)$$

Equation 9.2 is tested by Regression One in **Table 9.A1**. The estimated coefficient is very near the expected, –0.333. The constant term should be – 0.477 (the log of 1/3). While this is within the confidence interval, a clearly better fit is obtained by $D_2 = 0.50(MS)^{-1/3}$ (Equation 9.3), as we saw in Figure 9.3. This revised intercept would be –0.301 (the log of 0.5), and is closer to the regression-estimated constant.

Regression Two in Table 9.A1 tests Equation 9.4, which states that $D_2 = 0.50/N_S^2$. The regression output only partially supports the result, as neither expected coefficient is within the confidence intervals. However, as shown in Figure 9.4, the best fit derived from Regression Three is not greatly divergent from Equation 9.4. More importantly, we are on firm logical ground with both the slope of –1/3 in Equation 9.2 and, of course, the slope of 1/6 in the

---

[17] If graphed, the quantities derived from $(MS)^{-1/8}-[(MS)^{1/4}+1]^{-1/2}$ and $(1/3)(MS)^{-1/3}$ map almost perfectly on to an equality line; they are correlated at 0.994.

TABLE 9.A1 *Regressions for Deviation from Proportionality* (D_2)

	(1)	(2)
logMS	-0.322	
Expected: -0.333	(0.0250)	
	[-0.372 – -0.271]	
logN_S		-1.551
Expected: -2.0		(0.131)
		[-1.816 – -1.286]
Constant	-0.362	-0.514
Expected: see text	(0.0622)	(0.0474)
	[-0.488 – -0.236]	[-0.609 – -0.418]
Observations	295	295
R-squared	0.584	0.594

SPM, deriving N_S from MS. Thus we must have –2 in Equation 9.4. If we recalculate the intercept with the coefficient on logN_S forced to be –2, we obtain an intercept of –0.328, which (unlogged) is 0.470. This is so close to 0.50 that we would not allow the regression's estimated confidence intervals to override Equation 9.4.

10

All Politics Is National? How "Embeddedness" in a National Assembly System Shapes Votes and Seats in a District

In the 2015 Canadian election, the Green Party received 3.5 percent of the vote nationwide. Yet it won only one seat. The result is perhaps not a surprise. After all, the country uses the FPTP electoral system, and normally we do not expect small parties to gain many seats in such systems. In fact, what is perhaps most surprising is that the party ran some semblance of a national campaign despite being plausibly competitive in only a very few districts.[1] Why would a party run candidates and campaign where it can't win? One plausible reason, we suggest, is that it needs to show viability as a national party. It is not enough to emphasize local focus, or for a party to concentrate on a few places where it can win, because the local district is part of the national assembly election and most voters will be thinking of national politics.[2] That is the theme of this chapter.

The puzzle of national campaigning despite viability in only some districts is not only a feature of FPTP politics. In fact, most PR systems also use districts (although, by definition, districts in such systems will be multiseat[3]). In these systems, too, we may see parties entering in districts all around the country despite having a realistic chance at winning a seat in only a few places.

Consider the case of another Green Party, this time in Czechia (Czech Republic). In the 2006 election, this party won just 6.3 percent of the vote nationwide. The Czech electoral system is a simple PR system, with fourteen districts of highly varying magnitude, ranging from eight to twenty-five. The Green Party obtained its six seats (out of 200) in just five of these

---

[1] For instance, it ran a candidate in every district, and according to the CBC's *Tracking the Leaders* interactive map, the Green Party leader visited constituencies in several provinces across the country, in few of which it came anywhere near victory in either 2015 or the prior (2011) election (www.cbc.ca/news/multimedia/map-tracking-the-leaders-1.3081740).

[2] We do not claim that all parties act this way; there are, of course, strictly regional parties like the Bloc Quebecois in Canada or the Scottish National Party in the UK. We are referring to parties that claim to speak to national issues.

[3] A few otherwise PR systems have one or two districts that elect just one member (examples include the Åland Islands district in Finland, Madre de Dios in Peru, and the districts of Ceuta and Melilla in Spain).

districts. Nonetheless, there were only two districts in which the party failed to collect at least 5 percent of the vote. One of these (Moravia) was a district in which it won a seat, thanks to the very high magnitude, $M=23$. Yet the party won 6.7 percent of the vote in the lowest-magnitude district (Krlovy, $M=4$) despite having no realistic chance of a seat, and 6 percent or more in districts where magnitudes of ten to thirteen made a seat unlikely. This party was recognized from opinion polls as being assured of having sufficient nationwide support to enter parliament. Yet clearly many voters were willing to vote for this national party even in districts where a vote for it would be objectively "wasted," in that it would be unlikely to help the party win *in the voter's own district.*

The examples just given were of Green parties, a type of party found in many countries and advocating socially liberal and proenvironmental policies. They make good examples for the relationship between electoral systems and voting behavior because of their similarity in approach to politics across a wide range of countries (Spoon 2011, Belden n.d.). Perhaps one might object, however, that their voters are just idealistic and not motivated by winning seats. We doubt this – the Canadian Greens campaign around how they can make a difference in parliament, and the Czech party even entered into a coalition government following the 2006 election – but we can offer one more example from a very different type of party.

In Albania, the Republican Party, a conservative party emulating its American namesake, was a fairly minor party in the 2013 election. It won just 3.1 percent of the vote and three of the 140 seats. Albania also uses a simple PR system (first adopted in 2009, after a period of "mixed-member" rules). As in Czechia, district magnitude is highly variable: the twelve districts elect from four to thirty-two seats. The Republicans won one seat in each of three districts (with magnitudes of thirteen, fourteen, and thirty-two). Yet they obtained vote shares greater than their nationwide share in four other districts in which their prospects for seats would have been very bleak, including Kukis ($M=4$) and Gjirokastir ($M=5$).

In each of these cases, we see parties running and winning substantial vote shares even where they could not have expected to win. Each of these has seats elsewhere in the country, and therefore a reasonably secure hold on parliamentary representation. The conclusion we can draw from these examples, and many others we could have mentioned, is that voters are often motivated by national politics even when they vote in electoral systems where votes are used exclusively for allocating seats within self-contained electoral districts. The implication is that *all politics is national*, at least in the sense of electoral actors – party leaders, candidates, and voters – cueing on nationally viable parties even when they surely will not win locally. This chapter is about how the national affects the local. We analyze outcomes at the district level, but with a systematic focus on how the national electoral system shapes the local competition for seats and votes.

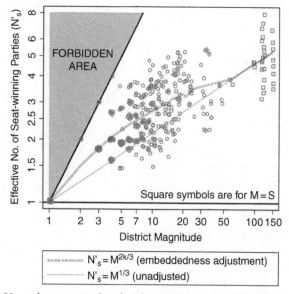

FIGURE 10.1 How the magnitude of a district shapes the effective number of seat-winning parties

Before turning to the logic, let us first see why the district level can be understood only with reference to the national. The following two graphs serve to illustrate the broader point. Figure 10.1 shows how the effective number of seat-winning parties in a district is related to magnitude. This graph is comparable to Figure 7.2, which showed the nationwide effective number of seat-winning parties (N_S) graphed against the Seat Product, MS. Indeed, inside a single district, the reasoning that led to $N_S=(MS)^{1/6}$ would lead to $N'_S=M^{1/3}$. But in Figure 10.1 this equation, plotted via the light solid line, fits only for nationwide single districts, where $M=S$ (plotted with square symbols). When districts are embedded in a larger country, they tend to a higher effective number of parties than the simple model would predict. Why is that? Because nationwide politics enters the game.

One might expect the district-level model to be simpler than the nationwide. But this is not so when the district is *embedded* in a nationwide context which affects the district. Indeed, the model here shows, via the thick dotted curve, a twisted path produced by the equation, $N'_S=M^{2k/3}$, where the parameter k depends on the relative weight of this district within the country's entire assembly. There will be many graphs in this chapter that have a thick dotted curve like this one. While the derivation of this specific curve will be explained later, we must emphasize at the outset that curves of this sort that we plot in this chapter (and in Chapter 14) are not post hoc best fits. Rather, they represent a logical model, plotting the y-axis variable at a given value of the x-axis

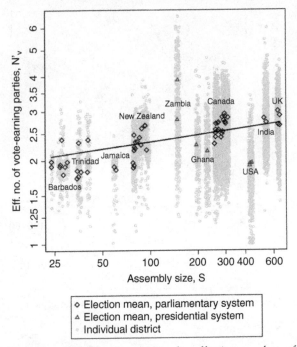

FIGURE 10.2 How the assembly size shapes the effective number of vote-winning parties in single-seat districts

variable and this new parameter, k, that will be central to the mission of this chapter and depends both on M and S.

The logical model curve shifts towards being identical to the straight line near the right side of the graph. Where the curve and line converge marks the shift from relatively small districts where $M \ll S$ to nationwide single district where $M=S$. The more complete logically derived model (which accounts for nationwide impact) can be seen to fit the average trend in both regions. Thus, Figure 10.1 reveals that *we need a somewhat complex model to make sense of the district level* effective number of seat-winning parties – even in a "simple" electoral system in which all seats are allocated in districts (i.e., without a second tier – a yet more complex matter that we return to later).

Our second preliminary graph is Figure 10.2. It shows something perhaps very surprising: the effective number of *vote*-earning parties at the district level in FPTP systems as a function of assembly size. It is generally held that the number of parties in a single-seat district tends to be around two; that is the claim of "Duverger's law." Let us focus initially on the diamond symbols in the graph, which show the mean value for each election in a parliamentary system. We can see that this mean tends to be around two, *as long as the assembly is small*. However, as assembly size increases, mean N'_V rises such that it tends to be 2.5 or greater in the largest countries.

The line in Figure 10.2 will be explained later. For now suffice to say that it again derives from the parameter k in order to reflect the impact of other districts on the votes constellation of any given district. We will explain the relationship in more detail later, after the logic of how this connection of the district and national features works. The broad point is that, even in – no, especially in – FPTP systems, the average degree of fragmentation of the vote is predicted not by the district magnitude so much as by the assembly size, which is obviously a nationwide factor. The average trend represented by the diamonds in Figure 10.2 could be possible only if many voters did not vote based on the district outcome – as standard coordination-based arguments (e.g., Cox 1997) would have it – but on national politics.[4] That is why this chapter is called "All politics is national?"; how districts are embedded in a national system predicts much of the variance in district-level N'_V.

Figure 10.2 shows each district in our FPTP elections with a light gray circle. The more a given area of the data plot looks like a gray smear instead of a series of discernible circles, the more clustered the observations are in that region. What is clear is that individual districts in any given election can vary wildly around the mean. No broad model could possibly claim to predict what a specific district's effective number of vote-earning parties will be. Nonetheless, there is a systematic relationship of district-level mean N'_V to assembly size, a point never before noted in the vast literature on whether "Duverger's law" accurately captures what goes on at the district level. Notably, the trend in India's two depicted elections (2004 and 2009) also follows the same pattern, despite the fact that India is generally considered as somehow "exceptional" to the general rule of how FPTP behaves. Clearly it is not, at the district level, once we take into account its large assembly size. In fact, if India is exceptional, then so is the UK, a country most political scientists probably think of as a fairly typical representative of its electoral system.

Far more deviant than the UK or India is the United States. The remaining symbols in Figure 10.2 are the triangles that mark the election means for presidential democracies. There are only three presidential countries included. Of all countries in the graph, the US is the most significant outlier. Its mean N'_V, lower than most elections in even the small country of Barbados, is far lower than we should expect for its large assembly. On the other hand, Zambia has one election with an unexpectedly high mean value, while Ghana is closer to fitting the parliamentary pattern. As we have seen before, presidential systems tend to be more variable, but with the exception of the US (and Zambia 2001),

---

[4] For such an argument on the Canadian case, see Johnston (2017).

those that use FPTP are not markedly different from the parliamentary cases. We will now turn to the logic of the national impact on the district level.

THE CONCEPT OF EMBEDDEDNESS

Scholars have claimed over many years that key processes leading to outcomes expected from Duverger's propositions actually occur at the district level. In recent years, there have been significant advances in analyzing district-level electoral data (Moser and Scheiner 2012; Singer 2013). The previous chapters have focused on *national* level measures of effective numbers of parties (seats and votes). Here we aim for a deeper understanding of the factors that impact the adaptation of party systems to the institutional context by focusing on the *district* level. The ultimate aim of this chapter is to tie the national and district levels together, to arrive at an understanding of how the districts in which votes are cast and seats allocated is embedded in the larger electoral system that elects the national legislature.

Everything we have done in the two previous chapters on the national level could be repeated in each district, as if it were a separate state with a nationwide single district. This approach *almost* works, but not quite: the number of parties consistently tends to be somewhat larger than expected, as we saw in Figure 10.1. This is so because nationwide politics interferes with the district-level politics.

The main conclusion of this chapter is that, indeed, at least in reasonably well-established parliamentary democracies with simple electoral systems, it may be true that the districts in which seats actually are allocated have their own local issues and personalities, yet *all politics is national*. By that we mean that a logical model of district-level vote fragmentation can be developed, and confirmed with regression analysis, based on the interplay between national electoral systems (the Seat Product, or its components, assembly size and average district magnitude) and the magnitude of the individual district. In other words, it is not quite accurate to say that the district level is decisive in Duvergerian dynamics. We can model the average trend in a district's effective number of parties, both seats and votes, by knowing its magnitude and the size of the national assembly in which it is embedded.

A key point is that two districts of a given magnitude will display different party-system competitive patterns according to the national systems of which they are a part. This is the sense in which politics can be national even when seat-allocation occurs entirely within local or regional districts. However, this does not mean that there is no room for local politics to enter as well; rather, it means that attempts to model how local electoral systems "project" to the national may be misguided. Rather, we find that we can project in the opposite direction: first model the national system, as we did in earlier chapters, and then model how it projects onto the districts.

We will undertake our analysis of district-level dynamics, and how the national electoral system shapes them, by reference to a dataset consisting of over 11,500 district-level results in 102 elections in sixteen countries. Our analysis will mainly focus on parliamentary (or parliamentary-leaning) executive formats. However, a key point is that – as we already saw at the national level – the district-level dynamics are not fundamentally different in presidential democracies. This is surprising, given how much presidencies are thought to shape the overall political process, but we are able to show that the same basic electoral-system factors shape parliamentary and presidential systems. The latter are, however, more variable, a point we shall return to at several points in this book – especially Chapters 11 and 12.

We use the Belden and Shugart (n.d.) dataset to test and refine several models of how institutions shape party-system fragmentation. Some of the models date back to the late 1980s or early 1990s (e.g., Taagepera and Shugart 1989a, 1993), others are of more recent vintage (Taagepera 2007), and several are original to our current joint work.

Taagepera and Shugart (1993) suggested that the actual number of parties that win at least one seat in each district (N'_{S0}, with the prime mark denoting the district-level measure), should be approximately *the square root of the district's magnitude.*[5] We already tested and confirmed this logical model graphically in Chapter 1 (Figure 1.2) and via regression in Chapter 7, because it is a key building block of the Seat Product Model for predicting nationwide effective number of seat-winning parties (N_S). The relationship of the actual number of seat-winning parties at the district level is our fundamental building block here as well. First, we must consider analytically the notion with which we opened this chapter: that appeals to national viability may affect vote-earning performance at the district level. This is important to consider because if it does so systematically, then we need to take it into account when attempting to predict the district-level effective number of vote-earning parties.

A Logical Model of a District's Embeddedness

In our earlier work (Taagepera and Shugart 1993) we argued that the simple model identified already in Chapter 1 as Equation 1.1,

$$N'_{S0} = M^{0.5},$$

would likely understate the relationship, because it tacitly presumes an isolated district not subject to nationwide, i.e., extra-district, pressures. We proposed an adjustment, based on how a given district is "embedded" in the nationwide electoral system. Here we explain the theoretical notion behind this concept of embeddedness.

---

[5] This is in full agreement with the nationwide $N_{S0}=(MS)^{1/4}$, shown in Chapter 7. Indeed, within the district S is the same as M, so that $(MS)^{1/4}=(M^2)^{1/4}=M^{1/2}$.

In practice we observe an "isolated", or nonembedded, district only in cases where $M=S$. In such cases there is a single nationwide district encompassing the entire assembly electoral system. Examples include Israel, the Netherlands, and San Marino. All other districts are embedded in a national system that consists of some number of other districts.

The notion of embeddedness is that parties that are smaller players in national politics, such as the examples we provided at the start of this chapter, may enter candidates and run campaigns even in low-magnitude districts where they are relatively weak. They do this perhaps to "show the flag" – i.e., to prove that they are in fact *national* parties. Once a party has been set up and is participating in the nationwide debate, and perhaps has won some seats somewhere, the costs to putting up at least minimal effort in other districts are lowered.[6] The theoretical notion of embeddedness is that these efforts and costs to entry are lower in a district of a given magnitude that is one of many districts in a wider assembly electoral system than they would be if the district were isolated.

Imagine a single nationwide district of just five seats; probably few small parties would bother. But now imagine a five-seat district in a 300-seat assembly where the party can win elsewhere, perhaps especially if some other districts have large magnitude. Now the party will tend to allocate some resources away from its strong areas to others, in order to make the point that it is a serious player on the national scene. If this resource-shifting happens, the votes and potentially the seats for other, larger parties, may be suppressed, relative to the "isolated" district of the same magnitude. Some parties other than the largest may win an additional seat in some districts (where $M>1$) beyond what they might have been expected to have won were the district isolated.

In parallel with such flag showing by small parties, nationwide competition by the top-two parties may also spill into districts. Consider two districts with lopsided support, so that seats are likely to divide up as four to one and one to four, respectively; hence $s'_1=0.8$ and $N'_S=1.47$. To appear to be making nationwide effort, it is in both party's interest to shift resources to winning a second seat where they are weak, even at potential cost of sacrificing a seat in their respective strongholds. Then these districts may shift to three to two and two to three, respectively, so that $s'_1=0.6$ and $N'_S=1.92$. Note that in such a case the number of seat-winning parties (N'_{S0}) does not increase. In contrast, small party flag showing might increase N'_{S0}, if it helps some party to win its first seat.

Drawing on this notion of embeddedness, Taagepera and Shugart (1993) argued, a parameter capturing the impact of national politics on the district must reduce to Equation 1.1 when $M/S=1$, but the exponent, 0.5, in that

---

[6] Our logic has affinities to Cox's (1997: 110–111) "economies of scale" argument for the formation of parties.

equation must increase as the M/S ratio becomes smaller. In this way the embeddedness parameter reflects the theoretical point that, the smaller the share of all seats that a given district represents, the more room there is for impact from other districts to affect this district's politics.

We have already seen in Chapter 7 that for the number of parties winning at least one seat, the model without adjustment for embeddedness, i.e., $N'_{S0}=M^{0.5}$, is a good fit. But this lack of necessary adjustment applies only to N'_{S0}. We show in this chapter that adjustment is absolutely needed to make sense of other outcomes of interest, including the *effective* numbers of both seats and votes (as Figures 10.1 and 10.2 at the start of this chapter showed). The details of the derivation of this embeddedness parameter, k, are complex. The resulting formula is:

$$k = 0.5 + 0.2076\log(S/M)/M^{0.25} \qquad (10.1)$$

The formula is baffling,[7] and those readers wanting to see our logic and many steps of calculation should refer to the appendix, where we spell it out in detail. Our next steps here are to show how the parameter, k, improves our prediction of the size of the largest party. From there we move on to the effective number of seat-winning parties, and then on to votes.

FROM THE NUMBER OF PARTIES OF ANY SIZE TO THE SIZE OF THE LARGEST

In order to provide the logical foundation behind the link shown in Figure 10.1, between N'_S and M, we must estimate the seat share of the largest party, s'_1. The *average* fractional seat share of the seat-winning parties must be $1/N'_{S0}$. That is, if there are four parties winning seats, each one averages one quarter of the seats. The fractional share going to the party with the most seats in the given district, s'_1, must be at least this average. The upper limit on s'_1 is 1, when that party wins all the seats.[8] In the absence of other knowledge, the expected average value is again the geometric mean:

$$s'_1 = N'_{S0}{}^{-.5}. \qquad (10.2)$$

That is, the seat share of the largest party in the district should be, on average, the inverse square root of the actual number of seat-winning parties. However, this expression ignores embeddedness. As a result, it would prove to be a poor fit

---

[7] The formula is different from (and, we believe, an improvement on) that in Taagepera and Shugart (1993), but the intuition behind it is the same. This k boils down to 0.5 when $M=S$. It reaches its maximum when $M=1$; then $k=0.5+0.2076\log S$.

[8] More precisely (as mentioned in Chapter 7), it is one, minus one seat for each of $N'_{S0}-1$ remaining parties. This additional complication adds no extra precision to our modeling enterprise, and is thus set aside. For discussion, see Taagepera and Shugart (1993) and Taagepera (2007:135).

to the data.[9] Thus we should run the regression instead with the embeddedness parameter included. When we do so, we are testing whether, instead of $s'_1 = N'^{-.5}_{S0}$, we might have $s'_1 = N'^{-k}_{S0}$.

In order to test the combined impact of N'_{S0} and the district's embeddedness on s'_1, we run the OLS regression on the logarithms with k included in the input variable:

$$\log s'_1 = \alpha + \beta(k\log N'_{S0}).$$

Because of the laws of logarithms and exponents, and if we find the expected α=0, this is equivalent to:

$$s'_1 = N'^{k\beta}_{S0}.$$

If a given district were isolated (i.e., nationwide PR), we already know from the way the national embeddness factor, k, is constructed that $k=0.5$. Thus if our expectations about the relationship between the number of seat-winning parties and the seat share of the largest are correct, we expect $\beta = -1$ to apply to the full sample (and, of course, we expect α=0), such that for any given district, the equation becomes:

$$s'_1 = N'^{-k}_{S0}. \tag{10.3}$$

When we run OLS regression, the result is:

$$\log s'_1 = -0.00016 - 0.990k\log N'_{S0}\,[R^2 = .954].$$

The result[10] offers clear validation of Equation 10.3, which states that the simpler proposed model ($s'_1 = N'^{-.5}_{S0}$) is valid for an isolated district (where k=0.5), but that in embedded districts the size of the largest party is indeed reduced according to the impact of extra-district politics.

Figure 10.3 is a scatterplot of the seat share of the largest party (y-axis) and the actual number of seat-winning parties in each district. The solid light gray line is the simple model, unadjusted for national politics, i.e., $s'_1 = N'^{-.5}_{S0}$ (Equation 10.2). It is obvious that the data trend is below this line. What explains this pattern? Here is where the nationally adjusted Equation 10.3 comes in. This equation is plotted with the thick dotted curve. Like its counterpart in Figure 10.1, this curve does not appear straight because it includes the embeddedness parameter, k. Therefore, it sags lower when the district contains a smaller share of the assembly's total seats. The curve – and

---

[9] If we run a regression to test Equation 10.2, we get: $\log s'_1 = -0.00061 - 0.594 \log N'_{S0}$. The 95 percent confidence interval is –0.622 to –0.566. Thus the logical value of –0.5 for an unadjusted model is not within the confidence interval. This establishes that we need the embeddedness adjustment.

[10] Summaries of regression results are found in the appendix to this chapter. The very high R^2 in this and some other results in this chapter are due to the large concentration of data points from M=1 districts, where N'_{S0} and s'_1 are constrained always to be one.

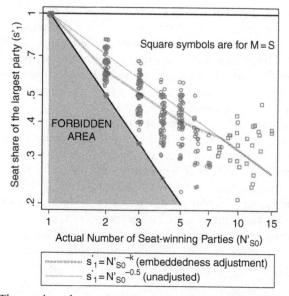

FIGURE 10.3 The number of seat-winning parties and the seat share of the largest party, district level

others like it in this chapter – is not a best fit; rather it represents the logical model.[11]

The observations that cluster well below the straight line are mostly from the lower-magnitude districts in which politics from outside the district has the most potential to impact the distribution of seats within a district. The extra-district political effects exert downward pressure on the size of the largest party. However, as we approach higher values of N'_{SO}, we are encountering more cases of districts that are large and thus represent a larger share of the assembly. By the time we reach $N'_{SO} \geq 7$, we have only cases of $M=S$, as depicted with the squares. At this point, the curve for Figure 10.3 has become identical to Equation 10.2 because there is no extra-district factor to account for when all seats are allocated in a single nationwide district.

Equation 10.3, and the graphed result in Figure 10.3, is consistent with parties' allocation of resources to districts where they are weak, as we hypothesized. However, the impact of such resource shifting is somewhat different from what we predicted in Taagepera and Shugart (1993). There, we suggested it would mean parties tending to win seats that they would not win if

---

[11] More specifically, it is a smoothed curve plotted through the result of Equation 10.3 for the mean value of k at any given value of N'_{SO}. The value of k differs for data points at a given value of the x-variable whenever they involve a different S.

the district were isolated, hence M^k parties instead of $M^{0.5}$. What we have instead is $M^{0.5}$ correctly identifying the trend in the number of seat-winning parties (N'_{S0}), but the seat share of the largest tending to be $s'_1 = N'_{S0}{}^{-k}$, instead of $s'_1 = N'_{S0}{}^{-.5}$. In other words, the effect of extra-district politics does not so much increase the chances of some party going from zero seats to one as it does the chances that one or more of the $M^{0.5}$ seat-winning parties, other than the largest, picks up an additional seat (or seats).[12]

The implication of this finding of the extra-district effect on the largest party is that the knowledge that some party other than the locally strongest is a significant player in national politics may increase that party's support. In fact, it is apparently the second party in the district that tends to benefit from the extra-district effect.[13] The upshot is that the gap between the two largest parties tends to be reduced significantly from what it would be if there were no extra-district effect. In other words, *national politics makes district politics more competitive than it might otherwise be* – another way in which all politics is national. For some details, see the chapter appendix.

Linking the Number of Parties, and Party Sizes, to the Effective Number

The next step is to derive the model that was shown in Figure 10.1 at the start of this chapter, linking the district magnitude and the effective number of seat-winning parties, N'_S. To complete these steps, we first need to connect the seat share of the largest party (s'_1) to district magnitude (M), and then we will connect it to N'_S. The first of these links should be to replace N'_{S0} in Equation 10.3 with $N'_{S0} = M^{.5}$, which would give us:

$$s'_1 = (M^{.5})^{-k} = M^{-.5k}. \tag{10.4}$$

When we run regression on the logs to test Equation 10.4, we find:

$$\log s'_1 = -0.00035 - 0.508(k \log M) \quad [R^2 = .912].$$

The relationship is shown in Figure 10.4, using the same symbol formatting as previous graphs: the solid light gray line represents the expectation without taking account of embeddedness ($s'_1 = M^{-0.25}$), whereas the thicker dotted curve represents Equation 10.4. Obviously we see a fair degree of scatter, but the pattern is confirmed; in particular, if we failed to consider a district's embeddedness, we would overstate the size of the largest party in most districts.

---

[12] If we graph the embeddedness parameter in the relationship of N'_{S0} and M, we find that it predicts too high. Often the value of N'_{S0} is greater than $M^{0.5}$ (see Figure 1.1), yet the average trend is closer to $N'_{S0} = M^{0.5}$ than it is to $N'_{S0} = M^k$. See chapter appendix for details.

[13] We do not attempt to model the size of the second party systematically, as doing so becomes cumbersome.

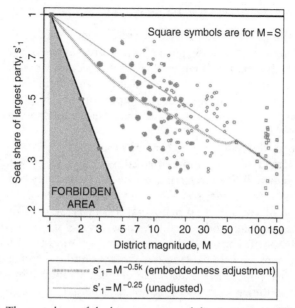

FIGURE 10.4 The seat share of the largest party and district magnitude, district level

Now we can proceed to the final step, from s_1 to N_S, and then to M. Previous analysis[14] has led to the equation, $N_S = s_1'^{-4/3}$, for nationwide values. Then we can proceed to the interlocking models, by trying:

$$N_S' = (M^{-.5k})^{-4/3} = M^{2k/3} \tag{10.5}$$

The regression equation that we obtain is:

$$\log N_S' = 0.00027 + .668(k \log M) \quad [R^2 = .937].$$

This is the curve depicted with the dotted curve in Figure 10.1 at the start of this chapter. It is clearly a better fit than the unadjusted model that does not take account of embeddedness (the solid line in Figure 10.1), which is $N_s' = M^{1/3}$.

Without the logic developed in this chapter, we would never have been able to explain the nonlinear pattern in the district-level results. With our concept of embeddedness, we are able to understand that the district-level effect depends not only on district magnitude, but also on the share of the assembly seats any given district represents. We have thus completed a chain of logical relationships for seat-winning parties at the district level. We are ready to turn to the votes.

---

[14] Discussed in Chapter 7; there the focus was nationwide, but there is no difference in the connection between N_S and s_1 at the two levels. Both quantities are already affected separately by embeddedness, hence the connection between the two remains the same.

HOW WE DERIVE VOTES FROM SEATS AT THE DISTRICT LEVEL

Up to now, this chapter has focused on the district-level distribution of seats. We have demonstrated how parties' seats are shaped by the nationwide system in which a district is embedded. In this section we turn our attention to the votes at the district level; as we did at the nationwide level in Chapter 8, we now deduce votes from seats. An important conclusion of this section is that the votes are affected by the district's embeddedness even more than the seats.

In particular, the system that is generally thought to be most predictable and "simplest" actually is much more affected by extra-district factors, and hence harder to predict. We are referring to the $M=1$, plurality, or FPTP system. Widely seen – from the so-called Duverger's law – as supporting the concentration of votes on two major parties, FPTP systems in fact are often more fragmented than moderate PR systems, *even at the district level*. Why is this? We offer an argument for this strange and – for most scholars of electoral and party systems – inexplicable result. What we find is that it is especially true under FPTP that politics in the district level is heavily shaped by the nationwide system. All politics is apparently national, *especially* when $M=1$ in a large assembly.

As we did in Chapter 8, we start thinking about the votes by reference back to the seats distributions. The basic reason is that it is seats that are physically constrained by institutions – principally district magnitude and assembly size. We build our models of district-level votes distribution using a concept that was already introduced in Chapter 8: the *pertinent vote-earning parties*. The concept is fundamentally the same in district as in national politics.

Pertinent Vote-Earning Parties at the District Level

At the national level (Chapter 8), we established that Equation 8.2,

$$N_{V0} = N_{S0} + 1,$$

was a reasonable estimate for the idea of "number of pertinent vote-earning parties," which we are unable to measure directly. In Chapter 8, we built our tests around the following:

$$N_V = (N_{S0} + 1)^{2/3}.$$

When we turn to the district level, of course, we need to take embeddedness into account. Before we can do so, we must recall (from earlier in this chapter) that we did not need to account for embeddedness to derive the district-level number of seat-winning parties, N'_{S0}. However, we did need it to connect the effective number of seat-winning parties, N'_S, to district magnitude, M (Equation 10.5). Therefore, the implication is that our logical model for the effective number of seat-winning parties, $N_S = N_{S0}^{2/3}$

(Table 9.2), could not work at the district level (i.e., as $N'_S = N'_{S0}{}^{2/3}$). However, the resolution that suggests itself is the following, with inclusion of the embeddedness function:

$$N'_S = N'_{S0}{}^{4k/3}.$$

This is confirmed by OLS regression.[15] The same relationship logically must hold for votes as for seats, meaning we should have $N'_V = N'_{V0}{}^{4k/3}$. In that case, what we expect is:

$$N'_V = (N'_{S0} + 1)^{4k/3} \tag{10.6}$$

We will be testing Equation 10.6 shortly. But wait! There is a complication, and it has to do with the $M=1$ districts – those districts that are supposed to be the most straightforward, according to the so-called Duverger's law. While the relationship between N'_S and N'_{S0} can vary with k, the national embeddedness function, when $M>1$, such variation is impossible when $M=1$. After all, in such a district it must always be the case that $N'_{S0} = N'_S = 1$, independent of how many other districts, of whatever magnitude, the assembly electoral system may contain. We showed in Figure 10.2, at the outset of this chapter, that a district's N'_V has a systematic relationship to the *size of the assembly* in which the district is embedded. A key remaining task of this chapter is to explain this relationship. First, however, let us test Equation 10.6 across the full range of simple electoral systems.

In Figure 10.5, we see the graph of Equation 10.6, in the thick dotted curve. The thick dotted curve plots, for the median value of k at any N'_{S0}, the regression result, which is an uncannily strong confirmation of the model:

$$logN'_V = -.00311 + 1.3355[klog(N'_{S0} + 1)] \quad [R^2 = .233].$$

With the expectation (Equation 10.6) being $4k/3$, we could hardly ask for a better approximation to the logical model. It is also clear that the unadjusted model (solid light gray curve) seriously underestimates what N'_V tends to be, for any given number of seat-winning parties. We must take embeddedness into account.

Despite the good overall fit of Equation 10.6, we should acknowledge that the estimate is visually high for $N'_{S0}=2$. Any attempt to adjust the model to make the curve dip down for cases where there are two seat-winning parties (and perhaps also for three-party districts) would make the model unnecessarily complex. The model fits $N'_{S0}=1$ well; it predicts $N'_V = 2.543$ where the actual mean $N'_V = 2.5954$. There are many more cases of $N'_{S0}=1$ than of $N'_{S0}=2$ (or $N'_{S0}=3$, for that matter). The implication is that either our sample of two-party districts is unusual in some respect, or that there is a systematic "balancing" factor when there are just two parties. Such

---

[15] We get $log N'_S = 0.0000 + 1.304(k \log N'_{S0})$ $[R^2=0.986]$.

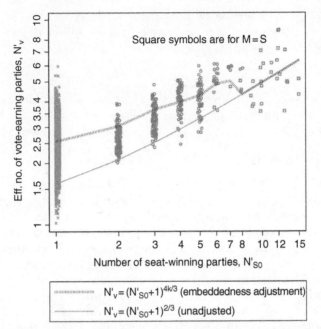

FIGURE 10.5 The actual number of seat-winning parties (N'_{SO}) and the effective number of vote-earning parties (N'_V), with incorporation of district-embeddedness function (k) The thin gray curve is the model without embeddedness: $N'_V = (N'_{SO}+1)^{2/3}$. The thick dotted curve represents Equation 10.7, incorporating embeddedness: $N'_V = (N'_{SO}+1)^{4k/3}$.

a factor would be a further generalization of embeddedness, in that it would imply that voters wanting to vote against the strongest party in their district may tend to boost the second party's votes, pushing N'_V below 2.5 for cases where exactly two parties win seats.

The striking thing is that no such second-party favoring is evident under $M=1$ (such districts represent the overwhelming share of $N'_{SO}=1$ cases); otherwise we would not see the large cluster of observations at $N'_{SO}=1$ for which $N'_V >3$. The implication is that voters face less pressure to boost the second party when only the largest can win than they do when both of them can.[16] While testing this voter response would take us well beyond the scope of this chapter, we offer it as a corrective to the usual assumptions about strategic voting–desertion of trailing parties or candidates to support the preferred one among the top two. Such desertion apparently happens less when $M=1$ than expected, and perhaps less than when two (but not more) parties win locally.

---

[16] There are no districts in our dataset that were contested by only a single party.

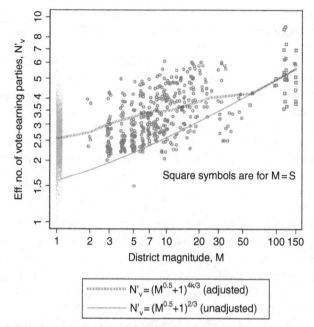

FIGURE 10.6 District magnitude and the effective number of vote-earning parties (N'_V), with incorporation of district-embeddedness function (k)

Now we are ready to connect N'_V to M. Given that we have $N'_{S0}=M^{0.5}$, it should be as simple as inserting $M^{0.5}$ in place of N'_{S0} in Equation 10.6; in other words:

$$N'_V = (M^{0.5} + 1)^{4k/3} \qquad (10.7)$$

In Figure 10.6 we graph district-level effective number of vote-earning parties (N'_V) against district magnitude (M). We see that we clearly must take into account embeddedness. If we failed to account for the assembly size, S, we would have to conclude that our effort at model-building had failed. The solid light gray line in Figure 10.6 shows such a model: $N'_V=(M^{0.5}+1)^{2/3}$, without embeddedness. This is visibly fairly accurate for $M=S$ (squares), but when $M<S$, the vast majority of district-level observations are above this line. The reason is embeddedness. Moreover, the curve for Equation 10.7 is not as steep as the unadjusted model, precisely because extra-district politics pushes up N'_V in lower-magnitude districts, which represent a smaller share of the system's total S seats, than it can when the district is a larger share of the assembly in which it is embedded.[17]

---

[17] In districts with three to five seats we again see our model with embeddedness predicting somewhat higher than the mean, probably due to the "two-party" effect that we discussed in reference to the trend in Figure 10.5. Most cases of exactly two parties occur within this magnitude range.

Nowhere, however, is the embeddedness factor more in evidence than when $M=1$. Once again, we see a high density of single-seat districts at values of $N'_V > 3$; evidently there are many districts that are quite "non-Duvergerian" in their result, yet there are also many such districts with very low values of N'_V. In other words, *the effective number of vote-earning parties is much less predictable precisely in those cases where the district magnitude is most constraining.*

We already saw at the start of this chapter, in Figure 10.2, that we can approximate the trend N'_V for FPTP systems when we graph it against assembly size. The line that we saw in Figure 10.2 represents the equation,

$$N'_V = 2^{(2+.8304\ logS)/3} = 1.587S^{0.08333} = 2^{2/3}S^{1/12}\quad [M=1].\qquad (10.8)$$

Equation 10.8 follows from Equation 10.6, $N'_V = (N'_{S0} +1)^{4k/3}$, when $M=1$ and hence $N'_{S0} =1$. (Recall that $k=0.5+0.2076\ log(S/M)/M^{0.25}$ simplifies to $k=0.5+0.2076\ logS$ when $M=1$. Hence $4k=2+.8304\ logS$. The rest is algebraic reformulation.) Thus, consistent with the theoretical claim that stands behind our embeddedness function, k, we see that *the size of the national assembly systematically affects mean district-level N'_V in FPTP systems.* The effective number of parties in an individual one-seat district is, on average, two, raised to an exponent in which the only variable input is the assembly size.

Of course, individual districts in any given election can vary wildly around the mean; every district has its own local issues and different interest groups within the constituency, as well as a unique set of candidates with their own personal vote. No broad model could possibly claim to predict what a specific district's effective number of vote-earning parties will be.[18]

What this analysis has shown is that when attempting to account for the district-level N'_V, one actually can start with a nationwide factor, assembly size. Districts then differ from a baseline predictable from knowing how many total districts there are in the election. This is a remarkable finding – national politics shapes the district level systematically, even under simple FPTP where the district's electoral rule is supposedly the most constraining.

APPLICATION TO PRESIDENTIAL DEMOCRACIES

The models and graphs shown in this chapter so far have been based solely on parliamentary democracies with simple electoral systems, aside from the FPTP graph (Figure 10.2), which included some presidential cases. In the case of

---

[18] One thing we can conclude is that the variance around the predicted values from our logical model is *not* accounted for by social diversity, as defined by Milazzo et al. (in press). The authors generously provided us with their data, and we find it explains precisely none of the deviation of a given district's N'_V from the value derived from Equation 10.8. (Details in our online appendix. www.cambridge.org/votes_from_seats)

presidential democracies, the assembly politics is not the only political game in the system, and it might be that the assembly electoral-system variables are swamped by the all-important competition for the presidency. Accordingly, we ran the regressions testing our logical models on a wider dataset including presidential democracies. The models continue to work, albeit with more scatter. *In no case is there a statistically significant difference between the parliamentary and presidential subsets.* The regressions for parliamentary and presidential systems are shown side-by-side in the appendix to this chapter.

That there is no systematic impact of presidentialism on the relationship between district magnitude and the effective number of parties is an important finding. It goes against much conventional wisdom about how presidential competition – such as the notion of presidential candidates' "coattails" – shapes assembly competition. We might have expected no ability of variables grounded purely in the assembly electoral system to predict patterns in party systems of presidential democracies. Already we expressed the idea that the Seat Product could predict the nationwide effective number of parties about as well in presidential systems as in parliamentary (Chapter 7). The impact of the legislative assembly electoral system extends to the district-level patterns as well. In Chapter 11, we will take this finding even farther – showing that even the effective number of presidential candidates can be predicted with astonishing accuracy (albeit imperfectly) by knowing the district magnitude and assembly size.

CONCLUSION

The findings of this chapter may come as a surprise to anyone familiar with almost any of the literature on electoral systems over the preceding five decades or more. It is well "known" that one-seat districts with plurality rule tend to have a "two-party" system, and that this effect is especially notable at the district level. Such a claim is pretty much the essence of the so-called Duverger's law. Meanwhile, according to the same common wisdom, PR electoral systems tend to have multiparty systems.

We show that this is a highly incomplete characterization. Duverger's propositions are overdue for an update, which we could provide only after constructing models based on nationwide assembly size (S) and mean district magnitude (M) – and, as in this chapter, extending and testing them at the district level. Specifically, we find that the districts in large countries with FPTP electoral systems actually tend to have a higher effective number of vote-earning parties (N'_V) than do the districts of moderate magnitude in many PR systems. More importantly, *this is as we expect*, based on our logical models.

In this chapter, we started with a very basic model of the number of parties, of any size, that can be expected to win in a district, given its magnitude.

TABLE 10.1 *District level equations for the Seat Product Model.*

District seats

$N'_{S0} = M^{1/2}$ [no k!]

$s'_1 = M^{-k/2}$ $s'_1 = N'^{-k}_{S0}$

$N'_S = M^{2k/3}$ $N'_S = N'^{4k/3}_{S0}$. $N'_S = s'^{-4/3}_1$

District vote-seat interaction

$N'_{V0} = (N'_{S0}+1)$

$v'_1 = (N'_{S0}+1)^{-k}$ $v'_1 = (s'^{-1/k}_1 + 1)^{-1/k}$

$N'_V = (N'_{S0}+1)^{4k/3}$ $N'_V = (s'^{-1/k}_1 + 1)^{4k/3}$ $N'_V = [N'^{3/(4k)}_S + 1]^{4k/3}$

District votes

$N'_{V0} = (M^{1/2}+1)$

$v'_1 = (M^{1/2}+1)^{-k}$ $v'_1 = N'^{-1/k}_{V0}$

$N'_V = (M^{1/2}+1)^{4k/3}$ $N'_V = N'^{4k/3}_{V0}$ $N'_V = v'^{-4/3}_1$

The basic models are shown in bold; the rest follows from basic laws (see Table 9.2) and algebra. District embeddedness function: $k=0.5+0.2076\log(S/M)/M^{.25}$.

This number tends to be the square root of the district magnitude (as shown already in Chapters 1 and 7), independent of the larger assembly electoral system in which the district is embedded. However, other key indicators of the district-level party system can be understood only by incorporating this "embeddedness" factor. This complex factor, dubbed "k" is based on the share of the total assembly represented by the seats elected in a given district. It thus is equal to the square root of the magnitude if there is only one district for the entire country's assembly (i.e., no embeddedness), and becomes a larger fraction as magnitude is smaller *and* the assembly is larger.

Table 10.1 offers a summary of the key equations developed in this chapter. They closely parallel those shown in Table 9.2 for nationwide outcomes, except for the fact that the impact of assembly size enters only through the exponent, where k is included (except for N'_{S0}!). Then in Table 10.2, we offer a demonstration of what the predicted values are from the key equations. All of the examples in Table 10.2 are based on an assembly of 270 seats (a value near the median for our sample). Further exploration of how the embeddedness function works out in practice may be found in the chapter appendix.

When we take embeddedness into account, we see that the largest party tends to be smaller, and the effective number of seat-winning parties higher, than would be the case without this factor. We suggest that this effect results from the impact of *nationwide politics* on the district, whereby parties other than the locally strongest bring in resources to try to blunt the main local party's advantage. Of course, to the extent that parties engage in this sort of behavior

TABLE 10.2 *Average expectations at various levels of* M, *when* S=270

M	1	2	5	10	20	45	90	135	270
$k=0.5+0.2076\log$ $(270/M)/M^{0.25}$	1.00475	.87189	.74051	.66710	.61096	.56237	.53216	.5183	.5
$s'_1 = M^{-k/2}$	1	.7392	.5511	.4639	.4005	.3429	.3020	.2805	.2467
$v'_1 = (M^{1/2}+1)^{-k}$	.4984	.4637	.4191	.3862	.3540	.3171	.2863	.2687	.2395
$N'_S = M^{2k/3}$	1	1.496	2.213	2.784	3.388	4.167	4.935	5.447	6.463
$N'_V = (M^{1/2}+1)^{4k/3}$	2.531	2.786	3.188	3.555	3.993	4.624	5.299	5.767	6.723

successfully, they tend to make local politics look somewhat more like national politics. This is what we mean by the phrase "all politics is national."

Our logical model of how embeddedness works allows for a more systematic understanding of N'_V. We can predict N'_V quite reliably by combining the concept of "strivers are winners, plus one," which we developed for the nationwide party system (Chapter 8), with the district "embeddedness" factor introduced here. When we take these steps, we see that the number of "pertinent" vote-earning parties in a district can be estimated as the number of parties that won at least one seat in the district, plus one ($N'_{S0}+1$). Then we can raise this quantity to the power, $4k/3$, where k is the embeddedness factor. Moreover, this works quite well for predicting the average even under FPTP, allowing us to conclude that the effective number of vote-earning parties when $M=1$ is strongly conditioned by the assembly size.

In other words, our *district embeddedness is an especially strong factor in FPTP systems.* In practice, this finding means that politics is quite "national" despite the presence of the district magnitude that is supposedly most conducive to local politics and to a Duvergerian "law-like" tendency towards two-party politics. The long-overdue update to these tendencies that we introduce is to reveal that a large assembly is a key factor in pushing N'_V well upward beyond two. We see this play out in Canada, India, and the UK. All politics is national – even in the one-seat districts of simple plurality electoral systems.

We have now completed Part III of the book, our main set of chapters devoted to the nationwide and district effects of electoral systems on the interparty dimension – i.e., outputs such as the degree of fragmentation of the votes and seats, the size of the largest party, and deviation from proportionality.[19] Our focus so far has been primarily on parliamentary systems, in which the balance of power in the assembly determines parties'

---

[19] We did not show a model for district-level deviation from proportionality, because details remain to be worked out, even as the basic steps followed in Chapter 9 (national level) can be replicated at district level. See our online appendix. www.cambridge.org/votes_from_seats

bargaining power for executive formation. We have noted that our models do indeed work for presidential systems, too, but scatter tends to be higher. Perhaps this is not surprising, given that executive power in such systems does not depend on the balance of partisan power in the assembly, but on a separate nationwide electoral contest. In Chapters 11 and 12, we explore the impact of variables unique to presidential systems. These are then followed by two chapters that go deeper into district-level politics, by analyzing the intraparty dimension.

Appendix to Chapter 10

CONSTRUCTING DISTRICT EMBEDDEDNESS EXPONENT k

We start this appendix with an unusual caveat: this is the one section in the book that the authors themselves hesitate reading over again. It feels like taking indispensable but bitter medication. Yes, the model is sound, and we need it, if we want to advance into the territory of nationally embedded districts, which was the basic theme of Chapter 10. The calculations have been checked and rechecked. But the reasoning is strenuous. Do not feel bad, if you give up and just decide to judge the tree by its fruits – the degree of agreement with actual district level data.

If districts were equivalent to mini-states with a single statewide electoral district ($M=S$), matters would be simple: just replace MS in the nationwide equations with M^2. But they are not. They are embedded in a wider nationwide context that intervenes so as to raise the effective number of parties[20] and depress the largest party's seat and vote shares. Let us make it more specific for the effective numbers of seat-winning and vote-earning parties.

The effective numbers of parties in a district unaffected from the outside would follow the nationwide models $N_S=(MS)^{1/6}$ and $N_V=[(MS)^{1/4}+1]^{2/3}$, but with $S=M$. Hence we would have $N_S=M^{1/3}$ and $N'_V = (M^{1/2}+1)^{2/3}$. Yet we actually observe higher values, as if the basic building block $M^{0.5}$ had been replaced by M^k, where k is larger than 0.5. How much larger, this should depend on how much M is smaller than S. The nationwide "interference" on district-level politics logically should be strongest when district magnitude is small compared to assembly size, yet larger than 1. At $M=1$, the number of seat-winning parties is bound to be one, with or without nationwide interference, although of course the effective number of vote-earning parties would still be

---

[20] We showed in Chapter 7 that the simple, unadjusted model for the number of seat-winning parties, $N'_{S0}=M^{0.5}$, fits well enough, and thus we keep to this simpler formulation. However, as discussed in the main text of Chapter 10, the adjustment derived in this appendix is needed to explain a host of other outcomes at the district level.

larger than one. At the opposite extreme, with a single nationwide electoral district ($M=S$) there is no interference from the outside.

This means that some function of M and S should be added to 0.5, the exponent in the basic building block. The embeddedness exponent then is:

$$k = 0.5 + f(M, S).$$

Replacing 0.5 with k (and hence 1 with $2k$) in the equations for district-level effective numbers of parties, they become

$$N'_S = M^{2k/3} \text{ and } N'_V = (M^{1/2} + 1)^{4k/3}.$$

Now it is a matter of determining the form of function $f(M,S)$ and hence k. The outcome, shown as Equation 10.1, is baffling – even to us:

$$k = 0.5 + 0.2076\log(S/M)/M^{.25}.$$

The path to reach this outcome is convoluted. We'll try to make it as simple as possible, but this is still one of the most complex parts of the book.

Try the simplest first: assume that $f(M,S)$ is a constant: $k=0.5+a$. But this cannot be all there is, because the supplement to 0.5 must vanish when M takes its highest possible value, $M=S$. Inserting $\log(S/M)$ is the simplest way to satisfy this constraint, given that $\log 1=0$. Then

$$k = 0.5 + a\log(S/M).$$

Next, we ask what happens when M takes its lowest possible value, $M=1$? Then the broad format is simplified to

$$k = 0.5 + a\log S \quad [\text{for } M = 1].$$

We could determine a empirically – except that it cannot be done with seats, because the logical $N'_S=1$ is satisfied with any value of k. This is why we must appeal to district votes data to determine the value of constant a. We will get to this.

For the moment, however, return to the broad format $k=0.5+a\log(S/M)$. For district level effective number of seat-winning parties, this means that $N'_S=M^{2k/3}$ becomes

$$N'_S = M^{1/3+(2/3)a\log(S/M)}.$$

In a logarithmic graph N'_S versus M, such as Figure 10.1, this pattern is an arc (the thick dotted curve) above the simple line $N'_S = M^{1/3}$ (shown in the graph as the thin straight line). The curve joins this line at $M=1$ and $M=S$, but the one incorporating nationwide embeddedness is higher throughout the range, $1<M<S$. How high above the line should this arc be? Here we have no logical answer. Empirically, this height can be simply regulated by dividing $a\log(S/M)$ by M^b and adjusting the empirical constant b. The broad format,

$$k = 0.5 + a\log(S/M)/M^b,$$

thus emerges from logical considerations and preference for maximal simplicity. To determine the value of constant b, we could use the $M>1$ data for either N'_S or N'_V – and they had better yield the same result! But first we must pin down the value of constant a.

Recall that at $M=1$ we have simply $k=0.5+a\log S$. Then $N'_S=1$, with or without nationwide impact, so it cannot give us any information about k. But for votes we have

$$N'_V = (M^{1/2} + 1)^{4k/3} = 2^{4k/3} = 2^{2/3+(4/3)a\log S}.$$

It is simpler to deal with the decimal logarithm of N'_V:

$$\log N'_V = \log 2[2/3 + (4/3)a\log S] = 0.201 + 0.401a\log S.$$

These coefficients, $0.20069=(2/3)\log 2$ and $0.40137=(4/3)\log 2$, emerge from the 0.5 in $k=0.5+a\log S$. This means they are theoretically set and not subject to empirical manipulation.[21] Is $\log N'_V$ really linearly related to $\log S$? Figure 10.2 shows that this is so indeed, even while scatter is huge – as one would expect for individual districts. The best fit is:

$$\log N'_V = 0.127 + 0.113\log S. \quad [R^2 = .17].$$

But the empirical intercept 0.127 differs from the required 0.201. So the equation must be recalculated with intercept stipulated as 0.201. This alters the best-fit line very little. The result is

$$\log N'_V = 0.201 + 0.0828\log S,$$

and hence (after taking the antilog of 0.201)

$$N'_V = 1.59S^{0.083}.$$

Combining $0.083\log S$ and previous $0.401a\log S$ leads to $a=0.2065$.

This is an empirical estimate. Does it have a logical foundation? This may well be so. The total number of candidates running in FPTP districts worldwide also increases with increasing assembly size.[22] This leads to hints that the exponent in the equation above might have to be $1/12=0.08333$ on logical grounds. Then constant a in $k=0.5+a\log(S/M)/M^b$ should be:

---

[21] The model is set up in terms of decimal logarithms. All numerical values, including that of constant a, would be off by a factor $\ln x/\log x=2.3026$ when natural logarithms are used.

[22] Why this is so might become more tangible in the light of the cube root law of assembly sizes (see Chapter 2). To the extent this law holds, the population of a district in system of FPTP would be close to $P'=S^2$. A larger district population might well engender more people to run as independents or minor party candidates.

$a = 1/(16\log 2) = 0.2076.$

We'll use this number rather than the empirically obtained a=0.2065. However, some kinks in the model that leads to this conclusion remain to be ironed out; so it's too early to present it in this book.

Now that constant a in k=0.5+$a\log(S/M)/M^b$ has been settled, it is time to address b. By trial and error we find that the average patterns in Fig. 10.1 (N'_S versus M) and 10.6 (N'_V versus M) are best satisfied when we set b at 0.25, approximately. Finally, the general formula for k, at any S and M, is

$$k = 0.5 + 0.2076\log(S/M)/M^{.25}.$$

To repeat: here 0.5 is the value in the absence of nationwide impact; $\log(S/M)$ assures that k remains 0.5 when M=S; the coefficient $1/(16\log 2)$=0.2076 emerges from logical concerns about the total number of candidates in M=1 elections; and $1/M^{0.25}$ results from empirical fit of district level effective numbers at given M. The broad format is determined by logical reasoning, while coefficient b=0.25 was found empirically and a=0.2076 was reinforced by incomplete logical considerations. The remaining challenge in logical model building is to reinforce the logic for a and explain why b=0.25.

EVIDENCE THAT EMBEDDEDNESS DOES NOT AFFECT
THE NUMBER OF SEAT-WINNING PARTIES

The goal here is two-fold. The first goal is to give us a feel of how k decreases as M increases, for a medium-size assembly. The second and more important goal is to present evidence that, in contrast to the effective numbers of parties and the largest seat and vote shares, the actual number of seat-winning parties (N'_{S0}) does not receive a boost from the district being embedded in a larger nationwide assembly electoral system. This contrast is rather surprising.

In **Table 10.A1** we show several values of district magnitude and what k would be for a hypothetical constant S of 270. We use 270 because it is approximately the mean for our sample of multidistrict simple PR systems. The first column indicates the magnitudes, and the second one the number of actual districts we have in the data sample with that M. (The actual districts, of course, may come embedded in a wide range of assembly sizes.) The third column then shows what N'_{S0} is predicted to be, using N'_{S0} =$M^{0.5}$. From the third and fourth columns we see the actual mean N'_{S0} for the districts in our sample (again, regardless of S), followed by the ratio of the actual value to that predicted from N'_{S0} =$M^{0.5}$. That these ratios tend to be close to 1.00 confirms the good fit of the *unadjusted* model for N'_{S0}; that is, not taking into account the impact of national politics on the district.

TABLE 10.A1 *How district magnitude shapes the number of parties, with and without embeddedness*

M	No. of cases	$N'_{S0} = M^{0.5}$	Actual mean N'_{S0}	Ratio, if $M^{0.5}$	k if $S=270$	$N'_{S0} = M^k$	Ratio if M^k
3	45	1.73	2.09	1.206	0.81	2.43	0.860
4	45	2.00	2.20	1.100	0.77	2.90	0.758
5	49	2.24	2.14	0.958	0.74	3.29	0.651
6	40	2.45	2.75	1.123	0.72	3.63	0.758
7	29	2.65	2.93	1.108	0.70	3.92	0.747
8	27	2.83	2.89	1.021	0.69	4.19	0.690
9	21	3.00	3.33	1.111	0.68	4.43	0.753
10	30	3.16	3.63	1.149	0.67	4.65	0.782
11	10	3.32	3.30	0.995	0.66	4.85	0.680
12	17	3.46	3.47	1.002	0.65	5.04	0.689
14	17	3.74	4.00	1.069	0.64	5.38	0.743
16	10	4.00	4.00	1.000	0.63	5.69	0.702
Mean				1.070			0.734

The last three columns show what the impact of nationwide politics would be, first by demonstrating how k decreases, for a constant $S=270$, from nearly 0.81 at low M (three-seat district) to 0.63 when $M=16$. If we were to continue with even larger magnitudes, while holding $S=270$, we would find $k = 0.58$ at $M = 35$, $k = 0.56$ at $M = 50$, and of course, $k=0.5$ if there were just one district with $M=S=270$. In the opposite direction we reach $k=1.005$ at $M=1$. Yes, k can surpass 1, at large S and low M.

The final column of Table 10.A1 shows very clearly that we do not need the adjustment for embeddedness (k) to predict N'_{S0}. All ratios of N'_{S0} predicted from M^k are clearly worse than the predictions from $M^{0.5}$. However, in this chapter, we saw that it is necessary to adjust for the embeddedness of the district when we are attempting to predict the effective numbers of parties and the largest seat and vote shares in a district. Hence the need for the calculations that produce this exponent, as outlined in the previous section of this appendix.

DISTRICT-LEVEL REGRESSION RESULTS AND HOW PRESIDENTIAL SYSTEMS ARE DIFFERENT (OR ARE NOT)

In this section we report the regression results of the district-level effects tested in this chapter. In all cases, the unit of analysis is the "list" within a district, even if this differs from party (i.e., where there are alliances). When $M=1$, the distinction does not matter (see Chapter 2), but for $M>1$ it sometimes does.

TABLE 10.A2 *Comparing regression results for parliamentary and presidential systems*

Output	Input	Parliamentary			Presidential			Significant difference?
		Intercept	B coeff.	R^2	Intercept	B coeff.	R^2	
N'_{S0}	$\log M$	.000399	.509	.954	(.0103)	(.554)	.8872	No
N'_{S0}	$k\log M$	−.000440	(.818)	.942	.00489	(.862)	.903	No
s'_1	$k\log N'_{S0}$	4.15e−06	−.958	.955	−.000723	−1.039	.941	No
s'_1	$k\log M$	−.000148	−.494	.912	(−.0098)	−.5734	.767	No
N'_S	$k\log M$	.0000396	.648	.937	(.00800)	.722	.848	No
N'_V	$k\log(N'_{S0}+1)$	−.00311	1.336	.233	−.169	1.613	.292	No
N'_V	$k\log(M^{0.5}+1)$	−.0123	1.369	.203	−.0564	1.308	.093	No

Parentheses indicate a result contrary to model; i.e., an intercept significantly different from zero, or a coefficient significantly different from our logical model prediction (for which see main text). Significance reported at $p \leq .05$.

We have three countries for which we have district-level data on the number and size of lists, but in which those lists may contain candidates of multiple parties: Brazil, Chile, and Finland (on the latter case, see the examples of alliances in Chapter 6). This matter is taken up in detail in Chapter 14, where we unpack the lists down to their component parties. For the purposes of this chapter, we are concerned with how the electoral system works on those entities to which the proportional allocation formula is applied: in simple PR systems, that is the list.

In Table 10.A2, we show the results for the parliamentary and presidential subsamples side by side. As noted in Chapter 10, for all of the district-level relationships tested, there is no evidence of a systematically different relationship under presidentialism. Table 10.A2 allows for a comparison the coefficients and statistical fit for parliamentary and presidential data samples. In the last column it indicates whether the difference across executive formats is itself statistically significant.[23] In all cases, the answer is *no*.

For the first outcome indicated, N'_{S0}, we show tests of the models both with and without embeddedness. We see that for the regression of N'_{S0} and $k\log M$, neither executive type produces the expected coefficient of −1.00. This confirms that we do not need to consider embeddedness for the actual

[23] Significant difference was determined by examining marginal effects across the range of the independent variable in a regression in which both samples were pooled, and differentiated with a dummy variable interacted with the independent variable (as recommended by Brambor, Clark, and Golder 2006).

number of seat-winning parties. Using the unadjusted log$M$ produces a better result, notwithstanding that the predicted parameters for presidentialism are just outside of the confidence intervals of the regression estimates.

The table also shows tests of several other output variables, sometimes with more than one input, in line with the way we introduced the logical sequences in this chapter. As explained in the chapter text, for all these other outputs, we do need to take into account embeddedness. In all cases, the results for presidential systems are statistically indistinguishable from those for parliamentary.

PART III

BRINGING THE PRESIDENT IN

11

Coattails Upside Down: How Assembly Elections Shape Presidential Elections

Up to now, we have largely glossed over potential differences between presidential and parliamentary democracies. We have seen that, in general, presidentialism is not so different from parliamentarism when it comes to how the assembly electoral system shapes the parties. This could be seen in Figure 7.1, which had each executive type plotted with a distinct symbol. We could see that the Seat Product Model (SPM) predicted the trend in the effective number of seat-winning parties (N_S) among the whole set of democracies. The presidential systems did not stand out as requiring a distinct model.

Nonetheless, it is true that presidential systems tend to be more variable. That is, there are more cases of extremely high party-system fragmentation (e.g., Brazil and Peru) than there are among parliamentary systems. There are also more cases of unusually low fragmentation without having a very low Seat Product (MS); the United States is one key example. This chapter and Chapter 12 delve further into some remaining puzzles about understanding how party systems work in presidential democracies.[1]

As a starting point, we pose the following question: Which output in a presidential democracy should be easier to predict starting from MS: (a) the effective number of vote-earning parties in assembly elections (N_V), or (b) the effective number of presidential candidates? If you answered "a" you would be in good company. However, it is actually the effective number of presidential candidates (which we will call N_P) that responds better to the Seat Product Model. Figure 11.1 shows this to be so. The left panel shows N_P while the right panel shows N_V. In each panel, the relevant logical model is plotted with a solid gray line. While the data points are scattered, clearly it is in the left panel that the trend is closer to the logical model. The model for the left panel is explained below; that for the right panel is Equation 8.1. The rest of the chapter is about explaining how the patterns depicted in Figure 11.1 come about.

---

[1] These chapters use our nationwide dataset (Li and Shugart n.d.).

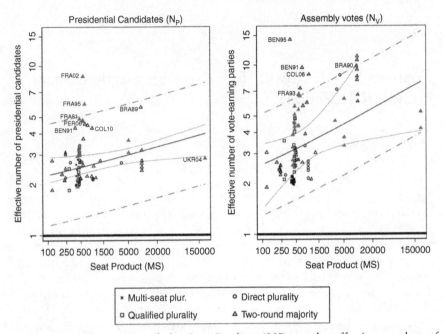

FIGURE 11.1 The impact of the Seat Product (MS) on the effective number of presidential candidates (N_P, left panel) and the effective number of vote-earning parties (N_V, right panel)

In both plots we have differentiated various institutional configurations of presidential and semipresidential democracy with different symbols. We also have labeled some specific elections that have substantially higher N_V or N_P than expected for their Seat Product.[2] In the right panel of Figure 11.1, the labeled points all come from nonconcurrent elections, meaning those that occur on a date different from that of the presidential election.[3] The relevance of this factor will be a major theme of Chapter 12. Dashed lines delimit values that are double, or half, the expectations of the respective model.

The symbols further differentiate the rules under which the president is elected; this, too, is a factor that we will come back to. Later in this chapter

---

[2] Note that data points from France are included, despite the country's assembly electoral system not meeting the definition of "simple." As we explain in Chapter 15, the French N_S is about what would be expected if it were simple (although N_V is less conforming to the SPM); thus we include it here to expand our sample to include one of the most important cases of significant presidency among all democracies.

[3] In defining the date, we mean the precise day and month, not merely the same year. In case of a two-round presidential election, elections are "concurrent" only if the assembly is elected at the same time as the first round of the presidential election. We have no cases of assembly elections occurring on the same day as a presidential runoff.

we will offer insights on what appears as a puzzle in Figure 11.1: there is no obvious pattern between how the president is elected and how high either N_P or N_V is.

If a symbol is filled in with light gray it is a semipresidential democracy, whereas the others are "pure" presidential. This distinction is discussed extensively elsewhere (e.g., Shugart and Carey 1992; Samuels and Shugart 2010) and our criteria for including a semipresidential system in this chapter and the next are explained in the chapter appendix.

The goal in this chapter is to explain patterns in those democracies in which a presidential election is a key event shaping the country's politics, thereby leaving out those countries that function as if they were parliamentary even when there is an elected head of state.[4] The model we develop in this chapter to derive N_P from MS assumes that the presidency is of central importance, either because the president fully controls the executive branch (as in "pure presidential" regimes) or because the presidency is especially important (even though there is also a premier accountable to the assembly, as in semipresidential systems).

The solid dark-gray diagonal in the left panel of Figure 11.1 represents the following model, derived through logic explained later in this chapter. It is:

$$N_P = 2^{1/2}[(MS)^{1/4} + 1]^{1/3} \tag{11.1}$$

Equation 11.1 is not a simple statistical best fit; it is a logical expression. Nonetheless, it is almost precisely the equation we obtain if we run a regression solely on the pure presidential systems. The regression outputs are shown in the chapter appendix. When we include the semi-presidential cases, the coefficients obtained conform to the model less precisely, although Equation 11.1 fits firmly within the 95 percent confidence interval of the expanded-sample regression (which is bounded by the solid light gray lines). In both cases R^2 is low (it is higher in the model with all cases), but we can be satisfied that the model is explaining the actual trend in N_P.

The finding in the left panel of Chapter 11.1 is remarkable, and must be emphasized:

The effective number of candidates receiving votes for the *presidency* can be predicted based on the *assembly* electoral system.

We should not be surprised that there is some wide scatter – as there is – because individual candidates for the office of presidency matter to the outcome of elections, often more than their party does (Samuels and Shugart 2010).[5] Yet the Seat Product Model explains the pattern.

---

[4] For instance, as noted in Chapter 7, we classify semipresidential systems in Finland and Portugal as if they were parliamentary. See the appendix for further detail.

[5] The biggest outlier in N_P is, by far, the French election of 2002, an extraordinary contest that we discussed in Chapter 3.

It is perhaps more remarkable still that the trend in N_P can be predicted better than N_V, which is shown in the right panel of Figure 11.1. In the plot for N_V our logical model from Chapter 8 is plotted as the solid dark-gray line: $N_V = [(MS)^{1/4} + 1]^{2/3}$. From the lighter gray curves we see just how wide the 95 percent confidence intervals are on a regression (shown in the appendix) for this relationship in presidential democracies. The party system for assembly elections in presidential systems is simply far more scattered than is the case in parliamentary democracies – or, importantly for the topic of this chapter, than is the case for the effective number of presidential candidates.

To illustrate numerically how much better the fit to model expectations is for N_P than for N_V, we can consider the ratio of actual values to model-predicted values for each outcome, and for both samples (pure-presidential only and the full sample). Taking all the individual elections plotted in each panel of the figure, and calculating a mean ratio of actual to expected, we find the following: in the pure presidential systems, the mean ratio for N_P is 1.0018 (standard deviation 0.260), while the mean ratio for N_V is 1.0637 (0.671). For the wider sample that includes the semipresidential systems, the mean ratios are, respectively, 1.081 (0.412) and 1.096 (0.634). In both cases, the mean fit is better (and the standard deviation lower) for N_P, but this is especially so for pure presidential. In the wider set, we see that both measures are farther off, on average, but still the fit for N_P is better.

The main task of the remainder of this chapter is to explain the logic behind Equation 11.1. Doing so is significant in light of the basic effort of this book, which is to push the boundaries of what we can explain in party-system fragmentation with sparse inputs, consisting principally of the mean district magnitude (M) and the assembly size (S). The specific importance of doing this for the fragmentation of the presidential contest (i.e., N_P), is that it means a sharp break from the standard approach to explaining party-system outputs. That approach takes N_P to be an input variable, entered into regressions to help explain the assembly party system. We already expressed our fundamental methodological objections to such approaches (see Chapters 1 and 7).[6] If we can predict the average degree of fragmentation, even in presidential elections, via purely institutional inputs, we would consider it an advance. That is, instead of considering N_P to be one of several inputs into the explanation of N_V and N_S, we take it to be *one of several outputs of the Seat Product Model*. (Recall the schematic in Figure 9.5.) Nonetheless, the interplay between N_V (or N_s) and N_P is somewhat complex. We expand upon this relationship in the rest of the chapter.

---

[6] These objections only increase when, as is the case in several prominent works, parliamentary elections are included in the same statistical tests with an impossible value of $N_P = 0$ entered into the regression. See our discussion in Chapter 7; see also Li and Shugart (2016).

HOW ASSEMBLY AND PRESIDENTIAL COMPETITION ARE RELATED

Common wisdom has it that presidential "coattails" help the president's party win votes and seats in assembly elections, too, at least when these elections are concurrent or when assembly elections follow a short time after a presidential election.[7] We do not deny that this is a perfectly plausible explanation – *for any given presidential election*. After all, the characteristics and experience of the one man or woman who will be chosen to lead the executive branch are a fundamental consideration that voters use in presidential elections. If they like the presidential candidate, voters may be more inclined to support with their assembly vote the party of that presidential candidate.

However, we should ask ourselves if the relationship might work the opposite way too. That is, do the rules of assembly elections (such as M and S) affect the votes for presidential candidates? Already, in Figure 11.1 and Equation 11.1, we suggested that the answer is "yes."

The model that leads to Equation 11.1 starts with thinking through a possible connection between N_P and N_V. We already are confident from Chapter 8 that N_V is connected back to the Seat Product, MS, even though the variability in presidential systems is considerably greater than is the case for parliamentary systems (as we saw in the right panel of Figure 11.1). If there is a systematic connection between N_P and N_V, we can conclude that it may be misleading to treat competition for the presidency as if it were an exogenous input, as many standard works do.[8] Instead, let us proceed to see how both are connected to MS. Doing so requires us to think systematically about the connection between N_V and N_P.

Figure 11.2 shows this connection, N_P graphed against N_V. We may be tempted to focus on the data first. However, for the sake of model building we should concentrate, instead, on three theoretical lines shown in light gray: $N_V=2$, $N_P=2$, and $N_P=N_V$.

We explain the logic as follows. First, suppose there were two equal-sized parties in the assembly election, meaning $N_V=2$. In such a case we should not expect N_P to differ much. There are only two partisan options, and this binary choice is likely to structure executive competition, too, implying $N_P=2$. As the assembly party system expands beyond $N_V=2$, each party might wish to present a candidate. Note that this expansion of the assembly party system could be, for present purposes, due to any factor. For instance, it could be that the effective number of parties increases in

[7] For an extensive treatment of "coattails" which also applies the notion to cases where assembly elections come shortly before presidential, see Stoll (2015).

[8] Examples include: Amorim Neto and Cox (1997) and Cox (1997), Mozaffar et al. (2003), Clark and Golder (2006), Golder (2006), Hicken and Stoll (2011), Elgie et al. (2014), and Stoll (2015).

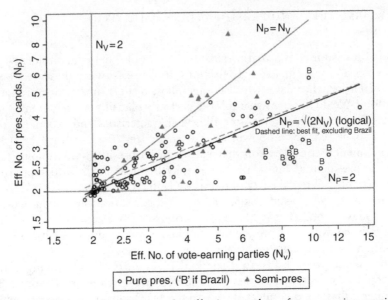

FIGURE 11.2 Relationship between the effective number of vote-earning parties in assembly elections (N_V) and the effective number of presidential candidates (N_P)

some country because existing parties split or new ones enter, despite a constant *MS*. What if the party system is more fragmented than $N_V=2$, even if it is a case where N_V is thus higher than expected, according to the Seat Product Model?

If voters followed their party preferences under a scenario of increased fragmentation of the assembly party system, then $N_P=N_V$ would result. However, with a single seat available, this would be a defeating strategy for most parties. If they behaved entirely "rationally" (in a restricted sense of the term) they should still gather behind only a few major candidates. If they gather behind two such candidates, then the result would remain close to the line $N_P=2$ even as N_V increases. The competition for the presidency is thus confronted by two contradictory trends, one of which pushes it towards fragmenting along with the assembly competition, the other that keeps pulling it back towards $N_V=2$.

The reality should be in-between the extremes of $N_P=2$ and $N_P=N_V$. In the absence of any further information on whether the fragmenting push or the consolidating pull weighs more heavily, our best guess would be the geometric mean of the extremes:

$$N_P = \sqrt{(2N_V)}. \tag{11.2}$$

In other words, as N_V increases, incentives for either pre-election alliance-formation or strategic voting (or both together) increase. Thus we expect $N_P<N_V$. Now we can think of $N_P=2$ as a (soft) lower limit, whereby the maximum coalescent or strategic behavior produces two equally competitive presidential candidates despite several significant players in the assembly arena. The upper limit on N_P is reasonably N_V, as it should be rare to have more options for president than for assembly, unless the latter has a very low effective number of parties. If $N_V<2$, then Equation 11.2 predicts $N_P>N_V$, suggesting competition for the presidency as a balance to assembly competition in which one party dominates.[9]

We can put this logical model to a visual test, by looking at the data shown in Figure 11.2. The dashed line indicates the logical model $N_P=\sqrt{(2N_V)}$. In the data plot, Brazilian elections are labeled with the letter "B" to distinguish them from the rest, while all other pure presidential systems are shown by unlabeled circles. Semipresidential cases are shown with shaded triangles. The reason for distinguishing the Brazilian elections is the same as one we have articulated in earlier chapters: the Brazilian electoral system is somewhat complex due to the prevalence of multiparty alliance lists. This feature means that the (actual or effective) number of parties in Brazil at the national level overstates the country's fragmentation.[10]

Figure 11.2 also plots a best-fit regression as a dashed line. We see that it is not much different from Equation 11.2, the logical model. For the actual regression result, which excludes the Brazilian data, see the chapter appendix. The fit of this model is better than we could have expected, as most of the variance in the number of presidential candidates is expected to come from current politics. These factors include the special characteristics of any given presidential candidate, as well as other factors besides the number of vote-earning parties in the assembly. The data points are scattered all around, mostly within the cone formed by lines $N_P=2$ and $N_P=N_V$. At very low N_V some occur well above the line, $N_P=N_V$, which now looks like only a soft upper limit.[11]

---

[9] On the notion of presidential voting as a balance to a dominant assembly party, see Zupan (1991), Fiorina (1992), and Shugart (1995: 329). The limiting case of single-party dominance under conditions of democratically competitive elections is one party, out of two running, winning all *seats*, thus $N_S=1$. By the model developed in Chapter 8, $N_V=(N_S^{3/2}+1)^{2/3}$, we predict for such a case $N_V=1.59$. That would mean two pertinent parties, the one that swept all seats, and one other competitor that managed to win none. In this two-party context, N_V is bounded at the upper end by 2.0, and we do not expect presidential contests to be more one-party dominant than those for the assembly, so the lower limit of expectation is $N_V=1.59$. Equation 11.2 would then yield $N_P=1.78$.

[10] We shall take up this topic further later in this chapter. In Chapter 14 we undertake a district-level analysis of the parties within alliances in Brazil and similar systems.

[11] The most striking of these cases among the pure presidential systems (circles) is Chile (2009): $N_V=2.6$, $N_P=3.1$, due to the presence of a nonpartisan presidential candidate who obtained around 20 percent of the vote. There are also some cases with higher N_V among semipresidential cases (triangles). All cases of $N_P>N_V>4$ come from France (1981, 1988, 2002, and 2007).

Where the assembly party system is restrictive in its options, we do find a higher effective number of presidential candidates than of parties earning assembly votes. As we suggested above, it may be that voters who have few options for assembly sometimes favor a minor party for president as a way of registering opposition to their main party options. Such a pattern occurs from time to time in the US, where a few elections have had significant third-party or independent candidates for president, but their support scarcely registered in the assembly voting (Shugart 2004).[12]

Figure 11.2 thus offers qualified support for the logical model of Equation 11.2. However, the real test of its logic is that represented by Equation 11.1; we have already found it to be promising (see Figure 11.1, left panel, and the chapter appendix). We now explain how we get from Equation 11.2 to the main logical model of this chapter, Equation 11.1. Table 9.2 gives us $N_V = [(MS)^{1/4} + 1]^{2/3}$. This means we can substitute in our model $N_P = \sqrt{(2N_V)}$:

$$N_P = \sqrt{(2N_V)} = 2^{1/2}[(MS)^{1/4} + 1]^{1/3}.$$

This is Equation 11.1, which was plotted as the almost straight line shown in the left panel of Figure 11.1.

Shaky propositions that interconnect in a quantitative way reinforce each other. By itself, $N_P = \sqrt{(2N_V)}$ is debatable, in view of substantial scatter that even extends beyond the supposed upper limit at $N_P = N_V$, on which the model is based. The multiple logical (best-guess) steps involved in $N_V = [(MS)^{1/4} + 1]^{2/3}$ add scatter. Their combination into $N_P = 2^{1/2}[(MS)^{1/4} + 1)]^{1/3}$ should pile up scatter to the point of submerging all logical connection. And yet the connection emerges – and pretty much agrees with actual best fit! This is a *tour de force*. It looks almost as if the individual parts of the total system were compensating for each other's deviations.

Brazil is a prime example. Its nationwide number of parties in assembly elections deviates from expectations based on *MS*, partly because of the complications introduced by multiparty alliance lists (the OLPR/SNTV hybrid discussed in the appendix to Chapter 7, and elaborated on further in Chapter 14). Because of its unusual party system, Brazil's data points are marked in Figure 11.2 – and its relationship between N_P and N_V deviates appreciably from the crowd. Yet when it comes to N_P versus *MS* (Figure 11.1), these two deviations seem to cancel each other out, and Brazil falls in line with the expectations. The key to this result is that *at the district level*, Brazil is not an outlier. Its effective number of *lists* is consistent with the models developed in Chapter 10, but as we shall see in Chapter 14, those lists often contain winning candidates bearing multiple party labels. These party labels are the ones counted

---

[12] Prominent examples include the US elections of 1968, 1980, 1992, and 2016, as well as the previously noted case of Chile 2009.

in the nationwide calculation of the effective number of parties, and thus the case appears deviant in Figure 11.2. Yet, strikingly, it is not deviant in Figure 11.1: when settling on presidential candidacies, the numerous parties in the system somehow come back into alignment with the logic of models devised for presidential systems that lack the various peculiarities present in the Brazilian case.[13]

This section of the chapter has demonstrated that we can derive a model for N_P in which the initial model-building step was N_V. Given that we found, shockingly, that the fit of the model for N_P is better than that for N_V, we should pause and ask if the order of the relationship might be

$$MS \rightarrow N_P \rightarrow N_V,$$

instead of

$$MS \rightarrow N_V \rightarrow N_P,$$

as we claimed in Figure 9.5. Such a claim would be even more outlandish than the one we are making with Equation 11.1, yet is it not plausible that the better fitting model is the one more proximate to the causal institutional factor? In a word, *no*.

Of all the effective-number quantities investigated in this book, the one on firmest theoretical logic is that connecting MS to N_S, the effective number of seat-winning parties. Our logical extension of the effect of MS on N_V was also found to be empirically sound in Chapter 8. In presidential democracies, as much as in parliamentary, the assembly size and the district magnitude constitute physical constraints on how much the number of parties can fragment. These constraints are not broken by presidentialism. More importantly, they do not directly constrain presidential candidates. Thus there is no direct link from MS to N_P, and thus should be expressed as

$$MS \rightarrow \quad N_V \rightarrow \quad N_P,$$

as indeed it was in Figure 9.5.

Why, then, are values of N_V more variable? The likely answer lies in the distinguishing feature by which an executive format moves away from parliamentarism to presidentialism (with those semipresidential systems with especially significant presidencies being intermediate in this distinction). If the system is parliamentary in its fundamental operation, the parties are forming, competing, and coordinating around the central institution that is solely responsible for determining executive power – the representative assembly to which a parliamentary cabinet is responsible.

---

[13] In a graph not shown here, N_P is found to be even more accurately represented by Equation 11.2 if we replace N_V with the mean district N'_V. Brazil is not an outlier in relation to N'_V. Further implications remain to be worked out.

On the other hand, when the system is fundamentally "presidentialized" (Samuels and Shugart 2010), political actors are relatively freer to create new vote-earning parties without destabilizing the executive. The latter depends on a presidency whose continuation in office is not threatened by fractious assembly politics. By the same token, political actors are also freer to deviate from their own party when the executive is presidential (Carey 2009), which may tend to reduce incentives to split a majority party when one is present, relative to the incentives under parliamentarism. Thus where the Seat Product or other factors encourage party fragmentation, presidentialism my exacerbate it (prime example: Brazil). Yet where the Seat Product or other factors lean towards few parties, presidentialism may help keep the number lower still (prime example: The United States). By these mechanisms, presidential systems are more variable, yet the Seat Product Model still affects assembly politics first.

In spite of that variation, we have seen that effective number of presidential candidates tends towards a MS-predicted value (Equation 11.1). Why might that be? An answer can be only speculative at this point, but perhaps the number of serious contenders for the executive expresses a broader tendency of alliances within the party system. Such a tendency would not be directly inferable from the effective number of assembly parties in the same way as it is in a parliamentary system.[14] However, those political groupings that nominate presidential candidates might reflect a more fundamental count of the political tendencies on the national scene via their competition for the most visible institution in the system. Perhaps future research that takes account of alliance patterns over time could disentangle the connections between N_V and N_P that this section has described and upon which we have built this chapter's logical models.

WHAT ABOUT ELECTION RULES FOR THE PRESIDENCY ITSELF?

At the start of this chapter, we differentiated, in Figure 11.1, various methods of electing presidents. We now address this factor, which would be seemingly important for explaining N_P, and perhaps by extension also N_V. The presidential election formula is, after all, the manner in which the winner of power over the executive institution is chosen. Nonetheless, only a weak visual pattern connects the rules of presidential election and N_P. The US presidency is the only one elected by a multiseat plurality rule, given the intermediary electoral college. The US, perhaps not surprisingly, has low N_P; moreover, it is possible that its low N_V for its MS (see right panel) is also largely

---

[14] In Chapter 15 (already foreshadowed at the end of Chapter 5), we see that India's highly fragmented party system has in common with Brazil's the formation of alliances that greatly reduce the number of competitors for the executive. The difference is that, being a parliamentary system, India's executive alliances are aimed at winning assembly seats first.

explained by the use of such a restrictive system to elect the presidency. Other countries that use direct plurality (depicted in both panels of Figure 11.1 as circles) or a qualified plurality (squares), such as Costa Rica, tend not to stand out as notably less fragmented than two-round majority (*contra* Shugart and Carey 1992; Mainwaring and Shugart 1997).

About half the presidencies in our sample are elected by two-round majority (triangle symbol in Figure 11.1), as are all our semipresidential cases. This rule might tend to inflate N_P, because it allows smaller parties to run in the first round to show strength, then support one of the top two in the runoff. Sure enough, some two-round majority presidential elections have high N_P. See, for instance, the elections at moderate MS but high N_P, such as some in France as well as Benin and Peru and other countries. Yet Brazil, which uses two-round majority, has only one election with fragmentation much higher than we expect based on its high Seat Product. That election was 1990, its first of the current democratic regime. The other Brazilian elections are quite close to the expectation of our logical model, notwithstanding the high MS. Thus sorting out the impact of the presidential election rule from that of MS is not straightforward. The challenge is especially great because the presidential election rule is changed more readily than is the assembly Seat Product, and some changes have been enacted only in response to increased fragmentation of presidential competition (Shugart 2007). On balance, it appears that the impact of the rule is greatest when MS is moderate; in such cases, the two-round system might encourage higher N_P than would be expected from the Seat Product.

We can probe the impact of the election method further by considering the ratio of a presidential election's observed value of N_P to what would be predicted by Equation 11.1. We will do this only for pure presidential systems, because we saw that they are better predicted by Equation 11.1, and because we are unable to compare the impact of plurality rule in semipresidential systems. The mean of this ratio for (pure) presidential systems that use plurality to elect their presidents is 0.971; the mean ratio for those using two-round majority is 1.110. While the direction of the effect is as expected, the difference of means is not significant (p=.102).[15]

While it is likely that the election method for the presidency has some effect on N_P, and indirectly on N_V, we do not attempt to model it. The election methods are several categories, rather than a quasi-continuous concept like MS. It is therefore difficult to specify a quantitative impact of presidential

---

[15] Perhaps this remains a surprise. We can take it one step further and investigate the difference of means in *presidential candidate vote percentages* in plurality and two-round majority elections (pure presidential only). We find only a small difference for the leading candidate (48.4 percent for plurality versus 44.2 percent for two-round majority). There is, however, a significant difference for the second candidate (40.0 percent versus 31.5 percent).

election rules, or their possible interaction with *MS*. Given the goals of this book, we prefer to work with quantities that lend themselves to model creation. We have seen in this chapter that even a statement as implausible as "the effective number of presidential candidates is systematically predictable from the assembly Seat Product" turns out to be astonishingly accurate. The rest – including the specifics of how the president is elected – is in detail.[16]

CONCLUSION

We have seen in this chapter that the assembly party system, and even the electoral system, plays a role in shaping the effective number of presidential candidates. This is a surprise, because it is generally assumed that there is a primary causality running the other way. In fact, it has become common for other scholars to treat the effective number of presidential candidates as if it were exogenously determined, and as if it were a major factor in shaping the assembly party system. Our results call this into question. We find that we can derive a quantitative logical model that predicts much of the variance in competition for the presidency from assembly factors – i.e., the Seat Product.

The advantage of discovering the effects reported in this chapter are that we now can say that electoral-system design can affect how fragmented the competition for the presidency is. Of course, we would not claim it can determine presidential politics. The institutional constraints located here do not take politics out of politics. After all, a presidential candidate with great charisma or tainted by serious scandal could cause a big fluctuation in the effective number of presidential candidates for one specific election. Such factors might also have repercussions for that candidate's party in assembly elections, through a more classic "coattail" effect. Moreover, several small parties might band together to present a joint presidential candidate, thereby generating a substantial difference between effective numbers of parties and presidential candidates. Yet even if there is not a determinative relationship for a single election, our results suggest that certain steps in electoral system design might make a difference in the long run. In particular,

---

[16] France is the most consistent outlier for N_P (and also has some high values of N_V). Why might N_P be so high in France? It could be due to France being our only case to use two-round systems for both president and assembly. We find (ahead, in Chapter 15) that N_S in France is consistent with a "simple" system, notwithstanding the second rounds. But N_V is less so. The parties can compete in first rounds for both institutions and retain their identity, while engaging in alliances for second rounds. No other country has this combination, and no other has a series of elections that have such high values of both N_P and N_V, despite modest *MS*. For a detailed treatment of the "four rounds" of any given election year in France since 2002, see Dupoirier and Sauger (2010).

if we want to minimize fragmentation of presidential competition, we would be wise to advise against very proportional systems for the assembly in a presidential democracy.

Such advice is not new (Mainwaring 1993), but it has not been shown before that the assembly electoral system and party system themselves could be so consequential, not merely to how presidents interact with assemblies, but also the constellation of votes for *presidential candidates themselves.*

Appendix to Chapter 11

DEFINITION OF "PRESIDENTIAL"

A presidential system is one in which the head of government is popularly elected and serves for a fixed term. Most definitions also include a criterion requiring the president to have some legislative powers (e.g., Shugart and Carey 1992). In most cases, classifying cases according to executive authority as either parliamentary or presidential is straightforward. However, semipresidential systems sometimes pose challenges. Broadly, a system is semipresidential if the president is popularly elected, but there is also a premier who (along with the cabinet) must maintain the confidence of the assembly majority (Samuels and Shugart 2010; Elgie 2011).

For our purposes – analyzing the impact of presidents on fragmentation of the assembly party system – we are most interested in isolating those presidencies that are sufficiently "powerful" to be the key political prize in the system. This is a distinction that crosscuts to a degree that between "pure" and "semi-" presidential types.

The operational rule we used in selecting cases of semipresidential as being "presidential" for purposes of this book is based on Shugart (2005b). This involves a series of questions posed about the powers stipulated in any given semipresidential constitution. We consider a country to be presidential if at least one of the following conditions is met:

(1) The president has initiative to name a premier *and* the cabinet forms without an investiture vote; *or*
(2) The president has initiative to name a premier *and* the president has a veto that requires at least three fifths of the assembly to override on regular legislative bills and/or the government budget.

The first condition establishes that the president generally dominates the process of selecting the head of government and cabinet, while the second one includes presidents who must bargain with the assembly to form the cabinet when their party lacks a majority, but who can prevent the majority from legislating over their heads.

Under this scheme, there are very few cases that would provoke controversy in coding. The semipresidential systems (and range of election years for which we have data) that count as sufficiently presidential to be included in Chapters 11 and 12 are: Armenia (1999), France (1967–2007), Georgia (2004–08), Poland (2001–2011), Sao Tome and Principe (1991–2010), Senegal (2001–2007), Taiwan (2008), and Ukraine (2006–2007). Two other semipresidential systems were already included in previous chapters as "parliamentary" based on their weaker presidents: Finland and Portugal.

REGRESSION RESULTS FOR PRESIDENTIAL SYSTEMS

In Table 11.A1, we report the results of five regressions on presidential democracies. The output variable in Regressions One, Two, and Three is the effective number of presidential candidates (logged), while in Regressions Three and Four it is the effective number of vote-earning parties (logged) in the assembly election.

Regression One tests Equation 11.2, for which we expect a constant term of 0.1505 (the log of the square root of two) and a coefficient on the effective

TABLE 11.A1 *Regression tests of models for presidential systems: the effect of the Seat Product* (MS) *on the effective number of presidential candidates* (N_P) *and the effective number of vote-earning parties* (N_V) *in assembly elections*

	(1) N_P, logged pure pres. (excluding Brazil)	(2) N_P, logged pure pres.	(3) N_P, logged all	(4) N_V, logged pure pres.	(5) N_V, logged all
N_V, logged	0.471				
	(0.101)				
Expected	0.500				
F test stat	0.795				
$[(MS)^{1/4} +1]$, logged		0.333	0.238	1.896	1.031
		(0.0764)	(0.100)	(0.235)	(0.445)
Expected		0.333	0.333	0.667	0.667
F test stat		0.9999	0.3499	0.0001	0.4215
Constant	0.185	0.139	0.238	−0.980	−0.297
	(0.0378)	(0.0705)	(0.0954)	(0.220)	(0.363)
Expected	0.1505	0.1505	0.1505	0.000	0.000
Observations		72	86	94	114
R-squared		0.088	0.039	0.466	0.270
rmse		0.0988	0.129	0.169	0.191

Robust standard errors in parentheses.

number of vote-earning parties (N_V) of 0.500. Regression One excludes the Brazilian elections for reasons explained in the main chapter. It includes both presidential and semipresidential systems. The expected values are reached, with minor deviation.

In Regressions Two through Five, the input variable is the input variable is the *MS*-based expected number of pertinent parties, $N_{V0}=[(MS)^{.25}+1]$. Regressions Two and Four are for "pure" presidential systems only, whereas Regressions Three and Five include semipresidential systems.[17] As explained in the main text of the chapter, and indicated in the table, our expectation for Regressions Two and Three, testing Equation 11.1, are that the coefficient should be 0.333. In Regression Two (pure presidential only) the result is precisely as expected. In Regression Three, it deviates, but the F test shows that the estimated coefficient is statistically indistinguishable from expectation. The expected constant on both Regressions Two and Three is again 0.1505, due to logic explained in the chapter. The estimated coefficients are not significantly different from the logical expectations, although the result for Regression Two is more in line with the quantitative prediction than is the case for Regression Three. (By coincidence, both the coefficient and constant in Regression Three are 0.238.)

For Regressions Four and Five we expect a coefficient on the input variable of 0.667. Actual estimates are quite far from this value, even if the estimated coefficient is statistically indistinguishable from the expected value in the case of Regression Five, as the F test indicates. We offer explanation and interpretation of these results in the main text of Chapter 11.

---

[17] Regressions Three and Five have more observations than their counterparts for presidential candidates because some countries hold assembly elections more frequently than presidential.

12

How Election Timing Matters in Presidential Democracy – And How It Does Not

In Chapter 11, we saw that the effective number of presidential candidates (N_P) has a logical connection to effective number of vote-earning parties in the assembly (N_V). Based on previously established relationships, that means N_P also is connected to the effective number of seat-winning parties (N_S) and from there all the way back to the Seat Product. Nonetheless, the ranges around the predicted values of N_V and N_S are wider in presidential countries. Could one reason be that N_V and N_S are affected by the typical cycle of presidential popularity? This is certainly what classic notions of presidential "coattails" would imply – presidents, when popular, help their parties. Yet the Seat Product Model sees party-system outcomes as derived from institutions. Where can presidents (and presidential candidates) and their typical cycles of popularity fit in?

Presidents are elected on new hopes and tend to enjoy a "honeymoon period." If assembly elections take place during the honeymoon, then the president's party, often the largest, receives an extra boost in votes and seats. These hopes often go sour, so that presidents frequently end their term less popular than in the beginning. Shugart and Carey (1992) called the late part of the term the *counter-honeymoon*. If new assembly elections take place during the counter-honeymoon, then the president's party could suffer, and an unusually small presidential party may result in the effective number of parties being above the normal. If so, then the range of fluctuation in N_V and N_S could widen, compared to parliamentary systems. We will now test this hunch for the effective number of parties in assembly politics (both N_S and N_V).

Figure 12.1 shows how the timing of an assembly election relative to the presidential election affects the accuracy of the Seat Product Model. The vertical axis is the ratio of a given election's observed effective number of parties to the value predicted given its Seat Product (MS). The left panel is for N_S, while the right panel is for N_V. In both panels, the horizontal axis is something we call Elapsed time (E), defined as the share of the total time between presidential elections that has elapsed when the assembly election is held. If the elections occur on the same day, i.e., concurrent, $E=0$. The closer the assembly election

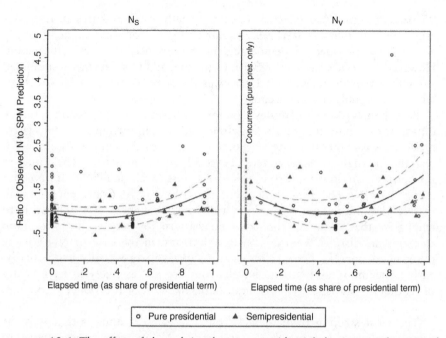

FIGURE 12.1 The effect of elapsed time between presidential elections on the ratio of observed effective number of parties to predicted value; seats (N_S, left panel) and votes (N_V, right panel)

date is to the *next* presidential election (but still before it), the more E approaches 1.0. As in Chapter 11, different symbols differentiate pure presidential from semipresidential systems; in the panel for N_V there is a further differentiation, using light gray x symbols, of the concurrent elections (all of which are pure presidential). The reasons for such differentiation – and for showing it only in the panel for N_V – will be explained later.

In both panels of Figure 12.1, curves show the estimated values from a regression in which the ratio of observed to predicted effective number is the output variable, and E is the input. More specifically, we enter E in quadratic form, i.e., E and its square. The reason for this formulation will become clear later in the chapter; the regression output is in the chapter appendix.[1] The dashed curves show the 95 percent confidence intervals of the regression.

The data and regression plots show a few things of interest to us in this chapter. First of all, through much of the range of a presidential term, an assembly election results in a value of either N_S or N_V that tends to be close to the SPM prediction. This can be seen by following the position of the horizontal line plotted for a ratio of 1.00, and whether this is within the regression's

---

[1] Concurrent elections are included in both regressions; details are in the appendix.

95 percent confidence intervals or not. Usually it is, and this justifies our repeated claim that *the SPM remains our best guess* for what either N_S or N_V will be in a presidential democracy, in the absence of other information. However, we sometimes have other information, and it is a further institutional variation, as shown in Figure 12.1: the elapsed time between presidential elections when the assembly election occurs.

Both panels show a "smiley" pattern, whereby the regression estimate dips near the midterm, and rises at either end. The upturn in the ratio, where observed N is higher than the SPM prediction, takes us significantly above 1.0 near the end of the president's term, especially in the case of N_V. The upturn in the honeymoon (low nonzero values of E) is just barely significant for N_V, but not at all for N_S. The concurrent elections are shown with a different symbol in the N_V plot and the regression lines are visually cut short of $E=0$ in order to emphasize that there is a break in the pattern for very early honeymoon elections, as distinct from concurrent elections, in the case of N_V. On the other hand, for N_S, there is no such distinction: statistically and visually, early honeymoon and concurrent elections are just as likely to have values of N_S that are statistically indistinguishable from the Seat Product prediction, on average.[2]

The most striking result demonstrated by these graphs is that it is the greatest values of E at which N_V (and less so, N_S) increases most, relative to the SPM. Thus it is during the counter-honeymoon, which we might define as $E>0.75$, that we are most likely to see inflated values of N_V. Why might this be? And how does this result call into question more common ways of understanding the impact of timing of elections on party systems in presidential systems? These will be the topics of the remainder of this chapter.

HOW THE PRESIDENT'S PARTY'S LUCK CHANGES OVER THE PRESIDENTIAL TERM

In the preceding section, we surmised that the observed variation in how well the Seat Product Model predicts the effective number of parties (votes or seats) is driven by relative boost and bust of the presidential party as the presidential term unfolds. This can be tested more directly.

Consider a quantity called the Presidential Vote Ratio (R_P), defined as the vote share of the president's party divided by the president's own vote share. We use the vote share of the president elected at the same time as the assembly, if

---

[2] The mean ratios observed for concurrent elections are 0.943 for N_S and 1.02 for N_V. For all nonconcurrent elections with $E<0.4$, the ratios are, respectively, 1.053 and 1.274; the difference for N_S is not significant ($p=.187$), while the difference for N_V is ($p=.025$). If we use earlier cutoffs on the set of "honeymoon" elections with which to compare to concurrent (e.g., 0.33 or 0.25), the pattern remains the same but the number of honeymoon elections in the comparison set becomes very small.

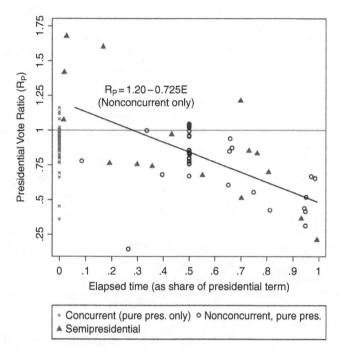

FIGURE 12.2 Relationship of elapsed time (E) between presidential elections on the presidential vote ratio (R_P)

elections are concurrent $(E=0)$, or the incumbent president for nonconcurrent elections (i.e., any $0<E<1$).

This ratio, R_P, is plotted against elapsed time in the president's term (E) in Figure 12.2. It shows a strong relationship. In the case of concurrent elections, plotted with light gray 'x' symbols, the tendency is for $R_P<1$. The observed mean when elections are concurrent is $R_P=0.908$, with a 95 percent confidence ratio of 0.876 to 0.940. In other words, leading presidential candidates tend to be more popular than their parties when elections are concurrent. Indeed, we can see a relative few data points above the line at $R_P=1$, in contrast to the large cluster of points just below this line.

The regression trend line, shown as a dark gray diagonal, is for nonconcurrent elections only. It shows a clear break in the pattern. That is, there is no continuous effect of timing on R_P from concurrent to early honeymoon elections; in fact, there is a sharp jump. If the assembly election is held after the winner of the presidency is known, we tend to have $R_P >1$ (even though a few individual elections defy the trend). The purely empirical regression result for nonconcurrent elections is:

$$R_P = 1.20 – 0.725E. \qquad (12.1)$$

To illustrate the effect, let us suppose that an assembly election is held one month following the election of a president to a five-year (sixty-month) term, for which $E=0.0167$. This is approximately the case in France, where a honeymoon electoral cycle has had a powerful effect on presidential support in the assembly (Dupoirier and Sauger 2010) since it was adopted in 2002 (Samuels and Shugart 2010: 175-179). From Equation 12.1, if $E=0.0167$, we expect $R_P=1.188$. If a hypothetical president had been elected with 35 percent of the (first-round) vote, we expect the president's party to win around 41.6 percent of the vote, on average, in this honeymoon election. Now suppose the election is at this same president's midterm ($E=0.5$). We expect $R_P=0.8375$, which for our president who received 35 percent of the vote would translate into only 29.3 percent for the party. The midterm penalty, well known from most US presidential terms, is a real, generalizable phenomenon.[3]

Finally, suppose there is a counter-honeymoon election, again with our hypothetical president who won 35 percent of the vote. If $E=.75$, we get an estimated $R_P=0.656$, which would imply only 23.0 percent of the assembly vote for the presidential party. The party tends to perform substantially worse relative to the president's own vote share, the later the election is held. As we see in Figure 12.2, this is not just a broad regression trend; every data point at $E\geq0.75$ is below the line, $R_P=1$. Moreover, there is no different pattern for pure and semipresidential systems. Across regimes with politically significant presidents (as defined in the appendix to Chapter 11), the impact of the timing of elections is an important factor in affecting the fate of the presidential party.

The timing of elections, or what Shugart (1995) referred to as the electoral cycle, is not generally considered part of the electoral system. However, we have seen in both Figures 12.1 and 12.2 that the timing matters for the effective number of parties, and for the performance of the president's own party. It is not that such an effect has gone unnoticed. Rather, it is the way in which it has been treated that deserves a corrective. In standard works since Amorim Neto and Cox (1997) and Cox (1997), the concept of relative timing has been examined through a very different variable, called *proximity*. This variable is held to affect how much the effective number of presidential candidates (N_P), entered in many common works as an input variable, impacts N_V. Already in Chapter 11, we showed that a different way of conceptualizing how N_P and N_V are related held promise, even allowing us to offer a model of the impact of the assembly electoral system on N_P (Equation 11.1). Now we turn to an analysis of how presidential votes constellations are related to those for assembly votes, with a specific focus on the counter-honeymoon elections.

---

[3] Due to the many US elections at $E=0.5$, it might be worth knowing if the overall effect depicted is substantially different without the US data points. It is not; dropping all US elections, we get $R_P=1.17 - 0.703E$. The difference is trivial.

Near the end of the chapter we offer a discussion of our conception of elapsed time, E, in contrast to the notion of *proximity* found in standard approaches.

Counter-Honeymoon Elections and the Relationship of N_P and N_V

We expect assembly elections that occur very late in a presidential term to experience greater fragmentation of the assembly party system. Our reasoning is that, as the next presidential election approaches, parties are jockeying for advantage in potential executive coalitions for the next term.[4] The counter-honeymoon logic is that parties that may later join forces behind a joint presidential candidacy emphasize their vote-earning potential in an assembly election that is no longer shaped by the now-distant prior presidential election.

The counter-honeymoon assembly election thus functions as almost a "primary" (Shugart and Carey 1992) in which the parties prepare the ground for launching or endorsing presidential candidates in an election that is coming up soon after. The implication is that it is those elections latest in a presidential term that should have the greatest ratio of N_V/N_P, where N_P is the effective number of presidential candidates when the sitting president was elected.

We explore this idea in Figure 12.3. This graph returns to the theme of Figure 11.2 in Chapter 11, where we compared N_P to N_V. The difference is that, instead of putting the two effective numbers on distinct axes, we now plot their ratio on the vertical axis and plot elapsed time, E, on the horizontal. This format allows us to see if an especially high N_V, relative to N_P, tends to occur in counter-honeymoon elections. We should expect such a high ratio if we are correct that the counter-honeymoon serves as a de facto primary in which multiple parties compete for the assembly, but many of them abstain from presenting their own candidate for the presidential contest.

The pattern is exactly as expected.[5] The plotted regression output (with its 95 percent confidence intervals) shows a sharp uptick on the ratio, N_V/N_P, when assembly elections are later than the midterm of the president. For the entire first half of time between presidential elections, the ratio is not significantly different from 1.0,[6] even though the estimated curve is similar to

---

[4] The logic articulated here is similar to that in Shugart and Carey (1992: 264–265), where the counter-honeymoon format is depicted as "quasi-parliamentary" because of "the primacy of the assembly elections and the parties represented in the assembly."

[5] Notwithstanding some anomalously high ratios in concurrent elections. All cases of $N_V/N_P > 2.5$ come from Brazil, whose patterns of N_V and N_P were discussed in Chapter 11.

[6] Despite our expressed reservations about using a future event in our estimations, perhaps some readers might wonder what would happen if we used N_P in the *next* election instead of the prior one. The answer is that it matters not at all. Regression results or a data plot would be almost identical. Thus the pattern of high N_V/N_P ratio in counter-honeymoon elections is not a result of unusually low N_P in earlier elections in our sample. It is a feature of the counter-honeymoon timing. Furthermore, it is not likely that counter-honeymoon elections tend to exhibit a sort of

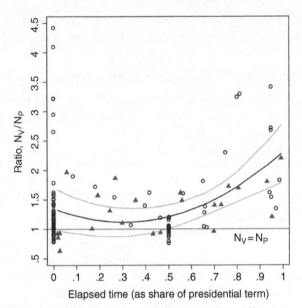

FIGURE 12.3 Effect of *Elapsed time* (*E*) on the ratio of the effective number of vote-earning assembly parties (N_V) to the effective number of presidential candidates (N_P)

the "smiley" pattern that we saw in Figure 12.1. For the regression output, see the chapter appendix.

The various patterns shown in this chapter suggest that for cases of concurrent or early-term elections and up till around midterm, the Seat Product Model is as accurate, on average, for presidential systems as it is for parliamentary. However, counter-honeymoon elections are different. They tend to feature higher than expected N_V (and to a lesser extent, N_S), and significantly higher ratio of N_P to N_V. The pattern likely results from parties' being relatively less concerned with the balance of partisan forces in the assembly than in demonstrating their strength for the upcoming presidential contest, when the latter will come shortly after an assembly election. Thus the counter-honeymoon pattern lessens the constraints of the Seat Product, as parties prepare to make their case to the electorate for the upcoming presidential contest.

THE NOTION OF "PROXIMITY"

What is counter-honeymoon for one presidential period is of course preparatory stage for the next period. While parties and voters usually

---

anticipatory coattail effect of the main contenders in the upcoming presidential election, as suggested by Stoll (2015). If this were the case, we might expect the N_V/N_P ratio to decline in the counter-honeymoon, because assembly voting would be dominated by the parties of the known leading contenders.

TABLE 12.1 *Asymmetry between assembly elections in late counter-honeymoon and early honeymoon*

	$E=0.75$	$E=0.25$	Difference	$E=0.99$	$E=0.01$	Difference
Act. N_S/Exp. N_S (Fig. 12.1)	1.12	0.85	0.27	1.47	0.94	0.53
Act. N_V/Exp. N_V (Fig. 12.1)	1.30	1.10	0.20	1.89	1.48	0.41
N_V/N_P (Fig. 12.4)	1.67	1.07	0.60	2.50	1.34	1.16

know the date of election, they do not know the outcome of the election to come, and this affects their decisions. Assembly elections in late counter-honeymoon – and, to a lesser degree, in the early honeymoon – lead to a larger effective number of parties than near midterm (or at concurrent elections). Thus a sort of a peak appears at elapsed time $E=1$ of the first period (which is $E=0$ for the next). At first glance this peak may look symmetric, which might be an appealing simplification. But at a closer look symmetry does not hold up.

As shown in Table 12.1, the quadratic fits in the onset of counter-honeymoon ($E=0.75$) are higher than in the end of honeymoon ($E=0.25$) for N_S and N_V (both normalized with respect to values expected from the *MS* model), as well as for N_V normalized with respect to N_P (see Figures 12.1 and 12.3). The contrast is boosted when we compare the quadratic fit extrapolations to immediately before and immediately after presidential elections ($E=0.99$ and $E=0.01$).

The existence of asymmetry makes sense, because the information available differs x months before and x months after the election. At both times the *date* of elections is known, leading to increased effective number of parties, compared to the quieter midterm. This accounts for the existence of the peak. But before the presidential election, parties and voters do not know its *outcome* – and maybe do not even know who might run. After the election they know who was elected president, with what percent of votes. Thus they behave in a different way in assembly elections before and after presidential election. This accounts for the asymmetry of the peak around the presidential election.

Why belabor what is so obvious? The future rarely is a mirror image of the past. We are compelled to do so because in the study of elections in presidential democracies a concept of "proximity" has emerged under which, indeed, x months before and x months after the presidential elections party system characteristics are supposed to be identical. This concept starts by correctly observing a peak in the number of parties around the time of presidential election, but then overdoes it by incorrectly assuming that the peak is symmetric, so that one can take the average of data x months before and x months after the election. This focus on mere "proximity" to presidential election (be it before or after) would correspond to presuming that all the differences shown in Table 12.1 are zero This conflation of "before" and "after" blurs data and hence limits predictive power. We consider it less than useful.

Yet, this concept has gained some currency, and so it has to be addressed. *Proximity* can be defined as:

$$\text{Proximity} = 2|(t_L - t_F)/(t_S - t_F) - \tfrac{1}{2}|,$$

where t_L is the date of legislative election, and t_F and t_S are the dates of first and second presidential elections, respectively. Its actual introduction (Cox 1997: 210) used more cumbersome subscripts, but to the same effect:

[The] formula expresses the time elapsed between the preceding presidential election and the legislative election . . . as a fraction of the presidential term . . . Subtracting ½ from this *elapsed time*, and then taking the absolute value, shows how far away from the midterm the legislative election was held. (Cox 1997: 210, our emphasis)

Cox presents the logic of his formula as follows:

The least proximal legislative elections are those held at midterm. This particular formula gives a proximity value of zero to these elections, which equates them with the *totally isolated* elections of nonpresidential systems. The most proximal nonconcurrent elections are those held *just before or just after* a presidential election. The formula above gives them a proximity value that approaches one, *the same value given to concurrent elections*. (Cox 1997: 210–211, our emphasis)

We object to the concept of proximity for two reasons. One is the reason stated at the start of this section, that x months before and x months after an event like a presidential election are not the same. The second is that there is scant evidence that a midterm election is "totally isolated" from a presidential election. The quadratic fits in Figures 12.1 indicate perennial influence, alternately boosting and depressing the number of assembly parties. In fact, the only way to isolate an assembly election from a presidential election is not to have the latter – as in a parliamentary system. A common empirical approach to explaining the effective number of parties, as used by Amorim Neto and Cox (1997), Cox (1997), Clark and Golder (2006), and others,[7] does indeed take midterm elections in presidential systems to be identical to elections in parliamentary systems.[8]

A well-established effect of timing of elections in the US and other presidential systems is that when assembly elections are at the midterm, there

---

[7] Other examples include Hicken and Stoll (2011); Mozaffar et al. (2003); Golder (2006); and Elgie et al. (2014).

[8] For parliamentary systems, these scholars enter a zero for *proximity* and interact it with a nonsensical value of $N_P=0$. For an extended critique see Li and Shugart (2016).

is a strong tendency for a decline in electoral support for the party of the incumbent president (Campbell 1960; Hinckley 1967; Tufte 1975; Kernell 1977; Erickson 1988; Shugart 1995). If timing of elections (whether measured by *proximity* or by our preferred *elapsed time*) is to have impact on the effective number of parties, it presumably works primarily through its effect on the size of the president's party.[9]

We already saw (Figure 12.2) that there is indeed a linear decline of the president's vote ratio (R_P) in nonconcurrent elections, because the president's party obtains lower vote totals as elections are held later in the incumbent president's term.[10] It is this decline that produces the pattern seen in Figure 12.1, wherein counter-honeymoon elections tend to have higher values of the effective number of parties than we would predict from their assembly Seat Product. By contrast, at the midterm, there is a tendency for N_V to dip, presumably because far from being isolated, such elections are "referendums" on the incumbent president. The president's support is slipping, although not as much as it likely will later still in the term.

For these reasons, we find greater predictive power in the continuous concept of elapsed time throughout the president's term, for which the counter-honeymoon elections take the highest values, and concurrent the lowest. Elections at the midterm, intuitively, take a value of one half in our measure. The standard approaches instead interact their notion of *proximity*, in which it

---

[9] In justifying an identical concept of *proximity* in their study, Clark and Golder (2006: 695) say: "The further apart in time these elections are held, the harder it is to imagine that presidential elections will significantly influence the behavior of voters and party elites in legislative elections." This claim is implausible: midterm decline is itself a product of voters and other actors responding to the outcome of the preceding presidential election – specifically, to the incumbent office-holder. Our linear decline in R_P strongly implies that behavior continues throughout the term to be conditioned by the outcome of the last presidential election, and how far back in time it was. Nonetheless, despite their claim, Clark and Golder estimate a regression in which midterm N_V can be higher than it would be if there were no presidential election at all, because they include a multiplicative interaction of N_P and *proximity*. Cox's regressions do not have this problem because he leaves out the constitutive terms of his interactions. So at least his result (midterm N_V no different from an otherwise identical parliamentary system) is consistent with his theory, whether or not it is plausible. Clark and Golder justify the inclusion of the constitutive terms solely on statistical practice, not on theory, and thus end up with results inconsistent with their theory, given that N_P, *proximity*, and their interaction are all found to be significant in the regression sample that contains their fully pooled results over the 1945–2000 period. (Thus the sample most similar to that which we use here, and in Chapters 7 and 8.)

[10] In introducing the concept, Cox (1997: 210) says that his approach to the impact of presidential variables, including proximity, "follows Shugart and Carey in general conception but differs in the details of implementation." However, he offers no apparent theoretical argument for why proximity should affect the number of assembly parties; Shugart and Carey (1992) and Shugart (1995) were concerned with the impact of timing on support for the president's party, not on the effective number.

is the midterms that have the zero value, with N_P. (See Li and Shugart, 2016, for further discussion.)

The notion in those works that employ the concept of *proximity* is that, the closer the dates of elections to each branch are to one another (regardless of which comes first), the more the presidential contest "influences" the assembly election. What they mean is that if there are several contenders for the presidency, there also will be more for the assembly; however, if presidential competition is confined to just two serious candidates, then the number of serious parties for the assembly likewise is held to a low level. This effect is, they say, minimized for elections farther in time from either the past or future presidential election, reaching zero at the midterm. This standard approach is not fruitful, partly because N_P itself turns out to be explained by the assembly electoral system, as we saw in Chapter 11, but also because of the inaccurate assumptions about how timing works, as reviewed in this section.

In this section, we have explained why the common notion of "proximity" employed by many works in the literature has key logical flaws. We already demonstrated earlier in the chapter how a continuous measure of elapsed time is superior. We also demonstrated the value of using a quadratic fit, because there is evidence of significantly greater fragmentation of the party system, relative to the Seat Product baseline, for elections late in a presidential term.

CONCLUSIONS: ARE PRESIDENTIAL SYSTEMS SPECIAL AND IF SO, HOW?

In one way, of course presidential systems are "special" – unlike parliamentary systems they have a separately elected presidency that serves executive functions. The executive is not simply the leadership of the party or coalition of parties that has earned sufficient assembly seats to govern. Yet in previous chapters, we have seen scant evidence of any systematic differences in the effects of presidentialism on the relationships examined. More scatter can be observed, but not a pattern requiring a different model or one with additional inputs (see Chapters 7, 8, and 10).

Now we are concluding the second of our two chapters focused specifically on presidential systems. We found in Chapter 11 that we could estimate the effective number of candidates in presidential elections from the assembly electoral system – a remarkable result that no other scholars have even considered, as best we can tell. In this chapter, we undertook an in-depth investigation of how the timing of elections to the two elected branches in presidential systems shapes party-system variables in the assembly.

In this chapter, we found that "elapsed time" does affect the number of parties in the assembly. Most significantly, the counter-honeymoon period (as defined by Shugart and Carey 1992) at the end of the president's term results in an effective number of assembly parties greater than expected from the Seat Product. This increase results from the late-term pressures that tend to push down the vote share of the president's party, relative to the president's own support when elected.

In the process of analyzing the impact of timing, we debunk the *proximity* approach to the presidential cycle and its impact on assembly parties. The latter assumes that election of a given president has exactly similar consequences for the assembly later on and prior to the presidential election. Since this approach has had some currency, it had to be addressed.

In sum, the effective number of assembly parties is predicted well, on average, by the Seat Product, *except for likely increase during counter-honeymoon elections*. These are the elections in which, along with waning support for the president's party, other parties are attempting to differentiate themselves with an eye towards the presentation of candidates for the *upcoming* presidential contest. Some of them subsequently may withdraw from the presidential coalition and form alliances with others. These incentives for parties – separate contests for assembly but alliances for presidency – tend to produce higher numbers of parties than foreseen by the Seat Product Model ratios of N_V to N_P.

If the Seat Product for the assembly election (Chapters 7 and 8) predicts the effective number of parties well in presidential systems, with the provisos we offer in this chapter about election timing, then this is good news for design of electoral systems in such democracies. We do not need to know just how many presidential candidates run, and their relative vote shares (i.e., the information summarized in N_P) in order to have a reasonably good idea what the assembly party rules should look like so as to produce a desired average pattern.

The applicability of the Seat Product in presidential systems turns the conventional wisdom on its head: most scholars and other observers assume that presidential competition shapes assembly parties and the outcomes of elections. We find that it is possible to give explanatory precedence to the assembly electoral rules: they shape competition for the presidency, and their timing impacts how constraining those rules are.

Appendix to Chapter 12

This appendix reports the regression results that are graphed and discussed in Chapter 12. Table 12.A1 shows three regressions, each with a different output variable. In Regression One, the quantity of interest is the effective number of seat-winning parties (N_S) normalized to the expectation from the Seat Product Model. In Regression Two it is the effective number of vote-earning parties (N_V), similarly normalized. In Regression Three it is the ratio of the effective number of presidential candidates (N_P) to N_V.

TABLE 12.A1 *Regressions for party system outcomes according to elapsed time in the presidential term*

	(1) $N_S/(MS)^{1/6}$	(2) $N_V/[(MS)^{1/4}+1]^{2/3}$	(3) N_V/N_P
Nonconcurrent		0.428** (0.206) [0.00600 – 0.850]	
Elapsed time (E)	–0.696 (0.450) [–1.632 – 0.240]	–2.307** (1.008) [–4.372 – –0.241]	–1.916** (0.678) [–3.331 – –0.501]
Elapsed time, squared	1.234** (0.592) [0.00288 – 2.466]	2.723** (1.041) [0.591 – 4.856	3.100*** (0.875) [1.276 – 4.925]
Constant	0.950*** (0.107) [0.727 – 1.173]	1.020*** (0.125) [0.763 – 1.276]	1.359*** (0.200) [0.942 – 1.777]
Observations	120	135	112
R-squared	0.112	0.135	0.161

Robust standard errors in parentheses.
95 percent confidence intervals in brackets.
*** $p<0.01$, ** $p<0.05$

TABLE 12.A2 *Regressions for the impact of elapsed time in the presidential term on the presidential vote ratio*

	(1) Presidential vote ratio (R_P)
Nonconcurrent	0.296*** (0.0932) [0.103 – 0.490]
Elapsed time	–0.725*** (0.129) [–0.992 – –0.458]
Constant	0.908*** (0.0220) [0.863 – 0.954]
Observations	118
R-squared	0.351

Robust standard errors in parentheses.
95 percent confidence intervals in brackets.
*** $p<0.01$

All three regressions include both concurrent and nonconcurrent elections. Only Regression Two has an indicator (dummy) variable to set concurrent apart from the rest. This is because including such an indicator in the other two did not affect the results (and the indicator itself was insignificant). The indicator is for nonconcurrent elections, rather than for concurrent, so that it captures the expected increase in the outcome variable in early honeymoon elections, relative to concurrent, and thus leaves the constant term to capture the value for concurrent elections (for which the *nonconcurrent* indicator and *elapsed time* variables are both zero).

In Table 12.A2, we report the regression output for the impact of election timing on Presidential vote ratio (R_P), calculated as the votes for the president's party, divided by the votes the president obtained in the concurrent presidential election, or the preceding one if nonconcurrent. The input variables are the indicator for nonconcurrent elections and the elapsed time (E).

PART IV

THE INTRAPARTY DIMENSION
OF REPRESENTATION

13

How Electoral Systems Shape Candidate Vote Shares

Up to now, this book has been principally about the interparty dimension of representation. That is, the focus has been on how different features of electoral systems – principally assembly size and district magnitude, but also electoral formula – shape the effective number of parties (votes and seats), as well as deviation from proportionality and other measures. In this sense, it is firmly in line with most of the literature on electoral systems. However, there is another dimension, mostly neglected until recently,[1] but of increasing importance to scholars and designers of electoral systems alike. That is the intraparty dimension, which is the focus of this chapter and the next. We show how, as with the interparty dimension, the votes of candidates on the intraparty dimension can be deduced from the constraints of seats available. In this sense, this chapter is also of methodological interest: it further demonstrates the power of assuming the mean of the conceptual extremes.

It is axiomatic that parties are collective actors, consisting of many politicians and other actors who associate with the party for purposes of enhancing their ability to win seats. Whenever $M>1$, a party typically may have more than one candidate running under its banner in a given district. The range of questions about how parties choose who their candidates will be, and how those candidates relate to voters and to one another form the essence of the intraparty dimension. We introduced various rules that shape the intraparty dimension in Chapters 1–6, and so they are not new to this chapter. In those chapters, we noted the distinction between open and closed lists, and showed how the single nontransferable vote and other nonlist systems for $M>1$ districts work. We offered examples in Chapter 6 of how alliances work when two or more parties combine on one list under either closed or open list systems. Now that we have established the main parameters of how electoral systems shape the interparty dimension, it is time to turn our focus to intraparty relations.

---

[1] Among scholars who have noted the relative neglect of the intraparty dimension are Lijphart (1985), Shugart (2005a), and Colomer (2011). Important pioneering comparative work was done by Marsh (1985), Katz (1986), Mainwaring (1991), and Ames (1995a, b).

We made the point in Chapter 2 that the simplest of all systems were the category of "list PR," in which each competing party presents a single list of candidates, and the electoral formula allocates M seats among them, in accordance with their relative vote shares. We noted that FPTP is the limiting case of a list having one candidate, and the allocation formula awarding the sole seat in the district to the highest vote-earner. As we elaborated further in Chapter 5, it need not matter whether voters choose a given list because they like the party as a whole or because they like one or more of the candidates – the sole candidate in the case of $M=1$. This is a pure categorical choice, with no opportunity to indicate a preference for one candidate of the party over some others. This is how closed-list systems operate, and for them, the intraparty dimension is primarily about candidate selection and campaign styles. It is not about competition for votes within a party.

As soon as we move to open lists, however, now the contest is one of competition on both dimensions. Voters may (or must, depending on specifics of a country's rules) select a candidate and not simply a party.[2] Lists are competing against one another for votes, but inside each list, candidates are likewise competing against one another. The key characteristic linking competition of candidates and lists together is that a vote for any candidate on an open list is also a *pooling* vote, in Cox's (1997: 42) typology: it counts for the list (of allied candidates) on which the candidate was nominated as well as for the specific candidate.

An open-list PR system remains "simple" by our definition because each list wins seats in proportion to its collective votes, within the constraints of district magnitude and allocation formula. Once the number of seats won by any given list has been put through the operation of the PR formula, then the winners within the list are simply its s highest vote-earners, where s is the number of seats won.[3]

Given that an open-list system means each candidate competing against list-mates for one of s seats the party wins, a question we devote this chapter to is: *Does the competition among candidates inside a list tend to follow a predictable pattern* as does the competition among lists within a district of a simple PR system? We will show that indeed there are such patterns. We can develop logical reasoning on the intraparty dimension in a way similar to what we have done for the interparty dimension – at least for some key aspects of intraparty relations.

There are also, of course, systems with $M>1$ but no lists. We outlined several of them in Chapter 3, but we have had little to say about them till now because of our focus on simple systems. Nonlist, $M>1$, formulas have the potential to

---

[2] As noted in Chapter 2, some open-list systems permit a voter to cast more than one preference vote. However, in the present chapter and Chapter 14, we will address only the single-vote systems.

[3] In this chapter, we do not explore flexible-list systems, a hybrid described briefly in Chapter 6.

break one of our defining characteristics of simplicity: the rank-size principle. This is so because it is possible for a party to have the most votes in a district yet not have the most seats, or more generally for parties not to win seats in order of their *collective* vote shares. The simplest of these nonsimple formulas, as we noted in Chapter 3, is the single nontransferable vote (SNTV). Under SNTV, the winners are the candidates who have the M highest vote totals, *regardless of their party affiliation* (if any). Because it is just a top-M candidate-based allocation formula, SNTV means that it matters how many candidates a party has, and how its votes are distributed among the candidates, as explained in Chapter 3. It does not matter how many votes a party has collectively; unlike any list system, votes do not "pool" on the list for the purposes of determining the interparty allocation of seats. The pure candidate-based aspect of SNTV introduces the incentive of parties to "manage" their internal competition.

Vote management means restricting the number of candidates, attempting to equalize candidates' votes, or other methods of shaping the competition (such as in the characteristics of candidates and how widely they appeal within the district). One key implication is that parties under SNTV will attempt to avoid having one candidate dominate the others nominated by the party in the same district. If one candidate is very popular, those are votes that the party would have benefitted from shifting to another candidate to help bring him or her into the district's top M vote totals.[4]

This imperative for parties to engage in vote management under SNTV is in stark contrast to the internal competition under open-list PR. Because of the pooling of votes on the list, parties in open-list systems can afford "laissez faire" competition. With seats first being allocated among lists before they are allocated to candidates, a party should want to have as many candidates as the law allows. Any votes obtained by a candidate benefit the party collectively, because they add to the pool of votes on which the list obtains seats. Moreover, a very popular candidate is an asset, as the votes he or she brings may increase the list's total seats and help elect less popular list-mates. Thus parties generally should not have reason to worry themselves at how unequal the vote shares of their candidates are, in contrast to parties under SNTV.

This distinction between *laissez-faire* competition under open-list proportional representation (OLPR) and incentives for parties to manage competition under SNTV has several implications that will form the basis of a logical model in this chapter, and of several other testable implications explored. Then in Chapter 14, we turn these logical implications onto a related aspect of electoral competition – that between sublist collective actors. We assume that sublist collective actors almost always exist in

---

[4] Coordination of candidates' personal vote totals has been central to the literature on SNTV, e.g., Batto (2008), Cox (1997: 100–114), Cox and Niou (1994), Cox and Shugart (1995), Grofman et al. (1999), Johnson and Hoyo (2012), Reed (1991), Swindle (2002), Thayer (1969).

a list-PR system. If those lists are open, these actors are competing against each other for the seats their combined list wins. We know from the extensive literature on SNTV that subparty actors, typically called "factions," are common in such systems. We will not explore the question of factions in SNTV further, as it is well-trod ground (e.g., Hrebenar 1986; Grofman, et al., 1999; Reed 2009). However, much less is known about OLPR with alliances, in which we often do not have party lists, per se, but alliance lists in which the list's candidates may be variously branded by different party labels. That is, the sublist collective actors are themselves parties. Before we can make sense of sublist collective actors, we need to understand the individual actors, that is the candidates, and their vote shares within a party or list. That is the focus of the rest of this chapter.

THE SCOPE OF OLPR AND SNTV AND WHAT WE CAN LEARN FROM THEM

Before we go farther on the topic, we might pause to ask, why study such systems at all? Are they not so rare that we should not bother? Is it not the case that most PR systems used closed lists? Is not SNTV a relic of history? Not quite, although open lists are less common than the categories of closed or flexible list, it is true. (Recall our discussion of flexible-list systems in Chapter 6; see Crisp et al. 2013, André et al. 2017, Cahill et al. n.d). Nonetheless, OLPR is found in the two largest countries that use PR: Brazil and Indonesia (Allen 2018), the fourth and fifth largest countries in the world. It is also used in several longstanding democracies in Europe, including Finland (von Schoultz 2017) and Switzerland.[5] Poland, the sixth largest country in the European Union, has used OLPR since it democratized in the 1990s (as discussed in Chapter 1), and other relatively large countries including Colombia and Peru use it.[6] Chile has used it whenever it has had democratic elections since the 1950s.[7] OLPR is also apparently spreading in Latin America, as since around 2000 at least three smaller countries in the region have replaced closed lists with open: Dominican Republic, El Salvador, and Honduras.[8] Thus it is far from being a marginal system.

---

[5] The system used in Switzerland, while meeting the criteria of open lists, is more complex. Voters may cast up to M preference votes, across lists (*panachage*, as mentioned in Chapter 2), and parties may run multiple lists in a district, and pool votes across them.

[6] Colombia has used OLPR (with a party option for closed lists instead) since 2006. Prior to that time it used SNTV. Data in this chapter included one election under each system. For details, see Shugart et al. (2007), Pachón and Shugart (2010), and Taylor and Shugart (2018). In the Peruvian case, a voter may cast two preference votes within a list.

[7] That is, in its two democratic periods, interrupted by the dictatorship of 1973–1989.

[8] The latter two cases permit the voter to cast up to M preference votes, with *panachage*.

It is true that SNTV is not currently used by any large democracy. However, it was used for decades in Japan. It was also used in Taiwan, and thus accounts of a sizeable block of East Asian democratic experience to date. The system was adopted for Afghanistan in 2005 (Reynolds 2006), and has been used in subsequent elections there. A system that is SNTV in its essential details is used in Hong Kong (Carey 2018), where it serves as a potential example for democracy activists in China (of which Hong Kong is a part, with a special status) as well as a thorn in the side of the Communist Party ruling that country.

A basic reason for studying these systems is not merely the scope of their use around the world, but because the logic of competition that they provide may be the key for understanding further aspects of the still-understudied intraparty dimension of representation. In the remainder of this chapter, we develop models of intraparty competition among candidates, showing that we can employ similar techniques of combining logic and empirical analysis as we have done previously on the interparty dimension.

HOW OLPR AND SNTV SHAPE THE NUMBER OF CANDIDATES AND COMPETITION BETWEEN THEM

In analyzing the intraparty dimension, we are interested in how electoral system features, specifically the district magnitude and the allocation formula, affect the behavior of parties as collective actors consisting of individual candidates. The two formulas we investigate are OLPR and SNTV, and each is used in a wide range of district magnitudes (with that range being greater empirically for OLPR).

The first question we will address is the question of how many candidates a party nominates. It is usually not in a party's interests to nominate M or more candidates if the system is SNTV. Given the absence of vote pooling, parties that spread their votes out across many candidates may fail to convert their collective votes into a proportionate number of seats. Thus parties under SNTV should tend to nominate fewer than M candidates, although it remains to be seen how many fewer. When the system is OLPR, the vote-pooling mechanism of any list system guarantees the party will convert its collective votes into a proportionate share of seats, within the limits of the district magnitude and whichever specific PR formula is used. Thus it has no reason to restrict the number of candidates.

Thus, we start with two basic premises about the expected number of candidates, c:

$c \geq M$ if OLPR;
$c' \leq M$, if SNTV.

We introduce here the prime mark ($'$) to differentiate quantities under SNTV from those under OLPR (which will be unmarked). To take these inequalities farther towards a logical model, we can stipulate that for OLPR, the number of candidates should rise 1:1 with magnitude. Sometimes the law restricts the number of candidates, and thus we would expect $c=M$. However, many countries, including Brazil and Finland, permit $c>M$, and as we have stated already, parties have clear incentive to nominate as many as they are allowed. Thus our expectation for OLPR is:

$$c = \beta M \quad \text{[OLPR]} \tag{13.1}$$

where β must be determined empirically and is equal to or greater than 1.0.

In the case of SNTV, many parties may follow the ultimate safe strategy and nominate only one candidate. In fact, parties that nominate just one candidate comprise a majority of our SNTV parties: 728 of 1271 (57.3 percent). These parties then have no need for further vote management among their candidates, because they have mitigated the problem of unequal votes distribution by having only one standard-bearer. For all other parties, then, we need a model that anchors at $c'=2$, $M=2$, given that we do not expect parties to nominate $c'>M$ and we have excluded $c'>1$ and hence $M=1$ from the model. We should expect c' to rise with M, but at a declining rate. Following our usual process of taking the geometric average when we lack other information, we start from the lower limit of 1 and the expected upper limit of M, and expect a slope of $M^{1/2}$. Thus we propose:

$$c' = (2M)^{0.05} = 1.4\sqrt{M} \quad \text{[SNTV, if } c' > 1]. \tag{13.2}$$

The expression obviously produces $c'=2$ at $M=2$, and then predicts a rise with M, but not the 1:1 relationship to M that we expect with OLPR.

When we run regressions to test Equations 13.1 and 13.2, we get $c=1.22M^{1.004}$ for OLPR and $c'=1.37M^{0.474}$ for SNTV (provided $c'>1$). While we had no specific expectation for the value of β in Equation 13.1, we confirm the expected slope of 1.0; that is, c really does rise 1:1 with M, on average. The regression for SNTV confirms the logical model of Equation 13.2 almost precisely. The output of these regressions is shown in the appendix to this chapter.

In Figure 13.1 we plot the result for the two formulas, OLPR in the left panel and SNTV in the right. Both panels are scaled to identical logarithmic axes in order to see at a glance the different patterns under the different formulas, even though the range of district magnitude is considerably lower under SNTV.

In the case of OLPR, the dashed line shows the average fit, $c=1.22M^{1.004}$. There is a bulge of data points at $M\geq6$ where many parties are seen with $c>M$; these represent the main range of M in Brazil and Finland, two countries that allow $c>M$.[9] In the SNTV panel, we see that $c'=1$ occurs at all observed values

---

[9] The data points in Figure 13.1, left panel, seem to form several parallel lines; we will not discuss them, other than to note that such a pattern is consistent with the predicted slope of M^1.

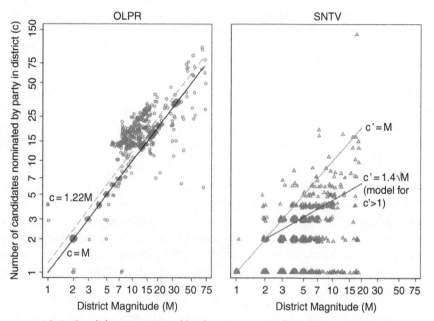

FIGURE 13.1 Candidates nominated by district magnitude under open list proportional representation (OLPR, left panel) and single nontransferable vote (SNTV, right panel)

of M, and we also see that the model fits the average pattern well for those that have $c'>1$, huge scatter notwithstanding. Surprisingly, $c'>M$ is sometimes observed. We will discuss later the reasons why parties might nominate more than M candidates even under SNTV, although it is worth noting that fewer than 5 percent of parties do so.[10]

Vote Management: Vote Distribution Across Candidates

Now we turn our attention to what, if anything, parties do to manage the distribution of votes across whatever number, c, of candidates they have nominated. To carry out this analysis, we will model the *preference-vote shares* of candidates at various ranks within their party (or list) at the district level. By preference votes, we mean the votes of candidates when there are two or more competing within a party, under any system in which voters cast votes below the level of the party, including OLPR and SNTV.[11] Just as vote and seat

---

[10] There is one data point in the right panel that looks like a sure mistake. It is not: The Liberal Party in the district of Bogotá, Colombia, really did nominate 141 candidates in a district with $M=18$ in 2002.

[11] The term, preference vote, is well established. See, for example, Marsh (1985), Katz (1986), Karvonen (2004), Renwick and Pilet (2016).

shares of parties are the standard means of measuring the relative success of parties – as in several of our preceding chapters – so the vote shares of candidates within a party are an obvious measure of candidates' performance relative to one another.[12]

We designate any given candidate's share of the preference votes as $P_r = V_r/V_p$, where V_r is the vote total of the candidate ranked r in votes in the party and V_p is the sum of the votes of all the party's candidates[13] running in the same district. For winning candidates, r ranges from 1, the first winner, to s, the party's "s^{th}" candidate (where s is the party's seat total in the district).

We will consider P_1 and P_s, the preference-vote shares of the first and last winners, respectively. The *first winner* is important partly because many parties have only one winner. In the case of OLPR, even if a party has several winners, it may have one "list-puller" who dominates the intraparty competition while others win seats largely due to the pooling of the list-puller's votes. In the case of SNTV, on other hand, the first candidate has further importance because if that candidate is overly popular, the party may fail to convert its (collective) votes into seats.

If we are interested in developing a more complete picture of the shape of intraparty competition, the *last winner* is also of interest. In a very fragmented party, it may be possible to win a seat with a very small share of the party's votes, while in other parties winning two or more seats, the last winner may have a share not far behind the first winner. Comparing first and last winners' votes offers us an indicator of incentives for intraparty equalization. We now build logical models of these quantities.

First Winner's Vote Shares

The more candidates a party runs in a district, the smaller the vote share of its first winner is likely to be. As is the case throughout this book, we want to do more than stipulate the direction of the effect. We seek to generate reasonably precise estimates of the relationship so that our models can be of use to electoral-system "engineers." Let c be the number of candidates the party has nominated in the district. When $c=1$, P_1 cannot be anything else but 1, and with $c>1$ it must decrease. The simplest format to satisfy these conditions is:

$$P_1 = c^b,$$

where P_1 is the preference-vote share of the first winner, and the exponent b must be negative. To derive an expected value for b, we consider what the

---

[12] This section of the chapter draws heavily on Bergman, Shugart, and Watt (2013); readers wishing detail on the dataset may consult the earlier article.

[13] Where, as in Brazil, a list-only vote is also permitted, such votes are not included in the denominator because such votes do not affect the order in which candidates are elected.

constraints are on the variables, in order to rule out values that are impossible on logical grounds. The value of the top candidate's share of preference votes, P_1, obviously can never exceed 1. It also can never be less than $1/c$ (the value when c candidates have equal votes). Thus we have a clearly limited range beyond which the quantity of interest would not be found. If a party has no collective incentive to intervene in its internal competition, as is the case with OLPR, there is no reason to expect actual values of P_1 to be closer to either limiting value. Some parties might have a dominant list-puller, whose pooled votes benefit the party: P_1 approaching 1. Other parties might nominate numerous candidates of equal popularity, secure in the knowledge that vote pooling means there is no risk from having over-dispersed votes: P_1 approaching $1/c$, which alternatively can be written as c^{-1}. Given no reason to expect the trend to be closer to one limiting condition than to the other – as is the case with OLPR's *laissez-faire* competition – we expect the average value. With logged variables the average is found by the geometric mean of the extremes:

$$P_1 = (1 * c^{-1})^{0.5} = c^{-0.5} \tag{13.3}$$

That is, under OLPR, we expect the first winner's share to be, on average, equal to the *inverse square root* of the number of candidates running under the party's banner.

What about SNTV? The model just derived applies to the situation in which the party has no collective incentive to intervene in its internal competition, that is OLPR. However, as we have argued theoretically, parties under SNTV have incentive to intervene. Such intervention is expected to include efforts to avoid a leading candidate who is overly popular, leading to a "vote equalization error." Thus the first winner's preference share under SNTV, which we shall denote as P'_1 (with the prime mark indicating SNTV), should tend to be systematically closer to $1/c$ than is the case for OLPR. But can we get at a more precise numerical prediction?

In the absence of any knowledge on just how effective SNTV parties would tend to be at vote equalization, our best "minimax bet" again would be the geometric average of extremes. Our average SNTV party has a $c=2$ (actually 2.08). Perfect equalization results in $P'_1=0.5$, whereas *laissez-faire* coordination would produce $P'_1=.2^{-0.5}=0.707$. The geometric average of 0.5 and 0.707 is 0.595, which can be obtained for $c=2$ when $b=-0.75$. Thus we expect:

$$P'_1 = c^{-0.75}. \tag{13.4}$$

Because our estimates for SNTV did not rely on absolutes – we estimated a prediction from a prediction – Equation 13.2 rests on a weaker logical foundation than does Equation 13.1.

We can turn to our empirical test, and run the following equation, using an interactive term to check that there is a significant difference in the slopes:

$$\log P_1 = \log a_1 + k_1 \log c + k_2 (\log c * sntv) + sntv. \tag{13.5}$$

The variable, *sntv*, is a dummy for that electoral system, and the interactive term tests for the expected difference of slopes; *a* is the regression's estimated constant term. The regression (see appendix) actually yields an absurd result for OLPR, in that it fails to respect the mandatory anchor point of $P_1 = 1$ when $c=1$. Instead it gives us:

$$P_1 = 0.88 c^{-0.408}.$$

The distribution of data gives us hardly any cases with just a single candidate, and therefore the regression will not anchor itself at the logically mandatory point, $P_1 = 1$, $c=1$. Thus we need to run it again with the intercept 0 imposed. For SNTV, where we do have many case of $c'=1$, the result is both relatively close to our expectation and respective of the anchor point:

$$P'_1 = 1.00 c^{-0.707}.$$

Our expected –0.75 is within the confidence interval.[14]

Because of the need to have an expression that respects the anchor point, we can run separate no-constant regressions, which results in:

$$\text{OLPR} : P_1 = c^{-0.45} \tag{13.6}$$

$$\text{SNTV} : P'_1 = c^{-0.72}. \tag{13.7}$$

Note that the result for SNTV is closer the logical model (Equation 13.4) than is the OLPR result. This is striking, given that we had somewhat weaker logical foundations for it than for Equation 13.3, the OLPR expectation. As for the OLPR model, it is, of course, "politics blind." This may especially be a problem for predicting vote shares on the intraparty dimension under OLPR. In this system, there is a strong premium on the personal vote, combined with no incentive of parties to manage their internal votes distribution. This means that a party under OLPR is likely to have at least one "star" candidate who has been nominated precisely because she can draw lots of votes. The implication is that once we introduce political factors – here the vote-seeking value of the main candidates, including the first winner – we have to expect that P_1 will be higher than what we derive from a model that does not address such considerations. Instead, our model addressed only the number of candidates. Given such a sparse model, it is remarkable that it comes so close!

As for SNTV, the "politics blind" feature of the model proves to be an advantage. This is actually not surprising, because parties intervene to attempt to prevent their leading candidate from being too popular. This is, of

[14] Specifically, –.7735 – –.6595.

course, politics – in the sense of party organization and campaign strategy. It is not, however, political talent or other personal vote-earning characteristics of the candidates themselves, whose votes we are modeling. Rather, it is political imperatives derived precisely from the one factor in our model: the presence of multiple candidates in a party that cannot pool its own votes across those candidates. Thus a model that takes no account of individual candidate characteristics is more accurate for SNTV, where parties seek to minimize differences among their candidates. It is, by contrast, less accurate under OLPR, where parties can adopt a *laissez-faire* approach to the characteristics and vote-pulling talents of their candidates.[15]

In Figure 13.2, we probe the models and the data distribution further. The graph shows all of the OLPR data points with light gray circles, and those for SNTV with gray triangles. The SNTV data points, in particular, are more clustered, resulting in their often looking like a blob rather than individual data points. In fact, this is as expected: SNTV behavior is much less variable because of the imperative of vote-management in order to avoid wasting many votes and electing fewer candidates than the party's collective votes could have allowed. On the other hand, the distribution of OLPR data points is much more scattered than for SNTV, at least when $c>2$. This is consistent with the *laissez-faire* approach that parties can afford when their candidates' votes in the district all pool. Thus we see some lists in which the leading candidate dominates, with 80 percent or more of the list's votes, even on lists with ten or more candidates. We see other lists where the leading candidate does not have even 10 percent of the list's votes.

Despite the wide variation in OLPR first-winners' shares, there is a distinct relationship, compared to that for SNTV. The SNTV parties' first winners tend to be distributed at lower values for all $c>2$, relative to those from OLPR. The SNTV data points have a notably stronger tendency to be closer to the minimum possible value of $1/c$ (the upper border of the forbidden area[16]), consistent with efforts by these parties to equalize votes. The dashed line is Equation 13.3, our model for OLPR: $P_1=c^{-0.50}$.[17] The solid dark-gray line is Equation 13.4, $P_1=c^{-0.75}$, our logical model for SNTV.

---

[15] Even so, it is noteworthy that the coefficient for SNTV is almost precisely the mean of –1.0 (where all candidates are equal) and the coefficient for OLPR (–.45). We expected just such a relationship between the two coefficients, except that we thought the one for OLPR, would be –0.5, giving us –1.5/2 =–0.75 for SNTV.

[16] It appears that some data points are in the forbidden area, but this is only due to the "jittering" of data points, which is necessary to prevent multiple points at the same values from looking like a single point.

[17] Even though –.5 is not, in fact, within the empirically estimated confidence interval for OLPR, we use it. Given the scatter in the actual data, the empirical result (–.45) is not superior to the one that has logic to back it up.

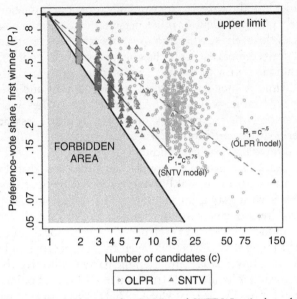

FIGURE 13.2 First winner's share under OLPR and SNTV: Logical models and data

Last Winner's Vote Share

To model the last winner's share, we start with SNTV, because its strategic imperatives make for a clear logical baseline. Just as parties under SNTV have the incentive to attempt to reduce the vote share of their leading candidate, they have a similar imperative to intervene in intraparty competition to equalize their candidates' votes. A hypothetical party that fully equalized across its candidates, all of whom won, would have a vote share of $1/c$ for each candidate. If our 1,271 parties competing under SNTV are, *on average*, successful at distributing votes equally across s candidates, then we should find:

$$P'_s = c^{-1}.$$

If this were the case, the average party would waste no votes. This is, of course, an unrealistic assumption, given that parties do not have perfect information about how their votes will be distributed across candidates, no matter how impressive their vote-management organization may be. Moreover, the last winner obviously has the same votes as the first winner for parties that win just one seat. Therefore, we might model the last winner's share as a fraction of the votes the party has left over *after accounting for its first candidate*. It is quite likely that parties need to factor into their management strategies the popularity of their leading candidate in the district. As we have argued, vote-management strategies under SNTV are partly aimed at reducing the leading candidate's intake of votes. A very popular candidate is a potential liability under SNTV, for any party seeking to win more than one seat. Nonetheless, there is only so much a party can do to undermine its own leading candidate. For these reasons, our logical model for the last winner's share is as follows:

$$P'_s/(1-P'_1) = 1/(c-1) \tag{13.8}$$

In words: the last winner's votes, as a share of the party's votes after subtracting those of its first winner, should be equal to the reciprocal of the number of its candidates after the first winner. This expectation assumes perfect equalization of votes of remaining candidates, which makes the model naïve, but forms a reasonable basis on which to build our logical model.

Now let us return to OLPR. Vote-pooling means that parties under this system do not have to worry that the distribution of their candidates' votes might undermine the collective performance of the party. Thus we should expect a higher share of P'_s for any given c. Equation 13.8, derived for SNTV would be a highly unlikely result for OLPR, because *laissez-faire* competition under the latter system means parties do not attempt to equalize votes among their candidates.

In the appendix, we propose two logical models for OLPR that take account of the *interparty dimension*. One is based on the expected relationship of the number of parties to district magnitude, $N'_{S0} = \sqrt{M}$ (as confirmed in Chapter 7), and the assumption that, under OLPR, parties nominate M candidates to their lists. The result of the logic is an expectation of:

$$P_s/(1-P_1) = [(c^{0.5}-1)(c-1)]^{-0.5}. \tag{13.9}$$

As detailed in the appendix, Equation 13.9 contains two terms on the right-hand side. The first, $c^{0.5}-1$, is based on estimating how many seats the average list holds, after accounting for the first winner, while the second, $c-1$, is based on the total number of remaining candidates (as in Equation 13.8).

The second approach to estimating P_s under OLPR takes account of the *actual* number of seats won by each list, as a function of district magnitude. While Equation 13.9 proves surprisingly accurate (as explained in the appendix), we will plot instead the results of an equation that is obtained from the known number of seats won, given that our focus on the intraparty dimension. That is, rather than incorporate any error of estimation from the interparty allocation of seats to lists, we can start with the known allocation. The adjusted model that we will plot here, and which is confirmed via regression (see appendix), is:

$$P_s/(1-P_1) = [(M^f-1)(c-1)]^{-0.5}. \tag{13.10}$$

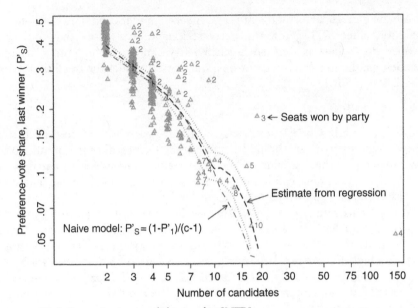

FIGURE 13.3 Last winning candidate under SNTV

where the exponent, f, on M in the first term on the right-hand side of the equation is the exponent that yields each individual list's *actual* number of seats won.[18]

We now proceed to graphs of last winner's shares under SNTV and OLPR. In Figure 13.3, we see a data plot for last winners in SNTV. The graph plots our naïve expectation for SNTV, Equation 13.8, as well as an estimate from a regression, which has a coefficient of –0.83 instead of –1.[19] The plotted equations are not straight lines, because we are plotting the equation with each party's actual value of P_1 plugged in, given that we are modeling what share P_s represents of the votes remaining after the first winner. The light dotted lines show the 95 percent confidence interval on the regression.[20] The naïve model is shown with the light dash-dot line.

As compared to the naïve model, then, parties under SNTV actually are not as good at equalizing. Or perhaps they are, if we relax the most "heroic" assumption of the naïve model, which is that parties nominate the correct

[18] That is, if $M=9$ and a given party won 2 seats, $f=0.315$, because $9^{0.315} = 2$.

[19] The regression is $\log[P_s/(1-P_1)]=-0.02 -0.830\log(c-1)$; $R^2=0.858$. The 95% confidence interval on the coefficient is $-0.919 - -0.741$. A no-constant version of the regression has a coefficient of -0.870.

[20] Both expressions that are plotted are algebraically modified so that they predict P_s after accounting for actual P_1. That is, the naïve model is plotted as $P_s=(1-P_1)/(c-1)$. The lines plotted are actually local regression (loess) curves, given that varying P_1 would otherwise imply multiple curves. The same is true of the lines plotted in Figure 13.4.

number of candidates, for how many they can elect with optimal intraparty vote distribution. In fact, parties may overnominate and then attempt to equalize among those they expect they can actually elect. To probe this idea impressionistically, we have indicated the number of seats won by all those parties that have an actual last winner's share that is above the regression's upper confidence estimate, or where the number of candidates is large, i.e., more than seven. We note that the parties with a higher than anticipated last winner's share also elected considerably fewer candidates than they had running. In fact, most of these win two seats, even if they have four or more candidates. Those with seven or more candidates and a very low last winner's share tend to have elected from $c/2$ to $c-1$ candidates through good vote-management strategy over a subset of their candidates. For instance, note the frequent occurrence of the number seven (and one case of eight and another of ten) in this area of the graph. These parties, then, had managed to suppress the votes going to their excess number of losers. We return to these questions of nominating and vote-management in more detail in Chapter 14.

Figure 13.3 thus shows that, despite the difference in coefficients, the naïve model is not far from the regression estimate, once we take the party's P_1 into account. In fact the naïve model, shown with the light dash-dot line, is barely below the regression's lower confidence bound when $c<4$, and again when $c>10$. Through the rest of the data plot, it is fully within the regression confidence bounds. Thus we see considerable evidence that parties under SNTV do indeed approximate the optimal vote management strategy, which is to ensure their winners' votes are not too disparate.

In Figure 13.4 we show a similar plot for OLPR last winners. Our logical model, Equation 13.10, which takes into account actual seats won by the list, is indicated by the black dash-dot curve. The lighter dashed curve is the empirical regression. The model and its regression test are both detailed in the appendix. What we see is that the actual pattern, as estimated via the regression, for last winner shares is somewhat higher than we expected. The difference is hardly so great as to prompt an adjustment to the model, which captures the trend well through most of the data, as well as the distinction with SNTV (when compared to Figure 13.3).

The reasons for the tendency for last winner shares under OLPR to be somewhat greater than we expect is likely due to the popularity of the candidates that parties nominate with expectation of their winning. That is, our model is blind to the personal vote-earning attributes of the candidates. It is based only on the expected number of seats a party would win, on average, and how many candidates it is expected to run. Parties may win more or fewer seats, nominate more (or less often, fewer) candidates, and some of those candidates are sufficiently popular as to stand out above the other nominees. In fact, parties may seek to prioritize the winning of candidates representing the party's constituent groups via their nomination strategy; they can increase the odds of certain candidates winning by ensuring that some of them represent specific

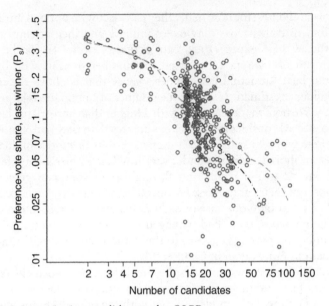

FIGURE 13.4 Last winning candidate under OLPR

constituencies.[21] To the extent that this is so, of course they are being less *laissez-faire* than we have assumed. Analysis of how the personal characteristics of winners and losers may produce the patterns observed in these graphs (or deviations from them) is a topic for further research.

CONCLUSION

In this chapter we have seen how the presence or absence of vote-pooling affects how votes are distributed across candidates in two basic types of system that entail intraparty competition for votes and seats. In both open-list proportional representation (OLPR) and single nontransferable vote (SNTV) systems, candidates stand in competition with others of the same party. The party is a collective actor that seeks to maximize the seats it wins, whereas candidates must amass a sufficient number of preference votes for themselves in order to surpass other candidates and win a seat.

The critical difference between OLPR and SNTV is in the relationship between these two goals: the party's and the candidates'. OLPR "pools" votes, and thus the party wins seats in proportion to the collective votes of its candidates (plus any votes solely for the list, if the ballot format of a given country permits such votes). Only after this seat total is known are seats

---

[21] Additionally, parties in their campaigning may boost the fortunes of a few of their key candidates (for instance, through the allocation of media time or party-provided finance).

allocated to the individual candidates, in order of their individual preference votes. This is the sense in which the system is "top s" on the intraparty dimension: the party gets s seats in the district, and the top-s candidates win them. As a result of the pooling of votes, we saw that parties tend to nominate at least M candidates. They can tolerate widely disparate vote totals for these candidates, because there is no risk of candidates spreading their votes too thinly for the party to achieve its proportionate seat total.

By contrast, SNTV is a top-M system on both dimensions. In fact, in a real sense there is no *inter*party dimension under SNTV, because the electoral system itself does not allocate seats to parties, only to candidates.[22] Thus a party wins as many seats in the district as it has candidates with top-M individual vote totals. We saw in this chapter the consequences of this distinction. In the case of SNTV, the party has an incentive to attempt to avoid too many votes going to its leading candidate. One step in this process is for a party to nominate a number of candidates close to the number it might elect. Many parties simply nominate one candidate, even when $M>1$, which obviates further vote management. Those that nominate more than one tend to keep the number below M, and we developed and confirmed a logical model that the number of candidates would tend to be, on average, $c'=(2M)^{1/2}=1.4\sqrt{M}$. Then, having two or more candidates, the party has incentive to equalize votes across whatever number of candidates it can realistically elect. Thus under SNTV we see parties engaging in managing of their internal competition, in contrast to parties under OLPR which benefit from *laissez-faire* competition.

In Chapter 14, we further investigate the behavior of parties in both SNTV and OLPR, with a focus on further consequences of vote management: how concentrated votes are on the party's winning candidates. We then take the analysis back to the interparty dimension, by examining cases under OLPR where lists consist of alliances of two or more parties.

Appendix to Chapter 13

This appendix displays the output of regressions discussed in Chapter 13, and explains detailed steps behind the model derived in the chapter for last winner's share.

REGRESSION RESULTS FROM CHAPTER 13

In Table 13.A1, we see regressions to test our expectations for the number of candidates (c) as a function of district magnitude (M). Both variables are entered as their decimal logarithms. Regression One is a test of Equation 13.1 for OLPR; we expect $\log(c) = a + 1.00\log(M)$. We have no specific expectation for

---

[22] See Shugart (2005a) for a more complete discussion of this point.

TABLE 13.A1 *Regression results for number of candidates and district magnitude*

	(1) OLPR No. of candidates (logged)	(2) SNTV No. of candidates (logged)
District magnitude, M (logged)	1.004***	0.475***
	(0.0313)	(0.0394)
	[0.942 – 1.065]	[0.397 – 0.552]
Constant	0.0878***	0.137***
	(0.0258)	(0.0259)
	[0.0369 – 0.139]	[0.0858 – 0.188]
Observations	762	543
R-squared	0.843	0.255

Robust standard errors in parentheses.
95 percent confidence intervals in brackets.
*** p<0.01

the value of a, other than that it must be not less than zero, as explained in the chapter text. The expected coefficient of 1.00 on log(M) is confirmed.

Regression Two is a test of Equation 13.2 for SNTV; we expect log(c) = 0.1505 + 0.50log(M), as explained in the chapter text.[23] Both expectations are within the 95 percent confidence intervals of the regression result, as indicated in the table.

In Table 13.A2 we test Equation 13.5, using an interactive term to check that there is a significant difference in the slopes for SNTV and OLPR. For the expectations and interpretations of the results, see the chapter text.

MODEL FOR LAST WINNER'S SHARE

For last winners, the model for SNTV is introduced in the chapter as Equation 13.8:

$$P'_s/(1-P'_1) = 1/(c-1).$$

This model is tested in Table 13.A3 as Regression One. Discussion and interpretation of the result was done in the chapter text.

For OLPR, the model is more complex, and we explain its logic here. We expect parties to nominate a full slate of candidates (M or more, if allowed); the expectation was confirmed (Table 13.A1, Regression One). As a result, they will have many losers, when M is large. Unlike in SNTV, then, there is no expectation of roughly equal vote shares among candidates after the first winner. In fact, because the last winner has many losing candidates trailing him or her, the vote share of the last winner should be well

---

[23] Note that 0.1505 is the decimal logarithm of the square root of 2.

TABLE 13.A2 *Regression results for first winner*

VARIABLES	Preference-vote share for first winner (P_1), logged
Number of candidates, logged ($\log(c)$)	-0.408^{***}
	(0.0152)
Interaction of $\log(c)$ X dummy for SNTV	-0.299^{***}
	(0.0360)
SNTV dummy	0.0455^{***}
	(0.0125)
Constant	-0.0543^{***}
	(0.0119)
Observations	2,033
R-squared	0.812

Robust standard errors in parentheses.
*** p<0.01

TABLE 13.A3 *Regression results for last winner*

	(1) SNTV $\log[P_s/(1-P_1)]$	(2) OLPR $\log[P_s/(1-P_1)]$	(3) OLPR $\log[P_s/(1-P_1)]$
$\log(c-1)$	-0.830^{***}		
	(0.0453)		
$\log[(c^{0.5}-1)(c-1)]$		-0.447^{***}	
		(0.0166)	
$\log[(M^f-1)(c-1)]$			-0.545^{***}
			(0.0147)
Constant	-0.0220^*	-0.0714^{**}	0.00628
	(0.0112)	(0.0320)	(0.0247)
Observations	386	384	384
R-squared	0.858	0.501	0.818

Robust standard errors in parentheses.
*** p<0.01, ** p<0.05, * p<0.1

above $1/(c-1)$, which is our naïve assumption for SNTV (where parties are assumed to have perfect equalization strategies among the "correct" number of candidates, after the first).

With OLPR, we expect, on average, $N'_{s0}=M^{0.5}$; it must also be the case, then, that on average, a party wins $s=M^{0.5}$ seats. We can attempt a model under this assumption. However, if the actual number of parties winning seats – and hence the mean number of seats won – deviates from these expectations, it will throw off our estimate of P_s. As it happens, this data sample has a number of parties per district that is, on average, closer to $N'_{s0}=M^{0.6}$. Because the number of seats per average party, times the number of parties winning seats must equal the magnitude, this means we have $s=M^{0.4}$. We thus can build the model either around the pure logical inputs, where we assume $N'_{s0}=M^{0.5}$, or around the empirically observed relationship between a given party's number of seats, s, and the magnitude of the district, M. Of course, the latter will be more accurate. But let us first do the purely theoretical logic.

Let us further assume that a party has $c=M$ candidates (although it tends to be slightly higher, in our OLPR data sample). This would make for a mean number of seats per party of $s=c^{0.5}$. Thus, after the first winner, a party has $c^{0.5}-1$ additional winning candidates.

Suppose its winners are well known and of approximately equal quality. This need not be the case, but is a simplifying assumption needed to keep the logical model tractable. If this were the case, the winners (after the first) might have vote shares around:

$$1/(c-1).$$

This is our "soft" upper boundary for the last winner's share. On the other hand, the minimum that the last winner would have is the same as the naïve model for SNTV, $1/(c-1)$. We can take the geometric average:

$$P_s/(1-P_1) = [(c^{0.5}-1)(c-1)]^{-0.5}.$$

This is Equation 13.9, introduced in the chapter. It is a complex expression, but it has a logical basis in both expected number of seats won by a party (on average) and expected intraparty vote distribution. When we test it via OLS, it is approximately confirmed. As shown in Table 13.A3, Regression Two, we get:

$$\log[P_s/(1-P_1)] = 0.071-0.447\log[(c^{0.5}-1)(c-1)] \quad (R^2 = 0.501).$$

The intercept, 0.07, suggests $P_s/(1-P_1) = 0.851$ (when unlogged) for $c=2$. This is illogical, as in such a situation the last winner must have 100 percent of the votes not won by the first winner. If we rerun the regression with the constant suppressed, we get a coefficient of -0.486, which is very close to the expected -0.5. This is remarkable, given how many assumptions have gone into it.

If we want to improve the calculations, we can use the actual exponent on M for a given number of seats won by the individual parties in the sample. This will allow the parameters in the model to vary with the actual success of parties on the interparty dimension, removing the prior "leap of faith" that our parties all average $M^{0.5}$ seats. The actual exponent on M, which we will call f, can be derived easily:

$$f = \log(s)/\log(M).$$

Then the previous steps are adjusted as follows. After the first winner, a party has $(M^f - 1)$ additional winning candidates. If they had equal votes then we would have $P_s = 1/(M^f - 1)$. This would be the "soft" upper boundary. We would thus have Equation 13.10:

$$P_s/(1-P_1) = [(M^f-1)(c-1)]^{-0.5}.$$

It is an even more complex expression, but it has a logical basis in both expected number of seats won by a party (on average) and expected intraparty vote distribution. When we test it via OLS, it is almost precisely confirmed (see Table 13.A3, Regression three):

$$\log[P_s/(1-P_1)] = -0.006 - 0.545\log[(M^f-1)(c-1)] \quad (R^2 = 0.814).$$

This constant, -0.006, is highly insignificant (we expect zero), and the coefficient, -0.544, is not far from the expected -0.5. Moreover, this adjustment has substantially improved model fit.

14

Pooling or Its Absence: Nomination and Alliance Behavior

This chapter extends the "vote management" theme of Chapter 13. It does so through two further tasks. First, we look further at the nomination behavior of parties under OLPR and SNTV. Recall from Chapter 13 that SNTV gives parties an incentive to manage intraparty competition, because of the absence of vote pooling. In OLPR, there are few incentives for such vote management, with a key caveat that we introduce as this chapter's second task.

As explored in Chapter 13, vote management can mean either restricting the number of candidates nominated by a party, or intervening in the competition between candidates in order to affect the distribution of votes among them. A party might pursue both vote-management practices in succession: first choose a number of candidates, then attempt to equalize across a realistically electable subset of them.

If parties have incentives to manage votes in either or both senses, then it has consequences for how concentrated the party's votes are on its winners. For instance, suppose a party nominates five candidates in an eight-seat district. During the course of the campaign, it becomes apparent that only three realistically can be elected. What might it do? It could seek to shift votes from two weaker candidates and encourage voters to give their votes to the three strongest ones, as equally as possible. In that way, it would tend to have the bulk of its total vote concentrated on its three winners.

If, on the other hand, the party had no such vote-management incentives – for instance, under OLPR – then it probably would have nominated (at least) eight candidates in the first place, and it would not worry about some candidates having weak vote-earning ability. It would allow *laissez-faire* competition, as we defined it in Chapter 13. The end result would be a smaller percentage of its votes concentrated on its winners than in the prior example.

The caveat to the *laissez-faire* assumption under OLPR is that sometimes "list" and "party" are not synonymous. That is, lists may be presented by alliances, in which case some candidates are from one party and some from others. All the parties and their candidates pool votes, but the candidates of the various parties win only if they obtain preference-vote totals in the list's – that is, the alliance's – top s (where s is the number of seats won by the alliance list).

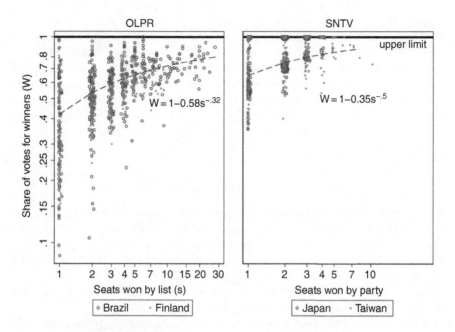

FIGURE 14.1 Share of votes for winning candidates (*W*) by number of seats (*s*), OLPR (left panel) and SNTV (right panel)

We demonstrated in Chapter 6 (in particular, Table 6.3) how this process works in Finland. In this chapter, we will explore the process in more detail, noting that for the parties inside an alliance list, the competitive incentives are *as if the system were SNTV*. Thus parties in alliances, and in particular the smaller partners, under OLPR, have incentives to manage their vote. That means they, too, should tend to concentrate votes on their winners.

To offer a preview of what we mean by vote concentration, consider the patterns shown in Figure 14.1. The figure contains two panels, with the left being OLPR systems and the right SNTV. In each panel, data points for two systems are combined: Brazil and Finland for OLPR and Japan and Taiwan for SNTV. The horizontal axis is the number of seats won by the list (OLPR) or party (SNTV).[1] The vertical axis is the share of the votes on the list or party won by the winning candidates.[2]

---

[1] The axis labels for SNTV stop at ten because we have no parties in such a system with more than ten seats won in a district. The scales remain the same, however, to allow ready visual comparison across systems.

[2] For present purposes – comparing electoral-system effects – we do not differentiate alliances from single-party lists in the OLPR cases. A statistical test shows no difference at the list level. Below we explore patterns for *parties* inside such lists.

The best-fit lines for logarithmic values are reported; the equations are empirical[3] (see the Appendix to this chapter). They are not logical models, but they represent the precise pattern expected: for any given number of seats won, the OLPR winners tend to have a lower share of their list's votes, while the SNTV winners have a higher share of their party's votes. The pattern suggests vote management by parties under SNTV – intervening to limit votes going to hopeless candidates – in contrast to the more *laissez-faire* competition under OLPR. We now turn to a fuller elaboration of the incentives behind the patterns shown in Figure 14.1. Then we turn our attention to multiparty alliance lists under OLPR.

HOW PARTIES CONCENTRATE THEIR VOTE – OR DO NOT

In Chapter 13, we investigated the number of candidates a party runs, for a given district magnitude, under either OLPR or SNTV formula. We further saw how individual candidates' preference-vote shares are shaped by the number of candidates, developing and testing logical models for both first and last winners. In this section, we look at a related aspect of vote management: *to what extent do parties under each system concentrate votes on whatever number of candidates they ultimately elect?*

The surest way to avoid maldistribution of votes within a party is to avoid nominating too many in the first place. We saw that in Chapter 13 that, on average, parties under SNTV tended to nominate $c'=(2M)^{0.5}$. This stood in contrast to OLPR, where vote pooling gives parties the luxury of nominating as many candidates as the law permits.

Ideally, parties under SNTV would nominate only as many as they believe they can elect. However, information may be uncertain about what that number is, or campaign context may work against the party's ability to elect all its candidates between the time nominations are settled and votes are cast. One strategy, then, would be for the party to play it safe and risk an *undernomination error*.[4] At the extreme, this means nominating only one candidate. We saw in Chapter 13 that many parties do have $c'=1$, even though some (unknown share) of these parties may have had enough votes to elect two or more candidates – provided they had been able to ensure relatively equal vote totals among them. Even some of those that have $c'>1$ may undernominate, having fewer than they could have elected but playing it safe.

Some of those parties that nominate $c'>1$ are sure to commit an *overnomination error*, having more candidates than they prove able to elect. Some may even do so deliberately, and have many excess candidates. A party

---

[3] The SNTV regression is run excluding parties that run only one candidate. (There are no such cases under OLPR.)

[4] For a full development of the concepts of errors under SNTV, see Cox and Niou (1994) and Cox and Shugart (1995).

under SNTV that nominates more than M candidates is clearly not pursuing a rational seat-maximization strategy. Even nominating M is usually overnomination, given that few parties will win M seats (when M is more than about two). Yet we saw from Figure 13.1 that parties having M or more candidates is surprisingly common, and at any $c'>1$, there is always the risk that the number is too many, for the party's voter support.

A question raised by this analysis is why a party under SNTV would ever nominate more than it can elect. Of course, one answer is that it may lack information about how many is the right number. However, there are so many cases of parties nominating "extra" candidates that uncertainty is probably not the sole explanation. Few nominate M and even fewer more than M. Yet, if M is much greater than two, there are many cases with well over s, the number of seats actually won. While we can't be sure of the reasons, two likely ones are (1) inability to control fully their own nominations, and (2) the need to groom future candidates and keep their supporters happy in the meantime.

Some parties may not be able to stop surplus candidates from running. Either they do not have legal control over their labels – as was the case in Colombia (Shugart, Moreno, and Fajardo 2007) – or the candidates whose endorsements they might deny would run anyway under another label or as independents (the latter having been particularly common in Japan). Parties may calculate that it is better to keep such candidates inside their tent than to let them undermine the party from outside,[5] even though their running may also undermine it from the inside! It is a tradeoff that SNTV makes especially acute.

Every incumbent will eventually leave office, it can be said safely. Thus parties need future talent, and some of these may run to test the waters even before there is an open slot for them. In the meantime, they are cultivating votes that may be useful to elect them as a party representative in the future. Again, it is a tradeoff: accept the risk that these candidates' running now may siphon some votes off the leading candidates and lead the party to commit an "error," versus having such a restricted field of candidates that the party looks unappealing to voters, especially those who will be needed in the future once an incumbent departs. For these reasons, parties under SNTV must engage in both forms of vote management that have been the focus of our analysis in Chapter 13 and so far in this one: restrict nominations (while sometimes remaining above their expected s), and attempt to equalize votes across their most viable candidates (while pushing the surplus candidates' votes down as best they can).

---

[5] Kasuya (2009: 100-101) mentions exactly such a logic for parties in the Philippines when they declare a "free zone", endorsing more than one candidate despite $M=1$ (which results in the same vote-management dilemmas as SNTV, $M>1$).

Now, having seen how parties in OLPR and SNTV differ in their vote-management practices, we turn to a class of open lists in which both tendencies are present. When lists are open and contain candidates of two or more parties, the intralist allocation is also an interparty allocation. That is, lists are of alliances, rather than strictly parties, and the multiple parties present on the list each win as many seats as they have candidates who place in the list's top *s* in preference votes. These systems, used in Brazil and Finland, are thus hybrids of D'Hondt (used to allocate seats among lists based on pooled votes) and SNTV (used to allocate seats to parties within each alliance).[6] In the next section, we consider how these systems of alliance lists affect both the interparty and intraparty dimensions.

ALLIANCES IN OPEN LISTS: THE INTERPARTY DIMENSION OF INTRALIST COMPETITION

We now turn our attention to patterns of alliance politics under OLPR. The chapter has two sections devoted to this topic. In this first one, we look at the interparty dimension of systems in which some lists contain candidates of two or more parties. In doing so, we ask how the hybrid of OLPR and SNTV results in systematically more winning parties than would be expected if all lists consisted of a single party's candidates. In the second section on alliance politics, we return to the intraparty dimension by looking at the nomination and vote-management behavior of parties competing with alliance partners.

In analyzing the interparty dimension of alliances, we are pursuing an extension of the themes of Chapter 10, which looked at district-level patterns of competition among parties. We find that our two fundamental quantities, M and S, once again predict how many parties appear in districts where alliance lists can contain two or more parties apiece. These quantities enter through the same district embeddedness factor, k, developed in Chapter 10. Thus, while alliance politics might seem arcane, this section of the chapter knits together some key findings of preceding chapters on both national and district-level party systems.

Alliances are very common in at least three OLPR systems: Brazil, Chile, and Finland.[7] In Chile, electoral competition is mainly between two nationwide

---

[6] The effects of the D'Hondt/SNTV hybrid on the interparty dimension was explored in the appendix to Chapter 7. Other rules are possible within open alliance lists. For instance, parties could be allowed to pool their own candidates' votes first before seats are allocated to candidates. Such a reform has been discussed in Finland (Raunio 2005:487), but not adopted. Alternatively, if more than a single preference vote is permitted, the intralist allocation could be MNTV (as defined in Chapter 3) instead of SNTV. Our analysis will consider only those where it is SNTV (and there is no sub-list pooling on the allied parties).

[7] For works that detail this feature of each of these systems, see: Machado (2009, 2012); Carey (2002), Siavelis (2002, 2005); Raunio (2005), von Schoultz (2018). There are also alliance lists in Poland (discussed in Chapter 1), but we lack sufficiently fine-grained data to include them in this analysis.

alliances, each of which consists of several parties. These alliances divide up the nominations among their component partners across districts. All districts have just two seats,[8] and lists contain no more than two candidates, thus two different parties in each alliance present candidates in any given district. In Finland and, especially, Brazil, district magnitude is higher. Moreover, lists frequently contain more candidates than the magnitude of the district. Further complicating the system, alliances may differ from district to district. Any two parties that are in alliance in one district may compete on separate lists in another district, and join with a different set of partners in yet another.

We already saw earlier in this book, in Table 6.3, an example from Finland of how competition among parties and their candidates might result in more parties than lists winning seats, given that lists may contain candidates of two or more parties. In that specific example, we saw four parties winning seats on three lists. We now turn to a systematic analysis of this tendency of the number of winning parties to exceed the number of winning lists. It might be that it would appear random – subject to the peculiarities of specific parties and candidates. On the contrary, this analysis shows that the patterns are predictable.

In district-level analysis in this book (Chapter 10), we have used the *alliance-list* as the unit of analysis. That is, in testing whether the actual number of seat-winning parties (N'_{S0}) and other quantities follows the expected logical relationship, we substituted "list" or "alliance" for "party." The reason for doing so is that if we are interested in effects on the "interparty" dimension, we want to count the electoral agent to which the electoral system directly allocates seats. In OLPR (as also in closed-list PR), that entity is the list, regardless of whether the candidates on it are all identified with the same label or some with distinct partisan labels.[9]

In Chapter 10 we confirmed the very first logical model mentioned in this book, Equation 1.1:

$$N'_{S0} = M^{0.5},$$

that is: the number of parties (of any size) that win in a district tends to be, on average, the square root of the district magnitude. Also in Chapter 10, we developed the concept of a district's embeddedness in the wider assembly electoral system; this effect is represented by our factor, k, which takes the assembly size into account. See Chapter 10 and its appendix for details.

---

[8] In 2015, Chile adopted an electoral reform that will increase district magnitude. See https://fruitsandvotes.wordpress.com/2015/01/14/chilean-electoral-reform/

[9] By contrast, at the national level, it is not possible to count electoral agents (actual or an effective number) based on alliances in Brazil or Finland, because the alliances are not consistent across districts. In Chile, on the other hand, one can make an accurate count of nationwide alliance lists because the partnerships into which parties enter are consistent across districts in any given election (and also have been quite stable across time).

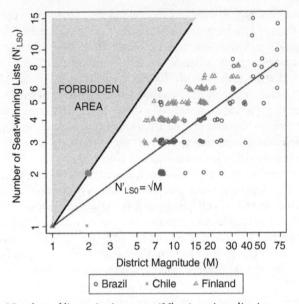

FIGURE 14.2 Number of lists winning seats (N'_{LS0}) against district magnitude

As the confirmation of Equation 1.1 in Chapter 10 showed, we do not need the embeddedness factor to account for N'_{S0}, but we do need it for all of the other district-level relationships investigated in that chapter, including the size of the largest party and the effective numbers of parties (both votes and seats). Here, with our focus on the *intralist* dimension, we perform three interrelated tests. The first is to verify that the number of *lists* winning at least one seat is around the square root of M for our three OLPR cases that use alliances: Brazil, Chile, and Finland. Our visual test of Equation 1.1 (Figure 1.2) excluded cases with a presidential executive. Thus it included Finland, but not Brazil and Chile.[10] Then we ask what the effect is of M on the number of *suballiance parties*, by which we mean the number we have once the alliances are disaggregated into their components. Finally, we do the same for the *effective* number of suballiance parties.

In Figure 14.2 we see the plot of the number of seat-winning lists, designated N'_{LS0}, and the district magnitude (M). The diagonal line in the graph corresponds to $N'_{LS0}=M^{0.5}$. A regression yields a coefficient of 0.543, rather than the expected 0.5, but this is an immaterial deviation from the expectation.[11] Finnish data points (triangles) tend to be high, but the overall

---

[10] As reported in the appendix to Chapter 10, the relationship is not statistically distinct in presidential systems.

[11] The reported result is a no-constant regression, because run with a constant the result violates the anchor point: $N_{LS0}=1.41M^{0.412}$. However, this result is due only to the inclusion of the Chilean

pattern is close to the expectation of Equation 1.1, when we use as our unit of observation the list. Now, what if we use the party, whether it presents its own list or is one of two or more components of an alliance list? We turn to this question next.

When lists may consist of two or more parties pooling their votes in alliance lists under OLPR, what should we expect for the number of seat-winning parties? In order to differentiate the concept of "party" here from the definition applicable more widely (where we use N'_{S0}), here we will use N''_{S0}, where the double prime mark signifies that we have now moved below the level of the district into the alliance lists. Thus N''_{S0} represents the district-level number of distinct party labels that win seats (whether on their own list or that of an alliance).

Given Equation 1.1, just confirmed on the number of *lists* even for cases where alliances are common, it must be that $N''_{S0} \geq N'_{LS0} = M^{0.5}$. The question is, how much greater N''_{S0} is than N'_{LS0}. We already have seen that the district embeddedness factor, k, is not needed for N'_{LS0} (as it was not needed for N'_{S0} in Chapter 10). Here we posit that N''_{S0} requires the incorporation of k:

$$N''_{S0} = M^k. \tag{14.1}$$

Equation 14.1 states that the number of distinct party labels winning in a district, on their own or alliance lists, is the district magnitude, raised to the district's embeddedness factor. In other words, the size of the assembly in which a district is embedded affects systematically how many *parties* win under alliance OLPR systems, even though it does not have such an effect on the number of *lists* that win. Before we see if this is correct, why might it be so?

The intuition is that parties decide whether to join an alliance in any given district *because they are viable elsewhere*, where they sometimes may run alone. Our theory of embeddedness, articulated in Chapter 10, is that parties bring resources in from districts where they are stronger to districts where they are weaker. This results in various district-level indicators being systematically different in a low-magnitude district of a large assembly than they would be in an "isolated" district of the same magnitude. The same logic should apply to parties under alliance OLPR, except that here the idea of parties "bringing in resources" means showing their flag in the district *through alliance partnership*. Many of these parties would not win seats in their weaker districts if they ran their own list. Worse, they might displace seats away from a potential partner to a party that both they and the potential partner like less (vote-splitting). By running on an alliance list, they pool their efforts. Moreover, if they play the "SNTV game" they can win a seat even on

districts, which as Figure 14.2 makes clear, almost always have $N_{LS0}=2$, whereas we might expect more cases of $N_{LS0}=1$ to balance it out. If Chile is dropped from the regression we get $N_{LS0}=1.17M^{0.478}$, with the constant insignificant. Moreover, if we use random effects, we get a $N_{LS0}=1.16M^{0.510}$, even with Chile included.

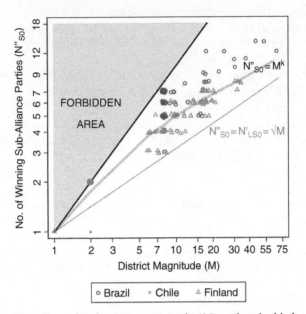

FIGURE 14.3 The effect of a district's magnitude (M) and embeddedness (k) on the number of seat-winning parties (N''_{SO}), whether running alone or on alliance lists

a vote share that would be too low to win if running their own list. Thus viability outside the district should lead to parties winning seats in districts through alliances. If so, then the embeddedness factor should affect N''_{SO}, the total number of such parties winning in a district, in line with Equation 14.1.

To run a regression to test Equation 14.1, we enter $k\log M$ as our independent variable, following similar procedures performed in Chapter 10. The result we obtain is:

$$\log N''_{SO} = 0.029 + 1.054 k\log M \quad [R^2 = 0.915; \ 233 \text{ obs.}].$$

The constant term, 0.029, is hardly different from the expected zero, and the coefficient on $k\log M$ includes the expected 1.00. Thus we can consider Equation 14.1 confirmed.

In Figure 14.3 we graph the result. This graph has the familiar kinky dotted line that we have seen several times in Chapter 10. It results from the varying k at different values of M. As in the preceding figure, we distinguish the data points of our three alliance OLPR cases with different symbols. We see that the kinky dotted curve, which represents our regression-confirmed Equation 14.1, follows the data points reasonably well. Moreover, even though not all seat-winning lists are alliance lists (except in Chile), we find that it is always the case that $N''_{SO} > M^{0.5}$, shown with the thin gray line, other than the relatively few cases in Chile where $N''_{SO} = 1$, and of course the Åland Islands in Finland, where $N''_{SO} = M = 1$.

Of course, we are not normally interested in the number of parties of any size that win. The size-adjusted number is of greater interest. For that we have the effective number, and thus we can apply it to suballiance parties just as we have previously to parties and party lists. What should we expect? From the sequence of logical models developed in Chapter 10, we have the steps needed to derive a quantitative model for the effective number of seat-winning parties. Equation 10.5 says:

$$N'_S = M^{2k/3}.$$

However, recall that the first link in this chain was Equation 1.1, $N'_{S0} = M^{0.5}$. We already know from Equation 14.1 in this chapter that for suballiance parties, $N''_{S0} = M^k$. This alters the entire sequence by having an additional k in the exponents we multiply as we substitute one equation into another.[12] When we do so, we obtain:

$$N''_S = M^{4kk/3} \tag{14.2}$$

The regression test produces the following equation:

$$\log N''_S = 0.010 + 1.403k^2 \log M \quad [R^2 = 0.831;\ 243\ \text{obs.}].$$

The coefficient, 1.4, is very close to the expected 1.33, which is in the coefficient's confidence interval. Thus the effective number of seat-winning parties below the level of alliances in our three OLPR countries in which multiparty lists are common follows the same logical pattern as in simpler list-PR systems. The provision for alliances inflates the party system at the district level, but not in a way that is chaotic or unpredictable, once we take into account the logic of embeddedness.

In Figure 14.4 we graph the result. The thicker kinky curve is the regression-confirmed Equation 14.2. The thinner dashed line is Equation 10.5, the equation that takes into account embeddedness of a district in the national electoral system, but does not take into account the further embeddedness of suballiance parties frequently winning seats on multiparty lists. Of course, there is considerable scatter, given that the intralist SNTV-style allocation need not follow from district magnitude; it is governed only by how many candidates of a suballiance party make it into a given list's top s. In particular, the highest-M Brazilian districts are higher than Equation 14.2 leads us to expect. Nonetheless, we able to approximate the pattern through our logical modeling techniques and so incorporate into our larger set of logical relationships a seemingly quirky allocation method like the combination of interlist D'Hondt and intralist SNTV used in Brazil, Finland, and Chile.

---

[12] Using the same sequence as in Chapter 10, only starting with Equation 14.1 instead of Equation 1.1, we have: $s'_1 = N'^{-k}_{S0} = M^{-kk}$; and $N_s = s_1^{-4/3} = (M^{-kk})^{-4/3} = M^{4kk/3}$.

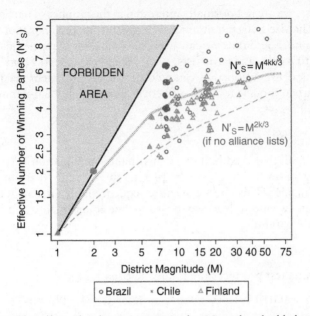

FIGURE 14.4 The effect of a district's magnitude (M) and embeddedness (k) on the effective number of seat-winning parties (N''_S), whether running alone or on alliance lists

TABLE 14.1 *Actual and effective numbers of lists and suballiance parties in Southern Savo, Finland, 2007*

$M=6$, $k=0.702$ (from $S=200$)

	Number of seat-winning lists $N'_{LS0}=\sqrt{M}$	Effective number of seat-winning lists $N'_{LS}=M^{2k/3}$	Number of suballiance parties $N''_{S0}=M^k$	Effective number of suballiance parties $N''_S=M^{4kk/3}$
Expected	2.45	2.31	3.52	3.25
Actual	3	3	4	3.6

For actual votes cast for winning candidates in this district, refer to Table 6.3.

We can return to the example from Table 6.3 and ask how alliance politics affected the outcome, and how the analysis of this section sheds light on the example. In that case, we had a six-seat district, Southern Savo in 2007, in which three lists won seats, including four parties. In Table 14.1, we apply the models of Chapter 10, for district-level *lists*, and of this chapter, for district-level suballiance *parties*. In a district of $M=6$, we expect the number of winning lists, N'_{LS0}, to be $6^{0.5}$=2.45 on average. Given that this quantity is a raw number, not the effective number, this means it could be expected to be two or three in any given election. In the actual case (shown in Table 6.3), we have N'_{LS0}=3. Because this actual whole-number value is larger than the expected average, we can expect that all other output values will be likewise somewhat higher than model predictions. But how much?

For other outputs at the district level (see Table 10.1), we need the embeddedness factor, k. For this M=6 district and Finland's 200-seat assembly, it works out to k=0.702. Thus we expect the effective number of seat-winning lists to be 2.31. In fact, it was 3.00, as each of the three lists won two seats. Now, we turn to the suballiance parties, and the models that we developed in this chapter. We expect the number of such parties, N''_{S0}=3.52 and the effective number, N''_{S}=3.25. The actual values in the example were 4 and 3.60, respectively.

Note that the one additional party winning due to alliance lists is in line with the expectation (3.52 being almost exactly one more than 2.45), adjusted for the chain of outputs having started with the actual value, N'_{LS0}=3. The effective number of suballiance parties in the example, 3.60, is only slightly larger than the expected. It is, however, *much larger than we would expect if there were no alliances* (2.31). In this way, what would seem like "randomly high" fragmentation in this district, or in others like it, if we ignored alliances, turns out to be very close to the alliance-adjusted expectation.

The results shown in this section offer insights into *how the intraparty dimension affects the interparty dimension*. For instance, if these countries did not use open lists with alliances, there would not be the opportunity for small parties to maintain their independent identity and vote-seeking activities while still pooling their efforts to common seat-winning entities (lists). It is remarkable that these seat-winning "entities" (lists) still tend to number $\sqrt{M}$, as Figure 14.2 showed for three countries that use such an electoral system.

The wider point is that when we count the number of parties, or estimate their effective number, at the *national* level, that number will be unusually high. The national counts routinely are based on the distinct parties and will include many that won only by having a relatively small vote share that happened to clear the top-*s* in some district-level list of the alliance in which they ran. Thus the open-list system, with alliances, generates a further fragmentation of the party system beyond even what high-magnitude PR supports. It does so because some of the parties are able to win, SNTV-style, by placing a successful candidate on an alliance list.

In Brazil, with its large magnitudes, the result is that the effective number of suballiance parties (N''_{S}) averages almost twice the effective number of lists (N'_{LS0}). When we look back at the nationwide level in Brazil, we see that the country's N_{S} tends to be 1.75 to 2.02 times what the Seat Product Model would predict. The implication from our findings in this section is that much of this excessive fragmentation can be traced to the district-level alliance politics, and their being embedded in such a large assembly. Brazil, one of the world's largest democracies and (in)famous for its high party-system fragmentation, looks less exceptional once we take into account how its electoral system affects alliances.[13]

Having established how the electoral system affects the (effective) number of lists and parties in systems where these two quantities are not necessarily the same, we now turn to the strategy of parties on the intraparty dimension. This next and final section returns to themes seen earlier in the chapter regarding nominations and vote concentration.

THE INTRAPARTY DIMENSION OF ALLIANCE POLITICS: NOMINATION AND VOTE-MANAGEMENT

Earlier in this chapter, we showed that parties under SNTV tended to concentrate their votes on their winning candidates, in contrast to parties under OLPR. Now we can run a similar analysis for parties in alliance lists, by turning to the intraparty dimension of parties on alliance lists.

The small parties in alliance should exhibit an SNTV-style logic. We previously have noted that parties under SNTV face the dilemma that their collective vote shares do not determine how many seats they win in a district (unlike in PR-list systems). Rather, the number of seats a party wins under SNTV is simply the number of its candidates who obtain top-M vote shares, where M is the magnitude of the district. For parties running on joint lists under OLPR, it is the same, except we need to refer to the top-s vote shares. That is, lists win their collective s seats based on their combined votes, and then in each list the top s candidates in preference votes are the winners. (The example in Table 6.3. demonstrated how this works.) A small party that fails to ensure it has a candidate with one of the s highest vote shares within the list will have a "sucker's payoff": its votes may have been critical to winning s seats (rather than $s-1$ or some smaller number), yet it wins no seats for itself.

As a result of these SNTV-style incentives in alliance lists, we should see small parties concentrating their votes on winners, whereas the larger ones should show relatively less concentration. (We cannot say there should be no concentration, because everyone is playing by SNTV rules on the intralist dimension; the challenge of vote management is less acute for large parties, given that they have more votes to pool and hence more room for error, but still present.)

---

[13] In Chapter 15 we make a similar observation about alliances under FPTP in the case of India.

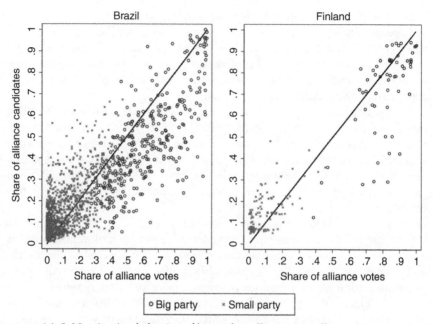

FIGURE 14.5 Nomination behavior of big and small parties in alliance lists: Brazil and Finland

Before considering concentration, which implies managing the vote across some number of candidates greater than the party can elect, we start with nomination behavior. We define as a "small" party any party that is in an alliance but is not the party with the most cumulative votes within the list. That is, every alliance list has one "big" party – the one with the highest intralist vote total – but a list may have more than one small party.

In Figure 14.5 we see the share of the list's total candidates contributed by the big party and any small parties in an alliance on the y-axis. On the x-axis is the share of votes accumulated by the big and small parties. The two-panel figure shows Brazil on the left and Finland on the right. Of interest here is whether small parties are tending to nominate conservatively, given that most of them will not elect more than one candidate on the list.[14]

Small parties are shown with light gray small x symbols, while the circles indicate the big party in each alliance. Because most of the small parties appear

---

[14] We recognize that causality can run in either direction between these variables. The votes obtained by a party should tend to increase as it has more candidates, all else equal. We place the candidate share on the y-axis because we expect that when alliance deals are struck, all parties to the deal have a reasonably accurate estimate of which one will be the larger, and thus the causality is stronger from (expected) vote share to candidate share, even though (actual) vote share is observed only after the election.

above the thick dark equality line, we can conclude that they tend to have a share of candidates that exceeds their share of the alliance's votes. This is true in both countries, but especially in Finland. Correspondingly, the big party tends to have a smaller share of candidates than votes. The evidence thus is that small parties tend to nominate more candidates than they plausibly could elect, even if all their candidates had equalized votes.

We might pause here and ask, why would a party overnominate to an alliance list? After all, in doing so, it risks the sucker's payoff, which we defined earlier as a party contributing to the number of seats the list wins (through vote pooling), yet electing no candidate of its own. Perhaps the answer is that a party does not look like a *party* if it nominates only one candidate. Even the small alliance partners need to show they are serious by nominating more than a token candidate.

This motivation is similar to the "show the flag" notion that we discussed in Chapter 10. There we developed models of how district-level outputs, such as the effective number of parties, are systematically affected by the district's embeddedness in a larger assembly. The logic for small parties overnominating to alliance lists is similar: both in districts within a larger assembly electoral system and in alliances within a district, parties have incentives to compete even for seats they will not win, in order to demonstrate their seriousness.[15]

As we saw in the preceding section of this chapter, open lists with provision for alliances systematically increase the number of parties (whether running on their own lists or in alliance). This pattern is possible only because of the ability of these parties, particularly the small ones, to manage their internal competition in what is essentially a system of SNTV on the intralist dimension. In the next step in our analysis of alliance politics, we tie these strands together by returning to the level of candidate competition.

Once a party has excess candidates on the list of the alliance it has joined, it must turn its attention to the next stage of competition – vote management. This is the phase in which intraparty competition for these parties is similar to the SNTV dynamics we investigated earlier. Thus we now replicate the analysis we did for OLPR and SNTV, only now turning our attention to parties within alliances under OLPR.

If a small party overnominates, then it might seek to concentrate its votes on a subset of realistically electable candidates. Thus we ask whether small parties in alliances show evidence of playing this SNTV-style vote-management

---

[15] Another motivation is that the alliance agreement struck with the bigger party may demand a certain minimum number of candidates, so as to bring additional votes to the list as a whole. The larger party may not object to its partner having several candidates, given that it is the most likely beneficiary of a partner playing the role of sucker. If we are right about parties wanting to "show the flag" even if it means overnominating, then the small party also does not object to its larger partner's demand for additional candidates, as whatever votes they pull for the alliance increase the perceived seriousness of the small party.

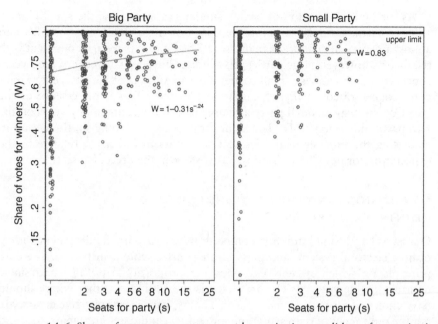

FIGURE 14.6 Share of party vote concentrated on winning candidates for parties in alliances: Big versus small parties in Brazil

strategy. Do they tend to concentrate votes on those candidates who actually won? Large parties, which face a less acute vote-management imperative, should be less likely to exhibit such concentration.

In Figure 14.6, we see the pattern for Brazilian parties in alliances. When we compare the big parties (left panel) with the small (right), we see a pattern similar to that we saw earlier in comparing OLPR to SNTV. Each panel includes the plot of a regression estimation. For the big parties, there is a significant increase in votes concentrated on winners the more seats the party wins, as we expect for OLPR parties. The best fit is $W=1-0.31s^{-0.24}$. For small parties in alliance, there is both the expected higher intercept and a totally insignificant effect of seats won; the best fit to this scattered plot is simply $W=0.83$.

Thus small parties in alliance behave even more like SNTV parties than parties in SNTV itself! That is, whereas we saw a small but significant upward slope for SNTV parties (Figure 14.1, right panel), there is no relationship between seats and vote concentration for small parties on alliance lists. The difference between big and small parties in Figure 14.6 is not great, but it is statistically significant. Even the big parties are playing an SNTV-style game with their partners, and have incentive to concentrate more than the list as a whole does (or than a single-party list would).

As for Finland, we do not have a similar graph because the small Finnish alliance partners rarely run more than two or three candidates on a list and almost always win no more than one seat. The Finnish pattern is consistent with the theory, however: large parties, on average, have 54.8 percent of their votes concentrated on winners; small parties have an average of 86.7 percent of their votes concentrated on their (usually one) winner. This is the essence of the "SNTV" strategy: a small party attempts to avoid wasting many votes on the intraparty dimension.[16] To the extent they succeed in doing so, they result in increasing the number of parties that win seats in a district, relative to the expectation for nonalliance settings, as we saw in the preceding section.

CONCLUSIONS AND IMPLICATIONS FOR DESIGN OF INTRAPARTY RULES

Our two chapters on intraparty competition have deepened our understanding of how electoral systems and party strategy affect vote distribution. The core principle on which systems like open list proportional (OLPR) and single nontransferable vote (SNTV) are based is the assumption that voters should have choice of more than just a party. That is, parties, as collective actors, are not the only agent of representation; individual candidates are agents, too, and voters may not be indifferent as to which candidates of a party represent them. So-called flexible-list systems (see Chapter 6) are also based on this principle, but they allow some combination of candidate-preference votes and party-provided list ranks to be mixed into the final determination of who gets elected to whatever seats a party wins. All of these systems – SNTV, open lists, and flexible lists – differ from closed lists, in that the latter system gives voters no choice within the party: the voter must accept or reject the list of candidates as a whole. Parties under closed lists still may nominate candidates so as to appeal to specific constituencies that prefer some candidates over others (see examples in Chapter 6), but the voter is not able to favor some candidate over another through any sort of intraparty vote.

We showed that there are fundamental differences in party strategies under OLPR and SNTV, with parties in the latter system exhibiting efforts to manage their competition. There are two principal ways to manage intraparty competition: restrict the number of candidates, and seek to equalize votes across whatever number of candidates the party expects to be able to elect. Under OLPR, on the other hand, parties can tolerate *laissez-faire* internal competition – if the party is concerned only with seat-maximization. The reason is that vote pooling on the list means that no increase in the number of candidates and no inequality of their vote totals can undermine the party's collective seat-winning potential when votes pool on a list.

---

[16] We are unable to carry out a similar analysis on Chile, because any party in an alliance has only one candidate, given $M=2$ and the restriction of lists to a maximum of two candidates.

Turning to alliance lists, we saw that parties under alliance lists engage in vote concentration as well. By playing the SNTV game, they can enhance their prospects of winning seats within the list. Despite the seeming idiosyncrasy of a given party's success or failure at vote concentration, we found that even the number of parties – whether with their own list or with candidates on an alliance – remains predictable. We see once again that our district embeddedness factor from Chapter 10 accounts for the number of parties under alliance open lists. Thus we saw that the interparty and intra*list* dimensions are connected.

The analytical tools and conclusions of this chapter likely apply more widely than to just those cases that have explicit multiparty alliance lists like the cases we focused on here. While systems of open alliance lists are not common, we suspect that many parties under OLPR consist of factions or other intraparty groupings that evolve to promote their preferred candidates. If so, then they should be observed to engage in similar strategies to avoid wasting their own votes. This would be a promising avenue for scholars of countries with OLPR systems (but no alliances of distinctly branded parties) to pursue – for instance, in Colombia, Indonesia, Peru, and other open-list systems.

For designers of electoral systems, the results of these chapters offer some implications. One is already well known, but has not been demonstrated as systematically and comparatively as we did: parties under SNTV tend to limit the number of candidates they nominate to fewer than the district magnitude, and to take steps to equalize votes among their candidates (or a realistically electable subset). In this way, SNTV considerably limits effective competition, compared to other systems that allow voters to cast preference votes for candidates below the level of the party. A survey of academic specialists (Bowler and Farrell 2006) revealed SNTV to be the least preferred system. We share the skepticism.[17] On the other hand, the same survey showed specialists tend to rate OLPR quite high.[18]

Our analysis offers some cautions to consider in designing OLPR systems. With large district magnitudes, the preference vote share of first winners can be very low. Our Figure 13.2 showed that under 15 percent of the party's combined vote is not uncommon when $M>15$; for last winners (Figure 13.4), the percentage is very often under 5 percent. Relatedly, in this chapter we saw that substantial vote shares for parties in OLPR tend to be cast for losing candidates. Perhaps this is not a problem. Voters may be indifferent among the candidates of the list they select, and with vote-pooling, no vote for a trailing candidate can help elect a candidate of a different list instead. On the other hand, the entire premise of systems that give voters a choice below the level of the list is that voters are not indifferent. Hence, high magnitude OLPR may leave many voters feeling unrepresented. It also may make the choice set

---

[17] It might be noted that both of us were among the 170 respondents surveyed.
[18] It ranked as specialists' third choice, after MMP and STV.

unwieldy, leading to suboptimal choices in the first place (Cunow 2014). One potential solution, aside from using smaller district magnitude, might be to restrict the number of candidates to fewer than M. Apparently no systems have such a provision, but it could be useful to limit intraparty vote fragmentation. Tentatively, we might propose a limit of $2+M^{3/4}$, rounded up.[19]

Even if voters might be relatively indifferent among candidates within one party, what if the list actually contains candidates from two or more parties? Alliance lists raise the stakes for voters who may prefer one of the competing parties on the alliance list over another: they now have some risk, a la SNTV, of spreading their votes in such a way that they hurt their favored party's chances. The process of connecting votes to party seats might even appear chaotic. Logical models and graphs introduced in this chapter showed that, far from being chaotic, there actually are predictable patterns for interparty competition within alliance lists. The evidence suggests that the number of parties – both actual and effective – can be very high for a given district magnitude when alliances are allowed, especially if assembly size is large (because of the effects of embeddedness on the individual district's politics). Thus if extreme party fragmentation is not desired, OLPR with alliances should be allowed only in relatively modest district magnitudes, unlike the very large districts used in Brazil and some parts of Finland.

Both SNTV and the hybrid of OLPR and SNTV (i.e., alliance lists) are relatively complex systems. Yet we have seen that their complexity does not prevent their being modeled, even on the intraparty/intralist dimension, using tools such as we have used for the interparty dimension in preceding chapters. The votes for candidates and sublist parties remain limited by, and largely predictable from, the constraints of available seats. In the next section of the book, we turn to questions of how well models for simple systems can be extended to account for other forms of complexity.

Appendix to Chapter 14

This appendix displays the results from regression discussed in Chapter 14.

Table 14.A1 shows the regressions for the equations plotted in Figure 14.1, which plot the share of votes for winning candidates (W) by number of seats (s)

---

[19] In a twenty-seat district, this would mean a limit of twelve candidates per list, which ought to be sufficient to provide choice without making that choice overwhelming. The same limit, with $M \leq 5$, would allow M candidates, or slightly more (thereby allowing *more* choice than most present cases of open lists have in very low-M districts). It might be noted that in our dataset, the highest M for which any party won all seats was five. (In countries where members who enter the cabinet must give up their assembly seats, there could be provision for a short supplementary list to be used only in cases where the number of candidates on the initial list proved insufficient.)

TABLE 14.A1 *Seats won by list or part and vote concentration, OLPR and SNTV*
Dependent variable: log(1–W); i.e., the log of votes accumulated by losing
candidates

VARIABLES	(1) OLPR	(2) SNTV ($c>1$)
Seats won by party/list, logged	–0.319***	–0.492***
	(0.0224)	(0.0597)
	[–0.363 – –0.275]	[–0.610 – –0.375]
Constant	–0.236***	–0.456***
	(0.0121)	(0.0229)
	[–0.260 – –0.212]	[–0.501 – –0.411]
Observations	801	374
R-squared	0.259	0.169

Robust standard errors in parentheses.
95 percent confidence intervals in brackets.
*** p<0.01

won by the list (OLPR) or party (SNTV). The dependent variable is first transformed, so as to be 1–W, which is then logged. We use the losers' votes (one minus winners' votes) because otherwise the regression would yield absurd values of W>1 for high values of s. We should never run regressions that would yield logically impossible values for our outcome variable; see Taagepera (2008), particularly p. 110.

In **Table 14.A2**, we see four regressions testing our models for how the number of lists and suballiance parties are affected by district magnitude. Regressions One and Two are for the number of seat-winning lists (N'_{LS0}); the expected value of the coefficient on logM is 0.5, and the constant is expected to be statistically indistinct from zero.

Regression One omits the case of Chile, where all districts have M=2. Results are consistent with logical expectations. If we include Chile, the regression yields a significant constant term that leads to absurd results (as noted in the chapter), due to how commonly we find two winning lists in Chilean districts. We can rerun the regression with the constant suppressed, in order to respect the mandatory anchor point of N'_{LS0}=1 when M=1. When we do so, it does not matter whether Chile is included or not; Regression Two includes the country in a no-constant regression.

Regression Three is for the number of *party labels* that win seats, whether on their own list or that of an alliance (N''_{S0}). Here, as explained in the chapter, we need to take the district's embeddedness factor, k, into account. Thus the input

TABLE 14.A2 *Regressions for number of list and parties at district level, systems with alliance lists*

	(1) No. seat-winning lists (excl. Chile)	(2) No. seat-winning lists (incl. Chile)	(3) No. of parties, including suballiance parties	(4) Effective No. of parties, including suballiance parties
District magnitude, logged	0.478	0.543		
	(0.0347)	(0.0276)		
	[0.398 – 0.558]	[0.481 – 0.606]		
Expected: 0.5				
k * magnitude, logged			1.054	
			(0.0370)	
			[0.971 – 1.138]	
Expected: 1.000				
k^2 * magnitude, logged				1.404
				(0.0884)
				[1.204 – 1.603]
Expected: 1.333				
Constant	0.0679		0.0294	0.0104
	(0.0448)		(0.0143)	(0.0254)
	[-0.0355 – 0.171]		[-0.00300 – 0.0618]	[-0.0471 – 0.0678]
Expected: 0				
Observations	178	231	233	243
R-squared	0.506	0.943	0.915	0.831

Robust standard errors in parentheses.
95 percent confidence intervals in brackets.

TABLE 14.A3 *Seats won by party and vote concentration, big versus small parties under OLPR in Brazil Dependent variable: log(1–W); i.e., the log of votes accumulated by losing candidates*

VARIABLES	(1)
Big party	0.278***
	(0.0553)
seats for party, logged	–0.0368
	(0.112)
Interaction	–0.199*
	(0.115)
Constant	–0.787***
	(0.0450)
Observations	667
R-squared	0.048

Robust standard errors in parentheses.
*** $p<0.01$

variable is the $k^*\log M$; the expected coefficient should be 1.000, which is confirmed by the regression result. The constant is statistically significant, but is close to the expected zero. In Regression Four, the outcome of interest is the effective number of parties, including suballiance parties (N'''_S); as explained in the chapter, now we need as our input variable, $k^{2*}\log M$; its expected coefficient is 1.333, which is within the 95 percent confidence interval of the regression's estimate of 1.4. The constant is approximately zero, and insignificant, as expected.

In **Table 14.A3**, we report a regression with an identical dependent variable as in Table 14.A1. In this case, the regression is for a single case, Brazil. It is an interactive specification, in order to test whether there is a significant difference in the patterns for big and small parties within alliances (as defined in the chapter). An inspection of the marginal effect of the big-party dummy shows that there is a significant effect for parties winning fewer than about three seats. The equations that result for big and small parties are plotted in Figure 14.6.

PART V

WHAT CAN WE EXPECT FROM MODELS OF ELECTORAL SYSTEMS?

15

Extending the Seat Product Model: Upper Tiers and Ethnic Diversity

In this final part of the book, we ask what we can expect from models of electoral systems. The topics include whether institutions alone are sufficient to predict the average trend in party systems, or whether many existing works on the topic are correct in their claims that electoral-system effects are operational only under certain conditions of social cleavages that produce demands for party fragmentation. Another key topic is the applicability of our models to complex electoral systems. This chapter takes up both of these topics, and the next takes the latter topic a step further by considering a wide range of features that introduce complexity, including second rounds, ranked-choice ballots, and thresholds. Then the concluding chapter wraps up with wider themes of electoral systems, and models of them, in the context of countries' politics, and the role of logical models in social science.

Our first task in this chapter is to extend the Seat Product Model (SPM). In Chapters 7–10, we developed and tested the SPM for simple electoral systems. This chapter introduces two main extensions: (1) the consideration of ethnic diversity; (2) the role of upper tiers of composite systems. We find that the added predictive power of including ethnicity is minimal (with few exceptions), and that our extended model can offer quantitative understanding of one major class of complex electoral system, two-tier compensatory PR (including mixed-member proportional; see Chapter 3 for definitions).

Both of these extensions are good news for both the science of electoral systems and practical, real-world, system design. Two-tier compensatory systems are common, and thus covering them under the SPM is an important advance. Moreover, while practitioners can, in principle, manipulate a country's electoral system when the current system is inadequate, a country's ethnic diversity is relatively fixed and is not subject to re-engineering, at least not absent redrawing national boundaries or engaging in unacceptable antidemocratic practices.

DEVELOPING AND TESTING AN EXTENDED SEAT PRODUCT MODEL

In the present section we introduce and test our extended version of the SPM. By introducing ethnic fragmentation and the upper tiers of compensatory PR systems, we can further compare the SPM with conventional approaches. Most such approaches include these variables (as well as variables specific to presidentialism – see Chapters 11 and 12). As was the case in Chapter 7, here our first modeling is concerned with predicting the effective number of seat-winning parties (N_S). In a subsequent section of the present chapter, we will extend the logic of Chapter 8 to test the ability of our extended SPM to predict the effective number of vote-earning parties (N_V).

Following common practice of standard regression analysis of party systems, such as Clark and Golder (2006), we will test whether our simple model for nationwide party systems can be improved if we account for social diversity. As with prior works, we use the *effective number of ethnic groups* (N_E).[1] This will allow us to determine whether the standard approaches are correct in claiming that features of the electoral system that generate permissiveness – that is, higher magnitude and upper tiers, as well as assembly size – are associated with a high effective number of parties only in the presence of social demand for many parties.

The other new factor added to the model in this chapter is the upper tier of composite systems. The largest set of such systems has an upper tier that is *compensatory* (Chapter 3). Taagepera (2007) devotes an entire chapter to complex systems, but ultimately concludes that it is impossible to understand how upper tiers affect seat distributions. This is an unfortunate limitation, standing in contrast to the conventional approaches. Since Cox (1997) and including Clark and Golder (2006) and Hicken and Stoll (2011), many scholars have estimated regressions in which there is a linear additive term for the percentage of seats in any upper tiers, typically along with an interaction for social cleavages.

In order to apply the SPM to two-tier compensatory systems, we first model how the basic tier (i.e., the component of the system excluding the upper tier) shapes party-system fragmentation. Logically, this should be through the product of the mean magnitude and the total size of the basic tier. We call this product the *basic-tier seat product*, which we will designate as MS_B, with the subscript B reminding us that it is the seat product of the basic tier alone. In this way, a simple (one-tier) system is one where the basic tier comprises the entire seat product ($MS=MS_B$).

How does the effect of an upper tier enter? If our hunch is right that the basic-tier seat product has the same relationship to the effective number of parties in

---

[1] Derived from Fearon (2003), which is the same measure used by Clark and Golder (2006) and by Li and Shugart (2016) in their attempt to replicate Clark and Golder's results on parliamentary systems.

systems with or without an upper tier, then the equation for a multitier system requires some adjustment to the basic-tier seat product that varies with the size of upper tiers. A compensatory upper tier could only increase the effective number of parties, relative to the N_S of simple systems with the same MS_B (i.e., $(MS_B)^{1/6}$). Thus the adjustment factor must be at least one. This gives us the following formula,

$$N_S = J^t(MS_B)^{1/6} \qquad (15.1)$$

where J is the base of the upper-tier adjustment factor,[2] which is raised to the power t, the upper-tier share; MS_B is the product of the average magnitude (M) of the basic tier and the total number of seats in that tier (S_B). Note that t and S_B are not two separate inputs; they are connected as $S_B = S(1-t)$. However, it is more convenient to enter them separately. The base, J, must be greater than 1.0, but its precise value is determined empirically. In the nationwide dataset we have, we can determine that we must have $J=2.5$.[3] The resulting formula is:

$$N_S = 2.5^t(MS_B)^{1/6} = 2.5^t[MS(1-t)]^{1/6} \qquad (15.2)$$

This model holds for $t \leq 0.5$, the usual range for upper-tier seat shares.[4] We emphasize that the logic behind Equations 15.1 and 15.2 applies only to complex systems that are compensatory – the "simplest" form of "complex" system. In Chapter 16, we will consider whether it also works for systems that have upper tiers that are not designed as compensatory.

Testing the Extended Model

We are ready now to perform regression tests of our extended model:

$$\log N_S = \alpha + \beta_1 \log(MS_B) + \beta_2 t + \beta_3 \log(N_E) + \beta_4[\log(MS_B) * \log(N_E)].$$

---

[2] We use J simply because it is the first consonant sound one hears in the word, *adjustment*.

[3] This value of the parameter is based on the sample of multitier compensatory systems for which Bormann and Golder (2011) report a known number of seats allocated in one or more upper tiers. For these cases, we ask, what would be the expected N_S (from the SPM) if we ignored the upper tier? We find that, for these systems, actual N_S is, on average, 1.27 times as large as it would be if we calculated the Seat Product from the basic tier alone. The mean upper tier in these systems represents 25 percent of the total assembly size. In Equation 15.1, therefore, we need a value of J such that $J^t=1.27$ when $t=0.25$. This can be calculated via the following steps:

$t \log J = \log 1.27$;
$\log J = 0.10/0.25 = 0.40$.

Therefore, we should expect a coefficient on t that is approximately 0.4, which is indeed what we find in the regressions (reported in Table 15.1). The inverse log of 0.4 is 2.51, hence the value of J in Equation 15.2. We test the underlying logic behind this complex set of steps later in this chapter.

[4] Purely empirically, Equation 15.2 could be well approximated by $N_S=(1+0.8t)(MS)^{1/6}$.

TABLE 15.1 *The extended Seat Product Model, including upper tiers, ethnic fragmentation, and systems with presidential executives*

	1	2	3
	All execs., established	All execs., any age since 1990	Full pooled sample
Seat Product (MS_B), logged	**0.171**	**0.173**	**0.166**
Expected coeff.: 0.167	(0.0251)	(0.0328)	(0.0237)
F test that coefficient on MS_B =1/6	0.866	0.852	0.981
Upper-tier ratio (t)	0.376	0.411	0.40006
Expected coeff: 0.40	(0.103)	(0.120)	(0.103)
F test that coefficient on t=0.4	0.825	0.926	0.9995
Eff. No. Ethnic Groups (N_E), logged	–0.0445	–0.0706	–0.189
	(0.269)	(0.318)	(0.275)
MS_B X N_E	0.0671	0.192	0.148
	(0.116)	(0.118)	(0.112)
Constant	–0.0661	–0.114	–0.0664
	(0.0749)	(0.108)	(0.0728)
Observations	376	197	432
R-squared	0.462	0.520	0.473

Of course, we expect β_1=1/6 (Chapter 7), while β_2=log$J$. From Equation 15.2, we should expect β_2=0.4, the decimal logarithm of 2.5. We have no specific expectations for β_3, but if the standard works in the field are correct, both should be positive and significant. Given the industry-standard expectation that the effect of a permissive system is felt only in the presence of demand via social heterogeneity, we will also seek to determine via analysis of β_4 whether there is a multiplicative effect of institutions and ethnicity.

In Table 15.1, we present three regressions. In Regression One, we consider only established democracies, defined as those that had their first democratic election before 1989. Regression Two includes elections since 1990, regardless of date of first election. Finally, Regression Three is our fully pooled model, including all postwar democratic elections in simple or two-tier compensatory systems for which the ethnic-diversity data were available.

Having models with and without newer democracies is important to test the breadth of applicability of the Seat Product Model. Clark and Golder (2006) report substantively different results for samples with and without the inclusion of post-1989 democracies. Thus the inclusion of newer democracies is an important check on the idea that the "context" of new democracies might temper or override electoral-system effects (Moser and Scheiner 2011; Ferree et al. 2013).

We see that in all of three regressions the coefficient on the basic-tier Seat Product (MS_B) is always near the expected one-sixth. The F tests reveal that in no case can we reject the null hypothesis that coefficient is equal to 1/6. Further, the coefficient on t (upper-tier ratio) is also near 0.4, as expected.[5] In addition, the constant terms are always statistically indistinguishable from zero, also as expected.

The coefficients reported in Table 15.1 confirm our expectation that the impact of the seat product is consistent across systems with and without compensatory upper tiers. We do not see any notable difference when we include or exclude newer democracies. Moreover, consistent with what Li and Shugart (2016) discovered in attempting to replicate Clark and Golder's (2006) findings, our results are not sensitive to whether or not we include India.[6] Unlike the conventional regression coefficients in the literature, those testing the Seat Product Model, as extended in this chapter, are remarkably stable.

As for the effect of ethnic diversity, β_3, the coefficient on N_E, is not significant in any of the three regressions, and the coefficient on $logN_E$ is actually negative. Moreover, β_4, the coefficient on the interaction term, is also insignificant, although it is positive in each model – especially in the samples that include the newer democracies (Regressions Two and Three), precisely the set where context aside from rules might have the greatest impact. For these reasons, and given the difficulty of analyzing interactions from just coefficients and standard errors (Brambor, Clark, and Golder 2006), we examined the marginal effects. We determined that the interaction is indeed significant – albeit barely – when $200>MS_B>15,850$.[7] Given that this range encompasses over 85 percent of all the elections included in Regression Three the finding appears to support the conventional expectation of permissive electoral systems having an effect on increasing N_S only under conditions of high heterogeneity, and perhaps especially so when we include younger democracies. We now explore this notion further.

In Figure 15.1 we compare the estimates of Regression Three against the institutions-only SPM. In the figure, we compare how different the predicted values are when we include ethnic fragmentation versus leaving the latter out. We see, plotted with the x symbol, the predicted value from the SPM

---

[5] Likewise, F tests show that we cannot reject the null hypotheses that these coefficients are 0.400.

[6] For reasons of space, we do not report models without India; in each sample reported in Table 15.1 any difference was trivial. We discuss the Indian case in some detail later in this chapter.

[7] A plot of the marginal effect is available at our online appendix www.cambridge.org/votes_from_seats. A further question is whether there is also an interaction of N_E with the upper-tier share, t. Other authors find such an interaction to be significant. Regressions of the extended SPM testing this show an extremely weak effect of this interaction. Thus the (small) impact of N_E on N_S apparently works through the basic-tier Seat Product more than through the compensation mechanism.

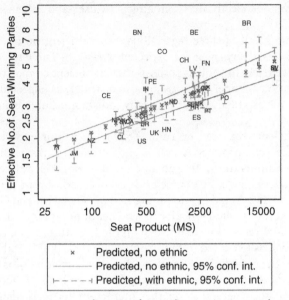

FIGURE 15.1 Comparing predictions from the institutions-only model to the predictions when considering ethnic fragmentation

(Equation 7.1), using only institutional variables.[8] The 95 percent confidence intervals, calculated from Regression Three in Table 7.2 (where we did not include ethnicity), are indicated with gray lines. Then, using capped bar plots, we see the 95 percent confidence interval on the predictions of Regression Three from Table 15.1, incorporating ethnicity. The country abbreviation is located at the actual value for that country, averaged over the elections in the sample (for visual clarity, although the regression estimates are derived from individual elections).

What we see is that inclusion of ethnicity does not substantially improve the fit of predicted to actual values in most cases. Only a few cases have actual values that are outside the 95 percent confidence interval of the institutions-only model while also being within the comparable interval for the model that includes ethnicity. One of these cases is India, a long-term democracy with very high N_E, which we discuss further below. In a few other cases, inclusion of the ethnic factor improves the prediction only because the country's low ethnic fragmentation helps account for a value of N_S that is even lower than its institutions would predict. This more accurately predicted lower N_S when accounting for low ethnic diversity is observed in one highly restrictive

---

[8] The figure shows only simple systems, due to the difficulty of graphing both MS_B and *Upper-tier ratio* on one axis. We return to analysis of two-tier systems later in this chapter.

electoral system, Jamaica, but also in some permissive systems, such as Poland and Portugal. Thus, from Figure 15.1, we can conclude that the Seat Product Model, based only on institutions, predicts the effective number of seat-winning parties at least as accurately for the large majority of democracies as does the combination of institutions and a widely used indicator of social diversity.

Extended Seat Product Model for Votes

Having dealt with seat-winning parties, we are now ready to test the connection between the Seat Product, MS, and the effective number of vote-earning parties for the extended sample. As in the preceding section, the analysis includes two-tier compensatory systems and a country's ethnic diversity. We already saw in Chapter 8, specifically in Figure 8.4, that the relationship between seat and vote fragmentation is not fundamentally different in two-tier complex systems. Thus it should be possible to derive votes from seats for the wider sample that includes the complex systems in the same manner as we did for simple (in Chapter 8). Combining our extended SPM (Equation 15.2) and our model for deriving N_V from N_S (Equation 8.3), we can test:

$$N_V = \{[2.5^t(MS_B)^{1/6}]^{3/2} + 1\}^{2/3} = [4^t(MS_B)^{1/4} + 1]^{2/3} \qquad (15.3)$$

(The "4" is rounded from $2.5^{3/2}=3.95$.) In Table 15.2, we report three regressions to test Equation 15.3 by pooling simple and two-tier systems. The first two are "institutions only," while the third brings in the ethnic factor. Because ethnic fragmentation data are missing on several countries, we show the institutions model both on the wider sample and on a sample restricted to those for which the ethnic data are available.

The dependent variable in each is the logged effective number of vote-earning parties ($\log N_V$) and the key independent variable in each is the *log of the number of pertinent vote-earning parties* ($\log N_{V0}$). Because this latter quantity is not directly measurable, as explained in Chapter 8, we estimate it from the Seat Product. That is, what is entered into the regression is the part of Equation 15.3 that is in the square brackets. We expect the coefficient on this input variable to be two-thirds (0.667). We see in Table 15.2 that the actual estimate ranges from 0.625 to 0.712 (thus −0.042 to +0.045, relative to the expected 0.667), depending on the sample. In all cases it is not statistically distinguishable from the expectation, as reported by the F test statistic in the table. Thus we can consider Equation 15.3 to be strongly supported on our pooled sample that includes two-tier proportional systems and presidential democracies.

Regression Three introduces the "industry standard" interactive effect of institutions and the *log of the effective number of ethnic groups* ($\log N_E$). We have no specific expectation for the coefficients on either $\log N_E$ or its

TABLE 15.2 *Three regressions for the effective number of vote-earning parties* (N_V), *including two-tier systems and the effective number of ethnic groups* (N_E)

	(1)	(2)	(3)
	Institutions only; incl. 2-tier and presidential	Institutions only; all systems with non-missing N_E	With N_E (interactive; all systems)
$\log N_{V0} = \log[4^t(MS_B)^{1/4}+1]$	0.625	0.675	0.712
expected: 0.667	(0.0614)	(0.102)	(0.1071)
F test that coeff = 2/3	0.500	0.935	0.673
$\log N_E$			−0.110
			(0.352)
$\log[(MS)^{1/4}+1] \times \log N_E$			0.566
			(0.475)
Constant	0.0291	−0.0158	−0.116
	(0.0508)	(0.0941)	(0.0965)
Observations	553	433	433
R-squared	0.395	0.317	0.403

interaction with $\log N_{V0}$, but if the standard works in the field are correct, both should be positive and significant. However, we find that neither is close to significant, and the coefficient on $\log N_E$ is actually negative. Nonetheless, when we examine the marginal effects, we find that the interaction of institutionally derived $\log N_{V0}$ and $\log N_E$ is significant as long as $\log N_{V0}$ is greater than about 0.60, meaning N_{V0} greater than 4.0.[9] This corresponds to a significant effect as long as $MS > 80$, for a simple system. Thus we find some support for the "industry-standard" interactive effect, which we should explore further.

What the regression output cannot directly tell us is how much of an improvement the inclusion of ethnic diversity offers over our institutions-only model. For all elections covered by the sample of Regression Three (Table 15.2), the mean ratio of actual to N_V predicted by our logical model is 1.042 (median 0.950, standard deviation 0.412). For the same sample, the mean ratio of actual N_V to the estimated derived from Regression Three is 1.053 (median 0.983, standard deviation 0.363). The improvement from including N_E is thus slight.

Of particular interest is whether the inclusion of ethnic diversity helps us understand individual countries that are relatively extreme on N_E. To probe the fit of our model (Equation 15.3) relative to the regression that includes the

---

[9] A plot of the marginal effect is available at our online appendix www.cambridge.org/votes_from_seats.

TABLE 15.3 *Comparing the logical model and the regression that includes ethnic effects*

Country	No. of elections	Mean N_V	N_E	Mean ratio of actual N_V to Equation 15.3	Mean ratio of actual N_V to Regression Three (Table 15.2)
		Lowest 25% of N_E			
Portugal	13	3.42	1.04	0.845	0.906
Poland	4	4.46	1.05	**0.991**	1.143
Netherlands	20	5.17	1.08	0.941	0.943
Germany	17	3.78	1.1	0.792	0.886
Norway	16	4.28	1.11	**1.054**	1.133
Austria	19	2.93	1.14	0.645	0.717
Denmark	25	4.85	1.15	**1.098**	1.22
		Highest 25% of N_E			
Israel	18	5.68	2.11	**1.087**	0.895
Macedonia	5	4.38	2.15	1.145	**1.022**
Brazil	6	9.62	2.22	1.954	1.564
Belgium	3	9.52	2.31	2.437	2.087
Switzerland	17	5.82	2.35	1.549	1.336
Latvia	4	6.67	2.41	1.5	1.444
Canada	21	3.27	2.48	1.101	1.026
Peru	5	5.36	2.76	1.586	1.351
Trinidad & Tobago	12	2.29	2.83	1.0004	1.007
Nepal	2	3.91	3.1	1.376	1.226
India	10	5.27	5.29	1.629	**1.146**

The ratio indicating the better-performing model is in bold if one model is within the range, 0.80–1.25, but the other is not, or if one is very close to 1.000 while the other is not.

ethnic effect (Regression Three from Table 15.2), Table 15.3 shows these ratios. The ratios start with the observed values of N_V for a given election and divide it by the predicted value from either Equation 15.3 or Regression Three (from Table 15.2). We then take a mean value of each ratio for each country and report these means in the table.

The cases included in Table 15.3 are those countries that have unusually low or high effective number of ethnic groups, relative to our full sample. A country is included in Table 15.3 if its value of N_E is in the lowest 25 percent of countries or the highest 25 percent, the ranges in which the effect of ethnicity is most likely to be felt. We see from the ratios for the set of relatively homogeneous or heterogeneous countries that the inclusion of N_E improves the prediction substantially only in a few cases. Among the low-N_E cases, the predictions of the two approaches tend not to differ greatly. However, the institutions-only model does better for some cases than does the incorporation of these countries' (low) ethnic diversity. Denmark, Norway, and Poland stand out as cases substantially better explained by our model (Equation 15.3).

In the high-diversity cases, again few are predicted better by inclusion of N_E. A case where the model including ethnicity performs a good deal better is India. This is striking, given how highly fragmented the system is, in spite of FPTP. Canada's N_V is predicted almost perfectly by the inclusion of N_E; however, the institutions-only model does only slightly worse. Several of our highest-diversity cases do indeed have unexpectedly high N_V, but are not predicted much better by inclusion of N_E than without it; examples include Benin, Brazil, Nepal, Peru, and Switzerland.

The case of Israel, our example of nationwide PR in Chapter 6, is predicted markedly better by institutions only, despite its very high N_V. We do not need to invoke the ethnic dimension, at least as measured by the proxy available to us for the wider sample, in order to understand how fragmented the vote is in Israel, on average. The very high Seat Product is sufficient to understand the country's high mean value of N_V.[10]

One case of high N_E is actually accounted for equally well by the institutions-only model (Equation 15.3) and by the model that includes ethnicity: Trinidad and Tobago, our example for FPTP in Chapter 5. Its ratios of almost exactly 1.0 from either model are consistent with the idea, common on the study of party systems, that even high diversity is not reflected if the electoral system is highly restrictive. Note, however, that *most of the mainstream literature would consider India's and Trinidad's electoral systems as equally restrictive*, as both have M=1. However, the Seat Product identifies India's larger assembly as making its system considerably more permissive; combined with its exceptional degree of ethnic diversity, we are able to account for its party-system fragmentation. We discuss the case of India in more detail below.

What we have shown here is that ethnic diversity of a country is a much less important factor in predicting its electoral fragmentation, as measured by either N_S or N_V, than is widely believed. While there is a statistically significant marginal effect, there are not many countries whose unusual degrees of ethnic diversity can be invoked as an explanation for why their mean values of N_V diverge from our Seat Product Model prediction. Contrary to much scholarship, then, *there simply is not much evidence that the effect of electoral systems is conditional on social factors* – at least not when these factors are measured by the effective number of ethnic groups, as has been the preference of many scholars. This does not mean that there is no effect of social diversity on party

---

[10] For a more nuanced account of the impact on its party system of changing social divisions over time in Israel, see Stoll (2013).

systems (Moser et al. 2018). It means only that this measure, N_E, widely used in the scholarly literature for exactly this purpose, is not able to detect such an effect in most democracies and – more importantly – that most countries are quite close to the prediction of our logical models, which are based solely on institutional factors.

The Seat Product Model and the Effective Number of Alliances: India

The Indian case is fundamental to checking on the accuracy of theories of the impact of electoral systems. India is the world's largest democracy. Perhaps, if a model of key democratic processes leaves India as an outlier, the model might need to be reconsidered. The case has long vexed scholars working on such topics. For instance, Riker (1982) resorted to a highly ad hoc approach to explaining why India was an "exception" to "Duverger's law."[11] More recent work also has had trouble with India, though the authors may not have been aware.

In Chapter 7, we reviewed the attempt by Li and Shugart (2016) to replicate the Clark and Golder (2006) regressions on the parliamentary subsample. Li and Shugart discovered that the Clark-Golder approach was not robust to the exclusion of the Indian case. Such lack of robustness is important because their approach assumes that ethnic diversity is an essential input variable, and that its effect is interactive with district magnitude. This is particularly a problem for proponents of the conventional method, given that India has by far the highest ethnic fragmentation of any of the countries that they (or we) have included. Fortunately, the coefficient of the Seat Product Model itself is robust to including or dropping the Indian case (as reported in Chapter 7). However, we should explore this case further, because it offers important lessons for Duverger's tendencies and the question of how parties adapt to the constraints of the first-past-the-post (FPTP) electoral system.

Many treatments of the so-called Duverger's law take the Indian case as an exception that must be explained. At one time the puzzle was the existence of a single dominant party, rather than the expected "Duvergerian" two-party system (Riker 1982). More recently, the puzzle has been the existence of an extremely fragmented party system, despite the continued use of FPTP.

Figure 15.2 shows Indian N_S over time, along with the mean prediction from the Seat Product Model. Focusing on the dashed trend line, we see that until the late 1980s, N_S was consistently below the Seat Product prediction. Then in the

---

[11] Riker argued that the then-dominant Congress Party was the Condorcet winner (i.e., would beat any single contender in a pairwise competition), but offered no evidence for the assertion, which is particularly debatable given that on the occasions when it has faced a grand alliance of most of the opposition, it sometimes has been defeated – including in 1979, before Riker's article was published, and again in some recent elections discussed in this section. See Ziegfeld (2018) for details.

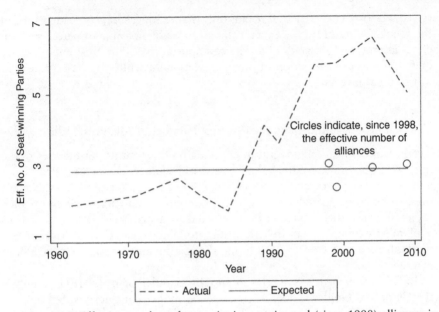

FIGURE 15.2 Effective number of seat-winning parties and (since 1998) alliances in India over time

more recent period, N_S has surged, remaining above 5.0 from 1996 through 2009. While India's assembly size has increased over time, the line for expected N_S remains flat visually because the increases have been small.

The period of Indian politics since 1998 has been marked by two major and some smaller *alliances*, each of which presents a single candidate in any given district (see the discussion near the end of Chapter 5). When we consider the individual parties that comprise these alliances to be distinct components for the calculation of the effective number, we obtain the strikingly high values tracked by the dashed line in Figure 15.2. However, one could be justified in starting from a different premise when calculating N_S. Indian voters are faced with a single candidate from each of the various alliances, because each presents a single candidate from just one of the alliance's component parties in each district. Thus we might want to know what the effective number would be if calculated it based on alliances.

The circles in Figure 15.2 represent the values of *effective number of seat-winning alliances* since 1998, the election at which the National Democratic Alliance first appeared. It is striking how closely the distribution of seats among these alliances approximates the predictions of the Seat Product Model. After all, the model is "blind" to the politics behind the effective number of components in the national legislature – whether those components are called representatives of distinct subcomponents (parties) or national alliances.

Looked at in this light, *India actually appears somewhat less exceptional than it is generally taken to be.*

As for the votes, we saw above in Table 15.3 that the effective number of vote-earning parties – here meaning the component parties, many of which are ethno-specific – is rather well accounted for by including the effect of N_E in addition to *MS* (Regression Three in Table 15.2). In other words, recent Indian elections have featured a very large number of parties, many of them representing specific ethnic groups, and a regression that takes into account the country's high ethnic diversity accurately accounts for N_V. These parties operate within large pre-electoral alliances, and the effective number of these alliances winning seats is well accounted for by the Seat Product Model (if we replace "parties" with "alliances"). Which is the better indicator – the alliances or the parties comprising them? We can only answer with, "better at what?" Both measures capture something important about the country's politics. Nonetheless, the management of business in parliament and the formation (or dissolution) of governing cabinets is done through the alliances (Heath et al. 2005: 152–154). It is thus striking that the SPM is quite accurate at predicting the effect of alliances, as if they were the parties in Indian parliamentary politics.

India is not the only case where this issue of whether to count alliances instead of their component parties arises. As we first noted in Chapter 6, electoral lists in proportional systems also sometimes consist of more than one party. If lists are open, voters are able to cast their vote for a candidate of one of the component parties rather than for the alliance as a whole. Should analysts count the parties or the composite alliances? When, as in the Indian FPTP case, alliances are consistent across districts and present only a candidate from one partner, it is possible to recalculate the effective number of alliances, rather than the component parties (as we saw in Figure 15.2). It is also possible to do the same in Chile, where a multiparty system is tempered by the existence of two major nationwide alliances. However, in some proportional-representation countries the set of parties that may be in alliance with one another differs from district to district, even in the same election. Chapter 14 offered a detailed discussion of pre-election alliances in PR systems.

DEVIATION FROM PROPORTIONALITY: INCORPORATING TWO-TIER SYSTEMS

In Chapter 9, we developed a formula that related deviation from proportionality to the Seat Product for simple systems. It is axiomatic that two-tier compensatory systems are "more proportional" than otherwise similar simple systems. That is precisely what a compensatory upper tier does, after all: reduce disproportionality! Let us see if we can specify how much.

We will extend Equation 9.3 for D_2 by including a parameter in a regression test for the upper tier, such that our extended equation will be of the form:

$$D_2 = 0.50 j^t (MS_B)^{-1/3},$$

where j is the base of the adjustment factor for the impact of the compensatory tier. As with its counterpart in Equation 15.1, we must estimate it empirically. It must be the case that $0<j<1$, because a compensatory tier can only deflate D_2 relative to what results from the basic-tier. When we run a regression to derive j, we find its value to be approximately 0.06, and thus the formula becomes:

$$D_2 = 0.50(0.06^t)(MS_B)^{-1/3} \qquad (15.4)$$

Recall that t and S_B are connected as $S_B=S(1-t)$.

The output of this regression is shown and explained further in the chapter appendix. In Figure 15.3, we plot the deviation from proportionality, D_2, for all of the two-tier compensatory PR systems. The main trend line plotted in black is Equation 15.4 for the mean observed value of t in our nationwide data sample, which is around 0.25. When an upper tier consists of a quarter of all assembly seats, Equation 15.4 becomes (with rounding):

$$D_2 = 0.25/(MS_B)^{1/3} \qquad (15.5)$$

We must emphasize that this is not a logical model! It contains multiple empirical steps. Only the 1/3 has a logical basis (see Chapter 9). Nonetheless, it suggests an elegant, albeit tentative, conclusion: it says that the "average" two-tier compensatory system reduces deviation from proportionality to half the predicted value for a system that has an identical basic tier but no compensation. The gray line near the top of Figure 15.3 represents values twice the predictions of Equation 15.4, which happens to be identical to Equation 9.3. No election is observed above this line, and thus the average prediction for simple systems may be an upper limit for two-tier systems.

A lighter gray line in Figure 15.3 shows values half the prediction of Equation 15.4. We see several elections are considerably below this line. From a design standpoint, this is not troubling. Electoral system designers would choose a two-tier PR system when they want to minimize deviation from proportionality; getting less disproportionality than they bargained for should not, therefore, be a problem. The useful finding here for practitioners is that the *upper* extent of disproportionality rarely is very much greater than we estimate its average to be in simple systems with the same (basic-tier) number of seats and mean district magnitude.

A further implication of this section is that the precise size of the upper tier may not matter greatly for proportionality, as long as it is not much below about 20 percent. The very large upper tiers of Germany, South Africa, and some other two-tier systems, are overkill. We had already suggested in Taagepera and Shugart (1989a: 131) that a compensatory upper tier need be

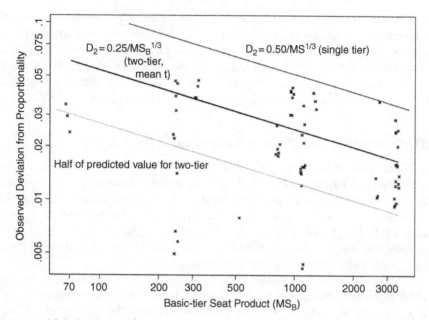

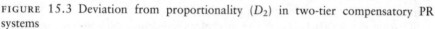

FIGURE 15.3 Deviation from proportionality (D_2) in two-tier compensatory PR systems

no bigger than the percentage Deviation from PR expected to result from the basic tier. We can test more directly the impact of the relative size of the compensation tier by turning to our district-level dataset, and disaggregating nationwide party-system outcomes into their basic-tier and upper-tier components. This is the task of the next section.

THE BASIC TIER IN COMPENSATORY SYSTEMS

In preceding sections of this chapter, we tested some models of party system outcomes in pooled samples that included simple and two-tier systems. Their results suggest the conclusion that the basic tier of the two-tier system works much like a simple system. Then the outcome (e.g., N_S or D_2) is adjusted by the application of upper-tier compensation. Up to now, however, the conclusion contains a bit of a leap of faith: we have not looked at the actual outcomes in the basic tier. We have only tested regressions in which the outcome variable was a nationwide indicator.

In this section, we return to our district-level dataset and perform tests on the basic-tier of complex systems directly. This procedure allows us to probe the process underlying the functioning of two-tier systems. We do so first by looking at the individual districts themselves. It might be expected that districts in two-tier systems would be fundamentally different from their counterparts in simple systems. After all, by definition, these districts are not the only way that parties can win seats. They can also win via the upper tier. After the district-level analysis we aggregate the districts within the basic tier, to see the extent to which upper tiers adjust the basic-tier outcome in a systematic way, as predicted by our extended Seat Product Model (Equation 15.2).

The Effective Number of Seat-Winning Parties in Basic-Tier Districts

It might seem as if the models of district-level party fragmentation that we developed in Chapter 10 for simple systems could not possibly extend to two-tier systems. By definition, the basic tier districts in compensatory PR systems is not decisive in determining the overall makeup of the assembly – in total contrast to the situation in simple, single-tier systems. Therefore, perhaps it follows that there would be little or no relationship between features of basic-tier districts and the representation of parties in that tier.

To give an idea of how models derived from single-tier systems need only one small adjustment to account for the pattern in basic tiers, we offer Figure 15.4.[12] It shows the districts of our two-tier systems, and the relationship of the effective number of seat-winning parties (N'_S) to district magnitude. Partially replicating Figure 10.1, this graph also plots the simple (single-tier) systems.[13] We can see quite clearly that the general trend is for the data points for two-tier systems to be somewhat higher than the main trend for simple systems.

The thick dotted curve takes into account the embeddedness of districts in the wider system, much as did Figure 10.1 and several other district-level graphs that we have seen. The remarkable aspect of this curve is that it captures the same relationship as Equation 14.2:

$$N'_S = M^{4kk/3}. \tag{15.6}$$

In the case of Equation 14.2, the quantity explained was the suballiance parties in the hybrid D'Hondt/SNTV countries – those open-list PR systems that often feature candidates of more than one party on the same list. Here it is parties, per se, but in systems where the district might be said to be "doubly embedded" – first it is embedded in a basic tier consisting of various other districts, and then it is embedded in a two-tier design in which some percentage of the assembly is elected via compensatory PR in national (or regional) districts.

Equations 14.2 and 15.6 both contain a double k, our embeddedness factor. This is because, *unlike with simple systems*, the number of seat-winning parties,

---

[12] Readers seeking more detail on these processes than we offer here are referred to our online appendix www.cambridge.org/votes_from_seats.

[13] Excluding the $M=S$ cases, in order to focus on the range that is relevant to the comparison to the two-tier systems.

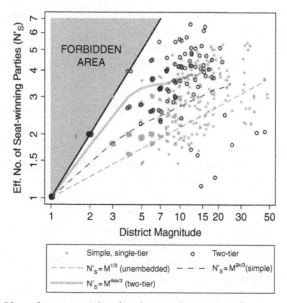

FIGURE 15.4 How the magnitude of a district shapes the effective number of seat-winning parties in the basic tier of two-tier systems, compared to simple systems

of any size, turns out to be $N'_{S0}=M^{k}$, instead of $N'_{S0}=M^{1/2}$, as it is with simple systems (Equation 1.1, tested in Chapter 7).[14] The implication is that parties in two-tier systems enter even in districts where they do not expect to win. They do so because winning the basic-tier district is typically not necessary to gaining representation, but entering is necessary to earning votes that may help it win seats in the upper tier.[15] By campaigning for and earning such votes, these parties are more likely to pick up a seat in a given basic-tier district even where they are relatively weak. Their ability to win seats is still constrained by the district magnitude, but it is boosted via the district's double-embeddedness in a more complex electoral-system design. We can see just how much it is boosted, on average, by comparing the thick dotted curve representing Equation 15.6 with the curve for simple systems (equivalent to Equation 10.5, and plotted with the dot-dash pattern), and the equation for a hypothetical unembedded district, plotted with the light gray dashed line.[16]

---

[14] The regressions supporting these results are included in our online appendix. www.cambridge.org/votes_from_seats

[15] The statement about entry is true for all cases in which the basic tier $M>1$. It is not strictly true for cases of MMP in which districts are $M=1$ and there is a separate party-list vote. Nonetheless, in most cases, even small parties enter the basic-tier districts with candidates whose presence helps the party "show the flag" for earning list votes.

[16] We see eight data points from two-tier systems below this line for the unembedded relationship. Two are from one Danish district in different elections, one is from Estonia, and all the others are

Both the D'Hondt/SNTV hybrid and the presence of an upper tier are forms of complexity. However, they lend themselves to modeling with the same theoretical approach that we applied to simple systems (Chapter 10). While such systems may seem as if they could not be modeled, in fact they can be.

The Basic Tier and the Upper Tier: Fitting the Components Together

The preceding section concerned individual districts of two-tier systems. This is one piece of the puzzle, but in order to understand the process of compensatory PR, we need to consider how the basic and upper tiers fit together as components of a two-tier system. The equations for two-tier systems overall – the Extended Seat Product Model (Equation 15.2) and the formula for Deviation from PR (Equation 15.4) – both make the following claim: the output (N_S or D_2) is a product of the basic-tier aggregate output, times the adjustment term. The adjustment term itself is a base raised to the tier ratio (the share of the total assembly elected from the upper tier): J^t for N_S and j^t for D_2. We can check the logic now in two steps.

The first step is to ask whether the output (N_S or D_2) in the basic tier conforms to the same relationship as the models for simple systems. In other words, we want to know whether the aggregate outputs of just the basic tiers of the two-tier cases conform to:

$$N_{SB} = (MS_B)^{1/6} \tag{15.7}$$

$$D_{2B} = 0.5(MS_B)^{-1/3}. \tag{15.8}$$

Once again, the addition of the B to our subscripts reminds us that these are quantities for the basic tier only. We run regressions (shown in the chapter appendix) to test both of these. We also graph the data and the lines formed by these equations in Figure 15.5, which consists of two panels. In the left we see the basic-tier effective number of seat-winning parties, N_{SB}, while in the right we see the basic-tier deviation from PR (D_{2B}).

We find that Equation 15.7 is confirmed precisely. So is the slope in Equation 15.8, although the intercept is somewhat higher than it was for the wider set of cases, including simple systems. The 0.5 constant term in our earlier equations for D_2 was empirically determined anyway; what is most impressive is the repeat of the expected exponent.

Having confirmed that the basic tier of compensatory systems works essentially equivalent to a simple system, we now ask whether the adjustment effect is as implied by Equations 15.2 and 15.4. In other words, does raising

---

from South Africa (which is noteworthy for its dominant party, notwithstanding its extremely proportional electoral system – see Ferree 2018).

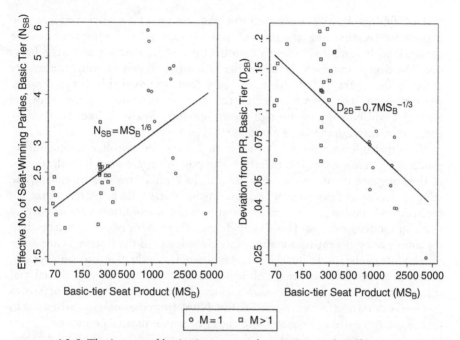

FIGURE 15.5 The impact of basic tier seat product (MS_B) on the effective number of seat-winning parties (N_{SB}) and deviation from proportionality (D_2)

a base coefficient to the upper tier ratio, t, accurately capture the tendency of the compensatory tier to adjust the basic-tier result? We can answer this by determining the mean adjustment factor in the two-tier systems that we have in our district-level dataset, the one we use in this section because it allows us to measure the impact of the two tiers separately. They are:

$$N_S/N_{SB} = 1.38;$$
$$D_2/D_{2B} = 0.36.$$

That is, after the application of compensation via the upper tier, N_S on average is 1.38 times what it was from the basic tier alone, whereas D_2 is 0.36 times as high. Given the previously estimated values of our adjustment factors, we ask whether the mean upper-tier ratio, which happens to be 0.364 in this dataset, yields the correct result:

$$J^{0.364} = 2.5^{0.364} = 1.396;$$
$$j^{0.364} = 0.06^{0.364} = 0.359.$$

The results are almost spot on. Therefore, by using the basic-tier district-level data and comparing to the nationwide, we have confirmed that the process is as we posited in developing Equations 15.2 and 15.4 earlier in this chapter.

This finding is highly relevant for the design of two-tier systems: the implication is that the number of parties (actual and effective) can be constrained by employing low or moderate district magnitude in the basic tier. The degree to which the upper tier will inflate this is broadly predictable through the share of all assembly seats that are available for upper-tier compensation. The degree to which the disproportionality arising from the basic tier will be reduced through the compensation seats is likewise broadly predicable, through the same parameter.

With this information, it is possible to understand two-tier compensation processes systematically. It is therefore also possible to estimate how the design of the components of two-tier systems can be crafted towards producing the relative degree of district-level and nationwide party system patterns that are desired.[17] Of course, there remains ample room for political variation away from the model estimates. This should be even more so for two-tier systems than for simple ones, for the reason that more complexity of the system means more uncertainty of the result. Yet the models shown in this chapter offer an advance, in that previously the best that political scientists could say was the directional statement: more compensatory seats means a higher effective number of parties and lower deviation from proportionality. Now, from the analysis carried out in this chapter, we can offer something closer to a quantitative prediction[18] if we know three parameters: the size of the assembly, the size of the basic tier,[19] and the mean magnitude of basic-tier districts.

CONCLUSION

This chapter extended the Seat Product Model (SPM) by considering two additional variables, ethnic fragmentation and upper tier share. Both variables are included in many standard regression-based accounts of electoral systems and party systems, and thus the SPM would be much less generalizable were it to ignore these factors. Fortunately for the applicability of the SPM, we have seen that accounting for ethnic fragmentation has much less impact than commonly believed, and that a compensatory upper tier can be included in the SPM with just one additional parameter.

What we have found is that even though the ethnic structure matters statistically for some of the outputs, its substantive effects are most often

---

[17] We have not considered the impact of relatively rare cases in which the upper tier is itself districted. These may not have different effects from cases of nationwide compensation if the basic tier is itself not too restrictive. However, for cases like MMP (basic tier districts of $M=1$) it is potentially consequential. Analysis of the Scottish Parliament system shows that our extended SPM predicts its N_S well, despite assuming erroneously that the upper tier is one district, but understates D_2. (See our on line appendix at www.cambridge.org/votes_from_seats).

[18] See Chapters 1 and 17 for discussion of direction hypotheses versus quantitative prediction.

[19] Recall that the tier ratio, t, is $S - S_B/S$.

negligible. This is a valuable insight, considering that the measurement of ethnicity is subject to serious controversy: see Stoll's (2008) discussion of the impact of measurement selection, Lublin's (2014) criticism of counting subthreshold groups, Potter's (2014) arguments regarding the mismatch of theory and data in the measurement of (district-level) diversity, and the extensive words of caution by Fearon himself (2003: 197–198, 200). Thus a parsimonious model that has good predictive power without the inclusion of ethnic variables should be preferred when the purpose is to predict nationwide party-system fragmentation under a given electoral system.

For two-tier systems, a small extension of the Seat Product Model allows us to include two-tier compensatory systems within its coverage. Through analysis of both the nationwide and district-level data, we find that two-tier systems affect N_S first through the seat product of the basic tier alone, and then through an inflation of this basic-tier value according to the share of the assembly that is elected in the upper tier. Larger upper tiers thus can be expected to inflate N_S more, relative to the impact of the basic tier. The relationship of N_V to N_S is equivalent across two-tier and simple systems, as already shown in Figure 8.4.

A key implication of our analysis is that *the basic tier of two-tier compensatory systems remains fundamental* to our expectations of how fragmented the party system will be. This need not have been the case; the existence of upper-tier compensation could have overridden the impact of the size of the basic tier and the average magnitude of its districts. Yet, for estimating what the effective number of parties tends to be, on average, the basic tier is indeed basic to the outcome.

The basic tier also remains fundamental to the impact of a two-tier system on deviation from PR, D_2. Compensation surely means that D_2 can be only reduced by the upper tier. As long as the upper tier represents at least a quarter of the total assembly, we can expect D_2 to be about half what would be expected if the basic tier were the entire assembly. However, it is quite likely to be even lower than that expectation. In other words, very large upper tiers appear to be unnecessary to produce a substantial reduction in disproportionality.

An informal iron law has been long observed in electoral system design: one can obtain more proportionality (which may be desirable) only at the cost of more fractured party landscape (which may be undesirable). Our Figure 9.4 confirms and quantifies this tradeoff, for simple systems. Two-tier compensatory systems relax this iron grip. For instance, a basic tier that does not encourage fragmentation, combined with a modest-sized compensatory tier (perhaps 25 percent of total seats), favors both a moderate effective number of parties and low disproportionality. We can have our cake and eat half of it too. In principle, simplicity is desirable, but the complexity of having two tiers pays off in practice – and to the extent expected in theory.

This chapter thus clarifies an important design principle, as there is often resistance to making districts large geographically or expanding assembly size in order to accommodate a large compensatory tier. If the compensatory tier can be considerably smaller than 50 percent of the total assembly and still provide adequate PR, then the basic tier can accommodate more compact districts within a reasonably sized assembly. These findings, it must be emphasized, refer only to compensatory upper tiers. Thus they may not apply to mixed-member majoritarian systems (as defined in Chapter 3) or other systems with noncompensatory upper tiers. In Chapter 16, we consider these and other complex systems.

Appendix to Chapter 15

This appendix reports results of regressions discussed in Chapter 15. In **Table 15.A1** we see a regression in which the output variable is Deviation from Proportionality (D_2) and the inputs are the basic-tier seat product (MS_B) and the upper tier ratio (t). Based on findings in Chapter 9, we expect a coefficient on MS_B of –0.333. We do not have a specific expectation for the coefficient on t, other than that it should be negative and significant. The constant term should be –0.301, so that when unlogged the equation derived from the regression matches Equation 9.3 for a simple system, i.e., $D_2=0.5/(MS_B)^{1/3}$. The results closely match the expectations, and lead us to Equations 15.4 and 15.5, reported in the main text of the chapter.

In Table 15.A2, we see the regressions on district-level outcomes in the basic tiers of our two-tier systems. All variables in each regression are entered as their decimal logarithms. Regression One confirms that the embeddedness

TABLE 15.A1 *The effect of two-tier systems on Deviation from Proportionality*

VARIABLES	(1) log(D_2)
(M_{SB}), logged	–0.342
Expected: –0.333	(0.0371)
	[–0.416 – –0.268]
tier ratio (t)	–1.209
Expect neg. sign	(0.205)
	[–1.620 – –0.799]
Constant	–0.317
Expected: –0.301	(0.120)
	[–0.558 – –0.0771]
Observations	342
R-squared	0.455

Robust standard errors in parentheses.
95 percent confidence intervals in brackets.

TABLE 15.A2 *Regressions for basic tier of two-tier systems: district level*

VARIABLES	1 No. of seat-winning parties $\log(N'_{SO})$	2 Size of the largest party $\log(s'_1)$	3 Size of the largest party $\log(s'_1)$	4 Effective No. of seat-winning parties $\log(N'_S)$
$k*\log(M)$	0.960*** (0.0508) [0.857 – 1.063]			
$k*\log(N'_{SO})$		−0.986*** (0.0574) [−1.104 – −0.868]		
$k^2*\log(M)$			−0.969*** (0.143) [−1.262 – −0.676]	1.271*** (0.162) [0.939 – 1.603]
Constant Expected: 0	−7.41e−06 (0.000172) [−0.000358 – 0.000343]	2.73e−05 (6.21e−05) [−0.000100 – 0.000155]	−0.000215 (0.000131) [−0.000484 – 5.33e−05]	0.000147 (0.000127) [−0.000113 – 0.000407]
Expected coeff.:	1.000	−1.000	−1.000	1.333
Observations	5,110	5,110	5,110	5,110
R-squared	0.963	0.947	0.860	0.902
rmse	0.0139	0.0107	0.0173	0.0185

Robust standard errors in parentheses.
95 percent confidence intervals in brackets.
*** p<0.01, ** p<0.05, * p<0.1

factor, k, is needed to understand the relationship of the number of seat-winning parties of any size (N'_{SO}) to district magnitude (M) – unlike in the case of simple systems (Chapter 9). The regression supports the expectation, $N'_{SO} = M^k$. Regressions Two and Three are for the output variable, size of the largest party (s'_1); in Regression Two the input is N'_{SO}. Following the same logic as in Chapter 9, we expect $s'_1 = N'^{-k}_{SO}$, which is supported by the result (because the expected −1 is within the 95 percent confidence interval of the estimated coefficient on $k*\log(N'_{SO})$.

When we take the next step, which is to connect s'_1 to M, we expect $s'_1 = (M^k)^{-k} = M^{-kk}$, which is confirmed (within the confidence interval) by Regression Three. Finally, because we have $N'_S = s'^{-4/3}_1$ (Table 9.2), we expect $N'_S = (M^{-kk})^{-4/3} = M^{-4kk/3}$; this is supported by Regression Four, where the

TABLE 15.A3 *Regressions on basic-tier effective number of seat-winning parties and deviation from PR*

	(1)	(2)
	Testing SPM in basic tier $\log(N_{SB})$	Deviation from PR in basic tier $\log(D_{2B})$
log_MB	0.166	−0.334
	(0.0700)	(0.104)
Expected:	**0.167**	**−0.333**
Constant	0.0124	−0.157
	(0.161)	(0.300)
Expected:	0	(empirical)
Observations	34	34
R-squared	0.337	0.463

Robust standard errors in parentheses.

estimated 1.271 is close to the expected 1.333 (and the latter is within the confidence interval).

In Table 15.A3 we see regression results to test whether our formulas for nationwide simple systems also work in the basic tiers of two-tier systems. Regression One is a test of the main claim of the extended SPM (Equation 15.1): that the effective number of seat-winning parties in the basic tier (N_{SB}) – i.e., prior to the application of nationwide compensation – is in fact equivalent to $(MS_B)^{1/6}$. We see that the expectation is confirmed almost precisely.[20]

Regression Two tests the effect of MS_B on deviation from PR (D_2). In line with our prior equations for nationwide deviation form PR (Equations 9.1, 9.2, 15.4, and 15.5), we expect the coefficient to be –0.333. Again, it is confirmed almost precisely. The constant term is estimated by the regression to be –0.0157, which unlogged is 0.697. This differs from the estimated 0.5 of Equations 9.2 (simple systems) and 15.5 (which pooled simple and two-tier). Moreover, the constant in Regression Two is not statistically significant. This is not a troublesome finding, as the constant in our equations for D_2 is empirically determined in all cases. What is important – and remarkable – is that we continue to get the expected –0.333 coefficient.

Both regressions confirm the logic of how two-tier systems work: first they shape party-system outcomes in the basic tier. Then the compensatory upper tier inflates N_S and deflates D_2.

---

[20] It narrowly misses the p=.05 standard of significance; it is actually p=0.055. This is trivial, especially in light of a virtual point confirmation of a logically determined parameter.

16

Complexities in Electoral Systems: Do Simple Models Work Anyway?

A theme of this book has been that we can develop logical quantitative expectations about the impact of electoral systems, *provided the system is relatively simple*. Many of the logical models we have devised and regressions we have undertaken have been based on systems we have classified as "simple," while others have included one class of complex system, two-tier proportional. Our reason for not attempting to model more complex systems is that, the more additional complications are added to rules, the more difficult it is to make meaningful predictions. Moreover, if we are unable to offer predictions as political scientists, committed as we are to logical quantitative models, we are even less able to offer advice to practitioners other than, "Keep it simple." Nonetheless, electoral system designers often do not keep things simple, either because they have sincere preferences for a system that is complex, or, more often, they must make compromises with other interests that have diverging preferences.

In Chapter 3, we identified several features of electoral systems that render them complex. We have already found that one of these, a compensatory upper tier, can be included in an extended Seat Product Model, making such systems broadly predictable in their impact on party systems (Chapter 15). Another complex system, the single nontransferable vote (SNTV), was a theme of Chapters 13 and 14, but we focused on its effects on intraparty outcomes, not its effect on the interparty dimension. Other complex rules have been left out till now. In this chapter we bring them back in, asking to what extent their effects on interparty outcomes could be systematically predicted. First we consider ranked-choice (transferable) voting, nontransferable voting, and two-round systems. We ask whether these more complex formulas nonetheless might be predictable almost as if they were simple systems. The answer for this set of complex systems is a cautious yes, except in the case of nontransferable voting systems.

Then we turn our attention to a common complicating feature found in many contemporary electoral systems, legal thresholds. We develop a logical model of the impact of legal thresholds. We find that it is successful for some types of systems, but not for others. In particular, as long as the system is otherwise simple in its structure or is a two-tier compensatory system, the Seat Product Model is generally more accurate than the threshold model. Yet for other more complex systems, the threshold model shows some promise. Understanding the effect that thresholds have (or do not have) is important, given that in recent decades many new systems have incorporated various threshold provisions.

SINGLE-TIER SYSTEMS WITH COMPLEX FEATURES: HOW SIMPLE?

In Chapter 3 we discussed several rules that introduce complexity aside from legal thresholds or composite, two-tier, systems. These latter features are discussed later in this chapter, but first we turn to rules that might render a single-tier system – one in which all seats are allocated in districts of some magnitude – too complex for the Seat Product Model to be useful.

More complex rules include two-round majority (or majority-plurality), and systems that use ranked-choice ballots: the Alternative Vote (AV, or instant runoff) and the single transferable vote (STV) variant of PR. Additionally, while we stated in Chapter 3 that SNTV is arguably the simplest electoral formula that could be used when $M>1$, it is not at all simple in the incentives it gives to parties attempting to maximize their own seat total, as we discussed in Chapters 13 and 14. In this section, we look at the main examples of each of these systems and ask whether the Seat Product Model performs well for them or not. We would not expect it to do well, because it was designed for simple systems (and, in its extended form, two-tier compensatory PR). However, it is an empirical question. Actually that question could be reframed as, do these more complex systems function *as if they were simple*?

In Table 16.1 we see seven single-tier complex electoral systems in six countries.[1] For each system, we compare the actual SPM predictions of their effective number of seat-winning parties (N_S) and seat share of the largest party (s_1) to the actual values. The intention here is to determine whether, were we to take any one of these systems' Seat Product, MS, and treat as if it were a simple system, would our predictions be off the mark? In order to facilitate making this determination, the cases are sorted in Table 16.1 according to increasing MS.

Single-Seat Districts with Complex Rules

The first entries in the table are for the three $M=1$ systems in Australia and France. The formulas used in these countries are quite different from one another, and from plurality. As introduced in Chapter 3, Australia uses the alternative vote (AV), with its ordinal ballots, whereas France uses the majority-plurality formula in two rounds. AV might be thought of as the closest system

---

[1] The French use of a two-round system was interrupted by the one-time use of list PR in 1986. For this reason, and the large expansion of assembly size, we show two electoral-system periods for France under a two-round system.

TABLE 16.1 *Single-tier systems with complex formulas: actual versus predicted effective number of seat winning parties (N_S) and seat share of largest party (s_1)*

Country	Years	No. of elections	Formula	MS	Actual N_S	N_S from SPM	Ratio for N_S	actual s_1	s_1 from SPM	Ratio for s_1
Australia	1949–2011	25	AV	134	2.48	2.26	1.10	0.505	0.542	0.93
France	1958–1981	7	Two rounds	497	3.50	2.81	1.25	0.453	0.46	0.98
France	1988–2007	5	Two rounds	577	2.85	2.89	0.99	0.497	0.451	1.10
Colombia	1991–1998	2	SNTV	756	3.09	3.04	1.02	0.5	0.434	1.15
Japan	1952–1993	16	SNTV	1936	2.76	3.53	0.78	0.531	0.388	1.37
Vanuatu	1983–2004	6	SNTV	146	3.79	2.29	1.66	0.456	0.536	0.85
Ireland	1954–2007	14	STV	601	2.79	2.91	0.96	0.478	0.449	1.06
Malta	1966–2008	10	STV	321	1.995	2.62	0.76	0.526	0.486	1.08

Are single-tier complex systems similar to simple systems? Values are mean for entire time period indicated

Note: Mean values for N_S in Colombia exclude 1994 and 2002, due to a large "other" category preventing accurate calculation.

one could have to FPTP (plurality) without having FPTP (e.g., Lijphart 1991), whereas most scholars see the French two-round system as meaningfully distinct from FPTP. In fact, when Duverger (1986) updated his "law" he included the two-round system along with PR as a system that promotes multipartism.

Despite the important distinctions between AV and two-round majority-plurality, the statistics in Table 16.1 suggest that if we pretended these were simple FPTP systems, our predictions would not be far off. The partial exception is the earlier period in France, where actual N_S exceeds our SPM-derived prediction by a factor of 1.25. Yet the seat share of the largest party, s_1, is spot-on, as are, essentially, both values for the more recent period in France and in Australia. What this implies is that the reason France tends to have a higher effective number of seat-winning parties, and lower seat share of the largest party, relative to Australia is not the electoral formula, but the very different assembly sizes.

Even with FPTP, we would expect France to have N_S closer to 3.0 than to 2.0, and a largest party just short of majority status, because its assembly is so large. Meanwhile, we would expect Australia to have N_S under 2.5, and generally a majority party, because its assembly is not so large. Thus we cannot say that AV and two rounds are fundamentally different from FPTP, in terms of their impact on the assembly party system, *once assembly size is considered*. Because there are so few actual examples of these systems, we would caution that one should not assume that their performance would be similar if adopted elsewhere.

The two systems diverge substantially from one another, however, if we look at the electoral party system. Using the *MS*-based formula derived in Chapter 8, we would expect Australia to have N_V around 2.68 for the elections shown in Table 16.1. The actual average is 2.90, only marginally higher. For France, on the other hand, the average over the 1988–2007 period would be expected, from the formula, to be $N_V = 3.27$. In reality it has been 5.49, dramatically higher.[2] The two-round system used in France encourages many parties to run in the first round, and then line up behind alliance partners before the second round – a game not possible in the AV "instant runoff." The result is to encourage fragmentation of the vote, making it all the more striking that the assembly party system results about where we would expect if it were a FPTP system.

With this information about higher electoral fragmentation in France, we can understand better now what we saw in Chapter 11, in which France had several outlier elections in its values of N_V (and also N_P, for presidential candidates, which we derive by way of N_V). We included France in Chapters 11 and 12 on the basis of the information revealed here, in Table 16.1, that shows its party system looks like that of a simple electoral system for the *assembly* parties (N_S). Thus the

---

[2] We base the calculation of actual N_V on first-round votes in France and first-preference votes in Australia.

French two-round system is de facto almost simple for seats, but not for votes, due to many parties entering first-round elections (for president as well as assembly). Many of these vote-earning parties likely would not exist, or would be more minor, if the system were simple FPTP, yet they are winning seats at about the rate we would expect from FPTP.

Multiseat Districts with SNTV or STV

As for the $M>1$ formulas in Table 16.1, two of three examples of SNTV show a largest party that is larger than expected (if we took the system to be simple PR). Correspondingly, Japan's N_S was much lower than expected, although Colombia's was near expectation and Vanuatu's tends to be smaller than expected. The advantage that large parties often obtain under SNTV is an established attribute of the system (Cox 1997: 243–249; Shugart, Moreno, and Fajardo 2007), because a governing party has superior access to resources that enable it to divide the vote efficiently – the vote-management strategies that we have discussed. (Apparently this is not possible in Vanuatu, where fragmentation is particularly high.)

It would seem that SNTV is easier to predict on the intraparty dimension (as we showed in Chapter 13) than on the interparty dimension. Perhaps this is unsurprising, given that SNTV is a purely candidate-based system, meaning that collective party vote totals are not relevant for determining the outcome across parties. Yet the system provides parties with strong incentives to organize themselves so as to avoid having excess candidates or too-unequal vote distribution among candidates. This is an easier task for large parties (due to resources permitting coordination) and also for small parties (coordinate on one). The middle-sized parties are likely to get squeezed, allowing SNTV to be simultaneously advantageous to large parties[3] and superproportional (Shugart, Moreno, and Fajardo 2007).

The statistics in Table 16.1 suggest that we should not treat SNTV as if it were just a simple PR system; for STV, on the other hand, there is somewhat more reason to treat it as such. For the country with the longest experience of STV, Ireland, both indicators are almost exactly as the SPM predicts, under the assumption of a simple system. The same can be said for the largest party size in Malta, even though from the SPM's perspective, the nearly pure two-party system in Malta is a surprise.[4]

The exercise in this section suggests that ranked-ballot and two-round systems, but not SNTV, perform in a way not fundamentally different from simple systems with the same Seat Product. We need to add the caution,

---

[3] Although, again, not in practice in Vanuatu.

[4] What about N_V? In Ireland, the votes also turn out almost precisely as the MS-based formula would lead us to expect (actual 3.18 versus expected 3.28). In Malta, considerably lower (2.07 versus 3.01).

however, that with these formulas being relatively rare, we are unable to say that another country, or subnational jurisdiction, adopting either of these formulas would have a similar experience.

Other Complex Formulas for Multiseat Districts

The systems listed in Table 16.1 do not completely exhaust the complex formulas used in single-tier systems with multiseat districts. We discussed several other examples in Chapter 3. Most of them are rare, but we will discuss briefly two other types: two rounds in multiseat districts and multiple nontransferable vote (MNTV), also known as bloc vote or unlimited vote.

In the set of countries for which we have data, there is one case of $M>1$, two-round majority-plurality. That is Mali, which had a period of democratic rule before a military coup in 2012. The first democratic election took place in 1992, with a second in 1997. For these elections, the mean assembly size was 138, and mean magnitude around 2.4. If we calculated a Seat Product from these values, it would be 323. By the Seat Product Model, then, we would predict $N_S=2.63$ and $s_1=0.484$. That is, those would be the predicted values *if Mali had used a simple system.*

Mali's system was not, however, simple – not only due to the two-round formula, but also due a further complicating characteristic: this formula was used in multiseat districts in which the voter was given a single party-list vote (Reilly et al. 2005: 170). As Taagepera (2007: 92) argues, for multiseat plurality, the mean magnitude should be first raised to the power, negative one, before calculating the Seat Product. This would imply, averaging the two Malian elections, a Seat Product of

$$M^F S = (2.4^{-1})138 = 58.1,$$

where the exponent, F, is an adjustment for allocation formula.[5] If we use this adjusted Seat Product, we would expect $N_S =1.97$ and $s_1=0.60$. Note the dramatic difference when we change the assumption of a simple system and account for the use of multiseat plurality (or, in this case, majority-plurality). We go from a largest party just short of half the seats to one that is expected to have a three-fifths super-majority.

In fact, the actual values, averaged over these elections, were $N_S =1.78$ and $s_1=0.73$. Looking at the individual elections reveals an even worse result, from the standpoint of a country's politics adapting to electoral-system design. In 1992 the country had $N_S =2.24$ and $s_1=0.496$; in the second election, the leading party, the Alliance for Democracy in Mali, capitalized on both incumbency and a large-party-favoring electoral system to give $N_S =1.31$ and

---

[5] For simple systems, including FPTP and the standard PR formulas, $F=1$, as explained by Taagepera (2007: 92).

s_1=0.87.[6] It is almost as if the political elites and voters responded to the system in 1992 as it were low-magnitude PR, but then in the second use of the system, the potential space for any significant opposition simply collapsed under an electoral system that left no room for parties other than the ruling one. Colomer (2014) commented before the 2012 coup that Mali had political institutions that weakened the viability of its democracy.[7] We can agree with this assessment, albeit retroactively.

Another rare form of multiseat district formula is multiple nontransferable vote (MNTV). In this system, the voter has votes for as many candidates as there are seats in the district. Is this equivalent to multiseat plurality, greatly advantaging the largest party? Or is it more like SNTV, encouraging strong candidate-centered politics? Our weaselly answer is, it depends. We offer two short case studies to demonstrate.

In Thailand, MNTV formerly was used for an assembly of 360 seats (increased to 390 in 1996) using a mean district magnitude of around 2.5. The system was in place in the 1980s and 1990s. In only one election of this period was s_1 larger than 0.30; in four of them it was under 0.25. Similarly, N_S was over 6.00 in several elections before falling to 4.32 in 1996; N_V was, of course, even higher. Although the effective numbers were lower at the district level – that is, much of the high fragmentation at the national level was a result of there being many regional parties (Hicken 2009: 110–112) – the system clearly did not contribute to nationwide consolidation of parties, as we might expect from a system that resembles a multiseat plurality system.

Studies of Thai party politics in this era emphasize how little party cohesion there was, and how correspondingly personalistic the politics was (Hicken 2009: 94–97). So, the Thai experience looks like a case both of highly candidate-centered politics (more akin to SNTV), and without any dominant party (unlike some actual SNTV cases, notably Japan). Clearly, many voters either did not use all the votes allotted them, or used them for candidates of different parties. The result was utter fragmentation, which was a contributing factor in the major constitutional reform of 1997 that sought to encourage consolidation of the party system (MacIntyre 2003: 118–119). As we will see later in this chapter, the MMM system adopted under the new constitution "worked" by that standard, although not by others.

Our second example of MNTV comes from the Legislative Council election in the Palestinian Territories of 2006. In this case, the system was even more complex; there was a nationwide party-list component in addition to the basic districts. It is the latter component that concerns us here. It consisted of sixty-six seats in districts that ranged in magnitude from one to nine, averaging 4.1. The contest pitted the established ruling party, Fatah, against Change and

---

[6] The party had 63 percent of the votes in 1997, up from 48 percent in 1992.

[7] Although Colomer's paper was published in 2014, a working paper version making this claim about Malian institutions was circulating months before the May 2012 coup.

Reform, a party put together for the election by Hamas, the armed militant Islamic Resistance Movement. In the separate party-list vote, Change and Reform bested Fatah only 44.5 percent to 41.4 percent. Yet Change and Reform won forty-five (68.2 percent) of the seats in the MNTV tier (and seventy-four overall, when its share of the sixty-six noncompensatory PR seats was added). Thus one party was strongly advantaged, earning over two-thirds of the MNTV-elected seats, almost as if it was a party-centered electoral system.

What explains the difference, relative to Thailand? In the Palestinian case, voters tended towards voting for the full slate of candidates of one party. This was even truer for Change and Reform than for Fatah (Abdel-Ghaffar, et al., n.d.). The result was that most districts were clean sweeps, and were especially likely to be so if Change and Reform was the party with the local plurality.[8] Thus we can conclude that when MNTV is used in a context in which the leading party has a strongly party-motivated constituency, it is almost as if it was multiseat block plurality. The result, in the Palestinian case, was a surprise sweeping victory by a party committed more to armed struggle than to parliamentary politics, and the process soon broke down into a spiral of violence.

By contrast, the Thailand case shows that the MNTV formula need not be so party-centric: if voters cast their votes based on individual candidates, seats in any given district may be won by multiple parties. These two cases of MNTV thus represent extremes of the possible outcomes. That such similar electoral formulas can produce such divergent results, depending on context, is probably a good reason to avoid using MNTV, and to prefer simplification.

Magnitude Variance in PR

Another potentially complicating feature in single-tier PR systems is magnitude variance. Taagepera (2007) suggested that highly unequal magnitude of districts could place a system outside the category of "simple." Most districted PR systems rely on existing administrative divisions to serve as electoral districts, and because these divisions vary in population, they may vary widely in magnitude, as well. How much does such variation complicate predicting their party fragmentation? We are unable to find any evidence that unequal M results in any worse performance of the SPM.[9] We now turn to the impact of thresholds, in either single-tier or composite systems.

---

[8] Abdel-Ghaffar, et al., (n.d.) show that, contrary to some claims in media sources, Fatah did not lose because it split and presented competing slates. There were some districts where independents who were Fatah defectors cost the mainstream party seats, but the overall loss was caused by Change and Reform being more popular, having voters more likely to cast most or all their available votes on its candidates, and the resulting ability to sweep most or all seats in several multiseat districts.

[9] The feature can be conceptualized as a deviation from a norm – here, equal M. If we apply the measure of deviation from proportionality (D_2, see Chapters 4 and 9) to each district's difference

A LOGICAL MODEL FOR IMPACT OF THRESHOLDS

The remaining forms of complex electoral system that we will investigate include those that have a legal threshold. A threshold may result in a party being ineligible to win seats even if it had sufficient votes to win were it not for the threshold. In other words, legal thresholds can counteract the effects of a large magnitude, a high share of compensation seats, a permissive formula, or other aspects of an electoral system that would favor the representation of small parties. In order to assess whether the Seat Product Model offers guidance to the party system that results from a given electoral system, even when a threshold intervenes between votes and seats, we need to attempt to develop a logical model of the impact of legal thresholds. We do so in this section. Then we pit the predictions of the threshold model against those of the SPM on several sets of complex electoral systems.

First Approximation to the Model of Thresholds

Suppose seats in the national assembly are allocated by nationwide proportionality, restricted by a nationwide threshold in terms of a minimal percentage of votes. How does this legal threshold affect the number and size of parties in the assembly?

A higher legal threshold can be expected to reduce the number of parties and thus increase the seat shares of the surviving parties. By so doing, it can also be expected to reduce the effective number of parties and indirectly prolong the duration of governmental cabinets. But going beyond directionality, to which quantitative extent would legal thresholds affect these quantities?

Our objective in this section is to construct a quantitatively predictive logical model, connecting the aforementioned outputs to the nationwide legal threshold. We will then test it on several classes of systems that employ legal thresholds, and compare the threshold model to the SPM.

The starting point for the SPM was the observation that, in a single district of M seats, at least one party must win seats, and at most M parties can win seats (see Figure 1.2 and Chapters 7 and 9). In an assembly of S seats, allocated by PR with no legal threshold, this corresponds to a range from 1 to S. When a sufficiently high legal threshold (T) is introduced, the plausible number of seat-winning parties is reduced. The number of parties reaching the threshold can in this way be at most the integer part of $1/T$. For instance, with a threshold of $T=4$ percent, at most $1/0.04=25$ parties could gain representation; whereas if the threshold were to be increased by 0.01 percent, to $T=4.01$ percent, we get $1/T=23.94$, and only 23 parties

from the system's mean M, and then regress this against the SPM prediction, we get R^2 of zero. Literally, 0.000. Magnitude variance has no measurable impact on either N_S or s_1. This does not preclude the possibility that it has other effects, for instance favoring certain parties over others (Monroe and Rose 2002, Kedar et al. 2016).

could surmount the threshold. On the average, this integer part is $(1/T)–1/2$, but as long as T is less than 20 percent, approximation by $1/T$ introduces an error of estimate of less than 10 percent. The number of seat-winning parties is thus restricted to the range,

$$1 < N_{S0} < 1/T.$$

As in the basic party size model, without any further information, our best guess is that the number of seat winning parties, N_{S0}, would be around

$$N_{S0} \approx (1/T)^{1/2} = T^{-1/2}.$$

[16.1; nationwide PR with electoral threshold larger than 1/S]

For this model to apply, the electoral threshold must equal or surpass $1/S$. If not, then $N_{S0}=S^{1/2}$ prevails, as it then imposes a more stringent limitation. The actual legal thresholds on top of nationwide PR always exceed $1/S$, except in the Netherlands, where they have equaled $1/S$ since 1935.

We can test Equation 16.1 via regression on the logs. When we do, it is at first not promising, as we obtain $\log N_{S0}=0.346–0.328 \log T$. The result is absurd, as it must be the case that if $T=1$ (i.e., 100 percent of the votes), only one party can win – the party that obtains all of the votes, which logically also gets 100 percent of the seats. Yet the regression result predicts $N_{S0}=2.2$ when $T=1$. We can re-estimate the regression by suppressing the constant term. When we do so, we obtain:

$$\log N_{S0}=-0.515 \log T.$$

This is obviously approximately Equation 16.1. Thus we have some confirmation of the logic. However, it must be considered weakly supported, relative to the SPM, because of the need to suppress the regression constant term. Such a step was not required for testing the effect of the Seat Product, *MS*. The difference in success of model testing may be because *MS* has a wide range and we had hundreds of elections to test it on. In the case of legal thresholds, we have a narrow range of T: excluding cases of no legal threshold,[10] the range is only 0.67 percent to 10 percent. We have only fifty-eight elections (in ten countries) on which to test it. Given the data limitations, then, we can be satisfied that the logic is valid and attempt to extend it to the more important quantities, N_S and s_1.

From Chapter 7 (and Table 9.2), we have $s_1=N_{S0}^{-0.5}$. Combining this relationship with Equation 16.1, we should have:

$$s_1 \approx T^{1/4}. \tag{16.2}$$

---

[10] We are unable to include these in our regression because Equation 16.1 applies only when $T \geq 1/S$.

The final step, to the effective number of seat-winning parties, is possible because of the formula $N_S \approx s_1^{-4/3}$ (see Table 9.2). Thus we expect:

$$N_S \approx T^{-1/3}. \qquad (16.3)$$

We can test these via regression on the logs. Once again, we must use no-constant regression. For both of these equations we have more elections with the complete data, giving us 159 observations. The results are:

$$\log s_1 = 0.265 \log T \quad \text{and} \quad \log N_S = -0.371 \log T.$$

These numbers are close enough to the predicted 0.250 and −0.333 to give the logic some credence, with the above caveats about the range of the data and the number of cases. Figure 16.1 shows graphs testing the Threshold models. The left panel shows the impact of thresholds on the seat share of the largest party (s_1), while the right panel shows the effective number of seat-winning parties (N_S). The straight lines represent Equations 16.2 and 16.3, respectively. (The dashed curves will be explained in the next section.) We see that both models capture the basic trend but need fine tuning. At large T, median s_1 is clearly lower than predicted, and correspondingly, median N_S is much higher. Where do these models go off balance?

Second Approximation to the Model of Thresholds

We saw that $N_{S0} = T^{-1/2}$ is largely confirmed, with regression producing an exponent −0.515. The next logical step, to s_1, introduces discrepancy, which does not seem to increase later, as we proceed to N_S. So let us take a closer look at this step.

In Chapter 7 we observed that the largest share cannot be less than the mean share, $1/N_{S0} = T^{1/2}$, nor larger than 1, thus $T^{1/2} \le s_1 < 1$. This "1" was an overestimate: at least one seat would have to be left to each of the other seat-winning parties. Yet this was such a minor adjustment that we could neglect it. When thresholds are imposed, this is no longer the case: with $T=0.10$, each seat-winning party must have not just one seat, but 10 percent of all seats! This is not peanuts! So the stipulation, $T^{1/2} \le s_1 < 1$, must be corrected. Subtracting the minimal share T for each party but the largest, we get

$$T^{1/2} \le s_1 < 1 - (N_{S0} - 1)T = 1 - (T^{-1/2} - 1)T = 1 - T^{1/2} + T.$$

The geometric mean of the extremes now predicts

$$s_1 = T^{1/4}(1 - T^{1/2} + T)^{1/2}, \qquad (16.4)$$

which reduces the largest share, compared to the previous $s_1 = T^{0.25}$. If the previous relationship between s_1 and N_S still holds, then

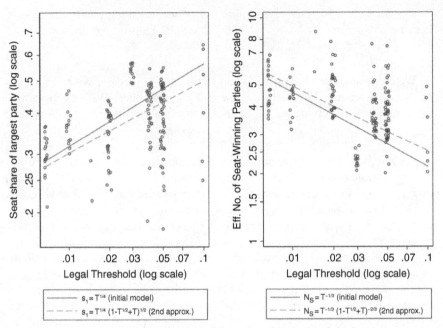

FIGURE 16.1 The effect of legal threshold on the seat share of the largest party (s_1, left panel) and the effective number of seat-winning parties (N_S, right panel)

$$N_S = T^{-1/3}(1 - T^{1/2} + T)^{-2/3}. \tag{16.5}$$

These relationships are shown as dashed curves in Figure 16.1. They are visibly closer to the average data pattern, compared to the straight lines, but still do not seem to go far enough. We may still miss some logical detail.

Despite their shortcomings, we will subject Equations 16.4 and 16.5 to empirical test alongside the Seat Product Model in the next section. In doing so, we break the various complex systems into distinct categories, whereas the graphs in Figure 16.1 (and the preceding regressions) pool all of the cases. We will see that the threshold model has value for some classes of complex systems, whereas for others the SPM is preferred.

IS THE THRESHOLD MODEL BETTER THAN THE SEAT PRODUCT MODEL?

In this section, we put the threshold model up against the Seat Product Model. We want to know if we are better able to explain the actual effective number of seat-winning parties and largest party sizes by knowing the system's threshold, or by using the Seat Product Model. We find that it depends on just how complex the system is. The closer it is to a simple system, the better off we are using the SPM, in general. However, as a system gets more complex, we find some more promise from the threshold model, but a highly complex system remains almost completely unpredictable.

Single-Tier PR Systems

We will start this contest of the models with the simplest electoral systems that nonetheless have thresholds. These are systems that allocate their seats in a single tier, yet have a nationwide threshold.

For each system shown in Table 16.2 we see the actual values for both N_S and s_1, as well as for MS and the threshold. We indicate a ratio for each model, calculated as actual value divided by predicted value. This allows us to see at a glance whether one model or the other is better at predicting the party-system measures of these electoral systems, which would be simple were it not for their thresholds.

If one model's ratio is notably better than the other, it is in bold for a given electoral system. If both are close to 1.00, both are in bold. The line at the bottom of the table shows us that, for all these systems as a group, the SPM performs better for N_S, while the threshold model performs better for s_1. In all these cases the threshold ought to be sufficient to override the effect of the Seat Product. Yet, surprisingly, the predictions of the threshold model are no better than those of the SPM. Elimination of small parties through imposition of thresholds does not seem to affect the largest share or the effective number of parties to any marked degree. Thus adding a separate threshold model to our prediction arsenal seems superfluous – unless further improvement can be made to the threshold model.

In general, the SPM performs as if the systems shown in Table 16.2 were simple, without a threshold. There are some notable exceptions, however, where the threshold model performs better. For instance, in Ukraine the very high Seat Product would imply an extremely fragmented party system (SPM-derived predictions of N_S =7.66 and s_1=0.217). The actual party system in these elections was quite close the prediction of the threshold model. In Turkey the threshold model is correct that the largest party should have about a majority of seats, whereas the SPM would predict it to be below 40 percent.

A system like Turkey's since 1995 contains an internal contradiction: on the one hand, a mildly permissive Seat Product, while on the other hand a highly restrictive threshold. We would caution that when a system is designed with such countervailing features, it would be hard to predict which way it will work out. We will return to a discussion of the unusual features of this Turkish system later in this chapter. The general picture of these single-tier systems is that we would place more confidence in the SPM than in the threshold model. At least when MS is not exceedingly high (as in Ukraine) or the threshold is not greater than 5 percent (as in Turkey), our best guess at the impact of the system on N_S or s_1 is to just ignore the threshold and treat it as a simple system.

TABLE 16.2 *Comparing model predictions to actual values for single-tier systems that have legal thresholds*

Country	Years	No. of elections	MS	Legal threshold (percent)	Actual N_s	Ratio for N_s from SPM	Ratio for N_s from T	actual s_1	Ratio for s_1 from SPM	Ratio for s_1 from T
Netherlands	1956–2010	17	22500	0.67	4.92	0.93	0.88	0.302	1.06	1.10
Israel	1951–1992	12	14400	1	4.41	0.89	0.89	0.381	1.26	1.26
Netherlands	1946–1952	3	10000	1	4.6	0.99	0.93	0.31	0.98	1.03
Israel	1996–1999	2	14400	1.5	7.16	1.45	1.64	0.25	0.83	0.76
Israel	2003–2009	3	14400	2	6.93	1.41	1.73	0.262	0.87	0.74
Ukraine	2006–2007	2	202500	3	3.36	0.44	0.94	0.401	1.85	1.04
Sweden	1948–1968	7	1888	4	3.11	0.88	0.95	0.488	1.25	1.19
Croatia	2000–2011	4	2114	5	2.99	0.84	0.97	0.385	1.00	0.90
Czechia	2002–2010	3	2858	5	3.76	1.00	1.22	0.345	0.93	0.80
Latvia	1995–2011	6	2000	5	5.43	1.53	1.76	0.258	0.67	0.60
Poland	2001–2011	4	5879	5	3.42	0.80	1.11	0.41	1.21	0.95
Slovakia	1998–2010	4	22500	5	4.93	0.93	1.60	0.318	1.11	0.74
Turkey	1983–1991	3	1921	10	2.71	0.77	1.07	0.526	1.35	1.06
Turkey	1995–2015	7	3625	10	3.04	0.78	1.20	0.48	1.24	0.96
		77				0.97	1.21		1.12	0.94

Now we will consider whether the threshold or Seat Product Model performs better for two-tier compensatory PR. Most of these systems have thresholds in addition to their composite electoral formula. Thus we need to consider the relative accuracy of both models.

Two-Tier Compensatory Systems

In Table 16.3, we carry out our contest between the SPM and Threshold models on the class of two-tier compensatory systems. This group includes the mixed-member proportional (MMP) systems of Germany and New Zealand, as well as systems with PR in both tiers (see Chapter 3 for definitions).

Leaving aside their threshold provisions, two-tier compensatory systems are the simplest systems among those that are composites of different rules. In Chapter 15 we developed an extended form of the SPM (Equation 15.2) that takes into account the Seat Product of the basic tier and the "tier ratio" (the ratio of seats in the compensatory tier to the entire assembly). If the table indicates zero for tier ratio, it is a remainder-pooling system (see Chapter 3 for definitions of the subtypes). Which performs better on these two-tier systems, the extended SPM, or the threshold model?

We see that for these systems it is a close call as to which model is better. The SPM is, on average, slightly better for N_S. However, the threshold model performs better for s_1. For individual countries there is a rather strong tendency of the threshold model to get s_1 closer to its actual values, but countries vary in which model does better for N_S. Thus, if asked how to estimate the impact of a proposed two-tier compensatory system, we would be inclined to turn to the SPM, in its extended form for N_S, but the threshold model for s_1. If we were to use both models, we might arrive at a reasonable range of what to expect from this class of complex system.

Composite Systems That Are Noncompensatory

Now we consider mixed-member majoritarian (MMM) systems, those in which the list-PR tier is noncompensatory (explained in Chapter 3). We do not expect the SPM to apply to these systems, but why not try? In Table 16.4, we perform the same contest as in the preceding section, but on the MMM systems.

We have fewer of these systems, and fewer elections within them, on which to base our test. Moreover, they do not comprise a coherent category. Only four of the systems shown in Table 16.4 are strictly MMM systems, in which there is no adjustment to list allocations based on how a party has performed in the districts where plurality or majority is used. These are Japan (since 1996), South Korea, Lithuania, and Thailand (in 2001 and 2005).

The other systems incorporate a partial compensation mechanism: Hungary, Italy, and Mexico. Each of these has been classified in some sources as MMP, but such a classification is misleading because the systems are neither designed

TABLE 16.3 *Comparing model predictions to actual values for two-tier compensatory systems that have legal thresholds*

Country	Years	No. of elections	MS_B	tier ratio (t)	Legal threshold (percent)	Actual N_S	Ratio for N_S from SPM	Ratio for N_S from T	actual s_1	Ratio for s_1 from SPM	Ratio for s_1 from T
Cyprus	1985–2011	6	522	0	2	3.56	1.25	0.89	0.353	0.77	1.00
Denmark	1953–1968	6	816	0.229	2	3.79	1.01	0.94	0.407	1.10	1.15
Denmark	1971–2005	14	1104	0.229	2	5.03	1.27	1.25	0.34	0.96	0.96
Denmark	2007–2011	2	1877	0.229	2	5.47	1.26	1.36	0.266	0.80	0.75
Bulgaria	1991–2005	5	1858	0	4	2.65	0.75	0.81	0.497	1.27	1.21
Sweden	1970–2010	13	3395	0.112	4	3.74	0.87	1.14	0.424	1.27	1.03
Germany	1953–1987	10	247	0.5	5	3.07	0.78	1.00	0.485	1.36	1.13
Germany	1990–2009	6	314	0.5	5	3.70	0.90	1.20	0.41	1.18	0.95
Iceland	2003–2009	3	567	0.143	5	3.84	1.17	1.25	0.381	0.93	0.89
New Zealand	1996–2011	6	69	0.433	5	3.29	1.09	1.07	0.436	1.00	1.01
		71					1.04	1.09		1.06	1.01

to offer full compensation, nor capable of it in practice. (The mechanism is different in each, further complicating conclusion drawing.)

For the pure MMM systems, the SPM (extend version, as if the system were MMP) does not perform too badly, but the mean of actual N_S is lower than expected and the mean of actual s_1 correspondingly higher. The variance from expectation is small enough, on average, that we might say just use the SPM were we asked to assess the impact of a proposed MMM system. On the other hand, that MMM would tend to result in lower N_S and higher s_1 is consistent with the design of the system, which is intended to boost larger parties.

Such consolidation of the party system was certainly the explicit goal of reformers in Thailand (MacIntyre 2003: 118–119), following their experience with extreme fragmentation under MNTV (reviewed earlier in this chapter). The Thai electoral reform to MMM was therefore a case of "mission accomplished"; in fact, more so than the averages in Table 16.4 imply.

In the first postreform election in 2001, N_S=3.06 and s_1=0.524. In the second election, the leading party, Thai Rak Thai, won over three fourths of the seats on just 56.4 percent of the vote, and N_S=1.65. Thai democracy broke down a few years later. Similar to the example we saw earlier with Mali, the adoption of a majoritarian system (in this case MMM) resulted in one party quickly attaining dominance. The electoral system turned dominance in votes into a near wipeout of the opposition in seats. These examples should give considerable pause to electoral-system designers in young or unstable democracies. Combining complexity and majoritarian features in such cases poses risks not worth taking.

Of our four examples of pure MMM, only one has N_S considerably higher than the SPM would predict, were it MMP. That case is Lithuania, which is also the only one with two-round majority in its single-seat districts. This factor may keep more parties in the game, despite the lack of compensatory allocation of the list-PR component. As for the threshold model, two of the MMM systems do not have a legal threshold. For the two that do, the threshold model is not especially useful in practice.

For the MMM systems that have partial compensation, the actual values (reported in the bottom part of Table 16.4) look unpredictable. This is perhaps not surprising, because each system has a *sui generis* design. This is precisely the situation in which we are unable to make predictions of effects. Actually, one might as well say the same for all the systems in Table 16.4. With MMM systems, whether or not they have partial compensation, small variations in the system might produce widely different effects. Unlike two-tier compensatory systems, including MMP, there is no coherent design to MMM systems that would make them conducive to generalization. The more that designers of systems choose unusual systems like MMM, the harder it is to know what to expect. We would suggest that MMM is best avoided for this reason. While it is plausible that MMP offers a "best of both worlds" (Shugart and Wattenberg, 2001), such a claim would be more difficult to sustain for MMM.

TABLE 16.4 *Comparing model predictions to actual values for two-tier noncompensatory systems that have legal thresholds*

Country	Years	No. of elections	MS_B	tier ratio (t)	Legal threshold (percent)	Actual N_S	Ratio for N_S from SPM	Ratio for N_S from T	actual s_1	Ratio for s_1 from SPM	Ratio for s_1 from T
Pure MMM											
Japan	1996–2009	5	300	0.38	0	2.62	0.716		0.545	1.442	
Korea	1988–2004	3	231	0.202	0	2.77	0.930		0.444	1.007	
Lithuania	1992–2008	5	71	0.496	5	4.18	1.302	1.356	0.398	0.954	0.926
Thailand	2001–2005	2	400	0.2	5	2.36	0.724	0.766	0.65	1.578	1.512
		15					0.918			1.245	
MMM with partial compensation											
Hungary	1994–2010	6	176	0.544	5	2.72	0.697	0.882	0.513	1.421	1.193
Italy	1994–2001	3	475	0.246	4	6.32	1.806	1.924	0.258	0.683	0.629
Mexico	2000–2009	3	300	0.4	2	2.78	0.745	0.692	0.446	1.199	1.265

WORKING AROUND COMPLEXITY: A CASE STUDY OF TURKEY

When a system has complex features, not only may outcomes be harder to predict, but also we may observe political actors undertaking unusual work-around solutions. We offer a brief example of this phenomenon from Turkey. As we saw in the section on thresholds, Turkey has the highest legal threshold, at 10 percent.

Were it not for the threshold, the Turkish system in place since 1995 would be mildly permissive, given *MS* over 3500. Moreover, it would seem to permit parties with regional concentration to win seats, given that the large assembly is divided into many multiseat districts. Yet regional parties are severely undercut by the fact that the threshold is not only high, but is applied nationwide. Despite the allocation of all seats in districts, as if it were a simple districted PR system, a party is barred from winning seats unless it clears 10 percent of the nationwide vote (Bahcik 2008) – even in cases where it might be the leading vote-winning party in a district.

The contradictory features of the Turkish system mean that in some years it has accommodated many parties, such as 1999 when $N_S=4.41$ and the largest party had just under 25 percent of the seats; five parties cleared the threshold. Yet in other years it has been enormously majoritarian in effect, such as 2002 when the leading party, the Justice and Development Party (AKP), won 66 percent of seats on only 34.3 percent of votes – a result that rates as the most exaggerated inflation of a leading party's support in our database for any country that uses a proportional allocation formula. The large overrepresentation of the AKP was made possible because only two parties cleared the threshold, and more than 40 percent of the votes were cast for parties that fell below the threshold, including one that narrowly missed, with 9.5 percent. By any objective democratic standard, Turkey has a threshold that is too high. It might even be said to be undemocratic – it is so restrictive.[11]

Two district-level examples demonstrate the perverseness of such a system. In 2002 in the district of Agri, the AKP won three of five seats on a mere 17.6 percent of the vote. The leading party in the district, the DHP, had 35 percent of the vote, yet won no seats. Two seats were won by the CHP, despite its having only 9.6 percent of the vote. The DHP was similarly shortchanged in Van, where it won 40.9 percent of the votes but no seats, while the AKP won six of the seven seats on only 25.8 percent and the fourth-place CHP the other seat on just 5.2 percent. These cases, where a party won a plurality of the vote but no seats, are extreme examples, but demonstrate how a legal threshold may leave an electoral system outside our definition of "simple" (see Chapter 2), by violating the rank-size principle by which the relative sizes of parties in voting are reflected in the allocation of seats. If the first party gets no seats, this basic

---

[11] It was challenged in the European Court of Human Rights (2008), which declined to rule against the provision. See http://hudoc.echr.coe.int/eng-press#{"display":["1"],"dmdocnumber":["837654"]} (accessed July 30, 2016).

concept of simplicity is obviously violated! These examples are a more extreme case of what we noted in Chapter 1 in Poland's 2015 election, where a list sometimes has district-level votes sufficient to elect one or more candidates yet wins none because of a nationwide threshold. Any single-tier districted system that has a nationwide threshold introduces the risk of such unusual outcomes.

Some Turkish opposition groups eventually found an ingenious way around the threshold, however, by taking advantage of a provision permitting independent candidacy (Bahcik 2008, Eccarius-Kelly 2008). The main party of the country's Kurdish minority, the Democratic Society Party, ran such candidacies in specific districts in which they have regional concentration. Running as parties, they would have been shut out by the high nationwide threshold, but running as individual candidates, they were able to compete and sometimes win.[12]

Table 16.5 offers an example of how this worked in the eight-seat district of Van in the 2011 election. The AKP earned 40.26 percent of the vote, which allowed it to elect four candidates from its (closed) party list. No other party that cleared the nationwide threshold had sufficient votes in the district for a seat. The remaining four seats were won by independent candidates, all of them Kurdish. These candidates combined for nearly half the district's votes (48.6 percent). They presented four candidates, whose votes were sufficiently equally divided to allow all four to be elected.[13] These Kurdish politicians thus used *SNTV-like strategies*,[14] such as we discussed in Chapters 13 and 14. It was as if the electoral system was two entirely different systems side-by-side: closed-list PR for parties that earn 10 percent nationwide, and SNTV at the local level for those who do not expect to clear the nationwide threshold. Using this strategy, Kurdish candidates were able to win twenty-six seats in the Turkish Grand National Assembly in 2007 and thirty-six in 2011 (5.1 percent and

---

[12] For purposes of determining a district's allocation, an independent candidate's votes are compared to the D'Hondt divisors of those party lists that have passed the nationwide threshold. Thus the independents are treated exactly as are the qualifying lists, except that any one independent's votes can never qualify for a second seat.

[13] They needed to avoid their fourth candidate falling behind the fifth D'Hondt divisor for the AKP. In the event, Gür was just under 7,000 votes ahead of this figure. How did the party achieve such even distribution? It was due to its local organization, which made it possible to visit Kurdish voters' homes and instruct them on which specific candidate to vote for in their area. Information from Giriş Tarihi, "Örnek pusula, şablon ve yorgan ipli seçim taktiği" [Tactics with Sample Ballot, Template and String], June 14, 2011. www.sabah.com.tr/yasam/2011/06/14/ornek-pusula-sablon-ve-yorgan-ipli-secim-taktigi [last accessed November 4, 2016]. The title of the article refers to campaign workers providing a string of a certain length to drape over the sample ballot and show the voter (particularly if illiterate) the location on the ballot of the name of the candidate for whom they should vote. Research and translation assistance provided by İpek Bahçeci.

[14] We acknowledge a comment from Steven Verbanck for first calling our attention to this practice. www.fruitsandvotes.wordpress.com/2007/07/22/turkish-ruling-party-gains-in-votes-declines-in-seats/#comment-2734

TABLE 16.5 *Example of how independents were elected in one Turkish district: Van, 2011*

Party or candidate	Votes	Votes %	Seats
Justice and Development	171,665	40.26	4
Kemal Aktaş	65,447	15.35	1
Özdal Üçer	51,357	12.04	1
Aysel Tuğluk	49,339	11.57	1
Nazmi Gür	41,212	9.67	1
CHP	15,945	3.74	0
MHP	12,734	2.99	0

Other parties totaling 18,703 votes and other independents totaling 3,974 not shown
Total votes cast: 426,402

6.5 percent, respectively).[15] These seats were won across sixteen and nineteen districts, respectively.

The example of the Kurdish opposition not only shows the steps political actors sometimes take to circumvent overly complex systems, but also reminds us that SNTV is the "simplest" system for multiseat districts (see Chapter 2). Running as if the system were SNTV, these political forces were able to be represented in an otherwise restrictive system. While the adaptation was ingenious, and looks like something out of a textbook on intraparty vote management (as discussed in Chapters 13 and 14), such strategy would have been unnecessary had Turkey adopted a simpler electoral system to start with.

CONCLUSIONS

In this chapter, we delved further into several electoral systems that we initially ruled out of our wider effort at developing systematic quantitative logical models. These systems were left out because they violate basic criteria for "simple" systems outlined in Chapter 2. The definition of a simple system states that all S seats in the assembly must be allocated within districts, and that the rule used in those districts must respect the relative vote shares of parties in the allocation of seats. The definition leaves aside those systems that have two tiers of allocation, two rounds of voting, ranked-choice ballots, or high thresholds, among other complex features. Only the simple systems readily lend

---

[15] In June, 2015, the Kurdish nationalists teamed up with a national left-wing party and jointly cleared the threshold. They did so again in November of 2015, when a snap elections was called because no government was formed in the assembly elected earlier in the year. A further postscript is that Turkish democracy came under severe stress in July, 2016, with a failed coup and widespread purge by the AKP afterwards.

themselves to quantitative logical modeling, such as represented by the Seat Product Model (SPM).

In Chapter 15 we had already seen how one type of complex system could be included in an extended version of the SPM: if it is a two-tier compensatory system its allocation principles still lend themselves to a general model. However, many other complex systems do not, leaving it an empirical question whether they might function *as if* they were simple. In the case of single-tier systems with nonsimple formulas, we found some evidence that they function like simple systems. For instance, both the French two-round system and Australia's Alternative Vote have tended to produce assembly outcomes that look like FPTP, once we account for their assembly sizes, as the SPM does. We were able to draw the same conclusion for the Single Transferable Vote, at least in the case of Ireland. However, because each of these system types is quite rare, we must be cautious about generalizing from the cases reviewed in this chapter. That the most prominent examples of AV and STV might work in practice much like FPTP and list PR, respectively, is encouraging, given the high regard many reformers and scholars have for these systems (Bowler and Farrell 2006). AV and STV may have some advantages over their simpler cousins while still having systematic effects on party systems, although, again, their rarity makes it hard to be sure.

Other single-tier complex systems, however, do not function as if they were just simple districted systems. The Single Nontransferable Vote, for one, seems to have outcomes as unpredictable on the interparty dimension from the SPM as they proved (in Chapters 13 and 14) predictable for their intraparty effects. Other, still more unusual and complex single-tier systems are even more difficult to understand systematically.

Then in this chapter we developed a model of how systems with legal thresholds shape assembly party systems. We pitted this model against the SPM for a several system types. We found that the SPM performs better than the threshold model in predicting the effective number of seat-winning parties in both districted PR systems (with thresholds of 5 percent or lower) and for two-tier compensatory systems. However, the threshold model performs slightly better for the largest party's seat share.

This chapter lets us draw some important conclusions for institutional engineering. Some degrees of complexity do not prevent our being able to make systematic predictions. This is useful information if we are called upon to advise electoral-system designers. While we maintain an overall preference for simplicity, some of the most common provisions incorporated into electoral laws – compensatory upper tiers and modest legal thresholds – apparently do not greatly upset the fundamental impact of variables like district magnitude and assembly size. Nor, perhaps, do ranked-choice ballots, a tool much admired by electoral-reform advocates and some political science experts on electoral systems. Other designs such as mixed-member majoritarian (MMM) systems, by contrast, do not lend themselves to systematic prediction of their effects.

The analysis in this chapter could be helpful, then, for practitioners of politics: *keep it simple, but if you must complicate, do so minimally.* Moreover, the experiences of some newer democracies reviewed in this chapter highlight the special risks that stem from introducing complexity aimed at making a system more majoritarian. We discuss these implications for practitioners further in our next, concluding chapter.

17

Conclusion: Substance and Method

This book has had two overriding ambitions, as sketched in its preface and in Chapter 1. One ambition has been within the subfield of electoral studies itself, and the other is for political science more broadly. We take up what we have achieved of our ambitions regarding electoral studies first, and then focus later in this concluding chapter on the wider contribution to political science.

CONTRIBUTIONS TO THE KNOWLEDGE BASE ON ELECTORAL AND PARTY SYSTEMS

The book has taken two principal measures of a country's electoral institutions, and from these logically deduced a whole chain of quantitative predictions for party-system outcomes. The two basic measures are the number of seats in the representative assembly ("assembly size," or S) and the number of seats in electoral districts ("district magnitude," or M) through which this assembly is elected. From just these two numbers, the application of rigorous logic permits the deduction of the number of parties in the assembly and in the electorate, as well as the size of the largest. These predictions agree with worldwide averages, which in turn supply a benchmark for country investigations. In doing so, we build on prior works, both our own (Taagepera and Shugart, 1989a, 1993; Taagepera, 2007) and others. Among the other building blocks are Rae (1967), who coined the term, district magnitude, in carrying out the first detailed quantitative examination of electoral systems and party systems, and Lijphart (1994), whose analysis was among the first to take the assembly size seriously.

From the product of M and S, we have a country's *Seat Product*. Based on a large pooled dataset of elections in old and new democracies, we are able, in Chapter 7, to confirm and extend the work done by Taagepera (2007) to show how remarkably accurately these two quantities predict the worldwide average pattern of the effective number of seat-winning parties (N_S).

A major extension, shown in this book for the first time, was to account for the effective number of vote-earning parties (N_V). Many works in the field see N_V as somehow conditioned by the electoral system, but nonetheless fundamentally see the electoral system as a sort of conversion box that takes in N_V and spits out N_S. We show that we can start with the quantity that is more constrained by institutions, N_S, and once we know that, a rather absurdly simple assumption gets us to N_V. That new concept, introduced in Chapter 8, is the idea of the number of pertinent parties. For this we drew on the $M+1$ rule (Reed 1991, 2003; Cox 1997). We reconceptualized it as $N+1$ (more precisely in our notation, $N_{S0}+1$). It is a starkly simplified assumption that there are N_{S0} seat-winning parties (of any size) and one serious striver that just missed, and added together, these comprise the parties that are "pertinent." From that we are able to offer a model of what N_V tends to be, on average. This is how *votes result from seats*, in addition to seats also resulting from votes.

In Chapter 9, we summarized four basic laws of party seats and votes, which we had explained and tested in the preceding chapters. We also extended the explanatory power of M and S to deviation from proportionality, as an application of the basic laws of party seats and votes.

Then we turned our attention, in Chapter 10, to the district level. It has been argued by many works that it is at the level of individual districts that "coordination" around some number of parties occurs and that the question of the national party system is one of how these district party systems project, or are "linked" (Cox 1997), into either a common national system or separate regional ones. We start from a different premise, and show that district-level party-system quantities can be deduced from the size of the nationwide assembly in which a district is "embedded." That is, we put the national assembly electoral system first, and understand a district as one component of the wider system.

Other findings of the book concern presidential systems. It has become standard wisdom in the field to understand the effective number of vote-earning parties in the assembly as being conditioned by competition for the presidency. Such an expectation is straightforward enough, but in reviewing the now-extensive literature to advance that line of reasoning, we were dissatisfied. We detail reasons for the dissatisfaction in Chapters 7 and 12, but two key reasons are worth emphasizing here.

One reason is that we aim for *predictive* models of how institutions work, but if one of the inputs is the effective number of presidential candidates, its means practically giving up the enterprise. It would mean that wherever presidents are important enough to shape assembly party competition, we have to know first one of the very things we are trying to predict – how many serious contenders are there for political power? Such number is surely not exogenous, but many approaches treat as if it were. In fact, we are able to show – remarkably – that we can predict the trend in the effective number of *presidential* candidates based on the *assembly* electoral system. While the scatter is high, because individual presidential candidates make a substantial difference in party support, a model based on the relationship of assembly and presidential competitors allows us to predict the latter, on average. In fact, the effective number of presidential candidates turns out to be more predictable from assembly institutions than is the effective number of parties in the assembly elections of those democracies that have politically important presidents.

The second dissatisfaction we felt with the standard literature is its claim that the impact of presidential competition is conditional on the temporal proximity of the presidential and assembly elections. Again, the idea is sensible, but we found it to be inadequately theorized, as explained in in Chapter 12. Instead, we returned to the notion of the timing of assembly elections as explaining shifts in electoral support for the presidential party (Shugart 1995), but not as a factor in assembly fragmentation. In fact, there is no systematic effect of the timing of assembly elections on the effective number of parties (votes or seats) for the assembly, with one important exception: late-term, or "counter-honeymoon," elections exhibit higher fragmentation. This high fragmentation, however, often gets reduced in presidential elections, as multiple parties coalesce in the short window of time between assembly and presidential elections, with the former being almost like a "primary" within groups of parties. Thus the results of Chapters 11 and 12 allow us to say that presidential democracies have party systems, and even numbers of presidential candidates, that can be predicted from the assembly electoral system – specifically, the Seat Product.

We further extended our logical modeling techniques to the intraparty dimension of representation. Chapter 13 explored how the intraparty dimension is like the interparty in one key respect: *the distribution of votes follows from the seats* for which parties and candidates are competing. Two prime examples of electoral systems that feature intraparty competition for votes – open-list PR (OLPR) and single nontransferable vote (SNTV) – systematically shape how many candidates a party tends to run in a district. The key distinction between these systems lies in whether they have vote pooling (as does OLPR) or not (SNTV). Patterns in the vote shares of candidates can be predicted, based on how many candidates a party puts forth. Chapter 14 extended this idea to include the extent to which votes are concentrated on winning candidates or are spread out with many votes cast for losers.

Moreover, in Chapter 14, we were able to account for votes and seats in electoral systems that are hybrids of OLPR and SNTV. Parties in such systems often present alliances, with one open list containing candidates from two or more parties. We again saw the impact of our two fundamental building blocks, M and S, which allowed us to make sense of high district-level fragmentation of the number of parties in systems where these parties run in alliance. Thus M and S prove useful for modeling key aspects of every broad topic covered in this book – nationwide party systems, how district-level competition is embedded in the national system, presidential competition, and intraparty and alliance politics.

Finally, we address the issue of complex electoral systems. Our basic models of nationwide effects (Chapters 7 to 9) apply to simple electoral systems, where all seats are allocated in districts, using simple formulas. Are they useless for the numerous actual systems that add several tiers, two rounds, legal thresholds, or many other complexities? Complex systems add but do not subtract. They still feature an assembly size and some basic district magnitude, which keep having an impact. Using work by Li and Shugart (2016), Chapter 15 extended the Seat Product Model to two-tier proportional systems, by adding one additional parameter, the share of seats allocated in compensatory upper tiers. We incidentally observed that interaction *with effective number of ethnic groups* does not substantially improve the fit of predicted to actual values in most cases.

We further found, in Chapter 16, that even some other more complex systems turn out to be explained well by *MS*, almost as if they were simple. There is something obviously quite fundamental about these two variables, mean district magnitude and assembly size. Many of those complex systems that have no upper tier still involve a definite number of seats in the assembly, all of which are allocated in districts of some (mean) magnitude. Thus they have a Seat Product. For such systems we simply asked: What would be the largest seat share and the effective number of parties for a simple electoral system with the same Seat Product? And how much would these results be off, compared to the actual figures in the complex system? The surprising answer: all too often, not much. When two countries have similarly complex (but single-tier) electoral systems, but one has a Seat Product of 100, while the other has 10,000, then the Seat Product turns out to be the cake and further complexities (like ranked ballots, second rounds, or moderate thresholds) often just amount to heavy icing on the cake.[1]

But What About the Politics?

Both of the authors of this book frequently receive comments from reviewers or other colleagues or from students that imply we leave the politics out. How can we, as political scientists, say everything comes down to some "mechanical" features of institutions, and to modeling that looks more like physics than what social scientists are accustomed to? Our response is that there remains plenty of room for "politics" if by that we mean the articulation of cleavages, organizing and maintaining political parties, campaigning and, of course, voting. Yet it is

---

[1] As we saw in Chapter 16, however, some systems like SNTV are hard to explain on the interparty dimension. And systems that have complexity aimed at enhancing majoritarianism similarly defy easy explanation.

true that little of these themes has filled the pages of this book. So maybe we do not think it is important. That would be the wrong conclusion to draw! What we aim to do is understand the institutional channels and constraints in which all of this sort of politics takes place. We offered numerous examples throughout the book of how context shapes the way systems work in practice, starting with our chapters offering short cases studies (Chapters 5 and 6) and at various other opportunities, including our exploration of especially complex rules in Chapter 16.

Rich country contextual analysis and sparse microfoundational models, and numerous other methodologies, have much to contribute. We hope that scholars of diverse traditions will take up the challenge and pick up where we are about to leave off. Why do these parties and not some others form? When a country has some sort of fundamental shock to its political party system, does that system later revert to the expectations set by our models? If so, how long does it take, and how does it come about? If not, is it a political problem, as perceived within the country, that the electoral system and party system are poor fits for one another (again, according to our models)? If so, does a movement for electoral-system change emerge and gain traction? If not, why not? We can illustrate some points of departure for these further analyses next, but the main message is that these questions cannot even be meaningfully asked unless we first have a baseline against which to measure country-level and election-level fluctuations. That is exactly what this book provides, as we said in Chapter 7: *a baseline* for understanding party and electoral politics, *not a threat* to those who study such topics.

Performance of the SPM for Specific Countries

In sum, the logically predictable impact of assembly size and district magnitude reaches even into many of the complex electoral systems. *At the level of worldwide averages*, it reaches seats and votes, national and district, parliamentary and presidential, interparty and intraparty, to a degree that looks impossible – except that it has logical foundation and empirical confirmation. But what good are mere worldwide averages? They supply a baseline for evaluating individual cases. For the first time, we now have baselines that go beyond "Anything goes."

Some readers may still be puzzled, however, by the lack of country-specific factors in the SPM. Partially in anticipation of such puzzled responses, in Chapter 15 we showed regression results that included a variable for one country-varying parameter, the effective number of ethnic groups. We found this had surprisingly little effect for most countries, once we fully specify the most important institutional variables, as in the SPM. Still, maybe there are other country-specific or even election-specific factors that explain N_S. Our response is – of course there are! The institutions set the parameters of the

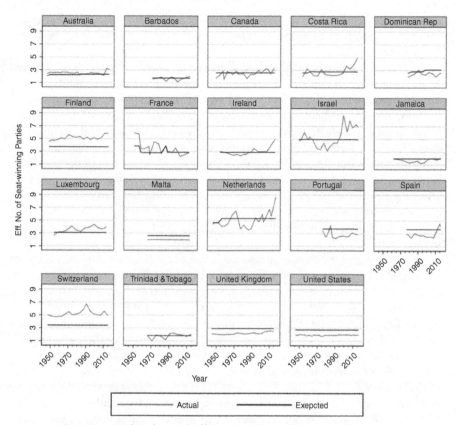

FIGURE 17.1 Expected and actual effective number of seat-winning parties (N_S) over time in long-term democracies with single-tier electoral systems

game, but not every move that the players of the game might make. This should not surprise anyone. After all, even in baseball, the same rules are compatible with distinctive national styles of play (Kelly 2007, 2009). So in electoral and party systems, after taking account of the institutional effects, there remains plenty of room for political actors to maneuver. That maneuvering space is, however, limited by the institutions.

We can visualize how national politics varies around the institutionally derived predictions. Figure 17.1 demonstrates the performance of the SPM for specific countries and how actual N_S fluctuates over time. The countries depicted here all had at least thirty-five years of consecutive democratic experience as of 2015; elections up to early 2017 are included. In addition, they are all either "simple" (as defined in Chapter 2) or are single-tier systems that we determined function as if simple (see Chapter 16). For each country plot, we see a solid black line, which depicts the expected N_S, given the country's assembly size and mean district magnitude. If the line shifts upward or downward, it is because of changes in either of these parameters that are sufficient to produce a change in *expected* N_S.[2] The gray line tracks the actual N_S, for each election.

We see a few countries that have systematically lower or higher than expected N_S – for instance, Spain's N_S is surprisingly low until 2016, and the US is low throughout, whereas N_S in Finland and Switzerland has been surprisingly high.[3] Most other countries fluctuate, with some elections below and some above. A few rarely deviate greatly from the expectation, such as Canada and, until 2016, Costa Rica and Ireland (despite the latter country's use of the nonsimple STV). Some countries that are notable for their very high N_S in recent elections, such as Israel and the Netherlands, also have prior periods when N_S was surprisingly low, given their Seat Product. It is certainly plausible that their party systems could consolidate somewhat again in the future, but there is no guarantee. And that is the point – politics is not determined by the Seat Product, but it is clearly shaped by it.

One theme that we have emphasized is that there is no need to take account of the executive type, or the number of presidential candidates (as is the case in several other authors' approaches), in order to derive a reasonably accurate prediction for N_S. Some of the countries shown in Figure 17.1 are presidential (Costa Rica, Dominican Republic, and the US), and one is a semipresidential system with a very important presidency (France).[4] None of these countries is any more out of line with its SPM prediction than are some nonpresidential systems. Party-system fragmentation may vary for any number of peculiarities of the country or an individual election. Yet if asked to guess what the effective number of parties would be in any given simple system, we would base our guess on the Seat Product, and not whether it was presidential or not, or had a given ethnic fragmentation, or any other factor. More often than not, we would be reasonably accurate, for most elections.

In Figure 17.2, we see a similar plot of multiple countries, this time showing countries with two-tier systems for some or all of the period. The dashed line shows the expected N_S from our extended Seat Product Model (Chapter 15), which applies to two-tier compensatory PR, as well as to simple systems. If there is also a solid black line, it marks any period under a single-tier system, allowing us to see whether the change of system corresponded to a change in N_S.

---

[2] The spike near the middle of the time series in France is due to the one election held under a PR system (1986). Whether by luck or otherwise, the actual N_S that year was almost exactly as predicted by the SPM.

[3] Some of Finland's high values can be explained by the use of the OLPR/SNTV hybrid. See Chapter 14, as well as the appendix to Chapter 7. The Swiss system also has alliance lists. Despite different rules from Finland's, the alliances may similarly enhance fragmentation.

[4] In addition, France elects its assembly by two-round majority-plurality (except in 1986), an electoral system that we do not define as simple. Yet in most elections, the SPM does well. See Chapter 16.

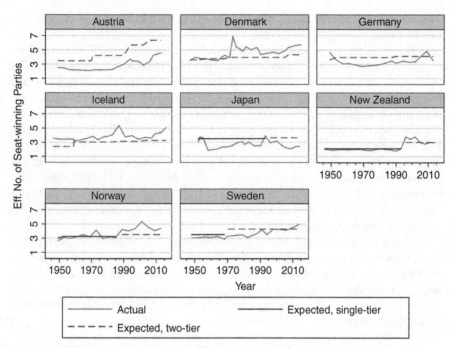

FIGURE 17.2 Expected and actual effective number of seat-winning parties (N_S) over time in long-term democracies with two-tier electoral systems

The overall pattern in Figure 17.2 is similar to that in Figure 17.1: few countries are systematically much higher or lower than expected. One that stands out as exceptional is Austria; even as the rules have been modified several times – note the shifts in the dashed line – actual N_S has lagged. Germany has had unexpectedly low N_S since the 1950s, with the notable exception of 2009. Japan's single-tier system was not simple (it was SNTV) and its postreform system is not compensatory (it is MMM); thus the "expected N_S" here should be treated with caution. We do not intend the models to be able to explain systems like these, and in Chapter 16 we saw that neither SNTV nor MMM could be covered well by the SPM. Nonetheless, we include Japan because it is a prominent example of democracy and of electoral reform. Japan's actual N_S has tended to lag behind what its Seat Product would imply, if we assumed these electoral systems were simple.

Other cases of reform look unexceptional from the standpoint of the SPM. For instance, New Zealand had almost the precise value of N_S that we would expect for decades under FPTP. When it shifted to MMP, there was an initial large increase in N_S, but then it came almost back to the new system's expected value. Changes from single-tier to two-tier PR in Norway and Sweden were quite modest in their effect on expected N_S; the actual value surged higher than expected in Norway, and lagged behind in Sweden before increasing.

The extension of the Seat Product Model to cover two-tier PR systems is one of the accomplishments of this book. In prior iterations of our work, we attempted and failed to do account for such systems. In Taagepera and Shugart (1989a) we attempted to develop an "effective magnitude" to take account of upper tiers and other complicating factors, such as thresholds. We now see that effort as a dead end; in fact, Taagepera (2007) said as much, but did not propose an alternative measure. Figure 17.2 shows that the SPM is approximately as reliable for two-tier PR as it is for simple systems. As with any country and any electoral system, individual elections will vary, and some countries will be chronically more or less fragmented than any broad model would predict. Yet the overall pattern is predicable. The politics play out within constraints set by institutions.

Systems that are still more complex, such as with high thresholds, noncompensatory tiers, or that use multiseat plurality or various *sui generis* combinations remain elusive to predicting outcomes. While we can model the impact of thresholds with some limited success, as we showed in Chapter 16, the main message is that the more complex the system, the harder it is to know how it will work in practice.

THIRTY YEARS AFTER

Thirty years ago we published a book, *Seats and Votes* (Taagepera and Shugart 1989a), that was hailed as a major advance in the study of electoral systems. So it was. Yet, we have practically nothing to cite from that book, and hardly any similar graph or equation to reproduce. This is a measure of later advance. Take just the central issue – the relationship between institutional inputs and outputs such as the number of parties.

In 1989 we were the first to graph the effective number of parties against what we called effective magnitude. On this basis we offered an empirical equation to connect N_V to M. This was the first attempt to express the fuzzy Duverger's "law" and "hypothesis" in such a way that quantitative predictions could be made, tested, and possibly refuted – something "Duverger's law" was safe against, due to is evasive nonquantitative character (see Chapter 7). We called our equation "Generalized Duverger's rule," and it was a major step forward toward quantitativeness. Yet, what did we miss? For one, we missed the role of assembly size, hopelessly trying to telescope its impact, along with district magnitude, into an "effective magnitude."[5] We graphed

---

[5] We correctly deduced S from cube root of population but used it for predictions only in the "Law of minority attrition." The latter still stands and has its uses (see Taagepera 2007, chapters on this law and on seat allocation in federal second chambers), but we do not need it for our purposes in this book.

N_V against M on regular scales rather than logarithmic, which could have given us ideas for logical modeling (cf. our introductory Chapter's Figure 1.2, albeit the latter addresses districts rather than the national scene). Above all, we had no logical model.

Several of the quantities we then highlighted (Taagepera and Shugart 1989a: 202) have found little or no use in the present book: number of issue dimensions, relative reduction in number of parties, break-even point, and advantage ratio. Among the relationships proposed (Taagepera and Shugart 1989a: 205), only those supported by a logical model have survived: the cube root law of assembly sizes and inverse square law of cabinet duration. (Hence we do not reproduce their derivation, but see respectively, Chapters 2 and 7.) Several other relationships, all empirical, could in hindsight be deduced as approximations based on logical models in the present book. This is how cumulative science proceeds, with many tracks that in retrospect turn out to be sidetracks.

PERSPECTIVES ON DESIGN PRINCIPLES FOR ELECTORAL SYSTEMS

In this book, we have seen that the range of variation in electoral systems is large, because some countries combine many different components. In extreme cases, a country (or other political jurisdiction) winds up with a system that is so complex that we are unable to say how it might work in practice. We reviewed some examples in Chapter 16 of what we termed overly complex systems. For such systems it is not feasible to develop a quantitatively predictive logical model, as has been the goal in this book.

Some actual systems are obviously the product of compromises among many different political forces. To some degree this is inevitable. The electoral system usually must be adopted by the very politicians who will be running for office under its provisions. (Even when approved by a referendum or some other arms-length process, it is generally elected office-holders who get the process started or make key proposals along the way.) Thus, while some degree of compromise with present political needs usually must happen when a new system is being designed, the complexities that sometimes result are regrettable. We believe that electoral systems should be designed for the long run (Taagepera and Shugart 1989b). Frequent tinkering is not wise, but the more the system is designed for the narrow needs of present power-holders, the more likely the system will be seen as inappropriate in the future.

Based on our analysis in this book, we can draw some broad conclusions about what are "best practices" in electoral-system design. The intention here is not to offer a one-size-fits-all model; that would be foolish. Rather, we sketch some principles of design about which the book has shown we can generalize. If we can generalize, we can be relatively more confident of recommendations if called upon in some specific design moment to offer answer to the question, "how might this work?"

Keep it simple. Ideally, an electoral system should avoid complexity. The simplest systems have a single tier of allocation and a common PR formula, with allocation taking place solely within districts. FPTP is included in this category (see Chapter 2), although we will admit a preference for even moderate degrees of proportionality over FPTP. The latter system almost necessarily entails substantial deviation from proportionality (Chapter 9), and is more prone than PR systems to manipulative practices like gerrymandering (Chapter 3). A good design presumably avoids either excessive disproportionality or opportunities for political chicanery, although what is "excessive" is normative. Moreover, there are equally good reasons to avoid being a purist about proportionality, which may invite high party-system fragmentation.

If complexity is needed, keep it limited. The compromises that must be struck to design an electoral system in real-world applications may require some complexity. If so, it remains our advice to keep such complexities limited. Our analysis in Chapter 15, and our Figure 17.2 in this chapter, showed that two-tier compensatory PR (a category that includes MMP) is about as easy to model accurately as simple, single-tier, PR. It is thus as simple as an electoral system can be while falling into the category of complex systems. Other complicating factors like thresholds turn out, according to our analysis in Chapter 16, to be not too troublesome for answering the "how might this work" question – provided the threshold is not very high. We suggest five percent or lower, because a too-high threshold invites partisan actors to seek work-around solutions.[6] Other relatively minor complications like ranked-choice voting (for either the Single Transferable Vote or its $M=1$ variant, the Alternative Vote) likewise do not render a system's output too difficult to predict through our quantitative logical models. We caution, however, that attempts to combine many complicating factors in one are unwise. For instance, having ranked-choice voting in low-magnitude districts with a compensatory PR tier, plus a threshold, would combine three complicating factors in one system. In such a hypothetical situation,[7] we are not able to say how the resulting system might work.

If the system is presidential, be careful. We do not take a stand on whether presidentialism[8] is itself a problematic institutional design. That question is outside the scope of this book, and is addressed in a separate literature (e.g., Shugart and Carey 1992; Cheibub 2007; Samuels and Shugart 2010). We were able to show in this book that assembly party systems can be modeled without including presidential variables as an input. Thus just knowing the assembly size and the mean district magnitude is generally sufficient to arrive at a reasonable

---

[6] See the Turkish example sketched in Chapter 16.

[7] The combination mentioned is not entirely hypothetical. Such proposals have surfaced from time to time in Canada and the Netherlands, and perhaps elsewhere.

[8] Including semipresidential, at least if the presidency is not extremely limited in its powers.

estimate of what the effective number of parties (or other output) is likely to be. Presidential systems are, however, more variable, presumably because specific election results may be shaped by the electoral coalitions assembled by particular presidents, even if the overall pattern of presidential democracies is not systematically different from parliamentary.

We would urge special caution in various aspects of electoral-system design for presidential democracies. The timing of elections, while not usually seen as a feature of the electoral system, has measurable impact on assembly elections. If elections are nonconcurrent, we can expect a substantial surge in the vote share won by the president's party if elections are early in the term (honeymoon), and a decline later. Elections very late in the term (in the counter-honeymoon) may be advantageous, however, in multiparty contexts: we showed evidence (Chapter 12) that such assembly elections function almost like primaries among parties that may choose to enter pre-electoral coalitions in the upcoming presidential contest. Such elections are, however, quite likely to result in higher levels of fragmentation than the SPM otherwise would predict. Thus it would be wise to use counter-honeymoon elections only with a moderate Seat Product. The timing of elections should be chosen carefully with an eye to desired impact, and not allowed to be essentially random, as can be the case when presidents and assemblies are elected to different term lengths. A high Seat Product also will tend to result in a higher effective number of presidential candidates, as we showed in Chapter 11.

On the intraparty dimension, also keep it simple. Aside from limiting interparty fragmentation, moderate district magnitude would also have benefits on the intraparty dimension. If lists are open, a high magnitude implies many candidates being elected with extremely small shares of their own party's votes (Chapter 13), and small margins over top losers. Additionally, many votes wind up being cast for losing candidates (Chapter 14), which may be undesirable if voters are not indifferent as to which of their party's candidates is elected. (The whole premise of open lists is that voters are not indifferent, and should be given a choice among candidates.) The implication then is that many winning candidates tend to represent very narrow slices of the electorate. Moreover, it is likely not possible for voters to process information on large numbers of candidates, and thus the cognitive demand on voters from high-magnitude open lists may be too high (Cunow 2014). If magnitude will be on the high side in order to allow for considerable interparty proportionality, it would be wise to restrict the number of candidates per party to something less than M.[9] We are aware of no countries that do this, but it should be considered, to keep the system more manageable and to encourage candidates to appeal more widely. In moderate magnitudes, allowing alliances in open lists is reasonable; however, with higher M, we would recommend against it, given

---

[9] Near the end of Chapter 14 we offered a proposal of this sort.

the complications for parties of estimating their seats in intralist allocation and the tendency to encourage substantially increased fragmentation of party labels (Chapter 14). Such enhanced fragmentation is predictable (based on M and S), so systems ought to be chosen under awareness of the likely outcome.

This book has shown that quantitative logical models can help us understand many aspects of electoral systems, including moderately complex ones. The further development of such models should help illuminate other aspects of electoral systems that we did not cover, and may also assist in advising processes of electoral-system design in new democracies, or where reforms are considered in ongoing democracies.

CONTRIBUTION TO SOCIAL SCIENCE METHODS

The book's direct contribution, as we have reviewed here, is to electoral studies: predicting so much from so little. It also has a contribution that we hope is broader for political science and other social sciences. We have made a centerpiece of this book the development of "quantitatively predictive logical models." The goal of these models is to connect a few variables at a time and then connecting these connections with each other. Having connections among connections is a hallmark of any developed science. While many natural sciences have bodies of quantitative interrelations, such are rare in social sciences. Philosophical arguments abound why this would be impossible in political science, or social sciences more generally. Yet we have shown it can be done: in a small slice of social phenomena, we offer a structure of quantitative interrelations, as indicated in Figure 9.5. Thus the book is a rare *scientific* book about politics, and should set a methodological standard for all social science.

Some of the methods we have used are not among the most usual in social sciences, even though they are familiar in natural sciences. We introduced the method in Chapter 1, and have followed it by developing models for the main questions of Chapters 7 through 16. Now we review the method and hope to point the way forward for further applications.

In Chapter 1, we introduced the idea that science walks on two legs (see Figure 1.1). One leg refers to determining how things *are*. This leads to careful observation, measurement, graphing, and statistical testing. The other leg refers to asking how things *should be*, on logical grounds. That question guides the first one. "How things are" assumes that we know which aspects of things are worth paying attention to. But we largely see only what we look for. It's asking "How things *should be*" that tells us *what* to look for.

This book's approach walks on both legs of science. And this is why it may look out of place in today's quantitative social science that often emphasizes fitting equations with many parameters entered simultaneously and limits its predictive modeling to the direction of a relationship: whether y goes up or down when x increases. Even in fine examples of social-science scholarship, typically the emphasis tends to be on whether the relationship goes in the expected direction to a statistically significant degree, neglecting *how much* it goes in this direction. Whether it goes in this direction to the expected extent is of course a moot question when nothing was expected apart from direction. We urge researchers to try and arrive at logical predictions of just *how much* the quantitative impact of a given variable *should be*. Doing so is not always feasible, we recognize,[10] and even the confirmation of a directional hypothesis can offer valuable insight. However, we should aim for better whenever we can.

In contrast, this book constructs logical models that make predictions that are quantitative, not merely directional. We do test these predictions by the usual statistical methods – but mostly when there is something more specific to test than the direction.

The notion of interaction of "should" and "are" is as old as social science. Auguste Comte, one of the initiators of social studies, put it as follows, two centuries ago, in his *Plan of Scientific Studies Necessary for Reorganization of Society:*

> If it is true that every theory must be based upon observed facts, it is equally true that facts cannot be observed without the guidance of some theory. Without such guidance, our facts would be desultory and fruitless; we could not retain them: for the most part we could not even perceive them. (As quoted in Stein 2008: 30–31)

This is a continuous interaction: "some theory" as guidance, some observation, some further model refinement ... The chicken and the egg evolve conjointly. These issues are discussed in more detail in *Making Social Sciences More Scientific: The Need for Predictive Models* (Taagepera 2008). Some basic tenets are worth pointing out here, making use of examples from this book.

Science is more than just learning facts. It deals with making connections among separate pieces of knowledge. Making connections among known facts can lead to new questions and new, previously unexpected vistas. Connections can be expressed in words, but they are more precise when they can be expressed in equations.

A fully developed science is not satisfied with isolated connections between factors. It aims at connections among such connections. In electricity, an array of mutually consistent equations connects voltage, current, charge, resistance, and force. In this book we establish a chain of quantitative connections that tie assembly size and district magnitude to various measures of the number of parties. The chain actually extends to further features that we barely touched on in this book: duration of cabinets (Taagepera 2007: 165–175), and

---

[10] In fact, we have presented some regressions in this book where only the direction or a vaguer quantitative notion could be expressed in a hypothesis. But we have aimed to minimize our use of such approaches.

dependence of assembly size on population of the country (Taagepera and Shugart 1989a: 173–183). The entire causal chain, from population to cabinet duration (Taagepera 2007: 187–200; Sikk and Taagepera 2014) passes through some of the linkages tested in this book. In contrast, empirical statistical analysis alone too often produces only disconnected relationships, piecemeal knowledge.

Quantitatively Predictive Logical Models

What are "logical models"? These are models one can construct *without any data input* – or almost so. Just consider how things should be or, as importantly, how they could not possibly be. When asked how many parties are likely to win seats in a twenty-five-seat district, we may rush to the Internet for data, or instead, proceed from the knowledge that no less than one and no more than twenty-five parties could win seats – knowledge so obvious we may consider it useless. Yet, knowing what is impossible leads us to what is most likely. The fictional Sherlock Holmes made note of the dog that did *not* bark.

We should aim at logical models that are "quantitatively predictive." In the previous case the prediction must not be just a vague "between one and twenty-five" but a more specific "around five." "Quantitative" does not have to mean "exact" – just much more specific than "between one and twenty-five." Constellations in the center of their possible range tend to occur more frequently, unless specific factors enter, to tilt them away from the center. In the absence of any other knowledge, our best guess is the mean of the possible extremes.[11]

This is an ignorance-based model (Taagepera 2008: 34–36). Normal distribution, so familiar to us, results from an ignorance-based model: How would pea sizes distribute in the absence of any knowledge about them? So does exponential growth model: if we do not know whether relative growth rate decreases or increases, our ignorance-based best guess is that it remains constant. Ignorance-based models are by no means the only types of logical models, but they frequently have come in handy in this book.

Logical models should not be just believed in. They must be tested with data. This book has done so, using several of the most extensive datasets ever used in the analysis of electoral systems.[12] But first we must have a logical model to test, and one that is quantitative – not just directional. "When district magnitude goes up, the number of seat-winning parties goes up" does not suffice. We need "In the absence of any other knowledge, the number of seat-winning parties will be around the square root of district magnitude."

---

[11] See Chapter 7 or Taagepera (2008: 120–127) for why the geometric mean is preferred in these applications rather than arithmetic mean.

[12] In the book's Preface, we thank several scholars who collected much of the data we use, and without which this book could not have been possible.

In the absence of any other knowledge – this is a central notion. Remarkably often it works. Sometimes it doesn't. Then we may be on the verge of discovering something new: What is it that we have failed to take into consideration? We began expecting that twenty-five-seat districts would tend to have five seat-winning parties, and that the resulting effective number would be the district magnitude's cube root, or 2.92. Yet data stubbornly hint at a slightly higher value for the effective number. Pondering this discrepancy makes us notice that we have neglected the nationwide impact on this particular district. We need to adjust for this embeddedness (see Chapter 10). This example shows there is interplay between logical models and data. Models are tested with data, and discrepancies between data and model suggest ways to refine the model.

According to Hawking and Mlodinow (2005), a good model has the following features:

- It is elegant. (This means simplicity, symmetry . . .)
- It has few arbitrary or adjustable components – it is parsimonious.
- It generalizes, explaining all available observations.
- It enables one to make detailed predictions; the actual data may possibly contradict these predictions and thus lead to a revision of the model.

How does one go on to build logical models? One learns it best by doing, because it's an art.[13] Each situation requires a different model. A model of (almost complete) ignorance is only one of many approaches. If there is one general advice, it is: *make it as simple as possible.* Albert Einstein reputedly added "and no simpler." How do we know when a model is overly simple? When it disagrees with good data. Cube root of district magnitude is a bit too simple for the effective number of parties when this district is embedded in a larger country.

Some of the greatest truths in life and science are very simple. Indeed, they are so simple that we may overlook them. And even when pointed out to us, we may refuse to accept them, because we say: "It cannot be that simple." (Maybe this was your initial reaction to $N'_{S0}=M^{1/2}$, when we first mentioned it in Chapter 1.) Sometimes it can be simple. This does not mean that it is simple to find simple truths. Moreover, combining simple building blocks can lead to quite complex constructs. Think about the equations for district-level votes, in this book.

Science Walks on Two Legs, but Too Often Social Sciences Try to Hop on One

Science largely consists of logical models that are tested with data, using methods that include statistics. Why is it necessary to dwell on this broad

---

[13] To develop such skills, a hands-on textbook, *Logical Models and Basic Numeracy in Social Sciences* (Taagepera 2015), is available at www.psych.ut.ee/stk/Beginners_Logical_Models.pdf. It has been tested with bachelors and doctoral students in North America and Europe. This section borrows from it.

methodology in a book on a very specific topic, votes from seats? The answer is that logical models too often have been neglected in electoral studies. Thus for some readers their use may look suspicious even when the results from both graphing and statistical regressions agree with the models.

Electoral studies are not alone in this respect. Social sciences all too often neglect to offer a quantitative estimate of *how things should be*. Rather than devising logically based models and then testing them, social sciences are often happy with directional hypotheses – statements that one variable should go up as another goes down, for example. Statistical methods are then used to test these directional predictions, and whether the variables entered are "significant." This can produce valuable insights, but these so-called "empirical models" are not really models at all. Some degree of fit results, but the *predictive* ability is minimal – and the resulting relationships do not interconnect. These cry out for elaboration, and a logic about *how much one variable increases as another decreases*, and *why the relationship takes the form we observe*.

In this book's introduction, we already set out the importance of "two legs" on which science must walk – the leg of "how things are" and the leg of "how things should be," logically (see Figure 1.2). In science the ideal role of statistics is to test logically based quantitative models. To do this, raw data most often must be transformed in the light of the model. For instance, to test the dependence of effective number of parties on the number of seats in the assembly and average district magnitude, we must first replace N_S, S and M by their logarithms, before linear regression could be applied. Failure to do so not only would lead to a lower correlation coefficient (more apparent scatter) but, more seriously, the output would fail to express the process through which these factors interact. Understanding how things are connected would be downgraded to a push-button exercise.

Too often, today's social sciences try to hop on one leg, in the manner depicted in Figure 17.3. The active leg is the one about "how things are," where patterns in the data area observed and statistical testing is done – too often with little or no graphing of the raw data. The other leg, regarding *how things should be* is often not engaged in the scientific "walk."

The excuse sometimes made for "empirical models" is that testing a directional relationship is itself valuable. We agree that it can be, but we should aim to do better. Every peasant in Galileo's time knew the direction in which things fall – but Galileo felt the need to predict more than direction. It does not suffice to predict that more seats available will increase the number of parties represented. One must specify *how many* seats are expected to lead to *how many* parties. Models should predict not merely the direction of processes but also their quantitative extent.

Developed science not only connects individual factors but also establishes connections among these connections. For such broader interlocking knowledge, one must enquire about how things *should be* connected. Ideally,

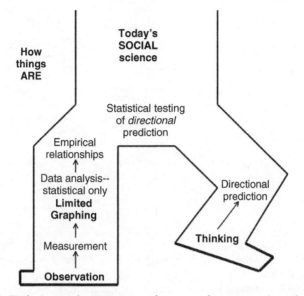

FIGURE 17.3 Today's social sciences too often try to hop on one leg, observation and empirical analysis, with no predictions beyond directional

this process leads to equations that are used over and over. In contrast, empirical regression coefficients, once published, are hardly ever used in any further work. They just take up space in large tables, but are not of intrinsic interest.

One doesn't hop very far on one leg. To continue its recent progress in addressing many important questions, the social sciences will have to reinforce the second leg on which science walks. They must strive to replace the "empirical models" with genuine *logical models* that can then be tested by statistical and other means. Quantitatively predictive logical models need not involve heavy mathematics, but they certainly need active thinking that is much more than the selection of an appropriate statistical approach (important though that is in itself).

Social sciences have made great progress in qualitative understanding and statistical description of patterns in social and political phenomena. Still, if social scientists complement statistical data analysis with logical models, the opportunities for scientific progress will open up even further. We hope that readers will agree that we have made significant progress in these pages in developing deeper quantitative understanding of many aspects of electoral systems. More importantly, we hope to inspire other researchers to make further advances in logical modeling of social phenomena, including electoral and party systems, but also many other topics.

References

Abdel-Ghaffar, O., Gordon, O., and Shugart, M. S., n.d., "How the Electoral System Rewarded Fervor in the 2006 Palestinian Elections," Unpubilshed paper, University of California, Davis.

Ahmed, A. 2013, *Democracy and the Politics of Electoral System Choice: Engineering Electoral Dominance*. Cambridge: Cambridge University Press.

Allen, N. 2018, "Electoral Systems in Context: Indonesia," in *Oxford Handbook of Electoral Systems*, edited by E. Herron, R. Pekkanen, and M. S. Shugart. New York: Oxford University Press.

Ames, Barry. 1995a. "Electoral Strategy Under Open-List Proportional Representation," *American Journal of Political Science* May.

Ames, Barry. 1995b. "Electoral Rules, Constituency Pressures, and Pork Barrel: Bases of Voting in the Brazilian Congress," *Journal of Politics* 57: 2 (May).

Amorim Neto, O. and Cox, G. W. 1997, "Electoral Institutions, Cleavage Structures, and the Number of Parties," *American Journal of Political Science* 44(1): 149–174.

André, A., Depauw, S., Shugart M. S., and Chytilek, R. 2017. "Party Nomination Strategies in Flexible-List Systems: Do Preference Votes Matter?," *Party Politics*. 23, 5.

Arter, D. 2014, "Clowns, 'Alluring Ducks' and 'Miss Finland 2009': The Value of 'Celebrity Candidates' in an Open-List PR Voting System," *Representation* 50(4): 453–470.

Bacik, G. 2008, "The Parliamentary Elections in Turkey, July 2007," *Electoral Studies* 27(2): 377–381.

Batto, N. F. 2008, "Strategic Defection from Strong Candidates in the 2004 Taiwanese Legislative Election," *Japanese Journal of Political Science* 9(1): 21–38.

Belden, C. R., n.d., "Do Electoral Rules Influence Small Parties' Policy Work? Analyzing Green Party Attention to Local Issues," Unpublished paper, University of California, Davis.

Belden, C. R., and Shugart, M. S., n.d., "District Level Party Systems Dataset." Unpublished, University of California, Davis.

Bergman, M. E., Shugart, M. S., and Watt, K. A. 2013, "Patterns of Intraparty Competition in Open-List, and SNTV Systems," *Electoral Studies* 32(2): 321–333.

Blais, A. and Shugart, M. S. 2008, "To Keep or Change First Past the Post: Conclusion" in *To Keep or Change First Past the Post*, edited by A. Blais. New York: Oxford University Press.

Blondel, J. 1968, "Party Systems and Patterns of Government in Western Democracies," *Canadian Journal of Political Science* 1(2): 180–203.

Boix, C. 2003, *Democracy and Redistribution*. New York: Cambridge University Press.

Bormann, N. and Golder, M. 2013, "Democratic Electoral Systems Around the World, 1946–2011," *Electoral Studies* 32(2): 360–369.

Bowler, S. and Farrell, D. M. 2006, "We Know Which One We Prefer but We Don't Really Know Why: The Curious Case of Mixed Member Electoral Systems," *The British Journal of Politics and International Relations* 8(3): 445–460.

Bowler, S., Farrell, D. M., and Pettitt, R. T. 2005, "Expert Opinion on Electoral Systems: So Which Electoral System Is 'Best'?," *Journal of Elections, Public Opinion, and Parties* 15(1): 3–19.

Brambor, T., Clark, W. R., and Golder, M. 2006, "Understanding Interaction Models: Improving Empirical Analyses," *Political Analysis* 14(1): 63–82.

Brams, S.J., and Fishburn, P.C. 1983, *Approval Voting*. Boston: Birkhäuser.

Cahill, C., André, A., Depauw, S., and Shugart, M. S., n.d, "The Incentives (or Lack of Incentives) to Cultivate a Personal Vote in Flexible-List Systems," Unpublished paper, University of California, Davis.

Cain, Bruce E., Ferejohn, John A., and Fiorina, Morris P. 1984. "The Constituency Service Basis of the Personal Vote for US Representatives and British Members of Parliament," *American Political Science Review* 78 (01): 110–25.

Calvo, E. and Murillo, M. V. 2012, "When Parties Meet Voters Assessing Political Linkages Through Partisan Networks and Distributive Expectations in Argentina and Chile," *Comparative Political Studies* 46(7): 851–882.

Campbell, A. 1960, "Surge and Decline: A Study of Electoral Change," *Public Opinion Quarterly* 24(3): 397–418.

Carey, J. M. 2002, "Parties, Coalitions, and the Chilean Congress in the 1990s" in *Legislative Politics in Latin America*, edited by S. Morgenstern and B. Nacif. New York: Cambridge University Press.

Carey, J. M. 2009, *Legislative Voting and Accountability*. New York: Cambridge University Press.

Carey, J. M. 2018, "Electoral System Design in New Democracies" in *Oxford Handbook of Electoral Systems*, edited by E. Herron, R. Pekkanen, and M. S. Shugart. New York: Oxford University Press.

Carey, J. M. and Hix, S. 2011, "The Electoral Sweet Spot: Low-Magnitude Proportional Electoral Systems," *American Journal of Political Science* 55(2): 383–397.

Carey, J. M., Hix, S., Htun, M., Mozzafar, S., Powell, G. B., Reynolds, A., 2013, "Political Scientists as System Engineers," *Perspectives on Politics* 11 (3): 827–833.

Centellas, Miguel. 2015, "Mixed-Member Election and Candidate Selection in Bolivia's 1993 and 1997 Elections," *The Latin Americanist* 59(1): 3–22.

Cheibub, J.A. 2007, *Presidentialism, Parliamentarism, and Democracy*. New York: Cambridge University Press.

Cheibub, J. A., Przeworski, A., Limongi Neto, F. P., and Alvarez, M. M. 1996, "What Makes Democracies Endure?," *Journal of Democracy* 7(1): 39–55.

Clark, W. R. and Golder, M. 2006, "Rehabilitating Duverger's Theory Testing the Mechanical and Strategic Modifying Effects of Electoral Laws," *Comparative Political Studies* 39(6): 679–708.

Colomer, J. M. 2004, "The Strategy and History of Electoral System Choice" in *The Handbook of Electoral System Choice*, edited by J.M. Colomer. London: Palgrave Macmillan.

Colomer, J. M. 2005, "It's Parties That Choose Electoral Systems (or, Duverger's laws Upside Down)," *Political Studies* 53(1): 1–21.

Colomer, J. M., 2007. "What Other Sciences Look Like," *European Political Science* 6: 134–142.

Colomer, J. M., ed. 2011, *Personal Representation: The Neglected Dimension of Electoral Systems*. Essex: ECPR Press.

Colomer, J. M. 2014, "Equilibrium Institutions: The Federal-Proportional Trade-Off," *Public Choice* 158(3–4): 559–576.

Cox, G. W. 1996, "Is the Single Nontransferable Vote Superproportional? Evidence from Japan and Taiwan," *American Journal of Political Science* 40(3): 740–755.

Cox, G. W. 1997, *Making Votes Count: Strategic Coordination in the World's Electoral Systems*. New York: Cambridge University Press.

Cox, G. 1999, "Electoral Rules and Electoral Coordination," *Annual Review of Political Science* 2(1): 145–161.

Cox, G. W. and Niou, E. 1994, "Seat Bonuses Under the Single Nontransferable Vote System: Evidence from Japan and Taiwan," *Comparative Politics* 26(2): 221–236.

Cox, G. W. and Shugart, M. S. 1995, "In the Absence of Vote Pooling: Nomination and Vote Allocation Errors in Colombia," *Electoral Studies* 14(4): 441–460.

Crisp, B. F., Escobar-Lemmon, M. C., Jones, B. S., Jones, M. P., and Taylor-Robinson, M. M. 2004, "Vote-Seeking Incentives and Legislative Representation in Six Presidential Democracies," *Journal of Politics* 66(3): 823–846.

Crisp, B. F., Olivella, S., Malecki, M., and Sher, M. 2013, "Vote-Earning Strategies in Flexible List Systems: Seats at the Price of Unity," *Electoral Studies* 32(4): 658–669.

Cunow, S. F. 2014, *Vote Choice in Complex Electoral Environments*. University of California, San Diego.

Dahl, R. A. 1961, *Who Governs: Democracy and Power in an American City*. New Haven: Yale University Press.

Dawisha, A. 2010, "Iraq: A Vote Against Sectarianism," *Journal of Democracy* 21(3): 26–40.

Denemark, D. 2001, "Choosing MMP in New Zealand: Explaining the 1993 Electoral Reform" in *Mixed-Member Electoral Systems: The Best of Both Worlds?*, edited by M.S. Shugart and M.P. Wattenberg. Oxford: Oxford University Press.

Doron, G. and Maor, M. 1991, "Barriers to Entry into a Political System: A Theoretical Framework and Empirical Application from the Israeli Experience," *Journal of Theoretical Politics* 3(2): 175–188.

Droop, H. R. 2012 [1869], "On the Political and Social Effects of Different Methods of Electing Representatives", in *Electoral Systems*, Vol. III., edited by D.M. Farrell and M.S. Shugart. London: Sage.

Dunleavy, P., and Caulier, J.-F. 2003, "Constructing the Number of Parties," *Party Politics* 9: 291–315.

Dupoirier, E., and Sauger, S. 2010, "Four Rounds in a Row: The Impact of Presidential Election Outcome on Legislative Elections in France," *French Politics* 8: 21–41.

Duverger, M. 1951, *Les partis politiques*. Paris: Armand Colin.

Duverger, M. 1954, *Political Parties: Their Organization and Activity in the Modern State*. New York: John Wiley and Sons.

Duverger, M. 1986, "Duverger's Law: Forty Years Later" in *Electoral Laws and Their Political Consequences*, edited by B. Grofman, and A. Lijphart. New York: Agathon Press.

Eccarius-Kelly, V. 2008, "The Kurdish Conundrum in Europe: Political Opportunities and Transnational Activism" in *Migration and Activism in Europe since 1945*, ed. by W. Pojmann. New York: Springer.

Elgie, R., 2011, *Semi-Presidentialism: Sub-Types and Democratic Performance*. Oxford: Oxford University Press.

Elgie, R., Bucur, C., Dolez, B., and Laurent, A. 2014, "Proximity, Candidates, and Presidential Power: How Directly Elected Presidents Shape the Legislative Party System," *Political Research Quarterly* 67(3): 467–477.

Elklit, J. 2005, "Denmark: Simplicity Embedded in Complexity (or Is It the Other Way Round?)" in *The Politics of Electoral Systems*, edited by M. Gallagher and P. Mitchell. Oxford: Oxford University Press.

Elklit, J., and Roberts, N. S. 1996, "A Category of Its Own? Four PR Two-Tier Compensatory Member Electoral Systems in 1994," *European Journal of Political Research* 30(2): 217–240.

Erikson, R. S. 1988, "The Puzzle of Midterm Loss," *The Journal of Politics* 50(4): 1011–1029.

Fearon, J. D. 2003, "Ethnic and Cultural Diversity by Country," *Journal of Economic Growth* 8(2): 195–222.

Ferree, K. E., Powell, G., and Scheiner, E. 2013, "How Context Shapes the Effects of Electoral Rules," *Political Science, Electoral Rules, and Democratic Governance*, ed. by M. Htun and G. B, Jr. Powell. Washington: American Political Science Association.

Ferree, K. E. 2018, "Electoral Systems in Context: South Africa" in *Oxford Handbook of Electoral Systems*, edited by E. Herron, R. Pekkanen, and M. S. Shugart New York: Oxford University Press.

Filippov, M. G., Ordeshook, P. C., and Shvetsova, O. V. 1999, "Party Fragmentation and Presidential Elections in Post-Communist Democracies," *Constitutional Political Economy* 10(1): 3–26.

Fiorina, M. P. 1992, *Divided Government*. New York: Macmillan Publishing Company.

Frederick, B. 2009, *Congressional Representation and Constituents: The Case for Increasing the US House of Representatives*. New York: Routledge.

Gaines, B. J. 1999, "Duverger's Law and the Meaning of Canadian exceptionalism," *Comparative Political Studies* 32(7): 835–861.

Gaines, B. J., and Taagepera, R. 2013, "How to Operationalize Two-Partyness," *Journal of Elections, Public Opinion, and Parties* 23(4): 387–404.

Gallagher, M. 1991, "Proportionality, Disproportionality and Electoral Systems," *Electoral Studies* 10(1): 33–51.

Gallagher, M. 2005. "Ireland: The Discreet Charm of PR-STV" in *The Politics of Electoral Systems*, edited by M. Gallagher and P. Mitchell. Oxford: Oxford University Press.

Gallagher, M., and Mitchell, P., eds. 2005a, *The Politics of Electoral Systems*. Oxford: Oxford University Press.

Gallagher, M. and Mitchell, P. 2005b, "Introduction to Electoral Systems" in *The Politics of Electoral Systems*, edited by M. Gallagher and P. Mitchell. Oxford: Oxford University Press.

Gallagher, M., and Mitchell, P. 2018, "Dimensions of Variation in Electoral Systems" in *Oxford Handbook of Electoral Systems*, edited by E. Herron, R. Pekkanen, and M. S. Shugart. New York: Oxford University Press.

Golder, M. 2006, "Presidential Coattails and Legislative Fragmentation," *American Journal of Political Science* 50(1): 34–48.

Golosov, G. V. 2009, "The Effective Number of Parties: A New Approach," *Party Politics* 16(2): 171–192.

Gouws, A. and Mitchell, P. 2005, "South Africa: One Party Dominance Despite Perfect Proportionality" in *The Politics of Electoral Systems*, edited by M. Gallagher and P. Mitchell. Oxford: Oxford University Press.

Grofman, B., Lee, S., Winckler, E., and Woodall, B., eds. 1999, *Elections in Japan, Korea, and Taiwan under the Single Non-Transferable Vote: The Comparative Study of an Embedded Institution*. Ann Arbor: University of Michigan Press.

Handley, L. and Grofman, B. 2008, *Redistricting in Comparative Perspective*. Oxford: Oxford University Press.

Hare, T. 1859, *Treatise on the Election of Representatives, Parliamentary and Municipal*. London: Longman, Green, Reader, and Dyer.

Hazan, R. Y., Itzkovitch-Malka, R., and Rahat, G. 2018, "Electoral Systems in Context: Israel" in *Oxford Handbook of Electoral Systems*, edited by E. Herron, R. Pekkanen, and M. S. Shugart New York: Oxford University Press.

Hawking, S. and Mlodinow, L. 2005. *A Briefer History of Time: A Special Edition of the Science Classic*. London: Bantam Books.

Heath, A., Glouharova, S., and Heath, O. 2005, "India: Two-Party Contests Within a Multiparty System" in *The Politics of Electoral Systems*, edited by M. Gallagher and P. Mitchell. Oxford: Oxford University Press.

Herron, E., Pekkanen, R.J., and Shugart, M.S., eds. 2018, *Oxford Handbook of Electoral Systems*. New York: Oxford University Press.

Hicken, A. 2009, *Building Party Systems in Developing Democracies*. Cambridge University Press.

Hicken, A. and Stoll, H. 2011, "Presidents and Parties: How Presidential Elections Shape Coordination in Legislative Elections," *Comparative Political Studies* 44(7): 854–883.

Hicken, A. and Stoll, H. 2012, "Are All Presidents Created Equal? Presidential Powers and the Shadow of Presidential Elections," *Comparative Political Studies* 46(13): 291–319.

Hinckley, B. 1967, "Interpreting House Midterm Elections: Toward a Measurement of the In-Party's "Expected" Loss of Seats," *American Political Science Review* 61(3): 694–700.

Hopkin, J. 2005, "Spain: Proportional Representation with Majoritarian Outcomes" in *The Politics of Electoral Systems*, edited by M. Gallagher and P. Mitchell. Oxford: Oxford University Press.

Hrebenar, R. J. 1986, *The Japanese Party System: From One-Party Rule to Coalition Government*. Boulder, CO: Westview Press.

Jacobs, K. 2018, "Electoral Systems in Context: The Netherlands" in *Oxford Handbook of Electoral Systems*, edited by E. Herron, R. Pekkanen, and M. S. Shugart New York: Oxford University Press.

Johnson, J. W. and Hoyo, V. 2012, "Beyond Personal Vote Incentives: Dividing the Vote in Preferential Electoral Systems," *Electoral Studies* 31(1): 131–142.

Johnston, R. 2017, *The Canadian Party System: An Analytic History*. Vancouver: University of British Columbia Press.

Jones, M. P. 2018, "Presidential and Legislative Elections" in *Oxford Handbook of Electoral Systems*, edited by E. Herron, R. Pekkanen, and M. S. Shugart. New York: Oxford University Press.

Kam, C. J. 2009. *Party Discipline and Parliamentary Politics*. New York: Cambridge University Press.

Karvonen, L. 2004, "Preferential Voting: Incidence and Effects," *International Political Science Review*, 25(2): 203–226.

Kasuya, Yuko. 2009. *Presidential Bandwagon: Parties and Party Systems in the Philippines*. Pasig City, Philippines: Anvil Publishing.

Katz, R. S. 1986, "Intraparty Preference Voting" in *Electoral Laws and Their Political Consequences*, edited by B. Grofman, and A. Lijphart. New York: Agathon Press.

Kedar, O., Harsgor, L., and Sheinerman, R. A. 2016, "Are Voters Equal Under Proportional Representation?," *American Journal of Political Science* 60(3): 679–691.

Kelly, W. W. 2007, "Is Baseball a Global Sport? America's 'National Pastime' as Global Field and International Sport," *Global Networks* 7(2): 187–201.

Kelly, W. W. 2009, "Samurai Baseball: The Vicissitudes of a National Sporting Style," *The International Journal of the History of Sport* 26(3): 429–441.

Kernell, S. 1977, "Presidential Popularity and Negative Voting: An Alternative Explanation of the Midterm Congressional Decline of the President's Party," *American Political Science Review* 71(1): 44–66.

Kollman, K., Hicken, A., Caramani, D., Backer, D., and Lublin D. 2016, *Constituency-Level Elections Archive*. Ann Arbor, MI: Center for Political Studies, University of Michigan [producer and distributor]. Web; 24 October 2016.

Laakso, M. and Taagepera, R. 1979, "The 'Effective' Number of Parties: A Measure with Application to West Europe," *Comparative Political Studies* 12(1): 3–27.

Lehoucq, F. 2004, "Costa Rica: Modifying Majoritarianism with 40 per cent Threshold" in *The Handbook of Electoral System Choice*, edited J. M. Colomer. London: Palgrave Macmillan.

Li, Y. and Shugart, M. S. 2016, "The Seat Product Model of the Effective Number of Parties: A Case for Applied Political Science," *Electoral Studies* 41(1): 23–34.

Li, Y. and Shugart, M. S. n.d., "National Level Party Systems Dataset." Unpublished, University of California, Davis.

Lijphart, A. 1985, "The Field of Electoral Systems Research: A Critical Survey," *Electoral Studies* 4(1): 3–14.

Lijphart, A. 1990, "Size, Pluralism, and the Westminster Model of Democracy: Implications for the Eastern Caribbean" in *A Revolution Aborted: The Lessons of Grenada*, edited by J. Heine. Pittsburgh: University of Pittsburgh Press.

Lijphart, A. 1991, "The Alternative Vote: a Realistic Alternative for South Africa?," *Politikon: South African Journal of Political Studies* 18(2): 91–101.

Lijphart, A. 1994, *Electoral Systems and Party Systems: A Study of Twenty-Seven Democracies, 1945–1990*. New York: Oxford University Press.

Lijphart, A. 1999, *Patterns of Democracy: Government Forms and Performance in Thirty-Six Democracies*. New Haven: Yale University Press.

Lijphart A, Lopez Pintor, R., and Sone, Y. 1986. "The Limited Vote and the Single Non-Transferable Vote: Lessons from the Japanese and Spanish Examples" in *Electoral Laws and Their Political Consequences*, edited by B. Grofman and A. Lijphart. New York: Agathon.

Loosemore, J., and Hanby, V. J. 1971, "The Theoretical Limits of Maximum Distortion: Some Analytic Expressions for Electoral Systems," *British Journal of Political Science* 1(4): 467–477.

Lublin, D. 2014, *Minority Rules: Electoral Systems, Decentralization, and Ethnoregional Party Success*. New York: Oxford University Press.

Lundberg, T. C., 2018, "Electoral Systems in Context: UK" in *Oxford Handbook of Electoral Systems*, edited by E. Herron, R. Pekkanen, and M. S. Shugart. New York: Oxford University Press.

Machado, A. 2012. *Alianças Eleitorais: Casamento com Prazo de Validade, o Caso das Coligações Brasileiras*. Rio de Janeiro: Elsevier Editora.

Machado, A. 2009, "Minimum Winning Electoral Coalitions under Presidentialism: Reality or Fiction? The Case of Brazil," *Latin American Politics and Society* 51(3): 87–110.

MacIntyre, A. J. 2003, *The Power of Institutions: Political Architecture and Governance*. Cornell: Cornell University Press.

Mainwaring, S. 1991. "Politicians, Electoral Systems, and Parties: Brazil in Comparative Perspective," *Comparative Politics* 24, No. 1 (October): 21–43.

Mainwaring, S. 1993, "Presidentialism, Multipartism, and Democracy: The Difficult Combination," *Comparative Political Studies* 26(2): 198–228.

Mainwaring, M. and Shugart, M. S., 1997. "Conclusion: Presidentialism and the Party System" in *Presidentialism and Democracy in Latin America*, edited by S. Mainwaring and M. S. Shugart. New York: Cambridge University Press, pp. 394–439.

Mair, P. 1997, *Party System Change: Approaches and Interpretations*. New York: Cambridge University Press.

Marsh, M. 1985, "The Voters Decide?: Preferential Voting in European List Systems," *European Journal of Political Research* 13(4): 365–378.

Massicotte, L., 2018, "Electoral Systems in Context: Canada" in *Oxford Handbook of Electoral Systems*, edited by E. Herron, R. Pekkanen, and M. S. Shugart. New York: Oxford University Press.

Matland, R. E., and Taylor, M. M. 1997, "Electoral System Effects on Women's Representation Theoretical Arguments and Evidence from Costa Rica," *Comparative Political Studies* 30(2): 186–210.

McAllister, I., and Makkai, T. 2018. "Electoral Systems in Context: Australia" in *Oxford Handbook of Electoral Systems*, edited by E. Herron, R. Pekkanen, and M.S. Shugart. New York: Oxford University Press.

McGann, A. J., Smith, C. A., Latner, M., and Keena, A. 2016, *Gerrymandering in America: The House of Representatives, the Supreme Court, and the Future of Popular Sovereignty*. New York: Cambridge University Press.

Milazzo, Caitlin, Moser, Robert G., and Scheiner, Ethan. In press. "Social Diversity Affects the Number of Parties Even under First-Past-the-Post Rules," *Comparative Political Studies*.

Mill, J. S. 1861, *Considerations on Representative Government*. London: Parker, Son, and Bourn.

Molinar, J. 1991. "Counting the Number of Parties: An Alternative Index," *American Political Science Review* 85: 1383–1391.

Monroe, B. L., and Rose, A. G. 2002, "Electoral Systems and Unimagined Consequences: Partisan Effects of Districted Proportional Representation," *American Journal of Political Science* 46(1): 67–89.

Moser, R. G., and Scheiner, E. 2012, *Electoral Systems and Political Context: How the Effects of Rules Vary Across New and Established Democracies*. New York: Cambridge University Press.

Moser, R. G., Scheiner, E., and Stoll, H. 2018. "Social Diversity, Election Rules, and the Party System" in *Oxford Handbook of Electoral Systems*, edited by E. Herron, R. Pekkanen, and M. S. Shugart. New York: Oxford University Press.

Mozaffar S., Scarritt J. R., and Galaich G. 2003. "Electoral Institutions, Ethnopolitical Cleavages and Party Systems in Africa's Emerging Democracies," *American Political Science Review* 97(3): 379–390.

Ordeshook, P. and Shvetsova, O. 1994, "Ethnic Heterogeneity, District Magnitude, and the Number of Parties," *American Journal of Political Science* 38, 100–123.

Pachón, M., and Shugart, M. S. 2010, "Electoral Reform and the Mirror Image of Inter-Party and Intra-Party Competition: The Adoption of Party Lists in Colombia," *Electoral Studies* 29(4): 648–660.

Passarelli, G. 2018, "Electoral Systems in Context: Italy" in *Oxford Handbook of Electoral Systems*, edited by E. Herron, R. Pekkanen, and M. S. Shugart. New York: Oxford University Press.

Potter, J. D. 2014, "Demographic Diversity and District-Level Party Systems," *Comparative Political Studies* 47(13): 1801–1829.

Rae, D. W. 1967, *The Political Consequences of Electoral Laws*. New Haven: Yale University Press.

Rahat, G. and Hazan, R. Y. 2001, "Candidate Selection Methods an Analytical Framework," *Party Politics* 7(3): 297–322.

Raunio, T. 2005, "Finland: One Hundred Years of Quietude" in *The Politics of Electoral Systems*, edited by M. Gallagher and P. Mitchell. Oxford: Oxford University Press.

Reed, S. R. 1991, "Structure and Behaviour: Extending Duverger's Law to the Japanese Case," *British Journal of Political Science* 20(3): 335–356.

Reed, S. R. 2003, "What Mechanism Causes the M+1 Rule? A Simple Simulation," *Japanese Journal of Political Science* 4(1): 41–60.

Reed, S. R. 2009, "Party Strategy or Candidate Strategy: How Does the LDP Run the Right Number of Candidates in Japan's Multi-Member Districts?," *Party Politics* 15(3): 295–314.

Reed, S. R. and Bolland, J. M. 1999, "The Fragmentation Effect of SNTV in Japan" in *Elections in Japan, Korea, and TaiFn Under the Single Non-Transferable Vote: The Comparative Study of an Embedded Institution*, edited by B. Grofman *et al*. Ann Arbor: University of Michigan Press.

Reilly, B. 2002, "Social Choice in the South Seas: Electoral Innovation and the Borda Count in the Pacific Island Countries," *International Political Science Review* 23(4): 355–372.

Reilly, B., Ellis, A., and Reynolds, A. 2005, *Electoral System Design: The New International IDEA Handbook*, International Institute for Democracy and Electoral Assistance.

Renwick, A., and Pilet, J. 2016, *Faces on the Ballot: The Personalization of Electoral Systems in Europe*. Oxford: Oxford University Press.

Reynolds, A. 2006, "The Curious Case of Afghanistan," *Journal of Democracy* 17(2): 104–117.

Riker, W. H. 1982, *Liberalism against Populism: A Confrontation Between the Theory of Democracy and the Theory of Social Choice.* San Francisco: W.H. Freeman.

Samuels, D. J. and Shugart, M. S. 2010, *Presidents, Parties, and Prime Ministers: How the Separation of Powers Affects Party Organization and Behavior.* New York: Cambridge University Press.

Samuels, D. J. and Snyder, R. 2001. "The Value of a Vote: Malapportionment in Comparative Perspective," *British Journal of Political Science* 31(3): 651–671.

Sartori, G. 1976, *Parties and Party Systems: A Framework for Analysis.* New York: Cambridge University Press.

von Schoultz, Å. 2018, "Electoral Systems in Context: Finland" in *Oxford Handbook of Electoral Systems,* edited by E. Herron, R. Pekkanen, and M. S. Shugart New York: Oxford University Press.

Shugart, M. S. 1995, "The Electoral Cycle and Institutional Sources of Divided Presidential Government," *American Political Science Review* 89(2): 327–343.

Shugart, M. S. 2004, "Elections: The American Process of Selecting a President: A Comparative Perspective," *Presidential Studies Quarterly* 34(3): 632–655.

Shugart, M. S. 2005a, "Comparative Electoral Systems Research: The Maturation of a Field and New Challenges Ahead," in *The Politics of Electoral Systems,* edited by M. Gallagher and P. Mitchell. Oxford: Oxford University Press.

Shugart, M. S. 2005b, "Semi-Presidential Systems: Dual Executive and Mixed Authority Patterns," *French Politics* 3(3): 323–351.

Shugart, M. S. 2007, "Mayoría relativa vs. segunda vuelta: la elección presidencial mexicana de 2006 en perspectiva comparada," *Política y gobierno* XIV(1): 175–202.

Shugart, M. S. and Carey, J. M. 1992, *Presidents and Assemblies: Constitutional Design and Electoral Dynamics.* New York: Cambridge University Press.

Shugart, M. S., Moreno, E., and Fajardo, L. E. 2007, "Deepening Democracy Through Renovating Political Practices: The Struggle for Electoral Reform in Colombia" in *Peace, Democracy, and Human Rights in Colombia,* edited by C. Welna and G. Gallon. Notre Dame: Notre Dame University Press.

Shugart, M. S. and Taagepera, R. 1994, "Plurality Versus Majority Election of Presidents: A Proposal for a 'Double Complement Rule'," *Comparative Political Studies* 27(3): 323–348.

Shugart, M. S. and Tan, A. C., 2016. "Political Consequences of New Zealand's MMP System in Comparative Perspective" in *Mixed-Member Electoral Systems in Constitutional Context: Taiwan, Japan, and Beyond,* edited by N. Batto, C. Huang, A. C. Tan, and G. W. Cox, pp. 247–277. Ann Arbor: University of Michigan Press.

Shugart, M. S. and Wattenberg, M. P., eds., 2001. *Mixed-Member Electoral Systems: The Best of Both Worlds?* New York: Oxford University Press.

Shugart, M. S., Valdini, M. E., and Suominen, K. 2005, "Looking for Locals: Voter Information Demands and Personal Vote-Earning Attributes of Legislators under Proportional Representation," *American Journal of Political Science* 49(2): 437–449.

Siavelis, P. M. 2002, "The Hidden Logic of Candidate Selection for Chilean Parliamentary Elections," *Comparative Politics* 34(4): 419–438.

Siavelis, P. M. 2005, "Chile: Unexpected (and Expected) Consequences of Electoral Engineering" in *The Politics of Electoral Systems,* ed. by M. Gallagher and P. Mitchell. Oxford: Oxford University Press.

Sikk, A., and Taagepera, R. 2014, "How Population Size Affects Party Systems and Cabinet Duration," *Party Politics* 20(4): 591–603.

Singer, M. M. 2013, "Was Duverger Correct? Single-Member District Election Outcomes in Fifty-Three Countries," *British Journal of Political Science* 43(1): 201–220.

Spoon, J. J. 2011, *Political Survival of Small Parties in Europe*. Ann Arbor: University of Michigan Press.

Stein, J. D. 2008, *How Math Explains the World*. New York: Harper Collins/ Smithsonian Books.

Stoll, H. 2008, "Social Cleavages and the Number of Parties: How the Measures You Choose Affect the Answers You Get," *Comparative Political Studies* 41(11): 1439–1465.

Stoll, H. 2013, *Changing Societies, Changing Party Systems*. New York: Cambridge University Press.

Stoll, H. 2015, "Presidential Coattails: A Closer Look," *Party Politics* 21(3): 417–427.

Swindle, S. M. 2002, "The Supply and Demand of the Personal Vote Theoretical Considerations and Empirical Implications of Collective Electoral Incentives," *Party Politics* 8(3): 279–300.

Taagepera, R. 1997, "Effective Number of Parties for Incomplete Data," *Electoral Studies* 16(2): 145–151.

Taagepera, R. 1999, "Supplementing the Effective Number of Parties," *Electoral Studies* 18(4): 497–504.

Taagepera, R. 2007, *Predicting Party Sizes: The Logic of Simple Electoral Systems*. Oxford: Oxford University Press.

Taagepera, R. 2008, *Making Social Sciences More Scientific: The Need for Predictive Models*. Oxford: Oxford University Press.

Taagepera, R. 2015. "La balanza inclinada: Probando la "ley" de Duverger en el nivel nacional," *De Política* 3, no. 4/5, 11–19.

Taagepera, R. and Ensch, J. 2006. "Institutional Determinants of the Largest Seat Share," *Electoral Studies* 25: 760–765.

Taagepera, R. and Grofman, B. 1985. "Rethinking Duverger's Law: Predicting the Effective Number of Parties in Plurality and PR Systems – Parties Minus Issues Equals One," *European Journal of Political Research* 13: 341–352.

Taagepera, R. and Grofman, B. 2003. "Mapping the Indices of Seats–Votes Disproportionality and Inter-Election Volatility," *Party Politics* 9(6): 659–677.

Taagepera, R. and Sikk, A. 2010. "Parsimonious Model for Predicting Mean Cabinet Duration on the Basis of Electoral System," *Party Politics* 16(2): 261–281.

Taagepera, R. and Shugart, M. S. 1993. "Predicting the Number of Parties: A Quantitative Model of Duverger's Mechanical Effect," *American Political Science Review* 87(2): 455–464.

Taagepera, R. and Shugart, M. S. 1989a. *Seats and Votes: The Effects and Determinants of Electoral Systems*. New Haven: Yale University Press.

Taagepera, R. and Shugart, M. S. 1989b. "Designing Electoral systems," *Electoral Studies* 8(1): 49–58.

Taylor, S. L. and Shugart, M. S. 2018. "Electoral Systems in Context: Colombia" in *Oxford Handbook of Electoral Systems*, edited by E. Herron, R. Pekkanen, and M. S. Shugart. New York: Oxford University Press.

Taylor, S. L., Shugart, M. S., Lijphart, A., and Grofman, B. 2014, *A Different Democracy: American Government in a 31-Country Perspective*. New Haven: Yale University Press.

Thayer, N. B. 1969, *How the Conservatives Rule Japan*. Princeton: Princeton University Press.

Tufte, E. R. 1975, "Determinants of the Outcomes of Midterm Congressional Elections," *American Political Science Review* 69(3): 812–826.

Vowles, J. 2008, "Systemic Failure, Coordination, and Contingencies: Understanding Electoral System Change in New Zealand" in *To Keep or To Change First Past The Post?: The Politics of Electoral Reform*, edited by A. Blais. New York: Oxford University Press.

Vowles, J. 2018, "Electoral Systems in Context: New Zealand" in *Oxford Handbook of Electoral Systems*, edited by E. Herron, R. Pekkanen, and M. S. Shugart New York: Oxford University Press.

van de Wardt, M. 2017, "Explaining the Effective Number of Parties: Beyond the Standard Model," *Electoral Studies* 45: 44–54.

Wolinetz, S. B. 2006, "Party Systems and Party SystemTtypes" in *Handbook of Party Politics*, edited by R. S. Katz and W. J. Crotty. London: Sage Publications Ltd.

Zittel, T. 2018, "Electoral Systems in Context: Germany" in *Oxford Handbook of Electoral Systems*, edited by E. Herron, R. Pekkanen, and M. S. Shugart, New York: Oxford University Press.

Zupan, M. A. 1991, "An Economic Explanation for the Existence and Nature of Political Ticket-Splitting," *Journal of Law and Economics* 34: 343–369.

Index